COURSE OF KABALAH

+

CURSO DE CÁBALA

Bilingual - Bilingüe

DR. ARNOLDO KRUMM-HELLER

"HUIRACOCHA"

1936

EDITOR'S NOTE:

The capitalization and punctuation have been duplicated (as much as possible) from the originals in order to preserve the Author's style. All pictures, footnotes, and the items in [brackets] have been added by the present Editor in order to help clarify and provide insight into this text's subject matter.

Course of Kabalah = Curso de Cábala (Curso de Cábala Ario-Egipcia)

© 2016 by Daath Gnosis Publishing (A.S.P.M.)
ISBN 978-1-365-32527-4
All Rights Reserved. Printed in the United States of America.

Based on the writings of Arnoldo Krumm-Heller.

First Edition September 2016
Second Edition December 2016

COURSE OF KABALAH[1]

DR. KRUMM-HELLER
(HUIRACOCHA)

Archbishop of the Holy Gnostic Church.

1936

CURSO DE CÁBALA[2]

DR. KRUMM HELLER
(HUIRACOCHA)

Arzobispo de la Santa Iglesia Gnóstica.

1936

---

[1] Full title: "Course of Aryan-Egyptian Kabalah"

[2] Titulo completo: "Curso de Cábala Ario-egipcia"

CURSO DE CABALA

DR. ARNOLDO KRUMM HELLER

Berlín – Heiligensee – Jagerweg 10 - Alemania

CONTENTS

ÍNDICE

CORRESPONDENCE COURSES

Of the Fraternitas Rosicruciana Antiqua, with [its] seat in Berlín-Keiligensee-Germany.

Dictated by its Commander for Hispanic-America

1st. **Esoteric Zodiacal Course.**—It makes available all the occult practices necessary to prepare the body so that the divine forces can penetrate into it. Its results are: physical Strength/Force and Health, Spiritual Power and Light. This Course constitute a revelation for oneself.

2nd. **Runic Course.**—What was yesterday [a] privilege of [the] initiated priests, especially in the application of the Magic Runes, is now in the hands of the sincere student. Its keys will permit one to reconstruct within oneself each of the characters of the **great Living Alphabet,** unfolding[3] the transcendental faculties and converting oneself into [an] arbitrator[4] of one's own destiny. With it one enters into possession of the most ancient dialect[5] of **Light.**

3rd. **Course of Aryan-Egiptian Kabalah.**—It is the bridge that connects the previous courses. Enclosed [in it are] all the keys and Arcana of the practical Kabalah.

---

[3] Literally 'desenvolver' means "unfold, unwrap; unwind; disentangle, extricate; develop; expound, explain"

[4] Literally 'árbitro' means "arbiter, arbitrator; mediator; umpire, referee"

[5] Literally 'idioma' means "Language, tongue, idiom (mode of speaking peculiar to a dialect or language), lingo (the language peculiar to a nation or country), speech.", but we have translated this term as 'dialect' throughout this text for uniformity.

CURSOS POR CORRESPONDENCIA

De la Fraternitas Rosicruciana Antiqua, con sede en Berlín-Keiligensee-Alemania.

Dictadas por su Comendador para Hispano-América

1.° **Curso Esotérico Zodiacal.**—Con él pone al alcance de todos las prácticas ocultas necesarias a fin de preparar el cuerpo para que penetren en él las fuerzas divinas. Sus resultados son: Fuerza y Salud física, Poder y Luz Espiritual. Este Curso constituye de por sí una revelación.

2.° **Curso Rúnico.**—Lo que hasta ayer fué privilegio de sacerdotes iniciados, sobre todo en la aplicación de la Magia de las Runas, queda hoy en manos del estudiante sincero. Sus claves le permitirán reconstruir en sí mismo cada uno de los caracteres del **gran Alfabeto Viviente,** desenvolver las facultades trascendentales y convertirse en árbitro de su propio destino. Con él entrará en posesión del más antiguo idioma de **Luz.**

3.° **Curso de Cábala Ario-Egipcia.**—Es el puente que une los Cursos anteriores. Encierra todas las claves y Arcanos de la Cabala práctica.

Since[6] the key[7] for the **Kabalah** is the **Tarot** (deck[8] of 78 cards), the objective of this Course is to teach [how] to read within each one of its 78 plates (which constitute the pages of the most ancient book of the world) wherein is contained all the mysteries of life: **Past, Present and Future,** they are in them; [afterwards you will] know enough to decipher it. The **Aryan-Egyptian Tarot** is the perpetuator of our own western tradition.

Conditions—(previous promise of silence): ESOTERIC ZODIACAL COURSE (12 lessons) 3 dollars. RUNIC COURSE (12 lessons) 3 Dollars.

Course of Aryan-Egiptian Kabalah, *free,* to all those who acquire a legitimate **Tarot** Deck, [the] cost of [which] is 5 Dollars; since these 78 colored cards are indispensable for study.[9] The only interest which is pursued in this Course is to divulge our own western tradition.

Doctor KRUMM-HELLER
Berlin - Heiligensee - Jagerweg 10 - Germany.

Como la llave de la **Cábala** es el **Tarot** (naipe de 78 cartas), el objeto de este Curso es enseñar a leer en cada una de sus 78 láminas, que constituyen las páginas del más antiguo libro del mundo, donde se guardan todos los misterios de la vida: **Pasado, Presente y Futuro,** están en ellas; basta saberlo descifrar. El **Tarot Ario-Egipcio** es el perpetuador de nuestra propia tradición occidental.

Condiciones—(previa promesa de silencio): CURSO ESOTÉRICO ZODIACAL (12 lecciones) 3 dollars. CURSO RÚNICO (12 lecciones) 3 Dollars.

Curso de Cábala Ario-Egipcia, *gratis,* a todos los que adquieran un Naipe **Tarot** legítimo, cuyo precio es de 5 Dollars; pues sus 78 cartas en colores son indispensables para el estudio. El único interés que se persigue con este Curso es divulgar nuestra propia tradición occidental.

Doctor KRUMM-HELLER
Berlín - Heiligensee - Jagerweg 10 - Alemania.

---

[6] Literally 'Como' means "as, like; by way of"

[7] Literally 'llave' means "brace; key; piston; lock; tap, faucet"

[8] Literally 'naipe' means "pasteboard, cardboard; playing card"

[9] Editor's note: This appears to be the 'Deutsches Original Tarot' or "Original German Tarot" first published by A. Frank Glahn (1865-1941) as a compliment to his book *Das Deutsche Tarotbuch* (1909) [*The German Tarotbook*]. This deck is also known under various other names including the 'Glahn Tarot', the 'Hermann Bauer Tarot' (from the name of a publisher of the deck, Hermann Bauer), and the 'Hans Schubert Tarot' (from the name of the apparent Designer and Artist who drew them according to Glahn's descriptions). Krumm-Heller refers to them as the 'Nordic Tarot' or 'Nordic Cards'.

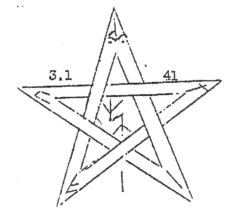

[Lesson 1]

M E S S A G E
from
the Sovereign Commander of
the Rosecross Order as [a]
Secret Course for the
dependent[10] brothers
of the S.S.S.

———

[Lección I]

M E N S A J E
del
Soberano Comendador de la
Orden Rosacruz como
Curso Secreto para los
hermanos dependientes
del S.S.S.

———

Beloved Disciple:

We have given to the disciples, after the Zodiacal Course, that of the Runes.

Now we follow with a new Course on Kabalah.

This obeys[11] a plan, [which has been] preconceived in advance.

In [a] similar way that the engineer, in order to accomplish their career, needs various studies, such as [how to design] roads, buildings, mathematics, drawing, etc., and then their work requires plans, in the same way the student who wants to be [a] lawyer[12] needs different studies, [of] Law and Codes, so too [does] the student of Occultism need to learn one subject after another, not for a final exam, but in order to get to consciously communicate with the Invisible World.

It may be the case that a student comes prepared from another previous life and for this reason nothing [is] set in stone[13].

Querido Discípulo:

Hemos dado a los discípulos, después del Curso Zodiacal, el de las Runas.

Hoy seguidos con un nuevo Curso sobre Cabala.

Esto obedece a un plan, de antemano preconcebido.

Del mismo modo que el ingeniero, para lograr su carrera, preciso diversos estudios, tales como caminos, construcciones, matematicas, dibujo, etc., y luego en sus trabajos necesita planos, de la misma manera que el estudiante que desea ser abogado necesita estudiar distinto, Derecho y Codigos, asi también el estudiante de Ocultismo, precisa aprender una materia tras otra, no para un examen final, sino para llegar a comunicarse conscientemente con el Mundo Invisible.

Se puede dar el caso de que un estudiante venga preparado de otra vida anterior y por esta razón nada precisa.

---

[10] Literally 'dependientes' means "dependant; dependent"
[11] Literally 'obedece' means "obey, take orders; mind; answer"
[12] Literally 'abogado' means "lawyer, attorney, barrister"
[13] Literally 'precisa' means "precise, accurate; necessary, requisite"

The courses [we are giving] are not for these [people], [they are] only for those few who are looking[14] for the Path.

In the Hermetic School of Papus we spent several years doing nothing but study.

Our ideal [situation] would be about fifty students in the Temple of the S.S.S. [Summum Supremum Sanctorium] in order to methodical study[15] the teachings every day.

But nowadays, this is very difficult.

There are few disciples who can take a trip to Germany, and with [just] a few [it is] not worth it.

There is, then, another way with[16] our Courses, and we are encouraged by the results actually[17] obtained.

Hundreds of disciples have achieved[18] the goal and all [of them] have reached Initiation.

All with perseverance[19] and with love for the cause.

Our subject matter is Kabalah and the High[20] Magic within it.

Para éstos no son los corsos, sino para aquellos[21] que van poco por el Sendero.

En la Escuela Hermética de Papus pasamos varios a años sin hacer otra cosa que estudiar.

Nuestro ideal seria tener una cincuentena de alumnos en él Templo del S.S.S. para dar en el diariamente ensenanzas metódicas.

Pero hoy por hoy, esto es dificilísimo.

Pocos son los discípulos que pueden emprender un viaje a Alemania, y con pocos no vale la pena.

No hay, pues, otro camino que nuestros Cursos, y el resultudo obtenido realmente nos alienta.

Centenares de discípulos consiguieron la meta y todos llegarán a la Iniciacion.

Todo de constancia y de amor a la causa.

Nuestro tema tema es Cabala y dentro de el Magia Superior.

---

[14] Literally 'van' means "go, proceed, move; travel; walk; suit; lead; drive; ride; see, view, perceive with the eyes; watch, observe; comprehend, understand; envisage, visualize; try, put on trial (Law); examine, inspect"

[15] Literally 'dar' means "give; present; deal; produce, yield; cause; perform; say; take; teach; lecture; start, begin; overlook; surrender"

[16] Literally 'que' means "that; than; but; for; since, because"

[17] Literally 'realmente' means "really, truly, actually; simply"

[18] Literally 'consiguieron' means "obtain, acquire, come by; procure, secure; earn, achieve"

[19] Literally 'constancia' means "constancy; certainty; proof, evidence"

[20] Literally 'Superior' means "superior, higher in rank or position; high; ranking; best; highest, top; advanced; over; farther"

---

[21] Originalmente "aqullos"

Let us begin with the Tarot, not as Papus has taught it, but with the modifications that further study and the Rose-Cross archives have suggested to us.

Much has been written about this particular [subject], but so far there is nothing good, nothing worthwhile.

This course will fulfill all the aspirations of the disciples.

The writers explaining the origin of the cards say that these were murals on the pyramid of Memphis and that the egyptians copied them onto little plates[22] in order to learn and to study the mysteries.

Students will see that each Arcanum is, effectively, a Key of Magic; and so much so that on each of them one can write an extended volume, such that each Arcanum encloses all the Occult Science.

Much discussion has started among the Initiates [about] the number of cards necessary in order to predict[23] the future.

There are games of 32 and those of 40 [cards], but 78 are necessary.

These 78 [cards] are divided into 26 Major Arcana and 52 complementary cards or Minor Arcana.[24]

We are going to teach with the 78 cards.

Principiemos por el Tarot no como lo enseno Papus, sino con las modificaciones que estudies ulteriores y los archivos Rosa-Cruz nos han sugerido.

Mucho se ha escrito sobre este particular, pero hasta ahora no hay nada bueno, nada que valga la pena.

Este curso llenará todas las aspiraciones de los discípulos.

Dicen los tratadistas explicando el origen de los naipes, que estos eran cuadros murales de la piramide de Menfis y que de allí los copiaron en laminillas los egipcios para aprender y estudiar los misterios.

Ya irán viendo los alumnos como efectivamente cada Arcano es una Clave de la Magia; y tan es asi que sobre cada uno de ellos puede escribirse un volumen extenso, ya que cada Arcano encierra la Ciencia Oculta toda.

Mucho se ha discutido entre los Iniciados el número de cartas necesarias para profetizar el porvenir.

Hay juegos de 32 y los hay de 40, pero son necesarias 78.

Estas 78 se dividen en 26 Arcanos Mayores y en 52 cartas complementarias o Arcanos Menores.[25]

Nosotros vamos a enseñar con las 78 cartas.

---

[22] Literally 'laminillas' means "lamellae, leaflets, flakes, platelets"

[23] Literally 'profetizar' means "prophesy, predict, forecast, foretell"

[24] Editor's note: Compare "…We have arrived at the conclusion that: all Kabalah is reduced to the 22 Major Arcana of the Tarot and [the] 4 Aces, which represent the 4 Elements of Nature…" from *Zodiacal Course* (1951) by Samael Aun Weor, in the chapter on Sagittarius.

---

[25] Nota del editor: Comparemos "…Llegamos a la conclusión de que: toda Kábala se reduce a los 22 Arcanos Mayores del Tarot y 4 Ases, que representan los 4 Elementos de la Naturaleza…" del *Curso Zodiacal* (1951) por Samael Aun Weor, en el capítulo sobre Sagitario.

It is necessary to establish a bridge between Astrology, Quirology and Cartomancy.

So, with these three disciplines we will realize a complete work, as these three constitute the Kabalah.

The origin of the cards is very difficult to prove.

Already in the 14th century, an Italian called the attention to the art of the spread.

Then we have seen that gypsies and ignorant people [who] occupy themselves with this Art [are actually] undermining it with their foolish chatter[26], until one day the astrologers saw that behind these cards something speaks and that it was something simply superb.

All peoples have used painted pictures[27] in order to synthesize their knowledge and so we have different kabalahs.

The first is the Nordic or Aryan Kabalah and [this] is what the Egyptians knew.

The jews took it with them, modified it or let us call it by its name: they falsified it and, disgrasfully, that of Papus is also falsified.

He suspected this but [he] did not get to know the Nordic [Tarot].

Today we are giving [something] to the disciple and beginning our study, for which we present a Practical Course: A male or female friend learns that we are students of [the] Kabalah and comes to us for us to tell them their future.

Es preciso establecer un puente entre la Astrología, la Quirosofía y la Cartomancia.

Así, con estas tres disciplinas realizaremos una obra completa, ya que estas tres constituyen la Cábala.

El origen del naipe es muy difícil de probar.

Ya en el siglo XIV, un italiano llamó la atención en el arte de echar las cartas.

Luego hemos visto que los gitanos y la gente ignorante se ocupaba de este Arte desprestigiándolo con sus charlatanerías, hasta que un día vieron los astrólogos que tras de esas cartas había algo y que ese algo era sencillamente soberbio.

Todos los pueblos se han valido de cuadros pintados para sintetizar su saber y asi tenemos cabalas diferentes.

La principal es la Cábala Aria o Nórdica y es esa que conocieron los egipcios.

Los judios al dar con ella, la modificaron o digamoslo por su nombre: la falsificaron y desgraciadanente la de Papas es tembien le falsificada.

El lo sospechaba pero no llegó a conocer la Nórdica.

Hoy la damos al discípulo y vamos a comenzar nuestro estudio, para lo cual presentaremos un Curso Práctico: Un amigo o amiga se entera que somos estudiantes de Cábala y viene a nosotros para que le digamos su porvenir.

---

[26] Literally 'charlatanerías' means "chatter, patter, small talk; palaver, idle or foolish chatter; quackery, charlatanry"
[27] Literally 'cuadros' means "square; stable, structure in which horses and other animals are housed; picture; painting; plot; table; chart"

We explain to them that people have taken to cards in order to get money, they have prostituted it, [and] that this is not a diversion nor a passtime[28], but something sacred that must begin with a prayer, for which please clasp your <u>hands</u> in [a] <u>prayerful</u> attitude.

Now [pay] attention!

If the <u>thumb</u> of the <u>right</u> hand is placed on the thumb of the <u>left hand</u>, [then] we have in front of us a <u>solar</u> person, whereas if the <u>thumb</u> of the <u>left hand</u> is <u>placed</u> on that of the the right, [then] the person in question will be **<u>lunar</u>**.

The <u>solar</u> [person] will be represented by <u>cups and pentacles</u>[29]; and the lunar [will be represented] by swords and clubs[30].

We separate the 26 Arcana from the 52 complementary cards.

Cards are being pulled from the 56 Arcana drawing from those that correspond to the requesting person: Pentacles - Cups, if [they] are solar; or Swords - Clubs if [they] are lunar.

If one pulls two Pentacles or two Cups in the first case and two Swords or two Clubs in the second row, [then] we will put these two cards in the respective centers of the two circles that we will form; leaving a space in the center in order to then put the 26 Major Arcana, then we repeat [this again], [and] we have to used all 78 cards.

Le explicaremos que las personas que han llevado las cartas al juego para sacar dinero, las han prostituido, que esto no es una diversion ni un pasatiempo, sino algo sagrado que debemos comenzar con una oracion, para lo cual le rogamos que junte las <u>manos</u> en actitud <u>orante</u>.

¡Atencion ahora!

Si el dedo <u>pulgar</u> de la mano <u>derecha</u> lo coloca sobre el pulgar de la <u>mano izquierda</u>, tenemos ante nosotros una persona <u>solar</u> mientras que si <u>coloca</u> el <u>pulgar</u> de la <u>mano izquierda</u> sobre el de la derecha, la persona en cuestion sera **<u>lunar</u>**.

La <u>solar</u> será representada por <u>copa y oro</u>; y la lunar por espada y basto.

Separamos los 26 Arcanos de las 52 cartas complementarias.

Se van sacando cartas de los 56 Arcanos, hasta sacar la que corresponden a la persona consultante: Oros - Copas, si es solar o Espadas - Bastos si es lunar.

Si se sacan dos Oros o dos Copas en el primer caso y dos Espadas o dos Bastos en el segundo seguidos, haremos con estas dos cartas los centros respectivos de los dos círculos que vamos a formar; dejando un espacio en el centro para poner luego un Arcano Mayor de los 26, pues repetimos, hemos de emplear las 78 cartas.

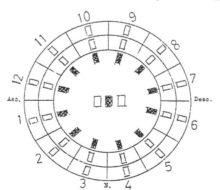

---

[28] Literally 'pasatiempo' means "pastime, hobby; entertainment; recreation, amusement"

[29] Literally 'oro' or 'oros' means "Gold, Gold Medals; Diamonds; Pentacles"

[30] Literally 'Bastos' means "clubs; coarse, rough; base, low"

We will form each circle with [the] central arcanum-card and twelve arcana in [a] circle.

Thus each circle is composed of 13 arcana.

By forming two circles we will used the 26 Major Arcana.

The central cards represent the consultanting [person].

In the same way that we form twelve houses in the horoscope, so too we will form them with the cards and we will equally have that the card on the left will be the Ascendant, that of the right the Descendant, the top [card is] the Midheaven and the bottom [card is] the Nadir.

Let us also considered the aspects: Sextile and Trine are good; Oppositions and Quadratures are bad.

We begin to form the first house, for which, in the first house, that is to say the first card [from those] we pulled [from the] two cards in the 52 complementary [cards].

Immediately we pull two others in the first card of the second circle [which] represents the past and present; and the second circle [represents] the future.

Now what remains is to know the meaning of each card and this is what we will study in the course for the next few lessons, because they will open up new horizons for us, since EVERY CARD ENCLOSES A GREAT MYSTERY.

Formaremos cada círculo con carta-arcano central y doce arcanos en círculo.

Así que cada círculo se compone de 13 arcanos.

Al formar los dos circulos habremos empleado los 26 Arcanos Mayores.

Las cartas centrales representan, al consultante.

De la misma manera que formamos en el horoscopo doce casas, asi también las formaremos con las cartas y tendremos igualmente que, la carta de la izquierda sera el Ascendente, la de la derecha el Descendente, la superior el Medio Cielo y la inferior el Nadir.

Considerados igualmente los aspectos: Sextil y Trígono son buenos; Oposiciones y Cuadraturas son malas.

Comenzamos a formar la primera casa, para lo cual, en la primera casa, es decir en la primera carta colocamos dos cartas en las 52 complementarias.

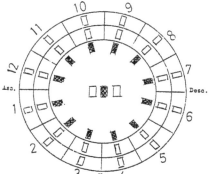

Inmediatamente colocamos otras dos en la primera carta del segundo círculo representa el presente y pasado y el segundo círculo el porvenir.

Ahora lo que falta es conocer el significado de cada carta y esto es lo que vamos a estudiar en el transcurso de las siguientes lecciones, pues ellas nos irán abriendo nuevos horizontes, ya que CADA CARTA ENCIERRA UN GRAN MISTERIO.

Card N° 1 for the brazilians has the name [of] "The Swindler[31]".

It should be 'the Magician [or Magi]', it is he who teaches us sacred Magic and he does not 'swindle'.

The Magician
Le Bateleur
1

On the head of the 'Swindler' is the symbol of infinity [and] on the table [is] a cup, jumbling[32] the pentacles with the sword and with the right hand he goes towards the gold or the money [that is, the coins or pentacles].

Magier

The Aryan card is very different: At the top is the Rune Fa ᚠ [like an F], that is to say, the creator, the factor, the father, the divine essence as [the] impulse of life.

The Magician holds, for this [purpose], the magic club [staff or wand] in his right hand, while in the left [hand] he carries the "Ang" symbol or the sword, the cup and the pentacle [which is on the table], being completed with the club [staff or wand] in his [other] hand.

The hebrew card says that the significance is 'earth', [but] no, it should say fire or "Light", because in the beginning was the Light of the Spirit.

The disciples, then, who compare[33] the hebrew and Aryan cards, will see the falsification made in those centuries, but [the law of] Karma permitted it and from this we rejoice, because with this comparative study one learns more easily.

La carta N° 1 de las brasileras tiene la denominación "El Escamoteador".

Debe ser el Mago, pues es él quien nos enseña la Magia sagrada y no escamotea.

Sobre la cabeza del Escamoteador está el simbolo del infinito sobre la mesa una copa, revuelto el oro con la espada y con la mano derecha va al oro o sea al dinero.

Muy distinta la carta Aria: Por encima está la Runa Fa ᚠ es decir el creador, el factor, el padre, la esencia divina como impulso de la vida.

El Mago tiene por eso el basto o sea la varilla de magia en la diestra, mientras que en la izquierda lleva el simbolo "Ang" o sea la espada, la copa y el oro, quedando completado con el basto en su mano.

La carta hebrea dice que el significado es la tierra, no, debe decir fuego o "Luz", pues al principio fue la Luz del Espiritu.

Los discípulos pues, que confronten las cartas hebreas y las Arias, verán la falsificacion hecha en aquellos siglos, pero Carma lo permitio y de eso nos alegramos, pues con ese estudio comparativo se aprende con más facilidad.

---

[31] Literally 'Escamoteador' means "scrambler; swindler; conjurer"

[32] Literally 'revuelto' means "scrambled, jumbled; unruly; troubled"

[33] Literally 'confronten' means "confront; collate, compare critically"

Card N° 2 takes on a name of [the] "Popess" and should be [the] "Priestess".

While in the hebrew [card] the left hand [is] on a closed book, in the Aryan she offers two keys and in the right [hand she has] a parchment[34].

It signifies <u>fame</u>, <u>reward</u>, <u>intelligence</u>[35], <u>the people</u>, <u>the masses</u> and <u>consultation</u>.

Of all these significances, the disciple [should] keep [in mind] the relationships with the rest [of the] cards according to the house.

The Popess
La Papesse

La carta N° 2 lleva en una el nombre de "Papisa" y debe ser "Sacerdotisa".

Mientras en la hebrea esta con la mano izquierda sobre un libro cerraio.en la Aria ofrece dos llaves y en la derecha un pergamino.

Ella significa <u>fama</u>, <u>recompensa</u>, <u>inteligencia</u>, <u>el pueblo</u>, <u>las masas</u> y <u>consulta</u>.

De todos estos significados el discípulo tiene que ver las relaciones con las demás cartas según las casa.

---

[34] Literally 'pergamino' means "sheepskin; parchment (the skin of sheep, goats, etc., prepared for use as a material on which to write; a manuscript or document on such material)"
[35] Literally 'inteligencia' means "intelligence, knowledge; wit; brains; abilities; comprehension, understanding"

A S P E C T S

A S P E C T O S

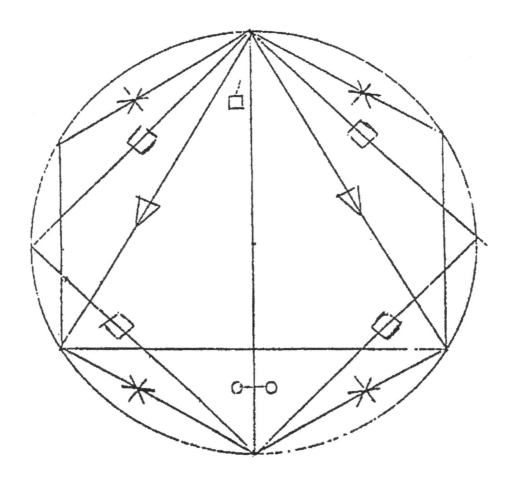

✳ = sextile = **very favorable** = 60°
    sextil = muy favorable = 60°

▢ = quadrature = **unfavorable** = 90°
    cuadratura = desfavorable = 90°

△ = trine = **favorable** = 120°
    trígono = favorable = 120°

O—O = opposition = **very unfavorable** = 180°
    opposición = muy desfavorable = 180°

P R E S E N T

P R E S E N T E

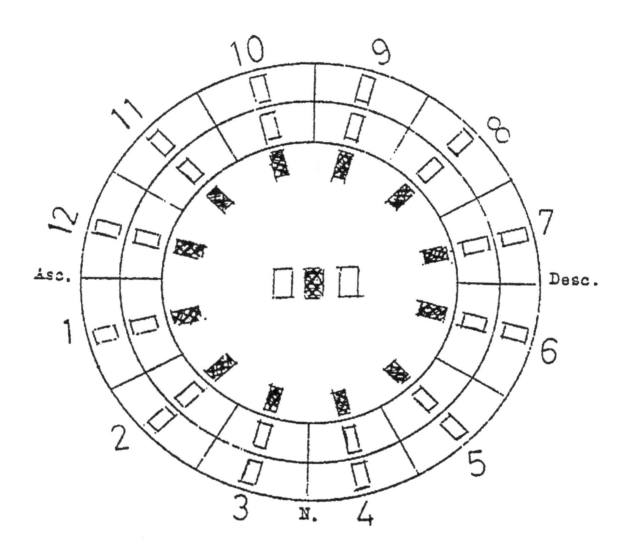

C A R D S

▦ = BASE-ARCANA [MAJOR ARCANA]

☐ = SIMPLE [MINOR ARCANA]

C A R T A S

▦ = ARCANOS-BASE [ARCANOS MAYORES]

☐ = SIMPLES [ARCANOS MENORES]

FUTURE

PORVENIR

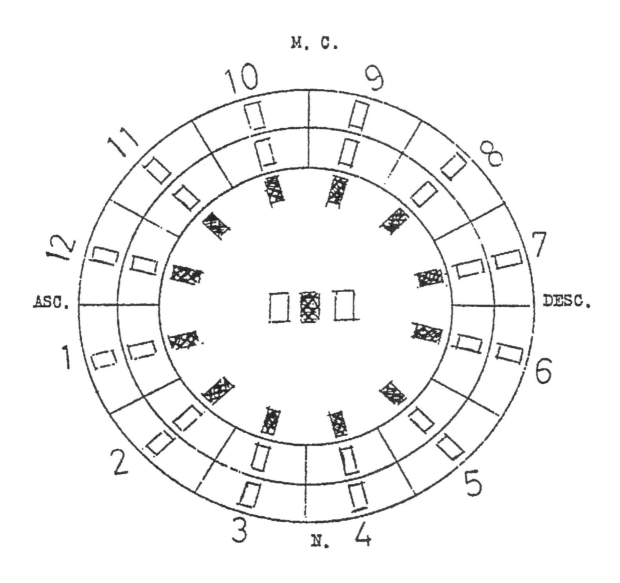

C A R D S

⊠ = BASE-ARCANA [MAJOR ARCANA]

☐ = SIMPLE [MINOR ARCANA]

C A R T A S

⊠ = ARCANOS-BASE [ARCANOS MAYORES]

☐ = SIMPLES [ARCANOS MENORES]

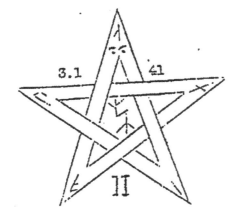

[Lesson 2]

M E S S A G E
from
the Sovereign Commander of
the Rosecross Order as [a]
Secret Course for the
dependent brothers
of the S.S.S.

———

[Lección II]

M E N S A J E
del
Soberano Comendador de la
Orden Rosacruz como
Curso Secreto para los
hermanos dependientes
del S.S.S.

———

Beloved Disciple:

Before proceeding with the comparison and description of the different cards we must teach the meaning of the houses to the disciple, [thus] when pulling the cards, one can more easily explain the significance.

We know from other studies or publications about Astrology that the:

First House: indicates the qualities of the person [in] question, [it] is the House of the SELF. Diseases of the head. The planet is Mars and the sign [is] Aries. It is also the House of the Ascendant and one must see [the] works of Astrology in order to know [its] significance.

Second House: is that of YOURS[36] [or YOUR POSSESSIONS/VALUES], it discloses the possibilities of fortune, sentiments and character. Diseases of the neck and throat. The planet is Venus and the zodiac sign [is] TAURUS.

Third House: refers to siblings, short voyages [with] relatives[37]. The planet is Mercury and the zodiac sign [is] GEMINI. Diseases of the stomach.

Querido Discípulo:

Antes de seguir adelante con la comparación y descripcion de las diferentes cartas debemos ensenar el significado de las casas para que el discípulo, cuando extiende las cartas, pueda con mas facilidad explicar el significado.

Ya sabemos de otros estudios o publicaciones sobre Astrologia que la

Primera Casa: indica las cualidades de la persona interrogante, es la Casa del SÍ MISMO[38]. Las enfermedades de la cabeza. El planeta es Marte y el signo Aries. Es también la Casa del Ascendente y hay que ver obras de Astrologia para conocer el significado.

Segunda Casa: es la del TU, da a conocer las posibilidades de la fortuna, los sentimientos y caracter. Enfermedades del cuello y garganta. El planeta es Venus y el signo zodiacal TORO.

Tercera Casa: se refiere a los hermanos, viajes cortos parientes. El planeta es Mercurio y el signo zodiacal GEMELOS. Las enfermedades del estómago.

---

[36] Literally 'TU' means "you, thou; your, thy, belonging to you, belonging to the person or persons being addressed"
[37] Literally 'parientes' means "kin, kindred, kinfolk; sib, sibling; relative, relation; dad; old man"

[38] Originalmente "Casa del YO"

Fourth House: discloses the relationship with parents, the homeland and the end of life. Diseases of the lymphatic system. The planet is the Moon and the zodiac sign [is] Cancer.

Fifth House: makes us see the odds in gambling[39] and speculation[40], the number of our children and their welfare. Diseases of the spleen. The sign is LEO and the planet [is] the Sun.

Sixth House: we have [here the] suspected[41] diseases, the servants, if we have them, and the clothes (dresses). Diseases of the intestines. The planet is Mercury and the zodiac sign [is] VIRGO.

Seventh House: can be considered as opposed to the first [house] and makes [us] see the relationships with our associates[42], with partners[43], public rivals and luck in general. Diseases, [of the] urinary tract and nerves. The planet is Venus and the astrological sign [is] LIBRA.

Eighth House: indicates to us whether inheritances, testament of wills, [testaments] of death and of destiny[44]; what may encourage[45] the children or widow after we die, if there is danger of [premature] death for the questioner. Sexual diseases. The planet [is] Mars and the Sign [is] SCORPIO.

Cuarta Casa: da a conocer la relacion con los padres, la patria y el final de la vida. Las enfermedades del sistema linfático. El planeta es la Luna y el signo zodiacal cáncer.

Quinta casa: nos hace ver las probabilidades del juego y especulaciones, el número da nuestros hijos y su bienestar. Las enfermedades del bazo. El signo es LEON y el planeta el Sol.

Sexta Casa: nos hace sospechar las enfermedades, los criados, si los tenemos, y la ropa (vestidos). Las enfermedades de los intestinos. El planeta es Mercurio y el signo zodiacal VIRGO.

Séptima Casa: puede considerarse como opuesta a la primera y hace ver las relaciones con nuestros socios, con la mujer, rivales publicos y suerte en general. Las enfermedades, vías urinarias y nervios. El planeta es Venus y el signo zodiacal LIBRA.

Octava Casa: nos indica si hay herencias, habla de testamentos, de la muerte y de la suerte que puedan correr los hijos o viuda despues de morir nosotros, si hay peligro de muerte para el interrogante. Las enfermedades sexuales. El planeta es Marte y el Signo ESCORPION.

---

[39] Literally 'juego' means "game, sport; court; gambling; set; service"

[40] Literally 'especulaciones' means "speculation (the contemplation or consideration of some subject; engagement in business transactions involving considerable risk but offering the chance of large gains, especially trading in commodities, stocks, etc., in the hope of profit from changes in the market price)"

[41] Literally 'sospechar' means "suspect, imagine to be so, believe to be true"

[42] Literally 'socios' means "member; partner, associate; sidekick; fellow"

[43] Literally 'mujer' means "woman; wife; inamorata"

[44] Literally 'suerte' means "destiny, fate, fortune, something which is to happen to a person; future course of events; luck, chance; condition, situation; sort, type, kind; stage"

[45] Literally 'correr' means "run, jog or move at a pace faster than that of walking; hurry; gallop; stream; blow; travel; publish"

Ninth House: represents great voyages, [and] education. It is the house of religion and philosophy. Diseases of the legs and fevers. The planet is Jupiter and the zodiac sign [is] SAGITTARIUS.

Tenth House: teaches us the honors that await us, our profession, and relationships with our chiefs[46]. Rheumatic diseases, [and those of the] arms and legs. The planet is Saturn and the zodiac sign [is] CAPRICORN.

Eleventh House: [here we] get to know our successes, [and our] protectors[47]. Diseases of the feet [or calves]. The planet is Saturn and the zodiac sign [is] AQUARIUS.

Twelfth House: points out our enemies, possibilities of entering into prison and also into hospitals. Diseases of the blood and feet. The planet is Neptune and the zodiacal sign [is] PISCES.

Let's look [at] why we put three cards into every house, one of the Base-Arcana [or Major Arcana] and two simple [or Minor Arcana].

We made two equal circles, one meaning the PRESENT, and the other [meaning] the FUTURE.

Now think about the significance of the house and of the three cards with a bit of imagination, [and] many things [can] be deduced, especially if you now put the cards in front of us into their respective houses, [then] we see the relationship with other houses and other cards.

If there is good or bad luck. This shows that it is good to know Astrology.

Novena Casa: representa los grandes viajes, la educacion. Es la casa de la religion y la filosofia. Las enfermedades de las piernas y las fiebres. El planeta es Jupiter y el signo zodiacal SAGITARIO.

Décima Casa: nos ensena los honores que nos esperan, nuestra profesion, y las relaciones con nuestros jefes. Las enfermedades reumaticas, brazos y piernas. El planeta es Saturno y el signo zodiacal CAPRICORNIO.

Undécima Casa: da a conocer nuestros éxitos, protectores. Las enfermedades de los pies. El planeta es Saturno y el signo zodiacal ACUARIO.

Duodécima Casa: nos senala nuestros enemigos, posibilidades de entrar a prision y también a hospitales. Las enfermedades de la sangre y pies. El planeta es Neptuno y el signo zodiacal PECES.

Fijémonos que hemos puesto en cada casa tres cartas, una de los Arcanos-Base y dos simples.

Hemos hecho dos circulos iguales, uno que significa el PRESENTE, y el otro el PORVENIR.

Ahora pensando en el significado de la casa y de las tres cartas con un poco de imaginación[48] se deducen muchas cosas, sobre todo si ahora puestas las cartas frente de nosotros, en sus respectivas casas, vemos la relacion con otras casas y otros naipes.

Si hay buena o mala suerte. Se ve que es bueno saber Astrologia.

---

[46] Literally 'jefes' means "boss, manager; chief, head, leader, ruler"
[47] Literally 'protectores' means "protector, guardian; defender; embankment"

[48] Originalmente "fantasia"

Concluding these explanations we can return to the significance of the cards and compare the hebrew with the aryan.

It is good to be aware[49] that when the head of the card falls [down, or it is reversed then this] is bad, [and on the other hand] it is good when [the card is] standing up [or upright].

We will see later that cards also contain the secret of the calendar, having [a] certain chronological key.

Already in the previous circular[50] we talked about the first cards and we must add that birds always mean the spiritual plane, the invisible world, which should always be placed high up and not like the hebrew card has it where the eagle is low, only the "Empress" is winged.

The 3rd card [in the Nordic deck] shows the eagle on a tree and is [being] interrogated by the Empress.

The cross always singifies matter and the Rose or flowers [always singify] the spirit.

In the first [card] we saw that the Magician is standing between roses.

Let's pass on to the 4th [card]: there we see four slaves who represent the Inferior Quaternary.

The Empress
L'Imperatrice 3

Herrscherin

Herrscher

Concluidas estas explicaciones podemos volver al significado de las cartas y comparar las hebreas con las arias.

Bueno es advertir aun que cuando la carta cae de cabeza es malo, bueno es cuando está de pie.

Veremos más tarde que las cartas encierran también el secreto del calendario, tienen cierta clave cronológica.

Ya en la circular anterior hablamos de las primeras cartas y debemos agregar que aves siempre significa el plano espiritual, el mundo invisible, que debe ser colocado siempre por lo alto y no como lo hace ver la carta hebrea donde el águila está abajo, sólo la "Emperatriz" está alada.

La carta 3/a. trae el aguila sobre un arbol y es interrogado por la Emperatriz.

La cruz significa siempre la materia y la Rosa o flores el espiritu.

En la primera vemos que el Mago esta parado entre rosas.

Pasamos a la 4/a: ahi vemos cuatro esclavos que representen el Cuaternario Inferior.

---

[49] Literally 'advertir' means "warn, caution; forewarn; point out; notice; admonish"

[50] Literally 'circular' means "circular, paper or leaflet intended for distribution"

It corresponds [to] the Rune OS, while the former [card or the 3rd card] has the value of DORN or THORN and I beg[51] the disciples to take the Zodiacal Course in order to draw [proper] conclusions[52].

The 4th [card] corresponds to the sign [of] Scorpio and to the planet Jupiter.

It is always a good sign when pulling a card in the same house as the planet.

The Emperor
L'Empereur   4

Upright [it] signifies blond/fair[53] and wealthy husband, takeover[54], hypocrisy; [being] on [the beneficial] side [of the] Law; reversed [it means] shipwreck, ill-will, abuse of force/strength and temporal.

Let's notice the position of the leg, in the hebrew [card he] has the right leg [raised], while the Aryan, the left [leg is] raised.

The disciples will see the connection with the Zodiacal Course.

Let's pass [on] to the 5th card. The hebrews call it "The Pope", while the Aryan [deck] designates it with [the title of] "Priest" and it is natural when the egyptians copied the cards [they] did not have a Pope and one can clearly see [in the hebrew card] the judeo-christian synchronicity.

Two slaves are seen kneeling before the priest in the [hebrew] one and three in the other, forming the superior principle [that is] the priest.

The Pope
Le Pape   5

Le corresponde la Runa OS, mientras la anterior tiene el valor de DORN o TORN y suplico a los discípulos tomen el Curso Zodiacal para sacar consecuencias.

La 4/a corresponde al signo Escorpion y al planeta Jupiter.

Buena señal es siempre cuando cae una carta en la misma casa del planeta.

De cabeza significa marido rubio y rico, toma de posesión, hipocresía; de lado Ley; al revés naufragio, mala voluntad, abuso de fuerza y temporal.

Fijémonos en la posicion de la pierna en la hebrea tiene la pierna derecha, mientras que en la Aria, la izquierda levantada.

Los discípulos veran la conexion con el Curso Zodiacal.

Pasamos a la 5/a carta. Los hebreos la llaman "El Papa", mientras la Aria la disigna con "Sacerdote" y es natural cuando los egipcios copiaron las cartas no había aún Papas y se ve claro el sincronismo judíocristiano.

Dos esclavos arrodillados frente al sacerdote se ven en la una y tres en la otra, formando el sacerdote el principio superior.

---

[51] Literally 'suplico' means "supplicate, appeal, pray; invoke, conjure"
[52] Literally 'consecuencias' means "consequence, outcome, effect; aftermath; consistence; issue, sequel"
[53] Literally 'rubio' means "fair, light; blond; dusky; blond, one who has light-colored hair"
[54] Literally 'toma de posesión' means "entry, inauguration, takeover"

[In the hebrew card] the pope blesses the inferior principles, bearing the Cross in the right hand, while in the Aryan [card] he signals with two keys pointing to heaven, to the stars, as [if] saying that in Heaven is the Key to the mysteries.

Everything [exists] under the Law, thus, the Rune is Rita - the Law

Upright the card is fortune, wealth, inspiration and teaching, reversed [it] signifies match[55].

Let's pass [on] to the 6th [card]. While the hebrew [card] puts the disciple beside a man and a woman, [and] names it "The Lover" showing cupid firing the arrow at the man, while in the Aryan [card] the arrow goes into void[56] and is fired by an Angel.[57]

The woman [is] completely dressed in the hebrew [card], [while] in the Aryan [card] a naked woman [is] shown.

———

El papa bendice, teniendo la Cruz en la diestra[58], a los principios inferiores, mientras en la Aria señala con dos llaves al cielo, a las estrellias, como diciendo que en el Cielo esta la Clave de los misterios.

Todo bajo la Ley pues la Runa es la Rita - la Ley.

Cayendo bien la carta es fortuna, riqueza, inspiracion y enseñanza, al revés significa casamiento.

Pasamos a la 6/a. Mientras la hebrea pone al lado del discípulo un hombre y una mujer, la llama "El Enamorado" se ve un cupido que dispara la flecha sobre el hombre, mientras en la Aria va la flecha al vacio y disparada por un Angel.

La mujer completamente vestida en la hebrea, señala en la Aria a una mujer desnuda.

———

---

[55] Literally 'casamiento' means "wedding, marriage; match; cassation"

[56] Literally 'vacio' means "empty, vacuous, hollow, void; vacuum, emptiness"

[57] Editor's note: Here Krumm-Heller has a different perspective on this card, putting the 'disciple' on the left, whereas traditionally the 'disciple' is in the middle between 2 women.

[58] Originalmente "distra"

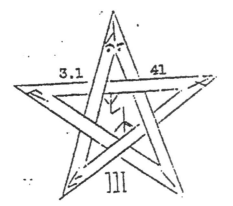

[Lesson 3]

M E S S A G E
from
the Sovereign Commander of
the Rosecross Order
as [a] Secret Course for
the dependent brothers
of the S.S.S.

———

[Lección III]

M E N S A J E
del
Soberano Comendador de la
Orden Rosacruz como
Curso Secreto para
los hermanos dependientes
del S.S.S.

———

Beloved Disciple:

Let us continue comparing the two cards [of Arcanum 6], the Aryan and [then] the Hebrew, and we see that:

In the Aryan [card the woman] is of [a] dark[59] color and the man [is] white.

Taurus is the Constellation and the Rune [is] Kaum.

The significance is "Divine Love". Upright it is the day, reversed [it is] night, as well as material love.

The 7th [card] shows us in both [cards] the "Chariot of Triumph" but in the hebrew [card] the feminine principle drives, in the Aryan [card there] is a male driver.[60]

The lions should be like in the Aryan [card] one white and the other black.

Querido Discípulo:

Seguimos comparando las dos cartas, la Aria y la Hebrea y vemos que:

En la Aria es de color negro y el hombre blanco.

Toro es la Constelacion y la Runa Kaun.

El significado es el "Amor Divino". De cabeza es el dia, al revés la noche, también el amor material.

La 7/a. nos senala en ambos el "Carro del Triunfo" pero mientras en la hebrea conduce el principio femenino, en la Aria es un hombre el conductor.

Los leones deben ser como en la Aria uno blanco y el otro negro.

---

[59] Literally 'negro' means "black, of the color black, or of pertaining to an ethnic group having brown to black skin and hair; dark"

[60] Editor's note: Here it appears that Krumm-Heller has not studied these cards carefully, because in Papus' deck (and in almost every case of the French Tarot) a man is driving the chariot.

While in the hebrew [the driver] has the magic wand in hand, in the Aryan [card the driver has] a whip [in one hand], and in the other hand there is a symbol of the cubic stone within the circle, that is to say, the symbol of transmutation.

The significance is triumph, success, good husband [or spouse], divine protection. Reversed it signifies disgust, struggles, enemies and intrigues.

The constellation is that of The Twins [which is Gemini]. The Rune is thus: ╳ [like an **X**[61] or] like a cross.

The 8th [card] shows in both the hebrew and in the Aryan [decks as] "Justice".

The difference is curious. In the hebrew [card] there is a dressed woman, justice, scale in hand; while in the Aryan [card] the scale works alone, by divine influence.

Upon one side[62] [is] a weight[63] and in [the] other, a man. In the right hand [is a] unsheathed sword.

In the Aryan [card is] justice as [a] woman [who] is naked and [with her] eyes closed, without [a] cross on her chest, not like in the hebrew [card].

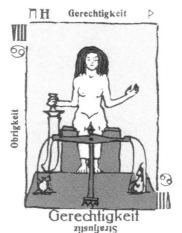

Mientras en la hebrea lleva en la mano la varilla magica, en la Aria un látigo, y en la otra mano hay un símbolo de la piedra cúbica dentro del circulo, es decir, el símbolo de la transmutacion.

El significado es el triunfo, exito, esposo bueno, protección divina. Se cae de cabeza significa disgusto, lucha, enemigos e intrigas.

La constelación es la de Los Gemelos. La Runa es así ╳ [como una **X**[64] o] como una cruz.

La 8/a. trae tanto en la hebrea como en la Aria "La Justicia".

Es curiosa la diferencia. En la hebrea es una mujer vestida, la justicia, la balanza en la mano, mientras que en la Aria la balanza trabaja sola, por influencia divinal.

Sobre un platillo un peso y en otro un hombre. En la mano derecha la espada levantada.

En la Aria la justicia como mujer esta desnuda y los ojos cerrados, sin cruz en el pecho, no como en la hebrea.

---

[61] Editor's note: Krumm-Heller says "The first letter was X, as if saying to us, the Cross in a twisting form, [and] all the others are derived from this letter." in his article *The Origin of Writing*, see the Editor's Appendix.
[62] Literally 'platillo' means "dish, bowl; scoop; scale; tray; basin; cymbal"
[63] Literally 'peso' means "weight, weighing, peso, burden, load, heaviness, heft, pressure, dead weight, kilo"

---

[64] Nota del editor: Krumm-Heller dice " La primera letra fue la X, como si dijéramos, la Cruz en forma de aspas, derivándose de esa letra todas las demás." en su artículo de *El Origen de la Escritura*, véase el Apéndice del Editor.

It is the justice of karma versus the justice of the code of the hebrews.

The Constellation is Cancer and its Rune is this: ᚱ [like an **R**] Rita.

The Hermit
L'Hermite 9

The 9th [card] shows the "HERMIT" as [the] plate in the hebrew [deck] and in the Aryan [it] is called "THE SAGE".

In the Aryan [there] is a woman with a lamp that illuminates everything, representing the criterion[65] of the sage.

The Rune is Hagal.

The symbolism which one may have here, signifies [being] on the good side [or upright is] wisdom and [a] successful[66] process, upsidedown [or reversed it signifies a] simple process, slander[67].

The 10th [card] is "The Wheel of Fortune".

In the hebrew [card] there is the sphinx sitting above the Wheel, while in the Aryan [card] the figure is shown looking from on high.

The dog takes in [its] hand the symbol of Mercury, the commerce of the jews and on the other side the lizard goes down.

The Wheel of Fortune
La Roue de Fortune 10

Es la justicia de carma frente a la justicia del codigo de los hebreos.

La Constelacion es Cancer y su Runa es asi: ᚱ Rita.

La 9/a trae como lamina en la hebrea el "ERMITAÑO" y en la Aria se llama "EL SABIO".

En la Aria es una mujer con una lampara que alumbra todo, representa el criterio del sabio.

La Runa es Hagal.

El simbolismo que pue de haber aqui, significa por el lado bueno, sabiduria y proceso ganado, al revés proceso simple, calumnia.

La 10/a con "La Rueda de la Fortuna".

En la hebrea esta la esfinge sentada por encima de la Rueda, mientras que en la Aria va mirando la figura desde lo alto.

El perro lleva en la mano el símbolo de Mercurio, el comercio del judío y por el otro lado va bajando la lagartija.

---

[65] Literally 'criterio' means "criterion, standard against which something is measured (i.e. standard or principle); canon, accepted principle"

[66] Literally 'ganado' means "gain, acquire; profit, earn; add; win; defeat; capture, possess; reach, arrive; prosper, succeed; flourish, thrive"

[67] Literally 'calumnia' means "calumny, slander, libel; defamation, slur"

In the Aryan [card] the dog goes without anything [in his hand] like a driver and instead of the lizard [there] is a serpent.

Its Constellation is VIRGO and its Rune is EH.

It signifies good position, augmentation of fortune and upsidedown [it signifies] failure and fatal disease.

The 11th [card] corresponds to Mars [and] is the same in both systems with only one small difference, but this is very revealing and proves[68] the hebrew character which is material.

[It] represents the card "Power", [or] force/strength and in the hebrew [it] says "divine force/strength", "moral force/strength", and "human force/strength" while the Aryan [card] just says "force/strength".

The aforementioned difference is that the hebrew [card], concerning the woman or about feminine force/strength, the card is material and [as such] it can never be infinite or eternal. Thus [they are] falsifying the card by adding this symbol.

The [upright] significance is as force/strength, tenacity and resolution. When upside down [or reversed] it announces accidents.

It corresponds to the planet Mars, that is to say only one aspect of force/strength.

En la Aria el perro va sin nada como conductor y en vez de la lagartija es una serpiente.

Su Constelacion es VIRGO y su Runa es EH.

Significa buena posicion, aumento de fortuna y al revés fracaso y enfermedad mortal.

La 11/a que corresponde a Marte es igual en los dos sistemas con solo una pequena diferencia, pero esa es muy reveladora y prueba el caracter hebreo o sea material.

Representa la carta "El Poder", la fuerza y en la hebrea dice "fuerza divina", "fuerza moral", y "fuerza humana", mientras la Aria solo dice "fuerza".

La diferencia aludida es que la hebrea, sobre la mujer o sea sobre la fuerza femenina, la carta es la material y esa nunca puede ser infinita o eterna. Al falsificar pues la carta agregaron ese simbolo.

El significado es pues fuerza, tenacidad y resolucion. Cuando cae de cabeza anuncia accidentes.

Le corresponde el planeta Marte, es decir solo un aspecto de la fuerza.

---

[68] Literally 'prueba' means "evidence, proof; test, exam; experiment, trial; audition; demonstration; correction"

The 12th [card] is "THE HANGED MAN" [who is] hung upside [down] in both, only in the Aryan [card he] is tied by both legs and in the other only by one.

Remember, disciple, the [vocalization] exercise from the Zodiacal Course, spelling[69] with the feet, [so] that the letters are not only entering the head but also through the feet. [70]

The Rune is /\ .

Upright it signifies warning[71], change and sacrifice, reversed [it signifies] discord[72].

The zodiacal sign is Libra ♎

The 13th card is "Death" [which], in the hebrew [deck], has [a] skeleton with [a] scythe mowing heads, while in the Aryan [deck it has a] being passing over a bridge, that is to say, passing from one life to another; the beings will be collected in the grave to rest and the Rune is SIG, that of Victory.

Hanged Man
Le Pendu   12

Death
La Mort   13

La 12/a. es "EL AHORCADO" colgado de cabeza en ambas, solo que en la Aria esta amarrado de las dos piernas y en la otra solo de una.

Recuerde el discípulo el ejercicio del Curso Zodiacal, deletrear por los pies, que las letras no sólo entran por la cabeza, sino también por los pies.[73]

La Runa es /ˌ.

Caída bien significa advertencia, cambio y sacrificio, al revés discordia.

El signo zodiacal es Libra ♎

La 13/a carta es de "La Muerte", tiene en la hebrea el esqueleto con la guadaña segando cabezas, mientras en la Aria pasa el ser sobre un puente, es decir, que pasa de una vida a otra; van a recogerse los seres a la tumba a descansar y la Runa es la de la Victoria SIEG.

---

[69] Literally 'deletrear' means "spell out; decipher"
[70] Editor's note: See the Lesson for Pisces "...you have to learn to derive the voice from the Feet in order to sense the vibration in them, that is to say, we must speak with the Feet. Whosoever does not know our studies will be smiling when they read this [phrase] of "speaking with the Feet", but we know that all Initiations do so. ...The modus operandi is as follows: The Disciple will sit comfortably, and after making a mental Prayer, one should lead the Vowels to the Feet, [that] is to say, think and pronounce the vowel "Iiiiiiiii" extending , vibrating, [and] seeking to mentally lead its pronunciation downwards, through the knees to the feet, so that it continues slowly [connecting and vibrating] with the other vowels..." from 'PISCES' in *Gnostic Rosicrucian Astrology* by Arnoldo Krumm-Heller.
[71] Literally 'advertencia' means "warning, caution; caveat, admonition; reminder; premonition"
[72] Literally 'discordia' means "discord, disharmony; dissension, disagreement"

---

[73] Nota del editor: Ver la Lección de Piscis "...hay que aprender a derivar la voz hacia los Pies para sentir en ellos la vibración, es decir, hay que hablar con los Pies. Quien no conozca nuestros estudios habrá de sonreírse al leer esto de hablar con los Pies, pero ya sabemos que todos los Iniciados lo hacen. ...El modus operandi, es el siguiente: Se sienta el Discípulo cómodamente, y después de hacer una Oración mental, tiene que llevar las Vocales a los Pies, es decir, piensa y pronuncia largamente, vibrándola, la vocal Iiiiiiiii, procurando llevar mentalmente su pronunciación hacia abajo, por las rodillas hasta los pies, y así se continúa despacio con las demás vocales..." de PISCIS en *Astrología Gnóstica Rosacruz* por Arnoldo Krumm-Heller.

[Upright] it signifies nothingness[74], conclusion of diseases and pains, that is to say: promise[75] of [good] health; and only [with the] head upside down [or reversed] is [it] bad.

The zodiacal sign is Scorpio ןןׁע

The 14th is the card of "Reincarnation", the substances of life pass from one jug[76] [or vessel] to another and [the cards] are the same in both systems.

Upright it signifies Temperance[77] and heartache[78], spirituality; and reversed [it signifies] disgrace[79].

The Rune is thus: ∧/

Significa la nada, conclusión de enfermedades y penas, es decir: esperanza de salud; y sólo caída de cabeza es mala.

El signo zodiacal es Escorpion ןןׁע

La 14/a es la carta de la "Reencarnación", pasa las substancias de la vida de un jarro al otro y están iguales en ambos sistemas.

Caída bien significa Templanza y penas de amor, espiritualidad; y al revés deshonra.

La Runa es así: ∧/

---

[74] Literally 'nada' means "nothingness, nought; nil, naught"
[75] Literally 'esperanza' means "hope, promise, expectation, prospect; anticipation; confidence"
[76] Literally 'jarro' means "mug; pitcher; tankard, large drinking vessel with a handle and a hinged cover"
[77] Literally 'Templanza' means "temperance, moderation, calmness"
[78] Literally 'penas de amor' means "pains/pangs of love, love pains, heartache, romantic woes"
[79] Literally 'deshonra' means "defile; discredit; disgrace, dishonor"

The 15th [card] is Baphomet, Lucifer.

In the hebrew [deck] the male goat signals[80] with one hand to heaven and the other to the earth.

The Devil
Le Diable　15

He is on a celestial globe, as [if] saying "[this] is the material aspect of the domain that has the sexes tethered[81] [or the domain that ties up the sexes]".

In the Aryan [card] we are signaled by the "Black Magician", each being is chained[82] [up] in order to separate them, and Lucifer has a torch in hand, [he is] seated between two light-giving[83] columns, but [he] does not decide the way.

Its Rune is God ᛦ and the zodiacal sign [is] Sagittarius.

The upright significance is: depression and loss; reversed [it signifies] illness and insanity.

It is the black magician who harms[84] us.

The 16th [card] is "Lightning [or the Ray]" in the Aryan [deck] while in the hebrew [deck it is] the "House of God".

La 15/a. es el Bafometo, Lucifer.

En la hebrea el macho cabrío señala con una mano al cielo y con la otra a la tierra.

Está sobre un globo celeste, es decir es el aspecto material del dominio que tienen los sexos amarrados.

En la Aria la señalamos con el "Mago Negro", cadá ser esta encadenado por sí separado, y Lucifer tiene una antorcha en la mano, sentado entre dos columnas alumbra, pero no decide el camino.

Su Runa es Dios ᛦ y el signo zodiacal Sagitario.

El significado es: caida bien, depresión y pérdidas; al revés enfermedad y locura.

Es el mago negro que nos hace daño.

La 16/a es en la Aria "El Rayo" mientras en la hebrea la "Casa de Dios".

---

[80] Literally 'señala' means "signalize, make prominent; mark, indicate, signal; particularize, specify"

[81] Literally 'amarrados' means "fasten, tie up, tether, moor (to fix firmly; secure)"

[82] Literally 'encadenado' means "catenate, link; chain, fetter; incarcerate; paralyze"

[83] Literally 'alumbra' means "light up, give light, shine, illuminate, enlighten"

[84] Literally 'daño' means "harm, injury, damage; hazard; jeopardy; bruise; nuisance; eradication"

In the hebrew [card] there is a single tower, [falling] matter and lightning kill human beings, it is the avenging God of the semites, it is the temple of Solomon destroyed while in the Aryan [card] there are two towers, through which the Lightning destroys matter, [while] the divine or superior representation remains intact.

The sign is Capricorn.

Upright [it] signifies good, prompt resolution and losses, reversed [it signifies] disgrace and deception.

The 17th [card] - In the hebrew [deck], with the name "Star", we have a naked woman and the Septenary indicated with 7 stars, [holding] two empty Jars[85] in hand.

In the Aryan [card] there is a clothed woman pouring liquid from two jars.

The woman is on an isolated Island.

The planet is Mercury and the Rune [is] SIG.

Upright it signifies hope, death of a relative and redemption; reversed [it means] theft[86].

En la hebrea hay una sola torre, la material y el rayo mata a los seres humanos, es el Dios vengador de los semitas, es el temple de Salomón destruído mientras en la Aria hay dos torres, que mientras el Rayo destruye la materia, permanece intacta la representación divina o superior.

El signo es Capricornio.

Significando caída bien, pronta resolución y pérdidas, al revés desgracia y decepción.

La 17/a. - En la hebrea tenemos con el nombre "Estrella" una mujer desnuda y el Septenario senalado con 7 estrellas en la mano dos Jarras vacías.

En la Aria esta una mujer vestida derramando liquido de dos jarras.

La mujer esta sobre una Isla aislada.

El planeta es Mercurio y la Runa **SIG**.

Caída al derecho significa esperanza, muerte de un pariente y redencion; al revés robo.

---

[85] Literally 'Jarra' means "jar; schooner; beaker; mug"
[86] Literally 'robo' means "steal, rob, thieve; remove; draw; walk away"

The 18th [card] we see in the hebrew [deck] a moon, [and] in the Aryan [deck], [we see] the sun.

In both [cards we have] the two dogs (the drivers[87] of the soul) who are found in all the mysteries and below the marine animal reminds [us] of [the] Cipactli of the mexicans.[88]

The dogs bark at the planets.

In both [cards] there are the two mountains through which the souls must pass.

The Rune is this ↑· [TYR]

Upright it signifies deception[89], occult enemies [and] harmful vices and backwards [or reversed it signifies] repentance.

The name of the Aryan [card] is "Blind Vices."

The zodiacal sign is Aquarius

The 19th [card] is called "THE SUN" in the hebrew [deck] and in the Aryan [deck] "Spiritual Life".

In hebrew there are two naked children illuminated by the sun in other words [illuminated] by the true light.

The Moon
La Lune   18

ʊTS   Betrug, Verrat, geheime Feinde   ↑
XVIII
Wasser, Schädliche Leidenschaft
Blinde Leidenschaft
Spätere Reue über Unrecht

The Sun
Le Soleil   19

La 18/a. vemos en la hebrea una luna, en la Aria el sol.

En ambos los dos perros, los conductores del alma, que encontrarlos en todos les misterios y abajo el animal marine recuerda a Cipactli de los mexicanos.[90]

Los perros ladran a los planetas.

En ambos hay las dos montañas por las cuales tienen que pasar las almas.

La Runa es así ↑· [TYR]

Caída bien significa engano, enemigos ocultos vicios daninos y al revés arrepentimiento.

El nombre de la Aria es "Vicios Ciegos".

El signo zodiacal es Acuario

La 19/a es llamada en la hebrea "EL SOL" y en la Aria "Vida Espiritual".

En la hebrea van dos ninos desnudos alumbrados por el sol o sea con la verdadera luz.

---

[87] Literally 'conductores' means "conduct; conductor, lead (Electricity); leader (of an orchestra, chorus, etc.); driver, motorist"

[88] Editor's note: Krumm-Heller mentions Cipactli in his 'The Zodiac of the Incas in Comparison with that of the Aztecs' where he says: "Ultimately, the constellation of Pisces corresponds to the Peruvian "Chokilla-Katua", the divine Fish, or also [called] "Challhua", Fish, and for the Aztecs the "Cipactli": a marine animal." see the Editor's Appendix in *Logos Mantram Magic.*

[89] Literally 'engano' means "deceit, double cross, betrayal; spoofing; cheat, deceive, swindle; betray, be disloyal"

---

[90] Nota del editor: Krumm-Heller menciona Cipactli en su 'El Zodiaco de los Incas en Comparación con el de los Aztecas', donde dice: "Por último, a la constelación de los Peces corresponde la peruana de Chokilla-Katua, Pez divino, o también Challhua, Pez, y la de los aztecas el Cipactli: animal marino."

In the Aryan [deck we have] a genie in the light [riding] on horseback, [who] is like [a] mediator, [or who] is the christonic force and both are symbolized [by] the fish, symbol of Christ.[91]

The Rune is this: ᛒ [BAR]

[Upright it] signifies [good] luck, money, marriage[92], fire and reversed [it signifies] prison[93].

En la Aria flota un genio a caballo en la luz, es como mediador, es la fuerza cristonica y en ambos están símbolizados los peces, símbolo de Christo.

La Runa es así: ᛒ [BAR]

Significa suerte, dinero, casamiento, fuego y al revés prision.

———

———

---

[91] Editor's note: Eliphas Levi gives the following description for this Card #19 in Ch.22 of *Ritual of High Magic*, "Hieroglyph, a radiant sun and two naked children [who] hold hands within a fortified enclosure. In other Tarots, substitute a spinner unwinding [people's] destinies; [and] in others a naked child mounted upon a white horse and displaying a scarlet banner."

[92] Literally 'casamiento' means "wedding, marriage; match; cassation"

[93] Literally 'prision' means "prison, jail; imprisonment"

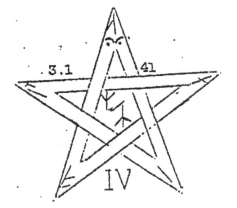

[Lesson 4]

M E S S A G E
from
the Sovereign Commander of
the Rosecross Order
as [a] Secret Course for
the dependent brothers
of the S.S.S.

———

[Lección IV]

M E N S A J E
del
Soberano Comendador de la
Orden Rosacruz como
Curso Secreto para
los hermanos dependientes
del S.S.S.

———

Beloved Disciple:

Card 20 represents "The Final Judgment".

In the hebrew [card] we see the angel announcing the Judgement with his trumpet.

The tombs open and the dead exit from there in order to present themselves at their judgement.

In it is the eternal feeling of fear of the jews.

The mother seeks to help the child.

The symbolism is very different in the nordic [card].

It is not the Judgement which is threatened, but instead it is the humans who are joyful ascending lifting [their] arms.

At the head [of the humans] the priest leads with the sign of life ([the] ankh).

It is saying, "life goes [on] to superior regions".

Querido Discípulo:

La carta 20 representa "El Juicio Final".

En la hebrea vemos al angel anunciador del Juez con su trompeta.

Se abren las tumbas y de ellas salen los muertos para presentarse a su juez.

En ella está el eterno sentimiento del temor de los judíos.

La madre pretende socorrer al hijo.

Muy distinto es el simbolismo de las nórdicas.

No es el Juez amenazador que viene, sino son los humanos que van ascendiendo levantando alegres los brazos.

A la cabeza va el sacerdote con el signo (ang) de la vida.

Es decir, la vida va a regiones superiores.

The significance of the card is "[good] fortune", public posts which honor us, "eternal life" and "verdict[94] of a pending trial".

The corresponding planet is Saturn and the Rune is an ancient symbol that is similar to an <u>M</u> signifying mystery.

In truth, a final judgment will always be a mystery to humans, but it turns out that this symbol among the Aryans signifies KARMA.

It is the law of karma, the judgment that awaits us and which is resolved through reincarnation.

Already [having arrived] at the final judgment we should finish this process [which is] represented in the Tarot cards and now [we have] in the hebrew [deck] the number 21 and only Papus puts a zero [for this card] in his work on the Tarot.

Here lies the great confusion for the kabalists, since card 21 of the hebrews represents "The Lunatic[95] [or the Fool]", [and] is only numbered in the Aryan [deck] with a zero.[96]

In the hebrew there is a dog that bites the staff[97] of the lunatic and [he] is heading[98] into an abyss.

The Lunatic
Le Fou   (0)21

El significado de la carta es "fortuna", púestos publicos con que nos honran, "vida eterna" y "sentencia de un juicio pendiente".

El planeta correspondiente es Saturno y la Runa es un símbolo antiguo que siendo parecido a una <u>M</u> significa misterio.

En verdad, que un juicio final sera siempre para los humanos un misterio, pero resulta que ese símbolo entre los Arios significa KARMA.

Es pues la ley de carma, el juicio que nos espera y que se resuelve[99] por la reencarnación.

Ya con el juicio final se deberia acabar ese proceso, representado en las cartas del Tarot y ahora resulta en la hebrea el numero 21 y sólo Papus pone en su obra del Tarot un cero.

He ahí la gran confusión para los cabalistas, pues la carta 21 de los hebreos que representa "El Loco", queda solo numerado en la Aria con un cero.[100]

En la hebrea hay un perro que muerde el bastón del loco y ese va a un abismo.

---

[94] Literally 'sentencia' means "sentence, judgement, judgment, verdict"
[95] Literally 'loco' means "crazy, batty, cracked, crazed, demented, insane, looney, loony, lunatic, mad, mentally unbalanced, nuts, nutsy, nutty, nutty as a fruitcake, off one's head, barmy, bats, berserk, bonkers, bunkers, crackers, deranged, loopy, wacky;"
[96] Editor's note: Samael Aun Weor says that Arcanum 21 is 'the Lunatic' or 'Transmutation' and that Arcanum 22 is 'the World' or 'the Crown of Life'.
   "Arcanum № 21 has been confused with Arcanum № 22 which is the Crown of Life. ARCANUM № 21 IS THE 'LUNATIC OF THE TAROT' or 'Transmutation'." from Ch. 21 of *Tarot & Kabalah*
[97] Literally 'baston' means "stick, staff; walking stick; cane; truncheon, rod representing authority; pallet"

[98] Literally 'va' means "go, proceed, move; travel; walk; suit; lead; drive; ride"
[99] originalmente "resieñve"
[100] Nota del editor: Samael Aun Weor dice que Arcano 21 es 'el Loco' o 'la Transmutatión' y el Arcano 22 es 'el Mundo' o 'la Corona de la Vida'.
   "El Arcano No. 21 ha sido confundido con el Arcano No. 22 que es la Corona de la Vida. EL ARCANO No. 21 ES EL 'LOCO DEL TAROT' o 'La Transmutación'." del Cap. XXI de *Tarot y Kábala*

The nordic [card] is different.

There is also a dog, but this [dog] jumps onto the side of the walker[101].

The dog is the leader[102] of the soul in all the very symbolic[103] mysteries among the ancients.

There is (in this nordic card) a threatening crocodile who impedes[104] the soul [from] falling into the abyss.[105]

The significance of the card is "errors of the Past".

It is not called "The Lunatic" [in the nordic/Aryan tradition], but "The Chaste Innocent" from [Richard Wagner's Opera] Parsifal.

The planet is Neptune and the Rune is that of Life.

Card 21 [of the Aryan] is now the hebrew [card] 22 and in this is the confusion.

In the hebrew 22 is a naked woman within a snake that bites its tail.

On the four sides are the 4 Evangelists: [the] Angel, Eagle, Lion and Bull. The Hebrew Kabalah has designated [it] with [the name of]: "The World."

Diferente es la nórdica.

También hay un perro, pero ese brinca al lado del caminante.

Es el perro conductor del alma de todos los misterios muy senalado entre los antiguos.

Hay en esta carta nórdica un cocodrilo amenazador que evita al alma caer en el abismo.[106]

El significado de la carta es: "errores del Pasado."

No se llama "El Loco", sino "El Casto Inocente" del Parsifal.

El planeta es Neptuno y la Runa es la de la Vida.

La carta 21 es ahora la 22 hebrea y en esto está la confusión.

En la hebrea 22 está una mujer desnuda dentro de una serpiente que se muerde la cola.

A los cuatro costados están los 4 Evangelistas Angel - Aguila - León y Toro. La Cábala Hebrea ha designado con: "El Mundo".

---

[101] Literally 'caminante' means "wayfarer; hiker; walker; tramp"

[102] Literally 'conductor' means "leading; conducting, conduct, conductor; driver, motorist"

[103] Literally 'senalado' means "indicated; signal; notable; signalize, make prominent; mark; particularize, specify"

[104] Literally 'evita' means "avoid, evade; obviate, prevent; shirk; preclude; save"

[105] Editor's note: Regarding the symbolism of the crocodile, Samael Aun Weor says, "THE CROCODILE IS SET, SATAN, THE "PSYCHOLOGICAL I", the Myself, always lying in wait to devour the one who allows himself to fall", in Ch. 21 of *Tarot & Kabalah*.

[106] Nota del Editor: En relación con el simbolismo del cocodrilo, Samael Aun Weor dice: "EL COCODRILO ES SETH, EL SATÁN, EL "YO PSICOLÓGICO", el Mí Mismo, siempre en espera de aquel que se deja caer para devorarlo", en Cap. XXI de *Tarot y Kábala*.

This card [is] very different from the painting on the nordic [version], it seems that the serpent is hidden behind the four figures and the dressed woman makes a movement we know from the 2nd Degree of Freemasonry.

The planet is the Sun, the King star and the [upright] significance is: "[good] Fortune", "success", and reversed, that is to say upside down [it signifies], "break and disputes".

The hebrew letter is shin [ש] and the Rune [is] that of Equilibrium.[107]

With this [we] complete the true Major Arcana and in them is the synthesis of all morality, of all religion and of the whole human being, for those who can decipher it.

It is the same as in Mystic Masonry which [is to say that] in the first three degrees are enclosed all the others, the others only serve to clarify or facilitate comprehension.

In both systems [card] 23 is the King of Clubs[108], and remembering the first card in which there is also a King with a cane or stick in hand, [being the] "Staff/Rod of Mary".

Today [it] is the Judge who gives his sentence, then the Penal Judgment [is given and] then [one receives] the observation [of] karma.

23 King of Clubs
Roi de Bâton

Esta carta muy distinta por la pintura en la nórdica, parece que la serpiente está escondida tras de las cuatro figuras y la mujer vestida hace un movimiento que conocemos del 2° Grado de la Masonería.

El planeta es el Sol, el astro Rey y el significado es: "Fortuna", "suerte", y al revés, es decir caída de cabeza, "rompimiento y disputas".

La letra hebrea es el schin [ש] y la Runa la del Equilibrio.

Con esto acaban los verdaderos Arcanos Mayores y en ellos está la síntesis de toda moral de toda religión y de todo el ser humano, para quienes saben descifrarlo.

Es lo mismo como en la Masonería Mística que en los tres primeros grados están encerrados todos los demás, sólo que los otros sirven para aclarar o facilitar la comprensión.

En la 23 de ambos sistemas tenemos al Rey de Bastos, y recordando la primera carta en que también hay un Rey con un bastón o palo "Varilla de Maria" en la mano.

Hoy es el Juez que da su sentencia después del Juicio Pinal después de observar el carma.

---

[107] Editor's note: According to Hebrew numbering 21 = ש and 22 = ת , so by saying 0 = ת and 21 = ש Krumm-Heller's ordering (which is probably also Glahn's) is not Kabalistically accurate.

[108] Literally 'Bastos' means "clubs; coarse, rough; base, low"

He is the Lord of Karma whom we know from theosophy.

We have seen that the hebrew cards always tend towards materialism, to the inferior planes [of matter], thus the Semitic King lacks the globe of the Empire[109], which represents the divine plane, the heavenly kingdom.

We note (for those who have the work[110] of Papus) that this [inferior tendency] continues [with] the different and misguided[111] numbering of the Master.[112]

This served as [a] theme for discussion when studying in his esoteric school in Paris, [in] which some [students] were never satisfied with the [explanations of the] Master in this case.

Es el Señor del Carma que conocemos de la teosofía.

Hemos visto que las cartas hebreas siempre tienden al materialismo, a los planos inferiores, por eso le falta al Rey Semita el globo del Imperio, que representa el plano divino, el reino celestial.

Hacemos constar a los que tengan la obra de Papus que ésta sigue la numeración didiferente y equivocada por el Maestro.[113]

Sirvió eso ya como tema de discusión cuando estudiamos en su escuela esotérica en París, que algunos nunca estuvieron conformes con el Maestro en este caso.

24 Queen of Clubs
Dame de Bâtons ה

---

[109] Literally 'Imperio' means "sway; imperial; empire"

[110] Editor's note: This seems to refer to *Le Tarot Divinatoire* (1909)

[111] Literally 'equivocada' means "wrong, mistaken; misguided; inadvertent; lost"

[112] Editor's note: Samael Aun Weor says that Papus adulterated the Authentic Kabalistic Teachings, "In this path we will have to live all the 12 Hours of which the Great Sage Apollonius spoke about. <u>The Black Magician "Papus" tried to disfigure the 12 Hours of Apollonius with teachings of Black Magic, liquidating all the millions of kabalistic volumes that drift in the world.</u> We have arrived at the conclusion that: all Kabalah is reduced to the 22 Major Arcana of the Tarot and [the] 4 Aces, which represent the 4 Elements of Nature. On such a simple thing, scholars have written millions of volumes and theories that would turn anyone "crazy" who had the bad taste of becoming intellectualized with that whole arsenal. <u>The worst of it is that, in questions of Kabalah, the Black Magicians seized what they found, in order to disfigure the teaching and lead the world astray.</u>" from *Zodiacal Course* (1951) in the chapter on Sagittarius.

[113] Nota del editor: Samael Aun Weor dice que Papus adulterado los Enseñanzas Auténtico Kabalístico, "En esta senda tendremos que vivir todas las 12 Horas de que nos habló el Gran Sabio Apolonio. <u>El Mago Negro "Papus" intentó desfigurar las 12 Horas de Apolonio con enseñanzas de Magia Negra, haciendo una liquidación de todos los millones de volúmenes kabalísticos que ruedan por el mundo.</u> Llegamos a la conclusión de que: toda Kábala se reduce a los 22 Arcanos Mayores del Tarot y 4 Ases, que representan los 4 Elementos de la Naturaleza. Sobre algo tan sencillo han levantado los eruditos, millones de volúmenes y teorías que volverían "loco" a todo aquel que tuviera el mal gusto de intelectualizarse con todo ese arsenal. <u>Lo peor del caso fue que en materia de Kábala, los Magos Negros se apoderaron de lo que encontraron para desfigurar la enseñanza y extraviar al mundo.</u>" del *Curso Zodiacal* (1951) en el capítulo sobre Sagitario.

Card 24 is the Queen of Clubs who [in the Aryan card], like the previous King, also bears the globe of the Empire, meaning that the difficulty of acting in [the] superior planes is not [a] masculine privilege, but women are spiritually our equals.

The [upright] significance is: "A Woman who protects us."

Reversed, [it signifies] a new man hinders[114] the work you intend to do [and] a woman [is] in our favor.

The planet is Saturn.

Card 25, just like 24 of Papus is: "The Knight [of Clubs]".

Which in the hebrew [card] only carries the Club, while in the nordic [card the knight also] holds [a] banner in the left hand.

25 Knight of Clubs
Chevalier de Bâton

The [upright] significance is: "Travel and separation" in a good sense.

Reversed [it signifies] "Difference with another person" and "obstacles that are opposed[115] to our plans."

The planet is not only Saturn but is also Mars, the warrior.

La carta 24 es la Dama de Bastos que como el Rey anterior lleva también el globo del Imperio, significando que esa dificultad de actuar en planos superiores no es privilegio masculino, sino que las mujeres son espiritualmente nuestras iguales.

El significado es: "Una Mujer que nos protegerá."

Al revés, un hombre nue obstaculiza la labor que pretende hacer una mujer a nuestro favor.

El planeta es Saturno.

La carta 25, así que la 24 de Papus es: "El Caballero"

Que en la hebrea sólo lleva el Basto mientras en la nórdica lleva en la mano izquierda la bandera.

El significado es: "Viajes y separación" en buen sentido.

Al revés "Diferencia con otra persona", y "obstáculos que se oponen a nuestros planes."

El planeta no sólo es Saturno sino que se une Marte, el guerrero.

---

[114] Literally 'obstaculiza' means "block, obstruct; balk, hinder"
[115] Literally 'se oponen' means "go against, oppose; object, demur"

[Card] 26 represents the Page [of Clubs], the servant[116]. Since this only shows [a] club[117] [or stick].

Its significance as the boaster[118] of [the] cards is: "Good news", and reversed, [it signifies] "bad[119] [news]".

The planets are Saturn and Mercury.

26   Page of Clubs   Valet de Bâton

Prior[120] to this figure we [should] have filled the interior circles in the wheel of the Present and of the Future.[121]

Now only with these cards can we say to someone else or ourselves [whether there is] luck, but we must go to the explanation of the simple cards [or minor arcana] which form the two exterior circles.

The position of the Clubs is very different in both systems.

La 26 representa el Paje, el muchacho. Ya éste sólo exhibe el palo.

Su significado para el echador de cartas es: "Buenas noticias", y de cabeza, "malas".

Los planetas son Saturno y Mercurio.

Ya con esta figura hemos llenado los circulos interiores en la rueda del Presento y del Porvenir.

Ya sólo con estas cartas podrianos decir la suerte a otra persona o a nosotros mismos, pero debemos ir a la explicacion de las cartas simples que formaran los dos circulos exteriores.

La posición de los Bastos en ambos sistemas es muy diferente.

---

[116] Literally 'muchacho' means "boy, lad, youngster; servant"

[117] Literally 'palo' means "pale, fence stake; stick, staff; handle; mast, long pole above the hull of a ship which supports the rigging and sails (Nautical); stalk, stem of a plant; wood; tree; ascender, part of a letter that extends above the baseline; descender"

[118] Literally 'echador' means "boastful; Castor (the twin brother of Pollux, related to the constellation of Gemini)"

[119] Literally 'malas' means "bad luck, absence of good fortune; bad; poor; mischievous, naughty; evil, wicked; disagreeable; sick; disgusting; hard, difficult; inconvenient; troubled"

[120] Literally 'Ya' means "already, by now; before, beforehand; anymore"

[121] Editor's note: For more information about these circles or wheels, see Lesson #1, pages 18-19

While in the hebrew cards the clubs are, for example, stationary[122] for 27, inclined to the left for 28, 29, 30, 31, 32, 33, stationary for 34, crossed[123] [for] 35, and the Ace [is] also stationary, all the nordic figures form symmetric-symbols, so for example, 27, [there] is a square in the center with three surrounding[124] triangles, 28 [has] four triangles, 29 [has] two squares and one more formed from the others[125], 30 [has] a square with an enclosed triangle, 31 [has] two triangles, forming the symbol of evolution, being the Star of King David. 32 [has] the five-pointed star, 33 [has] a square, 34 [has] a triangle, 35 [has] the Cross and finally 36 [has] a phallus.

[A] few hidden [or occult] considerations can not be formed merely from these figures and that is what should interest us most of all.

Now the disciples will compehend that the cards do not have prediction[126] as their principal objective, but [instead their objective is] to deepen our [understanding] in occult philosophy.

Let us consider[127] for a moment card 27 with the inferior quaternary and the superior triad, but not [while] simply excluding [the triad appearing] three times, which means to say that the superior principles are double and we did not know this from previous studies.

Mientras en las cartas hebreas los palos estan por ejemplo, en la 27 parados, en las 28, 29, 30, 31, 32, 33 inclinados a la izquierda 34 parados, 35 cruzados, y el As parado también, las nórdicas todas forman figuras simetro-simbólicas, así por ejemplo la 27, es un cuadrado en el centro con tres triángulos alrededor, la 28 cuatro triángulos, la 29 dos cuadrados y uno más formado por los anteriores, la 30 un cuadrado con un triángulo encerrado, la 31 dos triángulos, formando el símbolo de la evolución o sea la Estrella del Rey Davi. La 32 la estrella de cinco puntas, la 33 un cuadrado, la 34 un triangulo, la 35 la Cruz y por último la 36 un falus.

Cuántas consideraciones ocultas no se pueden formar solamente con estas figuras y eso es lo que nos debe interesar más que todo.

Ya comprenderán los discípulos que las cartas no tienen como objeto principal sacar la suerte, sino profundizarnos en filosofía oculta.

Pensemos por un momento en la carta 27 con el cuaternario inferior y la triada superior, pero no sencillas sino tres veces, lo que quiere decir que los principios superiores son dobles y eso no lo conociamos de estudios anteriores.

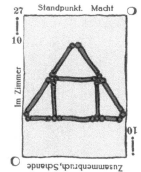

---

[122] Literally 'parados' means "stationary, motionless; idle; unemployed; lazy; stagnation, lack of movement, stillness; lack of activity or progress; apathetic person"
[123] Literally 'cruzados' means "crossed; cross; mongrel, crossbred (Botany, Zoology); double breasted; crusader, one who fights in a crusade, one who joins a medieval military expedition to recover the Holy Land from the Muslims; one who campaigns for the advancement of a cause"
[124] Literally 'alrededor' means "round, around; near, about"
[125] Literally 'anteriores' means "front; anterior, previous; prior, former; preceding, antecedent"
[126] Literally 'sacar la suerte' means "drawing of lots, casting lots, divining, telling the future, predicting fate"
[127] Literally 'Pensemos' means "think, deliberate, conceive in the mind; believe; contemplate, consider; ponder, reflect"

And the following instruction will give us the significance of the club cards.

It is not easy to keep all these things in the memory [at first] but little by little the disciple will become a good kabalist.

Ya la próxima instrucción nos dará el significado de las cartas de basto.

No es fácil guardar todas estas cosas en la memoria pero poco a poco si el discípulo será un buen cabalista.

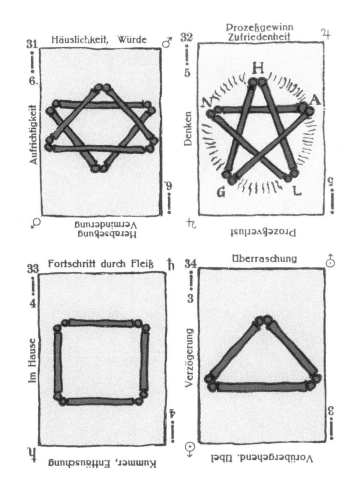

[Lesson 5]

M E S S A G E
from
the Sovereign Commander of
the Rosecross Order
as [a] Secret Course for
the dependent brothers
of the S.S.S.

———

[Lección IV]

M E N S A J E
del
Soberano Comendador de la
Orden Rosacruz como
Curso Secreto para
los hermanos dependientes
del S.S.S.

———

Beloved Disciple:

Some disciples wrote to me who do not have the hebrew cards (published in Brazil) [and who] desire to acquire them.

My opinion[128] [is] that it is not worth incurring[129] that expense.

The secondary objective of this Course is to provide[130] proof that the jews falsified the Kabalah, but what interests [us] primarily, is to know the significance of the nordic cards and then to enter into the Numeric Kabalah for the disciple to get a rounded knowledge of the Holy Kabalah.

Card 27 of Clubs [or the 10 of Clubs] signifies "Might[131]" whenever the triangle falls with the tip [pointed] up.

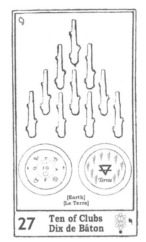

27   Ten of Clubs
    Dix de Bâton

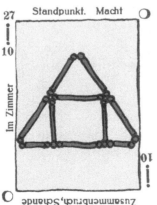

Querido Discípulo:

He escriben algunos discípulos que no teniendo las cartas hebreas, publicadas en Brasil, desean adquirirlas.

Yo opino que no vale la pena de hacer ese gasto.

El objeto secundario de este Curso es aportar la prueba de que los judíos falsificaron la Cábala, pero lo que interesa en primer término, es conocer el significado de las cartas nórdicas y luego entrar a la Cábala Numerica para dar al- discípulo un conocimiento redondeado de la Cábala Sagrada.

La carta 27 de Basto significa "Poderío" siempre que el triángulo caiga con la punta arriba.

---

[128] Literally 'opino' means "opine, express a view; hold a position; think that; assume that"

[129] Literally 'hacer' means "make; manufacture; create; construct, build; fashion, shape; compose; emit; wage, conduct (war, battle); prepare, do; cause; perform; effect; force; render; fabricate; behave, act in a particular manner; live through; be"

[130] Literally 'aportar' means "contribute, provide, bring, make"

[131] Literally 'Poderío' means "might, power, strength"

If [it] is reversed [it] always indicates "punishment[132]".

The square tells us that here the power is in matter, in the inferior principles, while in the 28 [there] are only[133] triangles, so this simply[134] signifies "Delayed[135] success" and reversed [it signifies] "Difficulties".

[Card] 27 has the Moon as [its] planet and 28 has Mercury.

[Card] 29 with its two squares clearly says that [the] significance [is] something material.

[It] is "Field trip[136]" and reversed [it signifies] "Insecurity", but can also be threatening[137] "Revolutions".

The planet is Venus.

[Card] 30, a triangle enclosed in a square, again[138] signifies to us our Septenary.

[Upright, it signifies] "Power" or reversed [it signifies] "Doubt", which means that Faith is the Great Power in opposition to Doubt.

This carefully[139] enclosed triangle is also "Harmony".

One can say that one of the superior principles is to care for the materials and this is why the [corresponding] planet is the Sun, which covers[140] everything.

---

[132] Literally 'penas' means "pain; emotional suffering or distress; penalty, penalize, punish"

[133] Literally 'puros' means "pure, uncontaminated, untainted; clean, free of dirt; absolute, utter"

[134] Literally 'solo' means "only, solely; exclusively; just"

[135] Literally 'Tardanza' means "backwardness, delay, tardiness"

[136] Literally 'Salida al campo' means "Field trip, Country outing, Outing to the countryside"

[137] Literally 'amenaza' means "threaten, menace; assault; loom up, impend"

[138] Literally 'vuelva' means "turn; return; again; back"

[139] Literally 'cuidadosamente' means "carefully, cautiously; meticulously"

[140] Literally 'ampara' means "cover, protect, shelter; harbor"

Si es al revés indicará siempre "penas".

El cuadrado nos dice que aquí el poder esta en la materia, en los principios inferiores, mientras que en la 28 son puros triangulos, por eso solo significa "Tardanza del exito", y al revés "Dificultades".

La 27 tiene como planeta la Luna y la 28 a Mercurio.

La 29 con sus dos cuadrados dice a las claras que significan algo material.

Es "Salida al campo", y al revés "Inseguridad", puede ser y también amenaza "Revoluciones".

El planeta es Venus.

La 30, encerrando con un cuadrado un triangulo, vuelva a significarnos con el Septenario nuestro.

"Poder" o de cabeza la "Duda", lo que significa que la Fe es el Gran Poder en oposicion de la Duda.

Es también "Armonia" ese triangulo encerrado cuidadosamente.

Se puede decir el de los principios superiores estan cuidados por los materiales y es por eso que el planeta es el Sol, que ampara todo.

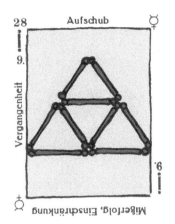

28 Aufschub ☿
9.
Vergangenheit
Mißerfolg, Einschränkung ♀

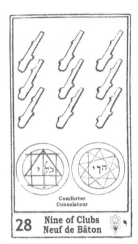

Comforter
Consolateur
28 Nine of Clubs
Neuf de Bâton

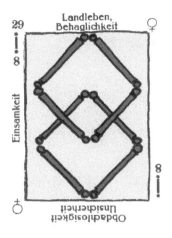

29 Landleben, Behaglichkeit ♀
8
Einsamkeit
Obdachlosigkeit Unsicherheit ♂

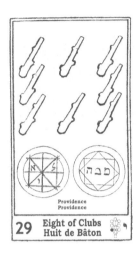

Providence
Providence
29 Eight of Clubs
Huit de Bâton

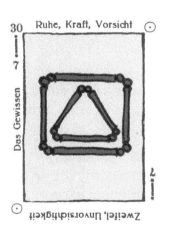

30 Ruhe, Kraft, Vorsicht ☉
7
Das Gewissen
Zweifel, Unvorsichtigkeit ☉

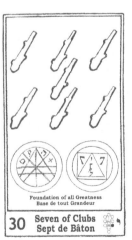

Foundation of all Greatness
Base de tout Grandeur
30 Seven of Clubs
Sept de Bâton

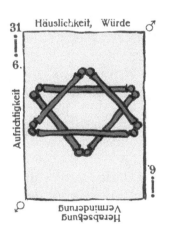

31 Häuslichkeit, Würde ♂
6.
Aufrichtigkeit
Herabsetzung Verminderung ♂

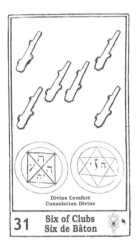

Divine Comfort
Consolation Divine
31 Six of Clubs
Six de Bâton

49

[Card] 31 is represented by the Six Pointed Star.

The superior triangle is that of the spirit, which fecundates[141] matter and [the] inferior triangle is where the matter rises to the spiritual world.

Significance of this card [is] "Dignity"and "Home Life". The planet is Mars.

[Card] 32 is man as microcosm, that figure which should be done with the feet on the ground and not with the head [pointed] downwards.

I believe this card has sometimes[142] suffered a printing error, because it is not correct[143] from my point of view.

Put in any manner, that is to say, no matter how [it] falls, [it always] means "Think".

The planet is Jupiter, the representative of the personality.[144]

[Card] 33 is the square[145] and signifies "Advancement by means of the work."

Modern authors have wanted to give a different significance to it, depending on how it falls and for this it can not have more meaning "Advancement through the Work."

[Card] 34 is the triangle and signifies "Surprise[146]" provided that the point [of the triangle] always goes up.

La 31 esta representada por la Estrella de Seis Pantas.

El triangulo superior es el del espíritu, que fecunda la materia y triangulo inferior es donde la materia asciende hacia el mundo espiritual.

Significa esta carta "Dignidad" y "Vida casera". El planeta es Marte.

La 32 es el hombre como microcosmo, que debe hacer esa figura con los pies en el suelo y no con la cabeza para abajo.

Creo que esta carta habra sufrido alguna vez un error de imprenta, pues no esta bien a mi modo de ver.

Puesta de todas maneras, es decir, no importa como caiga, significa "Pensar".

El planeta es Jupiter, representante de la personalidad.[147]

La 33 es el cuadrado y significa "Adelanto por medio del trabajo".

Autores modernos han querido darle una significacion diferente, segun como caiga y por eso no puede tener mas que ese significado del "Adelanto por el Trabajo.

La 34 es el triangulo y significa "Sorpresa" siempre que la punta vaya hacia arriba.

---

[141] Literally 'fecunda' means "fertilize, fecundate, impregnate"
[142] Literally 'alguna vez' means "ever, once, sometimes"
[143] Literally 'bien' means "well, excellently, in a good manner; appropriately, properly; nicely, pleasantly"
[144] Editor's note: According to Ch. 9 (Sagittarius) of Samael Aun Weor's *Zodical Course* (1951), Jupiter corresponds to "Chesed… The Divine Being. Atman…"
[145] Literally 'cuadrado' means "square, quadrate; chequered"

[146] Literally 'Sorpresa' means "surprise, act of surprising; astonishment"
[147] Nota del editor: Según Ch. 9 (Sagitario) del *Curso de Zodical* (1951) de Samael Aun Weor, Júpiter corresponde a "Chesed… El Ser Divino. Atman…"

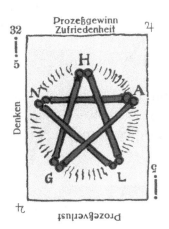

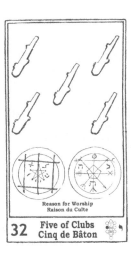

32   **Five of Clubs / Cinq de Bâton**

Reason for Worship / Raison du Culte

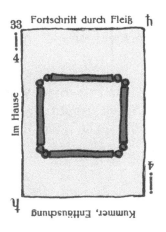

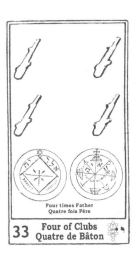

33   **Four of Clubs / Quatre de Bâton**

Four times Father / Quatre fois Père

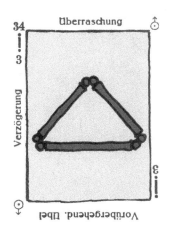

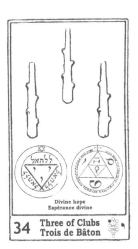

34   **Three of Clubs / Trois de Bâton**

Divine hope / Espérance divine

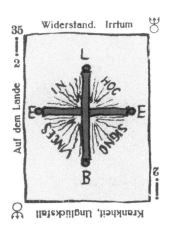

35   **Two of Clubs / Deux de Bâton**

Help of the Lord / Secours du Sauveur

When [it is pointed] down [it] signifies "Temporary discomfort".

The previous card had Mars[148] as its planet. The [card] 34 has Uranus.

[Card] 35 brings our Cross. [It] always signifies "Bonanza[149]" although with some[150] opposition, but under this sign [of the cross X or +] we have to conquer/overcome[151], as the legend says in latin.[152]

The planet [is Neptune] that is to say, the Trinity: Body, Soul and Spirit, about the Sun (the central force/strength) as the symbol says very clearly.

[Card] 36, the Ace [of Clubs], represents "Position", "The Office" and "Well being[153]" [when it is upright].

Reversed [it means] "Weakness" of the same.

It is enclosed between the Alpha and the Omega, which is to say, [for] man everything is vibration and [one] should vocalize in order to be personality.[154]

The planet is earth.

Para abajo significa "Molestias pasajeras".

La carta anterior tenia como planeta a Marte. La 34 tiene a Urano.

La 35 trae nuestra Cruz. Significa siempre "Bonanza" aunque con cierta oposicion, pero bajo este signo [del cruz X o +] hemos de vencer, como dice en latin la leyenda.

El planeta [es Neptuno] es decir, la Trinidad: Cuerpo, Alma y Espiritu, sobre el Sol (la fuerza central) como lo dice muy claramente el simbolo.

La 36, el As, representa "La posición", "El Oficio" y el "Bienestar".

Al revés "Debilidad" de lo mismo.

Está encerrada entre el Alfa y el Omega, es decir, el hombre todo es vibracion y debe vocalizar para ser personalidad.

El planeta es la tierra.

---

[148] Editor's note: This might be a typo for Saturn, based on the ordering Krumm-Heller gives to the other cards.

[149] Literally 'Bonanza' means "bonanza, rich mass of ore in a mine; boom, prosperity, good times"

[150] Literally 'cierta' means "sure, certain, definite; some"

[151] Literally 'vencer' means "get the best of, conquer, overcome, beat"

[152] Editor's note: This refers to the Legend of Emperor Constantine's conversion to Christianity. Constantine was marching with his army, when he looked up to the sun and saw a cross of light above it, and with it the Greek words "(ἐν) τούτῳ νίκα" ["In this, conquer"], a phrase often rendered into Latin as 'in hoc signo vinces' ["in this sign, you will conquer"].

[153] Literally 'Bienestar' means "well being, welfare"

[154] Editor's note: This may be refering to Chesed, Atman. Remember what was noted about this correspondence for card 32.

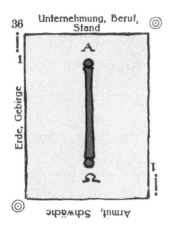

Card 37, "The King of Cups" is represented in the semitic cards by an egyptian priest, while on the nordic [card it] is a King with all his attributes.

The cloak[155] or toga of the superior Initiate, who has the chalice or the Holy Grail in hand.

The significance is "Protection by superiors" and if it falls upsidedown [then it] tells us "Beware of your superiors", different[156] against them in a given case.

The planets are double: Jupiter and the Sun

At the same time this tells us clearly [about] the great significance of this card bearing[157] the number 37.

Adding $3 + 7 = 10$, divine symbol. Man (one) enclosed in the (zero) [the] Cosmos, the Great All.

Now after concluding the explanations [of the cards], we will study the Numeric Kabalah and then we will see the importance of the [number] 10.

[Card] $38 = 3 + 8 = 11$. It is two ones, that is to say, the union of beings, here represented by a Queen wearing [a] white robe with blue (representing the sky) the celestial vault[158].

Jupiter is repeated as [the] planet, but in this case [it is] associated with the Moon.

La carta 37, "El Rey de Copas" esta representado en las cartas semitas por un sacerdote egipcio, mientras que en las nórdicas se ve un Rey con todos sus atributos.

El manto o la toga del Iniciado superior, quien lleva el cális o el Santo Grial en la mano.

El significado es "Proteccion por superiores" y si cae de cabeza nos dice "Cuidado de tus superiores", diferente contra ellos en un caso dado.

Los planetas son dobles: Júpiter y el Sol.

Al mismo tiempo esto nos dice a las claras el gran significado de esta carta. Lleva el numero 37.

Samando $3 + 7 = 10$, simbolo divino. El hombre (el uno) encerrado en el (cero) Cosmos, el Gran Todo.

Ya una vez concluídas las explicaciones, iremos estudiando la Cábala Numerica y entonces veremos la importancia del 10.

La $38 = 3 + 8 = 11$. Son dos unos, es decir, la unión de los seres, aquí representada por una Reina vestida de blanco con manto azul que representa el cielo, la bóveda celeste.

Se repite Júpiter como planeta, pero en esta vez asociado a la Luna.

---

[155] Literally 'manto' means "cloak, mantle"
[156] Literally 'diferente' means "different, distinctive; contrary; various"
[157] Literally 'Lleva' means "carry, transport; take; convey; wear; win; lead; bear; spend; hunch, hump; heave; carry off; deliver; live through; encroach on"
[158] Literally 'bóveda' means "vault, dome, arch"

Standing [up, meaning upright] or head [down, meaning reversed], this card is always favorable.   It is "The realization of our desires."

It is curious that in the four figures, the Chalice appears once held with the left hand, and with the right in the others.

In nordic [cards] the King takes it with both hands, the Queen with the right, and then the knights with the Left.

All this obliges us to meditate upon the significance.

The objective of this Course should not be to give[159] all the Keys, because then it would never end, but that all [persons] should consider[160] broadening[161] [these] deductions.

The Clubs, [or] green sticks, represent the vegetative life or the first years of life.

Now with the Grail, we receive the soul, the spiritual nourishment[162].   It is the second time that we educate ourselves.

Secure[163] in life and armed with instruction, we can launch ourselves into the conquest [of life with the] sword in hand in order to then attain victory[164], the prize, the spiritual gold represented by the Gold [or Pentacles] of the cards.

De pie o de cabeza siempre es favorable esta carta. Es "La realización de nuestros deseos".

Es curioso que en las cuatro figuras, el Cáliz aparece una vez tomado con la mano izquierda y otra vez con la derecha.

En las nórdicas el Rey lo toma con ambas manos, la Reina con la derecha, y los caballeros luego con la Izquierda.

Todo esto nos obliga a meditar sobre el significado.

No debe ser el objeto de este Curso dar todas las Claves, pues eso sería cosa de nunca acabar, sino que todos deben pensar en ensanchar las deducciones.

Los Bastos, palos verdes representan la vida vegetativa o los primeros años de la vida.

Ya con el Grial recibimos el alma, el alimento espiritual. Es la segunda época en que nos educamos.

Firme en la vida y armado con instruccion, podemos lanzarnos a la conquista espada en mano para luego lograr el triunfo, el premio, el oro espiritual representado por el Oro de los naipes.

---

[159] Literally 'dar' means "give; present; deal; produce, yield; cause; perform; say; take; teach; lecture; start, begin; overlook; surrender"
[160] Literally 'pensar' means "think, deliberate, conceive in the mind; believe; contemplate, consider; ponder, reflect"
[161] Literally 'ensanchar' means "enlarge; widen, broaden; extend, stretch"
[162] Literally 'alimento' means "nourishment, food; nutriment"
[163] Literally 'Firme' means "firm, set; secure; hard, fast; staunch; positive; sound; sign, mark, indicate; write one's name, autograph; ratify; witness"
[164] Literally 'triunfo' means "triumph, victory, success, win"

The cards [or four suits] represent the Four Gospels, [and] the four states of matter: <u>solid</u>, <u>liquid</u>, <u>gas</u> and <u>radiant</u>.

This Quaternary is also represented in the four figures: King, Queen, Jack[165] [or Page] and Lady or Knight.

We know of the Pegasus from Greek Mythology, the winged horse and poet.

We have similar mythological representations in all the mysteries which indicate [to] us that we should do nothing without the masses.

Poetry, in every way[166] [calls us] to conquer/overcome in life, and this poetry should also have its quaternary[167] development[168].

Back in the Clubs the horseman[169] [or knight] held the spear[170] [or lance], but the spear was only in the last three; in the Clubs [the horseman] carries the pennon[171], the banner as [a] guide.

The Knight of Cups [card 39], wields the spear [or lance], [and] provides[172] the cup of learning[173].

[The] following [cards have] Jupiter as [their] planet and now Mars is the warrior who accompanies him.

Representan las cartas los Cuatro Evangelios, los cuatro estados de la materia: <u>sólido</u>, <u>líquido</u>, <u>gaseoso</u> y <u>radiante</u>.

Este Cuaternario está representado también en las cuatro figuras: Rey, Reina, Sota y Dama o Caballero.

Conocemos de la Mitología Griega el Pegaso, el caballo alado y poeta.

Representaciones mitológicas parecidas tenemos en todos los misterios que nos indican que nada debemos hacer sin las masas.

De todo, formar o hacer poesía para vencer en la vida, y esa poesía debe tener también su desarrollo cuaternario.

Ya desde los Bastos tiene el jinete su lanza, pero esa lanza sólo en las tres últimas; en los Bastos lleva el pendón, la bandera como guía.

En el Caballero de Copas[174] [la carta 39], empuñada la lanza, brinda la copa de la enseñanza.

Sigue como planeta Jupiter y ahora es Marte el guerrero quien lo acompana.

39 Knight of Cups
Chevalier de Coupes

---

[165] Literally 'Sota' means "knave, jack, playing card with the figure of a knave; (Derogatory Slang) hussy, immoral woman"

[166] Literally 'De todo, formar o hacer' means "From every formating or making"

[167] Literally 'cuaternario' means "quaternary"

[168] Literally 'desarrollo' means "development; expansion; growth; unfolding"

[169] Literally 'jinete' means "rider, horseman"

[170] Literally 'lanza' means "lance, spear; pole"

[171] Literally 'pendón' means "pennon; banner"

[172] Literally 'brinda' means "offer, tender; present; express (goodwill, intent, etc.); dedicate; toast, propose or drink a toast"

[173] Literally 'enseñanza' means "education, teaching, schooling, instruction"

---

[174] Originalmente: "la Sota de Copas", pero el carta 40 es el Sota, y el 39 es el Caballero.

The [upright] significance is "Arrival of surprise", and reversed [it signifies] "Deception[175]".

In the following figure, card 40, we see the Chalice [is being] carried[176].

This is movement, [and] for this [reason] Jupiter [and] Mercury join [togther].

The [upright] significance is "An employment[177] is expected and the purpose is achieved." Reversed [it signifies] "Failed attempt".

Now in the next lesson we will continue explaining the Cups.

Certainly[178], we can indicate[179] that our body is a Cup, [it] is a Grail[180] that, first of all must always be ready and open to receive what [the] superior worlds want to put into it.

40 Page of Cups
Valet de Coupes

El significado es "Llegada de sorpresa", y al revés "Engaño".

En la figura siguiente, la carta 40 vemos llevando el Cáliz.

Es el movimiento, por eso se une a Jupiter, Mercurio.

El significado es "Se espera uno empleo y se logra el propósito". Al revés "Fracasa el intento".

Ya en la próxima lección seguiremos explicando las Copas.

Desde luego debemos indicar que nuestro cuerpo es una Copa, es un Grial que, antes que nada debe estar siempre dispuesto y abierto para recibir lo que de mundos superiores quieren poner en él.

---

[175] Literally 'Engaño' means "deceit, double cross, betrayal; spoofing; cheat, deceive, swindle; betray, be disloyal"
[176] Literally 'llevando' means "carry, transport; take; convey; wear; win; lead; bear; spend; hunch, hump; heave; carry off; deliver; live through; encroach on"
[177] Literally 'empleo' means "use; employment, occupation; business; investment; post, appointment"
[178] Literally 'Desde luego' means "certainly, of course"
[179] Literally 'indicar' means "indicate, show; point out; mark, signify; imply; exhibit, reveal; suggest"
[180] Literally 'Grial' means "grail, Holy Grail, legendary cup supposedly used during the Last Supper (considered to have supernatural powers)"

No one who has, although it is the lightest sentiment of aesthetics[181] will put wine in a dirty cups, everyone[182] cleans the cups that they intend to use and likewise we need to take care of our body in order to be clean, pure, and in order to receive superior influences, currents[183] [or streams of Cosmic Forces] or teachings.

—

Nadie que tenga, aunque sea los más ligeros sentimientos de estética pondrá vino en una copa sucia, sino que todo el mundo limpia las copas que pretende usar y asimismo debemos cuidar nuestro cuerpo para que sea limpio, puro, y para recibir influencias, corrientes o enseñanza superiores.

—

---

[181] Literally 'estética' means "aesthetics, branch of philosophy dealing with the nature or appreciation of beauty"

[182] Literally 'sino que todo el mundo' means "but the whole world"

[183] Literally 'corrientes' means "current, flow (of water, electricity, etc.); tendency, drift; tide; swim; rain"

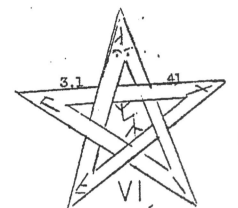

[Lesson 6]

MESSAGE
from the
Sovereign Commander of the
Rosecross
Order as [a] Secret Course
for the dependent brothers
of the S.S.S.

——

[Lección VI]

MENSAJE
del
Soberano Comendador de la
Orden
Rosacruz como Curso Secreto
para los hermanos dependientes
del S.S.S.

——

Beloved Disciple:

Continuing with the comparison of the two kabalistic systems, we find that the number 41 of the Tarot, with its 10 Cups are [in] completely different positions in one and [the] other method.

The hebrews put 4 Cups below, [this] is the Inferior Quaternary, the world of matter.

Above those four, there are three, then above those [there are] 2, and at the top, one Cup.

Thus [forming] a perfect pyramid of 10 Cups.

[They] represent the 10 Sephiroth.

Below there is a square separating the magic figures of the Moon.[184]

The Kabalist Rabbi who composed this card was very skilled, but it becomes hard to see the shock between these two worlds, the materialistic magic of the jews and the spiritualist intention of the initiated aryan priests.

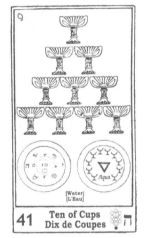

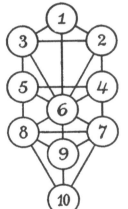

Querido Discípulo:

Al seguir la comparación de los dos sistemas cabalísticos, encontramos que el numero 41 del Tarot, con sus 10 Copas están puestos completamente diferente en uno y otro método.

Los hebreos ponen abajo 4 Copas, es el Cuaternario Inferior, el mundo de la materia.

Sobre esos cuatro hay tres luego sobre ellos 2, y en la punta una Copa.

Así que una pirámide perfecta de 10 Copas.

Representan los 10 Sefirotes.

Abajo hay un cuadrado separadas las figuras mágicas de la Luna.

Muy hábil ha sido el Rabino Cabalista quien compuso esa carta, pero se vuelve a ver el choque entra esos dos mundos, la magia materialista de los judíos y la intención espiritualista de los sacerdotes iniciados arios.

---

[184] Editor's note: This figure actually had 9 crescents (or Moons) and appeared on Papus' deck. The figure was one of Eliphas Levi's talismans for the 9 of Cups which was given in his *Major Keys and Clavicles*, and can be seen below in our corrected Daath Gnosis deck.

On the nordic card the Cups appear forming the Tree of Life.

In the bottom[185] there is a Cup, [which] is Cipactli, the Lord of Life, [they] are the waters upon the abyss mentioned in the Bible.[186]

So the Kabalist Rabbi also comprehended and took the Moon, which represents all liquid, thus water and in it is the foundation of[187] reason, which is the Moon, the planet of this card, what prevails here in the hebrew card [is] only the materialistic spirit.

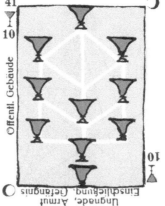

The Tree of Life, that is to say, humanity's path from the higher spheres, is indicated by the vertical line, which has two Cups almost like roots.

[This] is our spiritual origin and then, in the second Cup, this represents the astral world.

Like [ornaments] on a Christmas tree [we] will then put the Cups on the sides, crowning the last [one], [which] is the central sun, the divine realm, the superior "principle" from which everything emanates; for this [card] the significance is "Grace, Clemency, Might[188]". If it is reversed, it signifies the contrary.

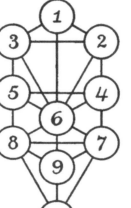

En la carta nórdica aparecen las Copas formando el Arbol de la Vida.

En el fondo hay una Copa, es el Cipactli, el Señor de la Vida, son las aguas sobre el abismo que menciona la Biblia.

Así lo comprendió también el Rabino Cabalista y puso la Luna que representa todo lo líquido, así que el agua y en ello está fundada la razón que sea la Luna el planeta de esta carta, sólo que prevalece acá en la carta hebrea el espíritu materialista.

El Arbol de la Vida, es decir, el camino de la humanidad desde las esferas superiores, está indicado por la línea vertical, que tiene casi como raíces dos Copas.

Es nuestro origen espiritual y luego en la segunda Copa esta representado el mundo astral.

Como en un árbol de Navidad van luego puestas las Copas por los lados, coronando la última, es el sol central, el reino divino, el "principio" superior del que todo emana, por eso el significado es La Gracia, La Clemencia, El Poderío. Si cae de cabeza es al revés, significa pues todo lo contrario.

---

[185] Literally 'fondo' means "backdrop, background; deep; ground, bottom; floor; fund; seat; term; long distance"
[186] Editor's note: This refers to the first 4 verses of Genesis.
[187] Literally 'en ello esta fundada' means "in it is founded"
[188] Literally 'Poderío' means "might; power, strength"

The number 42, or the 9 of Cups, has a Cup in the center and eight around [it], placed the center in such a way so as to form the center of the Cross.

The 9 has always represented humanity which has been revolving around the Self, [around] the Central Cross.

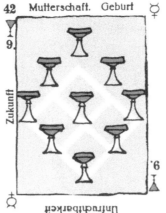

Exoterically, the Cross is matter, [and] esoterically [it is] the <u>Light</u>, [and] therefore, the Swastika Cross is the supreme symbol or [the symbol] of the Light from which everything is born[189] and this is why it signifies: "Birth, Fertility"; and reversed [it signifies] "Sterility".

The planet is Mercury.

Humanity has its material aspect, [it is] for this [reason that] we have a square formed by the cups.

The Cross then represents the Superior Triad and [so] we are once again forming a Septenary.

La número 42 o sea el 9 de Copas, tiene una Copa en el Centro y ocho alrededor, puesta la del centro de tal manera que forma el centro de la Cruz.

El 9 siempre ha representado la humanidad que gira alrededor del Sí Mismo[190], del Centro Cruz.

La Cruz es exotéricamente la materia, esotericamente la <u>Luz</u>, por eso, es la Cruz Swástica el símbolo supremo o de la Luz de la que todo nace[191] y es por eso que significa: Nacimiento, Fertilidad; y al revés Esterilidad.

El planeta es Mercurio.

La humanidad tiene su aspecto material, por eso tenemos formando las copas un cuadrado.

La Cruz representa entonces la Triada Superior y formamos así de nuevo un Septenario.

---

[189] Editor's note: Compare "From within the ineffable mystic idyll, commonly called "The Enchantment of Good Friday", we feel from the bottom of our hearts that in our sexual organs there exists a terribly divine power which can either liberate or enslave man. Sexual energy contains within itself the living archetype of the authentic Solar Man, which must take shape within us. Many suffering souls wish to enter the Transcendental Monsalvat, but unfortunately this is more than impossible due to the Veil of Isis or Adamic Sexual Veil. In the ineffable bliss of the Jinas paradise, a divine humanity certainly exists which is invisible to mortals' senses because of their sins and limitations, born of sexual abuse. It is written with characters of fire in the great Book of Life that in the Jaina or Jina Cross is miraculously concealed the untold secret of the Great Arcanum, the marvellous key of sexual transmutation. It is not difficult to comprehend that <u>such a Magic Cross is the same Swastika of the great mysteries</u>." from Ch.27 of *The Mystery of the Golden Blossom* by Samael Aun Weor

[190] Originalmente "del Yo"

[191] Nota del editor: Comparar "Dentro del inefable idilio místico comúnmente llamado "Los Encantos del Viernes Santo", sentimos en el fondo de nuestro corazón que en los órganos sexuales existe una fuerza terriblemente divina que lo mismo puede liberar que esclavizar al hombre. La energía sexual contiene en sí misma el arquetipo viviente del auténtico Hombre Solar, que debe tomar forma dentro de nosotros mismos. Muchas almas sufrientes quisieran ingresar en el Monsalvat Trascendente, más desgraciadamente esto es algo más que imposible debido al Velo de Isis, o Velo Sexual Adámico. Entre la bienaventuranza inefable de los paraísos Jinas, existe ciertamente una humanidad divina que es invisible a los sentidos de los mortales debido a sus pecados y limitaciones, nacidas del abuso sexual. Escrito está y con caracteres de fuego en el Gran Libro de la Vida, que en la Cruz Jaina o Jina se esconde milagrosamente el secreto indecible del Gran Arcano, la clave maravillosa de la Transmutación Sexual. No es difícil comprender que <u>tal Cruz Mágica es la misma Svástica de los grandes misterios</u>." del Cap. 27 en *El Misterio del Aureo Florecer* por Samael Aun Weor

Card 43 with eight Cups is curious.

The seven-pointed Star [is] formed in the interior [by the cups of the Aryan card], thus keeping the theosophical Septenary, but always in the center [is] the monad, the <u>Divine Spirit</u> which [is] absolutely missing[192] in the hebrew [card].

The hebrew [card] says that [it] signifies: "The Strange[193] Lover[194]", and below in [the] hebrew [card] it characterizes the <u>Shin</u> [ש][195] or that is [to say] the Prostitute[196] as the foundation of everything.

Papus has written extensively about the mystery of this letter and on Shin [ש] in his manuscripts on Sexual Magic, it is therefore good to meditate on this symbol.

In the nordic [card it is] missing all that, because the jews added this symbolism of their harvest[197].

For us [it] is Venus, Mary, the Mysterious Maya who is always [good] Luck, but [good] Luck in Competition[198].

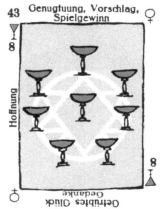

Curiosa es la carta 43 con ocho Copas.

Forma en el interior la Estrella de siete puntas, asi que sigue el Septenario teosofico, pero siempre en el centro la monada, el <u>Espiritu Divino</u>[199] que falta absolutamente en la hebrea.

Dice la hebrea que significa : La Amante Extraña, y abajo está en hebreo caracterizando el <u>Shin</u> [ש] o sea la Prostituta como base de todo.

Papus ha escrito mucho sobre el misterio de esta carta y sobre el Shin [ש] en sus manuacritos sobre Magia Sexual, es pues bueno meditar sobre ese simbolo.

En la nórdica falta todo eso, así que los judios agregaron ese simbolismo de su cosecha.

Para nostros es la Venus, la María, la Maya Misteriosa que siempre es Suerte, pero Suerte en el Juego.

---

[192] Literally 'falta' means "lack, want, need; deficit, shortage; default; mistake, error; bankruptcy"

[193] Literally 'Extraña' means "strange, odd; extraneous; foreign"

[194] Literally 'Amante' means "lover, paramour; mistress"

[195] Editor's note: This refers to Papus' deck which had a modification of Eliphas Levi's talisman for the 8 of Cups (the unadulterated talisman is on the right above). Papus had 2 of the 3 corresponding Hebrew letters removed so that only the Shin ש remained. For more information about Eliphas Levi's associations of talismans with the Tarot cards (specifically the Minor Arcana) see *The Occult and Kabalistic Philosophy of Eliphas Levi* Volumes 1 & 2.

[196] Literally 'Prostituta' means "prostitute, whore, harlot, person who provides sexual services for a fee"

[197] Literally 'cosecha' means "crop, harvest, yield (Agriculture); vintage; reap, gather in ripe crops"

[198] Literally 'Juego' means "game, sport; court; gambling; set; service"

---

[199] Originalmente "Ego Divino"

[Card] 44 brings (as is frankly natural) the Septenary, the Superior Triad and the Inferior Quaternary.

The planet of this Septenary (since it embodies both the spiritual and the material world) is the Sun which vivifies [or gives life to] everything.

The significance is "Happy Marriage" while the Triad is up; reversed [it signifies] "Marriage [that] does not agree".

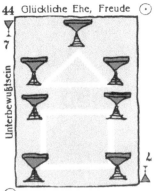

In [card] 45 [or the 6 of Cups], the Tree of Life becomes two triangles, a superior one with its three cups, and the other inferior with three others.

In the center is the Square with the Cross [or X] and everything [is] under the auspices of the planet Mars.

It is curious how the hebrew author has placed an ancient Rune at the center: the hammer of the God Thor.[200]

This symbol is found on many jars of Peru and Mexico, and often archaeologists have not known the significance of it.

[This] is the YULE symbol, that of Christmas.

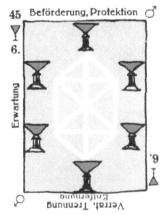

La 44 trae, como era natural francamente el Septenario, la Triada Superior y el Cuaternario Inferior.

El planeta de este Septenario, ya que encierra tanto el mundo espiritual como el material, es el Sol que todo vivifica.

El significado es Matrimonio Feliz, mientras la Triada está arriba; al caer al revés, Matrimonia aue no se aviene.

En la 45 vuelve el Arbol de la Vida: dos triángulos uno superior con sus tres copas, y el otro inferior con otras tres.

En el centro está el Cuadrado con la Cruz y todo bajo los auspicios del planeta Marte.

Es curioso cómo el autor hebreo ha puesto en el centro Una Runa antigua: es el martillo del Dios Thor.

Ese símbolo lo encontramos sobre muchos jarros del Perú y de Mexico, y muchas veces los arqueólogos no han sabido el significado de ello.

Es el símbolo YUL el de Navidad.

---

[200] Editor's note: This refers a symbol that is like an upsidedown T, given on the following page. It is unclear exactly what Krumm-Heller is referring to in Card 45, but there is a crescent figure on one of Eliphas Levi's talismans for the 5 of Cups, which can be seen below in our corrected Daath Gnosis deck.

[The Yule] is the symbol of the Light for the nordic peoples, as it is [for] the Toltecs and Incas.

The significance is "Protection and Salary Increase"; and reversed [it is] "Treason[201]".

[Card] 46 has the same symbol of the hammer.

Here we call attention to the students who possess the work of Papus on the Tarot which is not the same as [those] in the cards from Brazil, [since] they have different numbers, [let us] notice that the brazilian [cards] are good, and that the Teacher Papus is wrong.

The disciples [may] be surprised that I intended to amend the plan of my Teacher Papus.

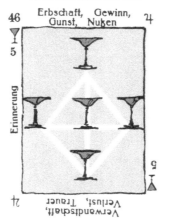

What can we do! ... everyone [in] the world can make mistakes, and if the Teacher was living, after giving my explanations, [I think he] would agree with me.

It is a pity that Papus never knew the nordic cards.

He was the son of spanish jews and jewish things always seduced him.

This card 46 [is] formed [by] four triangles with the Cross in the center, so [again it] follows the Septenary in [a] different form.

The planet is Jupiter, and the significance [is] "Heritage/Inheritance[202] or Gain"; [and] reversed [it signifies] the "Loss of a Relative".

Es el símbolo de la Luz para los pueblos nórdicos, como son los Toltecas e Incas.

El significado es Protección y Aumento de Salario; y al revés Traición.

La 46 tiene el mismo símbolo del martillo.

Llamaremos acá la atención a los estudiantes que poseen la obra de Papus del Tarot que no es igual como en las cartas del Brasil, son los números que difieren, teniendo que advertir que las brasileras están bien, y el que está equivocado es el Maestro Papus.

Se extrañaran los discípulos, que yo pretenda enmendar la plana a mi Maestro Papus.

¡Que le vamos a hacer! ... todo el mundo puede equivocarse, y si viviera el Maestro, después de darle mis explicaciones, me daría la razón.

Es una lástima que Papus nunca conociera las cartas nórdicas.

El fue hijo de judía española y las cosas judías siempre le sedujeren.

Esta carta 46 forma con la Cruz en el centro cuatro triangulos, asi que sigue el Septenario en diversa forma.

El planeta es Jupiter, y el significado Herencia o Ganancia; al revés la Pérdida de un Pariente.

---

[201] Literally 'Traición' means "treason, betrayal, treachery"
[202] Literally 'Herencia' means "heritage, inheritance; apanage, provision for the subsistence of royal descendants (as in land, regular income, etc.); heirdom; heredity"

Let us pass on to [card] 47, being the Quaternary only with the Cups at each end, the significance is: "New Relationships"; and reversed [it signifies] "A Traitor who tries to harm[203] us".

The planet is Saturn, the judge who rewards the good and punishes the evil.

[Card] 48, with its three Cups, represents the simple triangle.

[It is] curious that the hebrew author has put the Rune Sig[204] here, [symbolizing] "Victory", which proves that these cards [are] always taken[205] [from the] Runes.

The significance is "Wedding[206] Commitment[207]" and reversed [it signifies] "Unhappy[208] Love" or "Sweetheart who will not marry".

The planet [is] Uranus, the hidden luminary.

So, for the Occultist, [this] is always a card of [good] lucky.

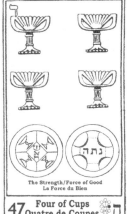

The Strength/Force of Good
La Force du Bien

47 Four of Cups
Quatre de Coupes

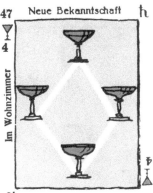

Goodness/Kindness
La Bonté

48 Three of Cups
Trois de Coupes

Pasamos a la 47 o sea el Cuaternario solamente con las Copas en cada punta, el significado es: Nuevas Relaciones; y al revés Un Traidor que nos trata de perjudicar.

El planeta es Saturno, el juez que premia al bueno y castiga al malo.

La 48 con sus tres Copas representa el triangulo simple.

Curioso es que el autor hebreo ponga acá a la Runa Zig, la Victoria, que nos prueba que estas cartas siempre llevaron Runas.

El significado es Compromiso de casamiento y al revés Amor es Desgraciados o Novios qae no se casan.

El planeta es Urano, el luminar oculto.

Así que para el Ocultista es siempre una carta de suerte.

---

[203] Literally 'perjudicar' means "damage, cause harm, cause injury; prejudice"

[204] Editor's note: Most likely this is refering to the Hebrew letter ל which is Krumm-Heller misinterpreted as a Rune.

[205] Literally 'llevaron' means "carry, transport; take; convey; wear; win; lead; bear; spend; hunch, hump; heave; carry off; deliver; live through; encroach on"

[206] Literally 'casamiento' means "wedding, marriage; match; cassation"

[207] Literally 'Compromiso' means "obligation, commitment; pledge, committal; date, meeting; compromise"

[208] Literally 'Desgraciados' means "miserable, unhappy; unfortunate, unlucky"

[Card] 49 is completely different in the two systems, because while in the hebrew there is a pitcher[209] in the middle with the symbol of Mercury with two snakes, the pitcher placed on a stone at the top of a mountain.

In the nordic [card there] are just two glasses in which one pours the liquid into the other.

In both the significance is the same: "Love and Desire", reversed [it] is reversed.

The planet is Neptune.

This card represents the two worlds: the spiritual world and the material [world], telling us that everything [we] have comes to us from a higher world, [and] everything we hope for [comes] from heaven and we still have it ......

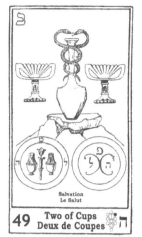

Just like card 50, the Holy Grail.

A cup in the center held by a hand in the hebrew [card] and a Grail in the nordic [card], but with rays coming from above and to fill it.

[It is] curious that the planet is the Earth and for [the] first time [we] see this [as] our planet amidst[210] the astrologic-kabalistic symbols[211].

La 49 es completamente diferente en los dos sistemas, pues mientras en la hebrea se ve un jarro en el centro con el símbolo de Mercurio con las dos serpientes, puesto el jarro sobre una piedra en la cima de una montaña.

En la nórdica son solo dos copas en que una vierte su líquido a la otra.

En ambas el significado es igual: Amor y Deseo, caiga como caiga.

El planeta es Neptuno.

Representa esta carta los dos mundos: el mundo espiritual y el material, diciéndonos que todo tiene que venirnos de un mundo superior, que todo hemos de esperar del cielo y nos queda el ......

Así[212] como carta 50, el Santo Grial.

Una copa en el centro tomada de una mano en la hebrea y un Grial en la nórdica pero con los rayos que vienen de lo alto y lo llenan.

Curioso es que el planeta sea la Tierra y por primera vez está nuestro planeta entre los significados astrológico-cabalísticos.

---

[209] Literally 'jarro' means "mug; pitcher; tankard, large drinking vessel with a handle and a hinged cover"
[210] Literally 'entre' means "between, among; in the middle, midst, amid; within, inside; by"
[211] Literally 'significados' means "significance, meaning, sense; purport"

[212] Originalmente "Als"

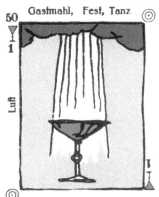

Gastmahl, Fest, Tanz.

Luft

Beginn einer Liebschaft

The meaning is "the Table of the Lord's Supper", or that "food will be provided for us", but it is the daily food that we receive from the Great God who filled this Grail-Earth with his gifts which he gives us [such as] his fruits, as a result of constant work and honor[213].

In this symbol of the earth is represented our common mother, Gaia [or Gaio], our mother, who is an inexhaustible[214] Chalice.

———

El significado es la Mesa de la Santa Cena, o sea que nos van a brindar una comida, pero es la comida diaria que recibimos del Gran Dios, que llena con sus dádivas este Grial Tierra que nos brinda sus frutos como producto de un trabajo constante y honrado.

En este símbolo de la tierra esta representada nuestra madre común, la Gea [o Gaio], nuestra madre, que es un Cáliz inagotable.

———

---

[213] Literally 'honrado' means "honest, truthful; honored; righteous; honorable, respectable; honor; grace"
[214] Literally 'inagotable' means "never failing; inexhaustible"

[Lesson 7]

M E S S A G E from the
Sovereign Commander of the
Rosecross Order as [a] Secret
Course for the dependent
brothers of the S.S.S.

———

[Lección VII]

M E N S A J E
del Soberano Comendador de
la Orden Rosacruz como Curso
Secreto para los hermanos
dependientes del S.S.S.

———

Beloved Disciple:

Querido Discípulo:

To Want[215] [or Will] – To Be Able[216] [or Capable] – To Dare and To Keep Quiet[217] is the motto of the Magician.[218] In the Club[219], the magic wand, resides the volitional agent, in the Cup [resides] the power [or ability to do] and today we continue[220] with [the] daring of the sword.

The disciple of Magic must have daring, but not be reckless, must always face danger, but not going [into battle] unarmed, therefore the third column is the column of the sword, for defense.

Card 51 – [is the] King of Swords, in the nordic card it has two more figures, which mean that we should never be alone in the fight, but rather always evoking the help of [the] superior planes.

Querer – Poder – Osar y Callar es la divisa del Mago. En el Basto, la varilla magica, reside el agente volitivo, en la Copa el poder y hoy seguimos con osadía de la espada.

El discípulo de Magia debe tener osadia pero no ser temerario, debe afrontar siempre el peligro, pero no ir sin armas, por eso la tercera columna, es la columna de la espada, de la defensa.

La carta 51. – Rey de Espadas, tiene en la carta nórdica dos figuras mas, que quiere decir que nunca debemos estar solos en la lucha, sino evocar siempre la ayuda de planos superiores.

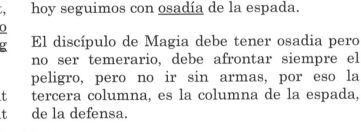

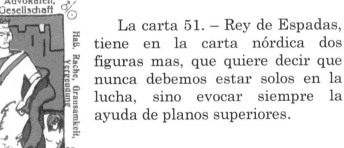

---

[215] Literally 'Querer' means "want, will; wish; like; feel like"

[216] Literally 'Poder' means "can, may, be able to; might; power, authority; might, puissance; capacity; ennoblement; warrant"

[217] Literally 'Callar' means "keep quiet; quieten; shut up"

[218] Editor's note: Compare Eliphas Levi "TO KNOW, TO DARE, TO WILL, TO KEEP QUIET – such are the four verbs of the magus…" from Ch. 1 of *Dogma of High Magic* and Samael Aun Weor "The four conditions needed in order to be a magician are the following: To Know [How] TO SUFFER, To Know [How] TO BE QUIET, To Know [How] TO ABSTAIN and To Know [How] TO DIE." from Ch. 1 of *Manual of Practical Magic*.

[219] Literally 'Basto' means "coarse, rough; base, low; ace of clubs"

[220] Literally 'seguimos' means "follow, keep track of; chase; pursue; continue; shadow; keep; run"

For [the] planet we have both the sun as well as Mars and the significance is a warning: "BE CAREFUL OF ATTORNEYS[221]". Reversed it signifies: "Evil men will cause you harm".

[Card 52, the Queen of Swords. Krumm-Heller does not give a description for this card, but we can assume (based on the rest of his associations) that the planets are Mars and the Moon.]

[Card] 53 [or the Knight of Swords] has [a] horse rider [who is] undressed[222] in the hebrew [card], [while] in the nordic [card the rider] is wearing armor.

Mars is the only planet and [it] signifies "War or Military[223]". Reversed, "Have done unthinkable things".

[Card] 54 follows[224] the knight [of swords] with [the Page of Swords] legs apart, ready for defense, while in the hebrew [card they] are still testing the blade[225].

The significance is: "There are spies after you". Watch out nonetheless[226] when it is reversed, the meaning is always the same.

Como planeta tenemos tanto el sol como Marte y el significado es una advertencia: "CUIDATE DE LOS ABOGADOS". Caída al revés significa: Hombres malos te causarán daño.

[La carta 52, la Reina de Espadas. Krumm Heller no da una descripción para esta tarjeta, pero podemos suponer (basado en el resto de sus asociaciones) que los planetas son Marte y la Luna.]

La 53 [o el Caballero de Espadas] que lleva en la hebrea al jinete desnudo, lo trae armado con coraza en la nórdica.

Ya es Marte sólo el planeta y significa Guerra o Militar. Al revés, Haber hecho cosas impensadas.

La 54 trae al caballero [de espadas] con [el Paje de Espadas] piernas abiertas, listo para la defensa, mientras en la hebrea está aún probando el filo.

El significado es: Hay espías tras de usted. Cuidado no importa como caiga, el significado es siempre el mismo.

---

[221] Literally 'ABOGADOS' means "lawyer, attorney, barrister; solicitor, one who offers legal advice to clients and may present petitions to the lower courts but is not a member of the bar"

[222] Literally 'desnudo' means "bare, bald; naked, nude; nudity, nakedness; undress"

[223] Literally 'Militar' means "military; soldierly; regimental; service"

[224] Literally 'trae' means "bring; carry; cover up; wear; get"

[225] Literally 'filo' means "phylum, basic subdivision used to classify living things, taxonomic category (Biology); sharp edge, edge"

[226] Literally 'no importa' means "never mind, it doesn't matter, it makes no odds"

51　King of Swords
Roi d'Épées

52　Queen of Swords
Dame d'Épées

53　Knight of Swords
Cavalier d'Épées

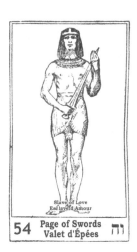

54　Page of Swords
Valet d'Épées

In the hebrew [card it] only says Dark[227] Lad[228] and also in the three previous cards [we were] warned that it is dark people in action.

There are reasons to consider this explanation as [something] erroneous.

[Card] 55 is the arch[229] of steel, that the disciple of Initiation should pass through, the planet is the Moon.[230]

[The swords] should not be [in the shape of a] pyramid like it is in the hebrew [card].

Upright it is "advantage, joy". Reversed [it signifies] the opposite.

It can not be "flowers" as the hebrew [card] says.

[Card] 56 has swords in three triangles and takes Mercury as [its] planet.

If [it is upright, then the] significance is "Justice and Confidence". The opposite if [it is] reversed: [although it] has good significance if the card falls into the circle of the Present.

[Card] 57 with 8 swords (placed as a symbol of evolution) brings Venus as [its] planet, [and its] significance: "Irresolution[231]" and "dispute".

En la hebrea sólo dice Muchacho Moreno y también en las tres cartas anteriores advierte que se trata de gente morena en acción.

Hay razones para considerar esa explicación como errónea.

La 55 es la bóveda de acero, por la que debe p[a]sar el discípulo de la Iniciación, el planeta es la Luna.

No puede ser pirámide como está en la hebrea.

Caída bien es ventaja, alegría. Al revés lo contrario.

No pueden ser "flores" como dice la hebrea.

La 56 trae las espadas en tres triángulos y pone a Mercurio como planeta.

Si significado es Justicia y Confianza. Lo contrario si cae mal: es buen significado si esa carta cae en el círculo del Presente.

La 57 con 8 espadas puestas como símbolo de la evolución trae como planeta a Venus, significa: Irresolucion y disputa.

---

[227] Literally 'Moreno' means "brown; brunette, person having dark hair skin and eyes; swarthiness"

[228] Literally 'Muchacho' means "boy, lad, youngster; servant"

[229] Literally 'bóveda' means "vault, dome, arch"

[230] Editor's note: The "Arch of Iron and Steel" is related to Masonic initiation. A French Masonic Ritual from the 1770s says:

"Question: How did you attain the mysteries of Masonry?
Answer: Through an arch of iron and of steel.
Q. What does it represent?
A. Strength/Force and stability of the Order."

For more information, see *Esoteric Studies in Masonry Volume 1* (2014) by the same Publishers.

[231] Literally 'Irresolucion' means "hesitation, indecision, irresolution"

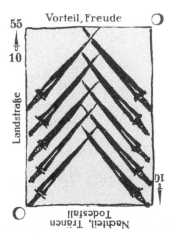

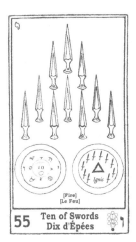

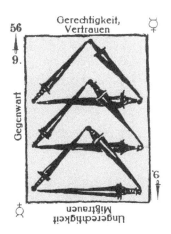

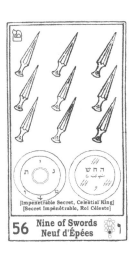

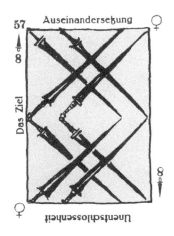

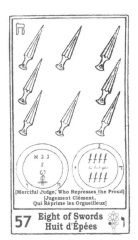

[Card] 58 has the swords in [the] form of [a] 7-pointed star.

[The] planet is the Sun and its significance is "Hope" and "Success". It always [signifies] the opposite, if it is reversed.

[Card] 59 with 6 swords brings two 6-pointed stars.

Mars returns to being the planet and the way the swords are positioned means the two worlds (the material and the spiritual), which must always act together.

Here is [how] our motto [is] described: "As above, so below."

The significance is "Security and Good Contract[232]", reversed [it signifies]: "Theft/Robbery and Disputes".

[Card] 60 [has the] 5-pointed star [in the Nordic deck] while the hebrew [card] carries the same attributes, but in the lower circle and the Sig Rune.[233]

This card proves once again that the egyptian cards are taken [from the] runes, but the jewish Rabbis (hating the nordic race) removed them.

The significance is: "Extension and. Augmentation[234]". Reversed [it signifies], "Loss and Decrease".

The planet is Jupiter.

La 58 tiene las espadas en forma de estrella de 7 puntas.

Planeta es el Sol y su significado es Esperanza y Exito. Lo contrario siempre, si cae mal.

La 59 con 6 espadas que lleva en dos estrellas de 6 puntas[235].

Marte vuelve a ser el planeta y la manera como están colocadas las espadas significa los dos mundos, el material y el espiritual, que deben actuar siempre unidas.

Aquí está descrito nuestro lema: "Lo que hay arriba hay abajo.["]

El significado es Seguridad y Contrato Bueno, al revés: Robo y Disputas.

La 60 como estrella de 5 puntas lleva en la hebrea los mismos atributos, pero en el circulo bajo y la Runa Sieg.

Esta carta prueba de nuevo que las cartas egipcias tratan[236] runas, pero que los Rabinos judíos, odiando a la raza nórdica, las quitaron.

El significado es: Extensión y Aumento. Al revés, Pérdida y Disminucion.

El planeta es Júpiter.

---

[232] Literally 'Contrato' means "agreement, contract; engagement"

[233] Editor's note: Again, Krumm-Heller appears to have misinterpreted a Hebrew letter ל as the Sig Rune.

[234] Literally 'Aumento' means "augmentation, growth, increase; addition, supplement; upturn, upward trend"

---

[235] Originalmente "5 puntas"

[236] Originalmente "traian"

58 — Hoffnung, Sieg — Kritik — Bedrückung, Unterwerfg.

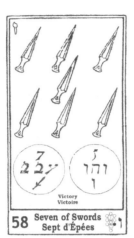

Victory
Victoire

58 Seven of Swords
Sept d'Épées

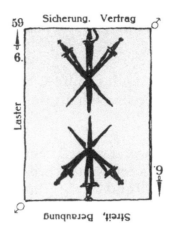

59 — Sicherung. Vertrag — Laster — Streit, Beraubung

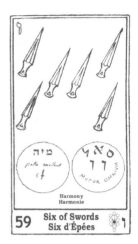

Harmony
Harmonie

59 Six of Swords
Six d'Épées

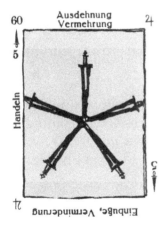

60 — Ausdehnung Vermehrung — Handeln — Einbuße, Verminderung

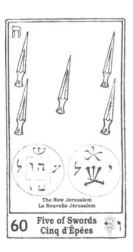

The New Jerusalem
La Nouvelle Jérusalem

60 Five of Swords
Cinq d'Épées

[Card] 61 brings four crossed swords in two pairs.

The planet is Saturn and the significance is: "Triumph over enemies". Reversed [it is] "Embarrassement/Hindrance[237]".

[Card] 62 brings the three swords forming a six-pointed star.

The planet is Uranus and signifies: "New Union", and if [it is] reversed, "Separation".

[Card] 63 with two swords signifies "Friendship", [it] is a very good card, but reversed [it] signifies "Infidelity", [that] is passing/fleeting[238].

The planet is Neptune, which makes one always think of something overseas and [now] let us pass on to the last [card] of the swords: the ACE [of swords, card 64], whose planet [is] the Sun.

In the hebrew [card] the sword is pointing upward, in the nordic [card] the opposite, [it is] pointing] down.

It is the Phallus [or sexual energy] which must be [used] to transmute ones forces and not to provoke[239] them.

The significance is "Dignity, Rank and Honors"; and reversed, "Attacks", [or] as the hebrew [card] says, "crazy Loves", [which] may also be acceptable [as an interpretation], but not in the nordic [cards] as the disciple will comprehend.

La 61 trae las cuatro espadas cruzadas de dos en dos.

El planeta es Saturno y el significado es: Triunfo sobre los enemigos.   Al revés Embarazo.

La 62 trae las tres espadas formando una estrella de seis puntas.

El planeta es Urano y significa: Nueva Unión, y si contrario, Separación.

La 63 con dos espadas significa Amistad, es una carta muy buena, aunque al revés significa Infidelidad, es ella pasajera.

El planeta es Neptuno, que siempre hace pensar en algo de ultramar y pasamos a la ultima de las espadas: el AS [de espadas, la carta 64], que tiene como planeta el Sol.

En la hebrea esta la espada senalando hacia arriba, en la nórdica al contrario, para abajo.

Es el Falus que debe transmutar sus fuerzas y no provocar con ellas.

El significado es Dignidad, Rango y Honores; y al revés Ataques, Amores locos, como dice la hebrea, puede ser también aceptable, mas no en la nórdica como lo comprenderá el discípulo.

---

[237] Literally 'Embarazo' means "pregnancy; embarrassment; hinder, prevent"
[238] Literally 'pasajera' means "transient, provisional, temporary, impermanent; passing, fleeting"
[239] Literally 'provocar' means "provoke, incite, instigate; stimulate, arouse; cause, induce"

61　Erfolg gegen Feinde　♄

In der Küche

Verlassenheit,
Unehel. Schwangerschaft　♄

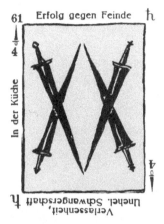

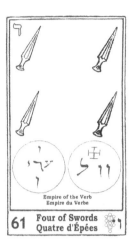

Empire of the Verb
Empire du Verbe

61　Four of Swords
Quatre d'Épées

62　Annäherung,
Neue Verbindung

Beschleunigung

Entfernung, Abbruch

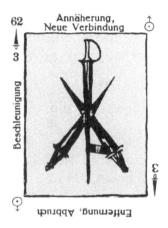

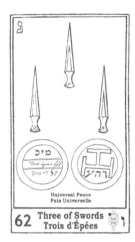

Universal Peace
Paix Universelle

62　Three of Swords
Trois d'Épées

63　Freundschaft,
Kameradschaft

In der Stadt

Treulosigkeit, Falschheit

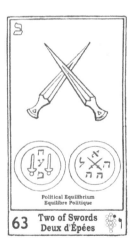

Political Equilibrium
Equilibre Politique

63　Two of Swords
Deux d'Épées

64　Rang, Würde, Ehrgeiz　◉

Feuer, Plötzlichkeit

Feindschaft, Angriff　◉

Force which Fecundates
Force qui Féconde

64　Ace of Swords
As d'Épées

Let us pass on, from this, to the Pentacles [or Gold Medals/Medallions], to the Sun, to the Host[240] that demands[241] respect, [and] silence.

KEEPING QUIET. The King seated on the Throne lifting up the Gold disc [being card 65, the King of Pentacles].

The planets are Mercury and the Sun, and it signifies: "[A] protective[242] man", and reversed "[a] man who discredits".

Mercury is always the planet of intellectuality.

Thus the Pentacles tell [us] that the intellect must convert itself into Wisdom.

[Card] 66 [has] Mercury and the Moon [for its planets and] signifies the same as the previous [card], except that here women are credited or discredited.

[Therefore its significance is: "[A] protective woman", and reversed "[a] woman who discredits".]

The Queen holds a flower in her right hand.

[This] is the symbol of the spirit that should regulate[243] our actions.

[Card] 67 carries a rider who seems tired[244], not like in the hebrew [card] who is shown [as if] arrogant.

Pasamos con esto a los Oros, al Sol, a la Hostia que pide respeto, silencio.

EL CALLAR. El Rey sentado en el Trono levanta el disco de Oro [o la carta 65, el Rey Oros].

Los planetas son Mercurio y Sol y el significado: Hombre protector, y al revés Hombre que descredita.

Mercurio es siempre el planeta de la intelectualidad.

Así que el Oro dice que el intelecto debe convertirse en la Sabiduría.

La 66 Mercurio y Luna significa lo mismo que la anterior, solo que aqui son mujeres que acreditan o descreditan.

[Por lo tanto lo significado: Mujer protector, y al revés Mujer que descredita]

La Reina lleva una flor en la mano derecho.

Es el simbolo del espiritu que deba normar nuestros actos.

La 67 lleva un jinete que parece rendido, no como en la hebrea que se muestra arrogante.

---

[240] Literally 'Hostia' means "Host, consecrated bread used during Communion (in Christianity)"
[241] Literally 'pide' means "ask, request, inquire; require, demand; invite; treat"
[242] Literally 'protector' means "protective; patronizing; protector, guardian; defender; embankment"
[243] Literally 'normar' means "regulate, regulating, standardize"
[244] Literally 'rendido' means "all in, tired, worn out, lobbied; submit, give in, surrender, yield; produce, supply; wear out; tire out, exhaust, make tired"

65 Wohlwollender, dienst-
fertiger Mann

Ordnung, Verstand · Aberglaube, Uebervorteilung

Ein bösartiger gefährlicher Mensch

65 King of Pentacles
Roi de Deniers

The Creating Father
Le Père Créateur

66 Edelmütige, verliebte
brunette Dame

Wissbegierde, Reiselust, Gastfreundschaft · Klatsch, Verleumdung, Bestechung, Neugierde

Ein ausschweifend, verdächtig. Frauenzimmer

66 Queen of Pentacles
Dame de Deniers

Master/Mistress of the children
Maitresse des Enfants

67 Nützliche Dinge

Scharfsinn, Beweglichkeit · Bestechung, Unredlichkeit

Faulheit, Sorglosigkeit

67 Knight of Pentacles
Chevalier de Deniers

Conqueror of Works
Conquérant des Œuvres

The planets are Mars and Mercury. And we know the significance.

[Card] 67. The significance is: "Useful Things" or the contrary [if] it is reversed.

[Card] 68, with Mercury as [its] planet, is a boy dressed as Harlequin[245].

The significance is: "Love with [a] lad", reversed [it] is: "Lad [who] is pretentious[246]".

[Card] 69, with 10 Pentacles shown[247] in [a] pyramid, [has] the Moon [as] its planet; significance: "Houses and Property"; reversed: "Maritime travel".

[Card] 70 [or the 9 of Pentacles] is very important because it brings all the planets and always signifies "Lottery Prize[248]".

Now we must look at what place [this card] falls [into].

[Card] 71, with Venus as [its] planet, signifies: "Idea for realization", and reversed: "Critical situation".

The 8 [of] Pentacles form a circle [in the nordic card], in the way they have put them in the hebrew [card it] is so incomprehensible and this is what all the Kabalists confess.

Los planetas son Marte y Mercurio. Y sabemos el significado.

La 67.[249] El Significado es: Cosas Utiles o lo contrario segun como caiga.

La 68 con Mercurio como planeta es un muchacho vestido de Arlequín.

El significado es: Amores con muchacho, al revés es: Muchacho es un pretensioso.

La 69 con 10 Oros puertos en piramide, su planeta es la Luna, significa: Casa y Propiedad; al revés: Viaje marítimo.

La 70 es muy importante pues trae todos los planetas y significa siempre: "Premio de Lotería".

Ahora hay que fijarse en qué lugar cae.

La 71 con Venus como planeta significa: "Idea por realizar", y al revés: Situación crítica.

Los 8 Oros forman un circulo, en la forma como se han puesto en la hebrea nos es incomprensible y asi lo confiesan todos los Cabalistas.

---

[245] Literally 'Arlequín' means "Harlequin (a comic character in *commedia dell'arte* and *the harlequinade*, usually masked, dressed in multicolored, diamond-patterned tights, and carrying a wooden sword or magic wand)"
[246] Literally 'pretensioso' means "pretentious, presumptuous, conceited"
[247] Literally 'puertos' means "harbor; port; gate; haven"
[248] Literally 'Premio' means "reward, prize, award; premium; accolade; wage"

[249] Originalmente "La 68."

68 Liebschaft mit jungen Burschen
B — Bedachtsamkeit, Achtsamkeit
Gedankenlosigkeit, Gleichgültigkeit — B
Eitelkeit, übermäßiger Aufwand

[Slave of Children or Works]
[Esclave des Enfants ou des Œuvres]

68 Page of Pentacles
Valet de Deniers

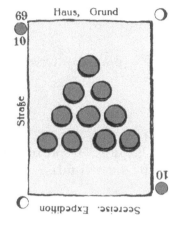

69 10 — Haus, Grund
Straße
Sbrcise. Expedition

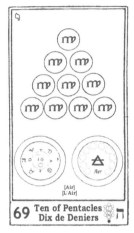

[Air]
[L'Air]

69 Ten of Pentacles
Dix de Deniers

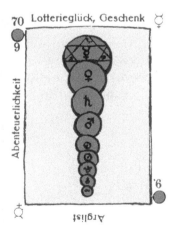

70 9 — Lotterieglück, Geschenk
Abenteuerlichkeit
Arglist

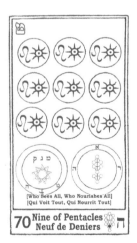

[Who Sees All, Who Nourishes All]
[Qui Voit Tout, Qui Nourrit Tout]

70 Nine of Pentacles
Neuf de Deniers

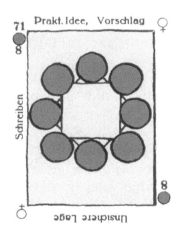

71 8 — Prakt. Idee, Vorschlag
Schreiben
Unsichere Lage

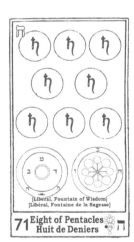

[Liberal, Fountain of Wisdom]
[Libéral, Fontaine de la Sagesse]

71 Eight of Pentacles
Huit de Deniers

[Card] 72 [or the 7 of Pentacles] also brings all the planets minus Neptune which means to say: "Less gained Overseas".

The same is [true for card] 73 [or the 6 of Pentacles] with Mars [as its] planet.

[Card 73] brings the planets in concentric circles and signifies: "Sparsity[250]."

In the way they are [placed] there is confusion.

[Card] 74 [or the 5 of Pentacles] with Jupiter as [its] planet, signifes: "Good or bad Loves" according to how [the card] falls.

[Card] 75 [or the 4 of Pentacles] with Saturn [as its planet] signifies: "Honorableness[251]"; and reversed [it signifies] the contrary.

[Card] 76, with 3 Gold Medals and Uranus as [its] Planet, warns us [of] "an upcoming trip" with favorable success or unfavorable [success], according to how [the card] falls.

[Card] 77 with 2 Gold Medals announces: "A card/letter".

Its planet is Neptune and we [now] have arrived at the last [card]: the ACE OF PENTACLES, which brings [us] back to the king of the first card with the Club [or Wand] raised.

Here, the wheel is enclosed.

The latter [card] is connected with the first [card of the minor arcana, Card 23, the King of Clubs].

La 72 [o 7 Oros] trae también todos los planetas menos Neptuno que quiere decir: Ganancia menos en Ultramar.

Lo mismo es la 73 [o 6 Oros] con el planeta Marte.

Trae en círculos concéntricos los planetas y significa: Escasez.

En la forma como están hay confusión.

La 74 [o 5 Oros] con Júpiter como planeta, significa: Amores Buenos o malos según como caiga.

La 75 [o 4 Oros] con Saturno significa: Honorabilidad; y lo contrario al revés.

La 76 con 3 Oros y Urano como Planeta nos advierte un próximo viaje con éxito favorable o desfavorable, según como caiga.

La 77 con 2 Oros nos anuncia : Una carta.

Su planeta es Neptuno y llegamos a la ultima: al AS DE OROS, que trae otra vez el Rey de la primera carta con el Basto levantado.

Aquí se cierra la rueda.

La última se conecta con la primera.

---

[250] Literally 'Escasez' means "scantiness,
sparseness; parsimony, stinginess; tightness;
shortage, dearth; famine; poverty"
[251] Literally 'Honorabilidad' means "honorableness, honor"

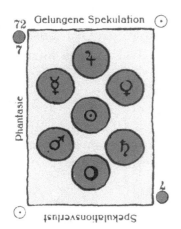

72 Gelungene Spekulation ⊙
7
Phantasie
Spekulationsverlust ⊙

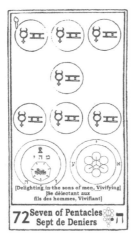

[Delighting in the sons of men, Vivifying]
[Se délectant aux fils des hommes, Vivifiant]

72 Seven of Pentacles
Sept de Deniers

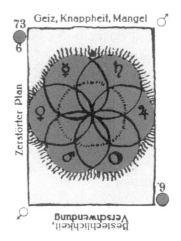

73 Geiz, Knappheit, Mangel ♂
6
Zerstörter Plan
Bestechlichkeit, Verschwendung ♀

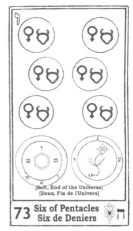

[Soft, End of the Universe]
[Doux, Fin de l'Univers]

73 Six of Pentacles
Six de Deniers

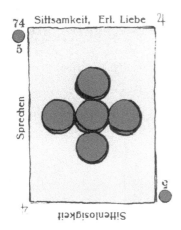

74 Sittsamkeit, Erl. Liebe 4
5
Sprechen
Sittenlosigkeit

[Supreme Being, Master of All]
[Être Suprême, Maître de Tout]

74 Five of Pentacles
Cinq de Deniers

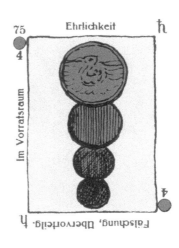

75 Ehrlichkeit ♄
4
Im Vorratsraum
Falschung, Übervorteilg. ♄

[Formidable Name, Who has Created Everything from a Word]
[Nom Redoutable, Qui a Tout Créé d'un Mot]

75 Four of Pentacles
Quatre de Deniers

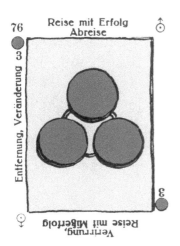

76 Reise mit Erfolg ☉
Abreise
3
Entfernung, Veränderung
Verrung, Reise mit Mißerfolg ♀

The Three Luminous Rings
Les Trois Anneaux Lumineux

76 Three of Pentacles
Trois de Deniers

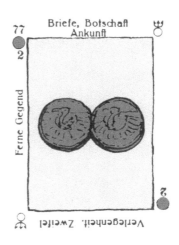

77 Briefe, Botschaft ♅
Ankunft
2
Ferne Gegend
Verlegenheit, Zweifel ♅

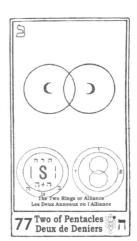

The Two Rings or Alliance
Les Deux Anneaux ou l'Alliance

77 Two of Pentacles
Deux de Deniers

Not so in the hebrew [deck] and [theirs] is an obligatory symbol.

[It] is Curious that the Pentacle [or Gold Medal] rests on the T TAU and thus forms the Rose-Cross.

Its planet is the Sun.

The significance is always "good" and always gives us "Success".

And with that, the disciples have the meaning of all the cards.

We recommend writing [this information] down in a notepad or better to learn them by heart, then it is easier to pull the cards.

—

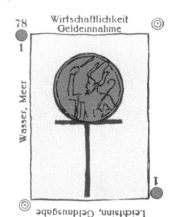

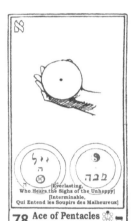

No es así en la hebrea y es un simbolo obligado.

Curioso es que el Oro descansa sobre el ⊤ TAU y así forma la Rosa-Cruz.

Su planeta es el Sol.

El significado es siempre bueno y nos ofrece siempre Éxito.

Ya con esto, los discípulos tienen el significado de todas las cartas.

Les recomendaríamos los apuntaran en una libreta o mejor los aprendieren de memoria, pues es más fácil entonces echar las cartas.

—

[Lesson 8]

MESSAGE
from the
Sovereign Commander of the
Rosecross
Order as [a] Secret Course
for the dependent brothers
of the S.S.S.

———

[Lección VIII]

MENSAJE
del
Soberano Comendador de la
Orden
Rosacruz como Curso Secreto
para los hermanos
dependientes del S.S.S.

———

Beloved Disciple:

So far we have learned the significance of the cards by their drawings and [by] the value of the Runes, but we also have to [learn the significance of] numbers [as one of our] study objectives.

You might think that these numbers only serve to order the cards [and so as] not to confuse them. No, the significance is much greater.

The hebrew alphabet, like many others, has its numeric value and each letter means something through the number representing its value.

The Kabalist maintains that the whole Universe is based on numbers and measurements, and only with mathematics and their esoteric philosophy can we understand the superior worlds and our relationship with them.

Written numbers are symbols, and [this is] a proof: The [number] 10 is composed of a line, the one (which is man), and zero, a circle (which is God).

Querido Discípulo:

Hasta ahora hemos aprendido el significado de las cartas por sus dibujos y el valor de las Runas, pero nuestros objetivos de estudio tienen también números.

Podría creerse qué esos números sólo servirían para ordenar las cartas para no confundirlas. No, el significado es mucho más grande.

El alfabeto hebreo, como muchos otros, tiene su valor numérico y cada letra significa algo por el número que representa su valor.

El Cabalista sostiene que, todo el Universo está basado en números y medidas, y solo con las matemáticas y su filosofía esotérica llegamos a comprender a los mundos superiores y nuestra relación con ellos.

Los números escritos son símbolos, y va una prueba: El 10 se compone de una raya, el uno, que es el hombre, y el cero, un circulo que es Dios.

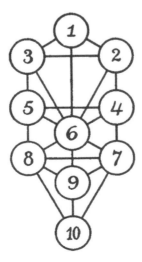

So 10 signifies: Ourselves in God or God in ourselves.

This constant struggle of being attracted to evil, by the devil, and the constant attempt to reach God, makes us fickle[252], [it] makes us appear as if being pursued[253] by [a] constant change of luck.

Man must rest[254] in God, [he] must try to achieve equilibrium in God.

10 is composed of $1 + 0 = 1$; and to analyze a name with the value 10 we must take into consideration both the one and the zero, [the] 'amen' of the 10 in itself.

Let's look [at] Card 10, 'The Wheel of Fortune'.

A wheel is never still, [it] is constantly changing.

We also know the 10 Sephira, the paths in order to reach God.

Once this is achieved, we gain[255] spiritual power which is taught to us [by] card number 11.

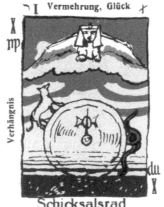

Asi que el 10 significa: Nosotros en Dios o Dios en nosotros.

Esa lucha, constante de ser atraído por el mal, por el demonio y el constante tratar de llegar a Dios, nos hace inconstantes, nos hace aparecer como seres perseguidos por el constante cambio de la suerte.

El hombre debe descansar en Dios, debe tratar de lograr el equilibrio en Dios.

El 10 esta compuesto de $1 + 0 = 1$; y al analizar un nombre con el valor 10 debemos tomar en consideración, tanto el uno y el cero, amén del 10 en sí.

Veamos la Carta 10, La Rueda de la Fortuna.

Una rueda nunca está quieta, va cambiando constantemente.

Conocemos también los 10 Sefirotes, los caminos para llegar a Dios.

Una vez logrado esto, ya contamos con poder espiritual que nos enseña la carta numero 11.

---

[252] Literally 'inconstantes' means "unsteady; inconstant; erratic; fickle"
[253] Literally 'perseguidos' means "pursuable, able to persist in it; able to continue in it"
[254] Literally 'descansar' means "rest, repose, relax; diversify; think over"
[255] Literally 'contamos' means "count, enumerate; calculate, estimate; compute (add, subtract, etc.); recount, tell, narrate"

Let us then first look [at] the value of the numbers below in order to be able to continue.

A	1	N	14
B	2	O	16
C	11	P	17
D	4	Q	19
E	5	R	20
F	17	S	21
G	3	T	9
H	8	U.-V.-W	6
I.-J	10	X	15
K	11	Y	10
L	12	Z	7
M	13		

Now let's go to the significance of these numbers:

1.–Willpower – Destiny
2.–Science
3.–Action – Marriage
4.–Realization.
5.–Religion
6.–Temptation
7.–Victory – Success
8.–Justice
9.–Wisdom
10–Change of Fortune
11–Spiritual Power
12.–Sacrifice – Penance[256].
13.–Transformation – Death.
14.–Regeneration
15.–Magic – Fatality
16.–Accident
17.–Truth – Faith, – Hope.
18.–Deception. – False Friends.
19.–[Good] luck – Friends
20.–Awakening and Reincarnation
21.–Successes – Occasions[257].
  0.–Deception – Disappointments

Veamos pues primero el valor de los numeros para poder seguir adelante.

A	1	N	14
B	2	O	16
C	11	P	17
D	4	Q	19
E	5	R	20
F	17	S	21
G	3	T	9
H	8	U.-V.-W	6
I.-J	10	X	15
K	11	Y	10
L	12	Z	7
M	13		

Ahora vamos a los significados de esos números:

1.–Voluntad – Destino
2.–Ciencia
3.–Acción – Matrimonio
4.–Realización.
5.–Religión
6.–Tentación
7.–Victoria – Exito
8.–Justicia
9.–Sabiduría
10-Cambio de Fortuna
11-Poder espiritual
12.–Sacrificio – Penitencia.
13.–Transformación – Muerte.
14.–Regeneración
15.–Magia – Fatalidad
16.–Accidente
17.–Verdad – Fe.–Esperanza.
18.–Engaño.–Falsos Amigos.
19.–Suerte – Amigos
20.–Despertar y Reencarnación
21.–Exitos – Acontecimientos
  0.–Decepción –Desengaños

---

[256] Literally 'Penitencia' means "penance, penitence"
[257] Literally 'Acontecimientos' means "event, occurrence; happening, occasion; affair"

[Inserted by the Editor, not in the Original]   [Insertada por el Editor, no en el Original]

Gnostic Ordering of Krumm-Heller's "Significance of these Numbers"

	Letter		Krumm-Heller's Association
1	א	A	1.-Willpower - Destiny
2	ב	B	2.-Science
3	ג	G	3.-Action - Marriage
4	ד	D	4.-Realization
5	ה	E	5.-Religion
6	ו	U, V, W	6.-Temptation
7	ז	Z	7.-Victory - Success
8	ח	H [Ch]	8.-Justice
9	ט	T	9.-Wisdom
10	י	I, J, Y	10-Change of Fortune
11	כ	C, K	11-Spiritual Power
12	ל	L	12.-Sacrifice - Penance
13	מ	M	13.-Transformation - Death
14	נ	N	14.-Regeneration
15	ס	X	15.-Magic - Fatality
16	ע	O	16.-Accident
17	פ	F, P	17.-Truth - Faith, - Hope
18	צ	[Sh, Sch]	18.-Deception. -False Friends
19	ק	Q	19.-[Good] luck - Friends
20	ר	R	20.-Awakening and Reincarnation
21	ש	S	0.-Deception - Disappointments
22	ת	[Th]	21.-Successes - Occasions

Ordenando Gnóstico de "Significados de esos Números" de Krumm-Heller

	Letra		Asociación de Krumm-Heller
1	א	A	1.-Voluntad - Destino
2	ב	B	2.-Ciencia
3	ג	G	3.-Acción - Matrimonio
4	ד	D	4.-Realización.
5	ה	E	5. -Religion
6	ו	U, V, W	6.-Tentación
7	ז	Z	7.-Victoria - Exito
8	ח	H [Ch]	8.-Justicia
9	ט	T	9.-Sabiduría
10	י	I, J, Y	10-Cambio de Fortuna
11	כ	C, K	11-Poder espiritual
12	ל	L	12.-Sacrificio - Penitencia
13	מ	M	13.-Transformación - Muerte
14	נ	N	14.-Regeneración
15	ס	X	15.-Magia - Fatalidad
16	ע	O	16.-Accidente
17	פ	F, P	17.-Verdad - Fe,-Esperanza
18	צ	[Sh, Sch]	18.-Engaño. -Palsos Amigos
19	ק	Q	19.-Suerte - Amigos
20	ר	R	20.-Despertar y Reencarnación
21	ש	S	0.-Decepción -Desengaños
22	ת	[Th]	21.-Exitos - Acontecimientos

[End of Editor's Insert]   [Fin del Inserción del Editor]

With this we have rejoined the meaning of [the numbers to] the cards, [and] we can extend our forecasts and analyze for the person who consults us.

Let us now look [at] the broader significance of each number and of the qualities of the person carrying this number.

One: Willpower, Destiny.

Willpower, Thelema, is a higher power without which we do not serve for anything.

[For] man [to have] Willpower [he] must have confidence[258] in himself, and [this number] emphasizes[259] that [the] persons who's sum is one, are always willful[260].

They are good manual laborers, Engineers, Technicians, but there is also much that employs their willpower in a bad sense.

Beware of them.

The Motto is "I Want[261] [or I Will]", "I Can".

Two: Science, Always [they] are intellectuals with [the] facilities of learning.

Good professors of teaching, Creators who possess the key of advancement.

[They] are Priests but are sometimes agitators.

[They] are beings of conscience/consciousness.

Con esto ya unido al significado de las cartas, podemos ampliar nuestros pronósticos y analizar a la persona que nos consulte.

Veamos ahora el significado más amplio de cada número y de las coalidades de la persona que lleve este número.

El uno: Voluntad, Destino.

La Voluntad, el Telema, es un poder superior sin el cual no servimos para nada.

El hombre Voluntad ha de tener confianza en sí mismo, y resalta que personas sobre las que sumando resulta el uno, siempre son voluntariosas.

Resultan buenos obreros manuales, Ingenieros, Técnicos, pero hay también habladores que emplean su voluntad en un mal sentido.

Cuidado con ellos.

El Lema es "Yo Quiero", "Yo Puedo".

El dos: Ciencia, Siempre son intelectuales con facilidades de aprender.

Buenos profesores de enseñanza, Creadores que poseen la llave del adelanto.

Son sacerdotes pero[262] a veces agitadores.

Son seres de conciencia.

---

[258] Literally 'confianza' means "trust, confidence; familiarity; reliance, dependence; faith, belief"
[259] Literally 'resalta' means "stick out, project; highlight, stresses"
[260] Literally 'voluntariosas' means "wayward; headstrong, wilful"
[261] Literally 'Quiero' means "want, will; wish; like; feel like"

---

[262] Originalmente "poro"

Motto: "Do not distract, do not scatter me in your things. Aim at an end and go forth[263]."

Three: Action. - Marriage.

Always or in general [they] are married.

In marriage [one] should listen to the advice of the intuitive woman, the woman has the intuitive sense and the man calculates with his intelligence [or intelligent understanding], [it] must be carried out [like this].

Many artists have the value 3.

Motto: "Alone I am not enough, I always go with [a] Woman [or a Spouse] in my [own] business."

Four: Realization.

Men [who's name add up to] 4 are politicians and philosophers.

Many socialists like Marx have that value.

4s can resolve big problems, from all the black and white parts, they seek to influence.

They have to be like the man in the card: calm[264], focused and thus [they] will triumph[265].

Motto: "Learn the past and shape the future."

Lema: "No se desconcentre, no se desparrame en sus cosas. Propóngase un fin y adelante.

El tres: Acción. - Matrimonio.

Siempre o por lo general son casados.

En el matrimonio deben escuchar los consejos de la mujer intuitiva, lo que la mujer haya sentido intuitivamente y el hombre calculado con su inteligencia, debe llevarse a cabo.

Muchos artistas tienen el valor 3.

Lema: No me basta solo, iré siempre con Mujer en mis asuntos.

El cuatro: Realización.

Los hombres 4 son políticos y filósofos.

Muchos socialistas a lo Marx tienen ese valor.

Grandes problemas tienen que resolver los 4, de todas partes blancos y negros, los pretenden sugestionar.

Tienen que quedar como el hombre de la carta, quietos, concentradas y así triunfarán.

Lema: Apreada del pasado y forme el porvenir.

---

[263] Literally 'adelante' means "go ahead!, keep going!; go! forward!; onwards; come in; yeah, yes; ahead, forward; onward, onwards; forwards; advance, progress; further, promote; overtake, surpass; forego, precede; put forward, propose"
[264] Literally 'quietos' means "halcyon, quiescent, calm, still"
[265] Literally 'triunfarán' means "triumph, defeat, win, succeed; celebrate a victory"

Five: Religion.

This comes from above as taught by the priest of the stars and everyone gets what they deserve.

Religious sentiment is innate in everyone, the question is [how] to resolve it inside [ourselves] and not put it on the priest in the confessional, since his blessing can not save us, everyone has their karma, their issues to resolve for themselves.

Motto: "Try to conquer the kingdom of heaven and everything else falls into place."

Six: Temptation.

Is [this] phrase, from the Lord's Prayer, cowardly: "Do not lead[266] us into temptation"?

On the contrary: Put us into temptation, Lord, in order to have a chance to struggle and fight.

Use[267] the whip[268] against yourself and [take] the wisdom into your hands and let a superior world inspire you.

The [people who's name adds up to] 6 are highly exposed to temptations, but the Motto should be: "Face[269] the devil, only then flee[270]."

El cinco: Religión.

Esa viene de lo alto como enseña el sacerdote de las estrellas y cada uno recibe lo que merece.

El sentimiento religioso es innato en cada uno, la cuestión es resolverlo por dentro y no ponerse las confesionales del sacerdote, pues ni su bendición puede salvarnos, cada uno tiene su karma, sus asuntos que resolver de por sí.

Lema: Trate de conquistar el reino de los cielos que todo lo demás viene por añadidura.

El séis: Tentación.

Es cobarde la frase del Padre Nuestro: "No nos pongas en tentación".

Al contrario: Ponganos en tentación, Señor, para tener ocasión de luchar y de combatir.

Toma el látigo contra tí mismo y la sabiduría en tus manos y deja que un mundo superior te inspire.

Los 6 están muy expuestos a las tentaciones, pero el Lema ha de ser: Enfréntate con el diablo, sólo así huye.

---

[266] Literally 'pongas' means "put, place; lay; insert; impose; mark; adjust; send; contribute; subscribe; perform; translate"
[267] Literally 'Toma' means "taking; capture; seizure; takeoff; intake; assumption; reduction; administration"
[268] Literally 'látigo' means "whip, lash, scourge"
[269] Literally 'Enfréntate' means "face, stand opposite; stand face to face; confront; clash"
[270] Literally 'huye' means "run away, flee, take flight, escape; abscond, evade"

Seven: Victory.

Climb into the chariot[271] of Victory, do not back down[272].

Have confidence in yourself and you will trumph.

You are born with a sacred number, so that your path will be easier than other people's.

The 7 can take any career [and] will always do well.

Their Motto: "I have confidence in my Victory, I think and want my success, for this [reason I] will triumph."

Eight: Justice and Equilibrium.

Judges and lawyers are good ones with this number, but the equilibrium must be between the body and soul.

Their struggle will always be with the tendency to equilibrate in all their affairs, and therefore their Motto will be: "Be just and always fair, this is [a] very big responsibility to carry".

Nine: Wisdom.

Do not be deceived[273] by scientific appearances, go much deeper into problems.

Your number is the number of humanity and you are responsible for it.

El siete: Victoria.

Móntate en el carro de la Victoria, no te achiques.

Ten confianza en tí mismo y triunfarás.

Has nacido con un número sagrado, de suerte que tu camino será más fácil que el de otras personas.

Los 7 pueden tomar cualquier carrora siempre les irá bien.

Su Lema: Yo tengo confianza en mi Victoria, yo pienso y quiero mi éxito, por eso triunfaré.

Los ocho: Justicia y Equilibrio.

Son los jueces y abogados buenos los de este número, pero el equilibrio ha de ser entre el cuerpo y el alma.

Su lucha sera siempre con la tendencia de equilibrarse en todos sus asuntos, y por lo tanto su Lema será: Ser justo y siempre justo, pues es muy grande la responsabilidad que llevan.

El nueve: Sabiduría.

No se deje engañar por las apariencias científicas, vaya más hondo a los problemas.

Tu número es el número de la humanidad y ante ella eres responsable.

---

[271] Literally 'carro' means "shopping cart; barrow; car; truck; carriage, cart"
[272] Literally 'achiques' means "lessen, reduce; dwarf, minimize; take in; humiliate, humble; bail, scoop out; pump out; kill; fasten, secure"
[273] Literally 'engañar' means "cheat, deceive, swindle; betray, be disloyal"

You can surpass[274] others if you want.

You can be a guide for many, since you have been born through clairvoyance.

9s are good occultists, but [they] must take [the] Motto: "I have everything inside and only in my interior [do] I look to solve problems."

—

Tú puedes sobrepasar a los demás si quieres.

Puedes ser guía pora muchos, pues has nacido para la clarividencia.

Los 9 son buenos ocultistas, pero han de llevar por Lema: Yo tengo todo por dentro y sólo en mi interior busco de resolver los problemas.

—

---

[274] Literally 'sobrepasar' means "bypass; exceed, surpass; transcend, excel"

[Lesson 9]

MESSAGE
from the
Sovereign Commander of the Rosecross
Order as [a] Secret Course
for the dependent brothers
of the S.S.S.

———

Beloved Disciple:

Today, [for a modern] Kabalist we have[275] Reichstein[276] [from whom we can] take some examples because he is an authority and [at the same time] we must certainly draw attention regarding[277] a work published on Kabalah in Spanish by a Mr. Jesús Iglesias Janeiro[278]: "The Consciousness of Numbers".

Mr. Iglesias ignores the most elementary laws and principles of Kabalah, he copied some jewish kabalists, but even they did not comprehend them.

[Lección IX]

MENSAJE
del
Soberano Comendador de la Orden
Rosacruz como Curso Secreto
para los hermanos dependientes
del S.S.S.

———

Querido Discípulo:

Tomamos hoy del Cabalista Reichstein algunos ejemplos por ser una autoridad y desde luego debemos llamar la atencion sobre una obra publicada en español sobre Cábala de un señor Jesús Iglesias Janeiro: "La Conciencia de los Números".

El señor Iglesias desconoce las más elementales leyes y principios de la Cábala, ha copiado algo de los cabalistas judíos, pero hasta a esos no los comprendió.

---

[275] Literally 'Tomamos' means "take, seize; accept; have; drink, eat; impound; touch; understand; draw; reduce; live on"

[276] Herbert Reichstein (1892-1944) wrote *Praktisches Lehrbuch der ariosophischen Kabbalistik [Practical Textbook of Kabalistic Ariosophy]* in 1930. The term 'Ariosophy' (meaning wisdom concerning the Aryans) is related to ideological systems of an esoteric nature. For more information about Reichstein's Ariosophy in English, see Ch. 13 of *The Occult Roots of Nazism* (2004) by Nicholas Goodrick-Clarke.

[277] Literally 'sobre' means "concerning, about; on, atop; onto, upon; super, above; in"

[278] Editor's note: Mr. Iglasias Janeiro later wrote *La Cábala de Predicción (1947)* which included an Egyptian Tarot deck that has been used (with slight modification to cards 21 & 22) in the books of Kabalah by Samael Aun Weor.

[Inserted by the Editor, not in the Original]

Correlation table between those numbers and letters with a short explanation in brief[279]

	Letter		Reichstein's Association
1	א	a	1. Will
2	ב	b	2. Knowledge
3	ג	g	3. Marriage, Community
4	ד	d	4. Act/Action
5	ה	e	5. Religion
6	ו	u,v,w	6. Sex, Temptation
7	ז	z	7. Victory/Triumph
8	ח	h, ch	8. Justice
9	ט	t	9. Wisdom
10	י	i, j, y	10. Change of Fortune
11	כ	c, k	11. Spiritual Power
12	ל	l	12. Sacrifice, Atonement/Expiation
13	מ	m	13. Transformation
14	נ	n	14. Self-Discipline
15	ס	x	15. Shocking Force (Magic)
16	ע	o	16. Catastrophes/Diasters
17	פ	f, p, ph	17. Truth, Faith, Hope
18	צ	sh, sch, ts, tz	18. Falsehood, Slander
19	ק	q	19. Happiness, Joy
20	ר	r	20. Awakening, Rebirth
21	ש	s	21. Success
22	ת	th	22. Failure, Illusion

[End of Editor's Insert]

[Insertada por el Editor, no en el Original]

Tabla de correspondencias entre esos números y letras con una breve explicación en breve[280]

	Letra		Asociación de Reichstein
1	א	a	1. Voluntad
2	ב	b	2. Conocimiento
3	ג	g	3. Matrimonio, Comunidad
4	ד	d	4. Acta
5	ה	e	5. Religion
6	ו	u,v,w	6. Sexo, Tentación
7	ז	z	7. Victoria/Triumpho
8	ח	h, ch	8. Justicia
9	ט	t	9. Sabiduría
10	י	i, j, y	10. Cambio de Fortuna
11	כ	c, k	11. Poder espiritual
12	ל	l	12. Sacrificio, Expiación
13	מ	m	13. Transformación
14	נ	n	14. Autodisciplina
15	ס	x	15. Fuerza de Choque (Magia)
16	ע	o	16. Catástrofes/Desastres
17	פ	f, p, ph	17. Verdad, Fe, Esperanza
18	צ	sh, sch, ts, tz	18. Falsedad, Calumnia
19	ק	q	19. Felicidad, Alegría
20	ר	r	20. Despertar, Renacimiento
21	ש	s	21. Exito
22	ת	th	22. Fracaso, Ilusión

[Fin del Inserción del Editor]

---

[279] Editor's note: Taken from Reichstein's *Praktisches Lehrbuch der ariosophischen Kabbalistik.* Remember that 21 & 22 should be swapped in order to obtain the Gnostic Correspondences.

[280] Tomado del libro *Praktisches Lehrbuch der ariosophischen Kabbalistik* de Reichstein. Recordar que para obtener las Correspondencias Gnósticas hay deben intercambiados el 21 y el 22.

He tried to make a Spanish Kabalah with the Spanish Letters[281], dividing the 28 letters into 4 groups[282] of 9 and with successive values.[283]

This is more than infantile and we recommend that before writing a work on the study of Kabalah, [that] one study some of the true Kabalists, because if his disciples employ his kabalistic values they will get[284] false results.

From our literature some Runes were plagiarized and then all those magic squares [he gives] are found in old booklets or grimoires.

It says in the preface [of his book] that it offers no presumption of originality.

No sir, it is very new, since the book is invented by its author and [is] composed by him, without knowing the real art of the Kabalah.

Let's pass on to our's:

First we must note that we always take, when it comes to Germans, the german or english names, the names in english.

The ex-emperor William is called "Wilhelm" in German and Wilhelm has a very different value than William.

El pretende hacer una Cábala Española sobre el Abecedario Español, dividiendo las 28 letras en 4 escalas de 9 y de valores sucesivos.[285]

Aquello es más que infantil y le recomendamos que antes de escribir una obra sobre Cábala estudie las de los verdaderos Cabalistas, pues si sus discípulos emplean, sus valores cabalísticos llegaran a resultados falsos.

De nuestra literatura plagió algo de las Runas y trae luego todos esos cuadrados mágicos que se encuentran en los libritos o grimorios antiguos.

Dice en el prefacio que lo que ofrece no presume de originalidad.

No señor, es lo más nuevo, lo de su libro, puesto que es inventado por su autor y compuesto por él, sin conocimiento de ese arte real de la Cábala.

Pasemos pues a lo nuestro :

Ante todo hay que advertir que hemos de tomar siempre, cuando se trata de Alemanes, los nombres alemanes o de ingleses, los nombres en inglés.

El ex-emperador Guillermo se llama "Wilhelm" en alemán y Wilhelm tiene un valor muy distinto de Guillermo.

---

[281] Literally 'Abecedario' means "abc book, primer; alphabet, series of letters used in a certain language"
[282] Literally 'escalas' means "ladder; scale; stopover"
[283] Editor's note: Regarding this author Samael Aun Weor says "There are those who figure out the numerical value of the letters in their own names and surnames. Iglesias Janeiro is a specialist in this, but we are not interested in this branch because it has not yet been studied in depth esoterically, in a scientific manner." from *Zodiacal Course* (1951), Ch. 9 'Sagitarius'
[284] Literally 'llegaran' means "arrive, come; reach; roll along; land; immigrate; invade; get; travel; vaporize"

[285] Nota del editor: "Hay quienes les sacan los valores numéricos a las letras del nombre y apellido propios. Iglesias Janeiro es especialista en esto pero a nosotros realmente, no nos interesa este ramo, porque no está estudiado esotéricamente a fondo, en forma científica." del *Curso Zodiacal* (1951), Cap. 9 'Sagitario'

Let's analyze[286] the poet Friedrich Schiller with his german letters[287]:

```
F   r   i   e  d  r   i  ch
17  20  10  5  4  20  10 8

            Sch  i   l   l   e  r
            18  10  12  12  5  20
```

If we add those values contained in Friedrich 94 and in Schiller 77   94 + 77 = 171.

It [gives] 171 [which] is added back in order to to have theosophical values and we get 1 + 7 + 1 = 9

From 171 we should reduce it [by] 9 and 162 remains for us.

We have said that to reduce the theosophical number of any amount, [we] always receive[288] a value divisible by 9 which is the number of humanity.

The kabalistic value of 9 is of the highest importance, uniting[289] [it with] one [which corresponds to] "God", we have the 10 Kabalistic Sephiroth.

This is a very curious thing, but what [did] the ancient kabalists know to construct their science?

In our case, we have seen that the first and last name Schiller gave us 171, minus 9 = 162, divided by 9 = 18.

Analicemos al poeta Federico Schiller por sus señas alemanas:

```
F   r   i   e  d   r   i  ch
17  20  10  5  4   20  10 8

            Sch  i   l   l   e  r
            18  10  12  12  5  20
```

Si sumamos estos valores tenemos en Friedrich 94 y en Schiller 77   94 + 77 = 171.

Estos 171 se vuelven a sumar para tener los valores teosóficos y nos resultan 1 + 7 + 1 = 9

De los 171 debemos rebajar esos 9 y nos quedan 162.

Ya hemos dicho que al rebajar el número teosófico de cualquier cantidad siempre resta un valor divisible por 9 o sea el numero de la humanidad.

El 9 como valor cabalístico es de la más alta importancia, uniendo el uno "Dios" tenemos a los 10 Sefirotes Cabalísticos.

Es una cosa muy curiosa esa, pero que la conocían los antiguos cabalistas el construír su ciencia.

En nuestro caso hemos visto que el nombre y apellido de Schiller nos dió 171 menos 9 = 162 dividido por 9 = 18.

---

[286] Literally 'Analicemos' means "analyze, examine; dissect; anatomize"
[287] Literally 'señas' means "address; trace, sign"
[288] Literally 'resta' means "remainder; subtraction; receive; return; deduct"
[289] Literally 'uniendo' means "unite, join, link, connect; mate; incorporate; interlock"

The Kabalist should not do[290] anything without God and since the kabalistic value of God is the ONE; [then we] always have to add it: 18 + 1 = 19

19 is therefore the kabalistic value of the German poet.

Let's see what the [value] will be for Juan Sanchez:

```
J  u  a  n   S  a  n  ch e  z.
10 6  1  14  21 1  14 8  5  7
```

The ch is always a problem for us and not all the Kabalists calculate it equally, some as c [with a] value [of] 11 and [others] as h [with a] value [of] 8, producing 19, and then it would be worth 10.

We have considered [it] as [the] ch in spanish, but not in mayan last names in Mexico; then its value [is] 10 for their chi.

Juan values at 31 and Sanchez [at] 56; 31 + 56 = 87   8 + 7 = 15 + 1 = 16

From 87 we reduce [it by] 15 = 72, [and then] add the divine 1, resulting [in] 7 + 2 = 9 + 10.

So abstractly Juan Sanchez has 10 at birth.

Now [we] need to add the value of his birth.

Let's suppose [he was] born the 22nd of february 1894.

---

[290] Literally 'hacer' means "make; manufacture; create; construct, build; fashion, shape; compose; emit; wage, conduct (war, battle); prepare, do; cause; perform; effect; force; render; fabricate; behave, act in a particular manner; live through; be"

El Cabalista no debe hacer nada sin Dios y como el valor cabalístico de Dios es el UNO; siempre hay que agregarlo 18 + 1 = 19

El 19 es pues el valor cabalístico del poeta aleman.

Veamos cuál será el de Juan Sánchez:

```
J  u  a  n    S  á  n  ch · e  z.
10 6  1  14   21 1  14 8    5  7
```

La ch es siempre un problema para nosotros y no todos los Cabalistas la calculan igual, unos como c valor 11 y como h valor 8, dan 19, y entonces valdría 10.

Nosotros la hemos considerado como ch en español, mas no en apellidos mayas en Mexico; entonces vale 10 por el chi de ellos.

Juan vale pues 31 y Sánchez 56 ; 31 + 56 = 87   8 + 7 = 15 + 1 = 16

De los 87 debemos rebajar 15 = 72, agregado el 1 divino, resalta 7 + 2 = 9 + 10.

Asi que Juan Sánchez tiene al nacer abstractamente el 10.

Ahora falta sumar el valor de su nacimiento.

Supongámosle nacido el 22 de febrero de 1894.

Adding up $2 + 2 + 2 + 1 + 8 + 9 + 4 = 28$, again [this reduces to] 10.

Returning to the example of Schiller.

The second kabalistic law says that uniting the values of the name with dates of birth, gives the future. Karma plus horoscope.

Schiller was born on 10/11/1759, being $10 + 1 + 1 + 1 + 7 + 5 + 9 = 25$.

Adding everything [together, we have] $94 + 77 + 25 = 196$ $1 + 9 + 6 = 16$ remove this 16 from the 196 [and the] result is 180.

This number divided by 9 gives us 20 plus the $1 = 21$. 21 signifies <u>Success</u>.

This number is one that can be used to do all Schiller's horoscope, always taking into consideration the dates of new events, [with] Success, nonetheless, prevailing[291].

Let's do an analysis of Mussolini, since Schiller, despite his immense fortune died in misery struck[292] by failure and fear that the same will occur[293] to Mussolini:

```
B   e   n   i   t   o
2   5   14  10  9   16

        M   u   s   s   o   l   i   n   i
        13  6   21  21  16  12  10  14  10

    = 56                    = 123
```

Suman $2 + 2 + 2 + 1 + 8 + 9 + 4 = 28$, otra vez 10.

Volvamos al ejemplo de Schiller.

La segunda ley cabalística dice que unidos los valores del nombre a las fechas del nacimiento, dan el porvenir. Carma plus horóscopo.

Schiller nació el 10.-11.-1759 o sean $10 + 1 + 1 + 1 + 7 + 5 + 9 = 25$.

Sumando todo $94 + 77 + 25 = 196$ $1 + 9 + 6 = 16$ rebajados estos 16 de los 196 restan 180.

Este número dividido por 9 nos da 20 más el $1 = 21$. El 21 significa <u>Exito</u>.

Este número es el que los puede servir para hacer todo el horóscopo de Schiller, siempre tomando en consideración las fechas de nuevos acontecimientos, prevaleciendo, sin embargo el Exito.

Hagamos un analisis de Mussolini, pues Schiller, a pesar de su inmensa suerte murió en la miseria golpeado por el fracaso y temo que a Mussolini le pase igual:

```
B   e   n   i   t   o   M   u   s   s   o   l   i
2   5   14  10  9   16  13  6   21  21  16  12  10
                            n   i
                            14  10
      = 56                          = 123
```

---

[291] Literally 'prevaleciendo' means "obtain; reign, prevail, prevailing"

[292] Literally 'golpeado' means "kicked; struck, strike, hit; knock; beat up on; thump, bang, batter"

[293] Literally 'pase' means "come in, enter; permit, pass; hand over, transfer, deliver; move from one place to another, relocate; conduct; pass; traverse, cross; give, bestow; send, dispatch; insert, put in; slip by; strain, filter through a sieve; swallow; overlook, ignore; smuggle"

56 + 123 = 179   179 or being [reduced to] 17. These must be reduced [179 minus 17] and becomes 162, divided by 9 gives us 18 + 1 = 19

19 is luck and joy as karma and [one] can not deny that the unknown journalist Mussolini, has had no luck, nor joy, for many years.

If we add the values of his first and last name, [and] date of birth 29 of july of 1883 = 38 − 9 = 29   29 + 179 = 208 = 10 reduced from 208 = 198 / 9 = 22 + 1 = 23 or 5 signifying Religion.

As [he] behaved [like] an enterprising[294] warrior sustained largely by the Vatican here is the danger of Religion.

It is known that Mussolini, in private, is a religious man, but after following the application of numbers to his life, his success is not constant in this year 1936 = 19 and that will remain true[295], but when you add the number 1 [it] predicts failure, and that failure awaits [him] from the war in Africa where [he] will never able to satisfy his ambitions.

We are not [making] friends by making[296] ourselves prophets, but the numbers calculated by the dates of departure of his troops, battles, etc., are not favorable for the future.

56 + 123 = 179   179 o sean 17. Estos hay que rebajar y quedan 162, dividido por 9 nos da 18 + 1 = 19

El 19 es suerte y alegría como carma y no se puede negar que el periodista desconocido Mussolini, no haya tenido suerte y alegría durante muchos años.

Si sumamos los valores de su nombre y apellido, la fecha de su nacimiento (29 de julio de 1883 = 38 − 9 = 29   29 + 179 = 208 = 10 rebajado de los 208 = 198 : 9 = 22 + 1 = 23 o 5 significa Religión.

Como se trata de una empresa guerrera sostenida en gran parte por el Vaticano ahí está el peligro de la Religión.

Se sabe que Mussolini, en lo privado es un hombre religioso pero siguiendo después la aplicación de los números a su vida, no es constante su éxito en este año 1936 = 19 y ese le seguiría fiel, pero al agregar el número del 1 presagia un fracaso, y ese fracaso lo espera por la guerra en Africa donde nunca logrará satisfacer sus ambiciones.

No somos amigos de meternos a profetas, pero los números calculados por las fechas de la salida de sus tropas, batallas, etc. no le son favorables al porvenir.

---

[294] Literally 'empresa' means "enterprise, undertaking; venture, gamble; business, company; firm; task; employer; employment; car dealership"

[295] Literally 'fiel' means "faithful, loyal, true; religious; accurate; dependable"

[296] Literally 'meternos' means "put, place; insert; shove; introduce; enclose; intrude; involve; engage; yank off; gather; deal, give; wager, bet; gamble; invest; cause, make happen, bring about; score, earn a point (in a game, etc.)"

On the contrary, complications caused by his ambitions will bring failure, except if (in the future) [he] intuitively takes [different] dates in order to [give] his resolutions more favorable numerical values and [if] he sees the religious danger.

In this present course, [it] is not possible to explain[297] all the kabalistic laws and we might reduce them only to give general directions[298], [which we have] already [given to] the disciple, with the value of the Runes and [those of the] symbolic pictures of the cards, making a combination that will give unfailingly[299] exact results.

The issue[300] is not taking into consideration [just] one of the things, but reuniting all [things] and if, finally, you take into consideration the astrological horoscope and kabalistic measurements[301] [then] everything will be complemented and all the factors will be dominated[302], then one can predict the future with absolute confidence.

———

Al contrario, complicaciones provocadas por sus ambiciones le traerán fracasos, salvo que en el porvenir intuitivamente tome fechas para sus resoluciones con valores numericos más favorables y vea el peligro religioso.

En el presente curso no es posible agotar todas las leyes cabalísticas y hemos de reducirnos únicamente a dar directivas generales, ya el discípulo, con el valor de las Runas y cuadros simbólicos de las cartas, hará una combinación que le dará indefectiblemente resultados exactos.

La cuestión es no tomar en consideracion una de las cosas, sino reunir todas y si se toma por último en consideración el horóscopo astrológico y medios cabalísticos se complementa todo y dominando todos los factores sí se puede predecir el porvenir con absoluto acierto.

———

---

[297] Literally 'agotar' means "exhaust, use up; wear down; distress; frazzle; impoverish"
[298] Literally 'directivas' means "directive; directorial; managerial; executive"
[299] Literally 'indefectiblemente' means "unfailingly, in an unfailing manner"
[300] Literally 'cuestión' means "question; issue; point; affair, business"
[301] Literally 'medios' means "middle, mean; average; half; mesial, medial; measure; gauge; span; meter"
[302] Literally 'dominando' means "dominate, control, rule, command"

[Lesson 10]

M E S S A G E
from the
Sovereign Commander of the Rosecross
Order as [a] Secret Course
for the dependent brothers
of the S.S.S.

—

Beloved Disciple:

We have already spoken of sympathies and of antipathies between persons and these can be found through the analysis of their kabalistic values.

Let's look [at]: RUPERTO LUNA [who] wants to marry LUISA MORENO.

Let's get their kabalistic values:

```
L  U  I  S  A      M  O  R  E  N  O
12 6 10 21 1      13 16 20 5 14 16
   (50)              (84)
```

$$50 + 84 = 134 - 8 = 126 / 9 = 14 + 1 = 15$$

Let us suppose that Luisa was born on the 15th of April in 1916, then we would add them together: $1 + 5 + 4 + 1 + 1 + 9 + 6 = 27$

We add the kabalistic values of the name and birth date.

$$134 + 27 = 161 - 8 = 153 : 9 = 17 + 1 = 18$$

[Lección X]

M E N S A J E
del
Soberano Comendador de la Orden
Rosacruz como Curso Secreto
para los hermanos dependientes
del S.S.S.

—

Querido Discípulo:

Hemos hablado ya de simpatías y de antipatías entre personas y esas se pueden conocer por medio del análisis de sus valores cabalísticos.

Veamos: RUPERTO LUNA pretende casarse con LUISA MORENO.

Saquemos sus valores cabalísticos :

```
L  U  I  S  A      M  O  R  E  N  O
12 6 10 21 1      13 16 20 5 14 16
   (50)              (84)
50 + 84 = 134 - 8 = 126 : 9 = 14 + 1 = 15
```

Supongamos que Luisa nacio el 15 de abril de 1916, entonces tenemos qué sumar: $1 + 5 + 4 + 1 + 9 + 1 + 6 = 27$

Sumamos los valores cabalísticos del nombre y nacimiento.

$$134 + 27 = 161 - 8 = 153 : 9 = 17 + 1 = 18$$

Reducing the theosophical numbers results in the [following] value for the name:

[1+2]   [1+0][2+1]
3 + 6 + 1 + 3 + 1 = 14

[1+3][1+6][2+0]
4 + 7 + 2 + 5 + 5 + 7 = 30

14 + 30 = 44 = 8

The kabalistic value of the name is 8 and through this [number, we] will always be [able to determine] the best days of the month, 8, 17 and 26, because the kabalists have the following number correspondences with the days [of the month]:

BASE VALUE	BEST DAY OF THE MONTH			
1	1	10	19	28
2	2	11	20	29
3	3	12	21	30
4	4	13	22	31
5	5	14	23	
6	6	15	24	
7	7	16	25	
8	8	17	26	
9	9	18	27	

In the above explanations we have seen that 14 signifies REINCARNATION, TEMPERANCE and HEARTACHE as well as SPIRITUALITY.

30 signifies POWER, FAITH, HARMONY, [and] has the SUN as [its] planet, so Luisa Moreno is a good girl[303] for marriage.

Let's pass on to Ruperto Luna:

R   u   p   e   r   t   o   L   u   n   a
20 6 17 5 20 9 16   12 6 14 1
             = 93   = 33

93 + 33 = 126 − 9 = 117 / 9 = 13 + 1 = 14

---

[303] Literally 'muchacha' means "girl, gal, lass"

Reduciendo a números teosóficos el valor del nombre resolta:

$$\overset{(1+2)}{3} + 6 + 1 + \overset{(1+0)}{3} + \overset{(2+1)}{1} = 14 \quad \overset{(1+3)}{4} + \overset{(1+6)}{7} + 2 + \overset{(2+0)}{5} + 5 + 7 = 30$$

$$14 + 30 = 44 = 8$$

El valor cabalístico del nombre es 8 y por eso serán siempre los días mejores del mes los 8, 17 y 26 pues los cabalistas tienen la siguiente correspondencia de numeros con los días:

VALOR BASE	MEJORES DIAS DEL MES			
1....	1	10	19	28
2.........	2	11	20	29
3..	3	12	21	30
4.........	4	13	22	31
5.........	5	14	23	
6.........	6	15	24	
7.........	7	16	25	
8.........	8	17	26	
9.........	9	18	27	

En las explicaciones anteriores hemos visto que 14 significa REENCARNACION, TEMPLANZA y PENAS DE AMOR como también ESPIRITUALIDAD.

El 30 significa PODER, FE, ARMONIA, tiene como planeta el SOL, asi que Luisa Moreno es una buena muchacha para el casamiento.

Pasemos a Ruperto Luna:

R   ü   p   e   r   t   o   L   ü   n   a
20 6 17 5 20 9 16=93 12 .6 14 1 = 33
93+ 33 = 126 ~ 9 = 117 : 9 = 13 † 1 = 14

Let us suppose that Ruperto was born the 5th of May in 1910. So we have: $5 + 5 + 1 + 9 + 1 + 0 = 21$

We add kabalistic values of the name and birth [together] $126 + 21 = 147 - 12 = 135 / 9 = 15 + 1 = 16$

Here let's also reduce the theosophical numbers of the name:

$$2 + 6 + 8 + 5 + 2 + 9 + 7 = 39$$
$$3 + 6 + 5 + 1 = 15$$
$$39 + 15 = 54 = 9$$

The kabalistic value is 9. So the best days are 9, 18 and 27.

In the cards we have seen that 39 signifies the Cup of Learning[304], Surprise, [it is] also therefore very favorable.

Here we have the planets Jupiter and Mars, when they are protected by the Sun [it] is very good.

So we have seen that Luisa Moreno and Rupert Luna will have a very happy marriage.

Now you do the math for your own case.

When the disciple is [an] Astrologer, [they] must combine the two factors: Astrology and Kabalah.

Supongamos que Ruperto nació el 5 de Mayo de 1910. Así tenemos : $5 + 5 + 1 + 9 + 1 + 0 = 21$

Sumamos los valores cabalísticos del nombre y nacimiento $126 + 21 = 147 - 12 = 135 : 9 = 15 + 1 = 16$

Vamos, a reducir aquí también los números teosóficos del nombre:

$$2 + 6 + 8 + 5 + 2 + 9 + 7 = 39$$
$$3 + 6 + 5 + 1 = 15$$
$$39 + 15 = 54 = 9$$

El valor cabalístico es el 9. Así que los mejores días son 9 18 y 27.

En las cartas hemos visto que 39 significa la Copa de Ensenanza, Sorpresa, también pues, muy favorable.

Aquí tenemos al planeta Júpiter y Marte, cuando éstos estan protegidos por el Sol es muy bueno.

Así que hemos visto que Luisa Moreno y Ruperto Luna tendrán un matrimonio muy feliz.

Ahora tú saca la cuenta en tu propio caso.

Cuando el discípulo es Astrólogo, debe combinar los dos factores: Astrología y Cábala.

---

[304] Literally 'enseñanza' means "education, teaching, schooling, instruction"

The numbers have their colors like this:

1.- Violet, Yellow
2. Dark violet, gold and white.
3. Light yellow, blue and green.
4.- Dark red
5.- Blue and Violet
6.- Yellow
7.- Purple, Coffee, Red/Scarlet[305].
8.- Dark blue, black.
9.- Light blue, gray
10.- White
11.- Iridescent[306].
12.- Dark Purple, blue, gray.
13.- Light red, red
14.- Dark yellow, yellow, blue, green.
15.- Blue
16.- Red
17.- Light violet, violet, dark green, light yellow
18. Light green, green, white, violet
19.-Light yellow, yellow-red, orange[307].
20.- Green
21.-Yellow-green, orange
22.-Black, gray.

We have given a synthesis of the Numeric Kabalah, but the kabalists are also the lords[308] of the mantram.

They know sacred words which we find in all the kabalistic works without knowing their significance, until we see that [they] are the ancient names of the runes.

Los numeros tienen sus colores así:

1.- Violeta, amarillo
2.- Violeta obscuro, dorado y blanco.
3.- Amarillo claro, azul y verde.
4.- Rojo obscuro
5.- Azul y Violeta
6.- Amarillo
7.- Púrpura, Café, Colorado.
8.- Azul obscuro, negro.
9.- Azul Claro, gris
10.- Blanco
11.- Irisado.
12.- Púrpura obscuro, azul, gris.
13.- Rojo claro, rojo
14.- Amarillo obscuro, amarillo, azul, verde.
15.- Azul
16.- Rojo
17.- Violeta claro, violeta, verde obseuro, amarillo claro
18.- Verde claro, verde, blanco, violeta
19.- Amarillo claro, amarillo-rojo, anaranjado.
20.- Verde
21.- Amarillo-verde, anaranjado
22.- Negro, gris.

Hemos dado una síntesis de la Cábala Númerica, pero los cabalistas son también los señores del mantram.

Ellos conocen palabras sagradas que encontramos en todas las obras cabalísticas sin saber el significado, hasta que vimos que son los nombres antiguos de las runas.

---

[305] Literally 'Colorado' means "colored; dyed; red, having a red coloring; scarlet"
[306] Literally 'Irisado' means "iridescent, colorful, shining with all the colors of the rainbow; chatoyant, having a changing luster"
[307] Literally 'anaranjado' means "orange, orange-colored; made or consisting of oranges"
[308] Literally 'señores' means "messieurs, term of respect for a man, mister, sir; gentleman, lord, overlord; senior, elder, old, older"

Let us continue to give the copy:

Damos a continuación la copia:

NAMES AND RUNE EQUIVALENTS

Fehu	–	Animals
Urur	–	Bull
Thurisar	–	Giant
Ansur	–	Handle
Raidu	–	Rite
Kauna	–	Wound
Gebu	–	Giving
Winju	–	Joy
Hagla	–	Hail[309]
Naudir	–	Danger
Isar	–	Cold
Jara	–	Year
Pertru		
Elgir		
Ihwar	–	Taxus Yew
Sowelu	–	Sun
Tiwar	–	God
Berkana	–	Birch
Ehwar	–	Colt
Mana	–	Man
Lagur	–	Lake
Ingwar	–	Goddess
Dagar	–	Day
Ochala	–	Inheritance

NOMBRES Y EQUIVALENCIAS DE LAS RUNAS

Fehu	–	Animales
Urur	–	Toro
Thurisar	–	Gigante
Ansur	–	Asa
Raidu	–	Rito
Kauna	–	Herida
Gebu	–	Dádiva
Winju	–	Alegría
Hagla	–	Granizo
Naudir	–	Peligro
Isar	–	Frío
Jara	–	Año
Pertru		
Elgir		
Ihwar	–	Tejo Taxus
Sowelu	–	Sol
Tiwar	–	Dios
Berkana	–	Betul
Ehwar	–	Potro
Mana	–	Hombre
Lagur	–	Lago
Ingwar	–	Diosa
Dagar	–	Día
Ochala	–	Herencia

---

[309] Literally 'Granizo' means "hail, small pellets of ice or frozen vapor"

NOMBRES Y EQUIVALENCIAS DE LAS RUNAS

ᚠ	Fehu	— Animales
ᚢ	Urur	— Toro
ᚦ	Thurisar	— Gigante
ᚨ	Ansur	— Asa
ᚱ	Raidu	— Rito
ᚲ	Kauna	— Herida
ᚷ	Gebu	— Dádiva
ᚹ	Winju	— Alegría
ᚺ	Hagla	— Granizo
ᚾ	Naudir	— Peligro
ᛁ	Isar	— Frío
ᛃ	Jara	— Año

ᛈ	Pertru	
ᛇ	Elgir	
ᛉ	Ihwar	— Tejo Taxus
ᛊ	Sowelu	— Sol
ᛏ	Tiwar	— Dios
ᛒ	Berkana	— Betul
ᛖ	Ehwar	— Potro
ᛗ	Mana	— Hombre
ᛚ	Lagur	— Lago
ᛜ	Ingwar	— Diosa
ᛞ	Dagar	— Día
ᛟ	Ochala	— Herencia

[Lesson 11]

MESSAGE
from the
Sovereign Commander of the Rosecross
Order as [a] Secret Course
for the dependent brothers
of the S.S.S.

———

Beloved Disciple:

We have seen, in the study of the Kabalah, the symbolic figures of the nordic cards, their relationship with the Runes and with numbers, and finally, with Mantrams themselves.

Let us now, in order to finish this study, see how they relate with dreams[310], since the Kabalah is said to be all encompassing.

Kabalah is, therefore, 'the Science of correspondence'.

Better said, 'the science which teaches us how all things of this plane or world correspond to others [things] from the same womb[311] in [the] superior planes, most especially in the astral plane'.

Many imaginative drawings [are] recorded in our brain, forming different pictures which we project (even unconsciously) into the astral plane and this plane is where they are energized[312] and come alive.

[Lección XI]

MENSAJE
del
Soberano Comendador de la Orden
Rosacruz como Curso Secreto
para los hermanos dependientes
del S.S.S.

———

Querido Discípulo:

Hemos visto, por el estudio de la Cábala, las figuras simbólicas de las cartas nórdicas, su relación con las Runas y con los números, y ultimamente, con los Mantrams mismos.

Ahora nos queda, para finalizar esta estudio, ver la relación que guardan con los ensueños, ya que la Cábala puede decirse que lo abarca todo.

Cábala es pues, la Ciencia de la correspondencia.

Mejor dicho, la ciencia que nos enseña cómo todas las cosas de este plano o mundo corresponden a otras del mismo matriz en planos superiores, muy especialmente, en el plano astral.

Cuantos dibujos grabamos imaginativamente en nuestro cerebro, forman cuadros diversos que proyectamos aun inconscientemente en el astral y en este plano es donde se vigorizan y toman vida.

---

[310] Literally 'ensueños' means "dream; fantasy; reverie, day dream"
[311] Literally 'matriz' means "womb, uterus; matrix, environment in which something develops"
[312] Literally 'vigorizan' means "invigorate, energize, enliven; arouse; strengthen; reanimate"

If we knew how to invigorate[313] in the astral each picture of those which we forge[314] in our imagination until they are made objective, [then] we would be true creators and we would fully[315] enter into the work of the Magician.

Numbers are the factors[316] of a Law that permits[317] us to know the value of everything in superior planes because in each one of them is the living Number as [its] value.

KABALAH is the knowledge of the PHYSICAL, the superlative knowledge of the METAPHYSICAL and the knowledge of correspondence between the two.

For example: We have the knowledge of ASTRONOMY, ASTROLOGY is [also] known to us and yet we know [that a] relationship exists between the stars and their influence upon human beings both in Medicine as well as in [the] Natural Sciences.

We also have, on the one hand, synthesis and on the other, analogy.

Thus the Kabalah goes into the study of the inductive method of isolated phenomena in relation with the deductive totality.

In the same way, conclusions are reached in [the] inverse sense, that is to say, from the totality or conjunction of the phenomena to the isolated or particular phenomena.

Si cada cuadro de los que forjamos en nuestra imaginación supiéramos vigorizarlos en lo astral hasta hacerlos objetivos, seríamos verdaderos creadores y entraríamos de lleno en la labor del Mago.

Los números son los factores de una Ley que nos dan a conocer el valor de cada cosa en planos superiores porque en cada una de ellas está el Número vivificado como un valor.

CABALA es el conocimiento de la FISICA, el conocimiento superlativo de la METAFISICA y el conocimiento de correspondencia que existe entre ambas.

Por ejemplo: Tenemos el conocimiento de la ASTRONOMIA, nos es conocida la ASTROLOGIA y aún sabemos la relación existente entre las estrellas y su influencia sobre el género humano tanto en Medicina como en Ciencias Naturales.

Además tenemos, por un lado la síntesis y por otro la analogía.

Así la Cábala va hacia el estudio del método inductivo de los fenómenos aislados en relación con la totalidad deductiva.

Del mismo modo estrae conclusiones en sentido inverso, es decir, de la totalidad o conjunto de los fenómenos hacia los fenómenos aislados o particulares.

---

[313] Literally 'vigorizarlos' means "invigorate, energize, enliven; arouse; strengthen; reanimate"
[314] Literally 'forjamos' means "forge, fashion; trump up; build"
[315] Literally 'de lleno' means "fully, squarely, full in the face"
[316] Literally 'factores' means "factor, agent; factotum"
[317] Literally 'dan' means "give; present; deal; produce, yield; cause; perform; say; take; teach; lecture; start, begin; overlook; surrender"

Since Official Science [does] not even admit [the existence of] the superior planes, it is logical that it realizes[318] nothing from correspondences.

Scientists of this branch of knowledge can not admit that the plane of this world can correspond [to] another plane in heaven (as they call the superior world), another plane, without having a prior belief regarding it.

The day will come, and perhaps it is not far off, in which men from the forefront[319] of science (those who are most free from scholastic prejudices) will give officially or otherwise, the first demonstrations of something superior because [with] the science of today [it will] not occur.

[It] was precisely in the Ancient Mysteries where these sciences of correspondence were taught and they were taken to the classrooms and colleges[320].

Read [about it], because Aristotle, the Neoplatonists, Plotinus and ultimately Swedenborg [all studied it].

The latter must have been saved [by] the wisdom of the Kabalah and have liberated it from the black veil of oblivion[321], in order to come to us.

In Mexico and Egypt, the ancient religons[322] represented their deities with animal figures, because they knew with certainty that everything that exists in this world corresponds to something similar in the corresponding superior plane.

Como la Ciencia Oficial no admite aun los planos superiores, es lógico que nada sepa de correspondencias.

Los científicos de esta rama del saber no pueden admitir que el plano de este mundo pueda corresponder en el cielo como ellos llaman al mundo superior, otro plano, sin tener sobre él una previa creencia.

Día llegará, y tal vez no esté muy lejos, en que hombres de la vanguardia científica, aquellos que estén más exentos de prejuicios escolásticos, den ya oficialmente de uno o de otro modo, las primeras demostraciones de ese algo superior porque la ciencia de hoy no pasa.

En los Misterios Antiguos, era precisamente donde se enseñasan estas ciencias de correspondencia y ellas eran llevadas a las aulas y colegios.

Léase, pues a Aristoteles, a los neóplatonicos, a Plotino y en última instancia a Sweneenborg.

A este último le debemos haber salvado la sabiduría de la Cábala y haberla libertado del negro velo del olvido, para que llegara hasta nosotros.

Los cultos antiguos en México y Egipto, representaban a sus Deidades mediante figuras de animales, pues ellos sabían con toda certidumbre que todo cuanto existe en este mundo corresponde a algo similar en el plano superior correspondiente.

---

[318] Literally 'sepa' means "know; realize; can; learn; hear; savor"

[319] Literally 'vanguardia' means "advance guard, vanguard"

[320] Literally 'colegios' means "college; institute; school"

[321] Literally 'olvido' means "oblivion, state of complete forgetfulness; omission; forgetfulness, absentmindedness"

[322] Literally 'cultos' means "cult, worship, religion"

A bird, a dog, a serpent, a fish, a letter or a number, signified for them that there is something very similar which exists in the higher [worlds], in the supraphysical world.

For this reason, Mexican Theosophy, where those pictures still exist in the pure state, asserts[323] with far more exactitude than those things adulterated from Egypt.

Bulls, men, women and children, [a] pair of living beings, were a powerful symbology.

If a telegraph in its transmission has a point and a line, you know you've transmitted an A.

If you continue placing points and lines, [then] the name ANA [can] be given, ie that of a woman who has this name and nothing more.

But when an Egyptian put a Fish, this sign signified Science.

It is clear [for] everyone who dreams of a fish or sees it, that it signifies something that concerns or anticipates[324] this in relation to a scientific thing.

The gypsies, who have popularized[325] these things, have written books with [the] significance of dreams and oracles, but they are plagued with errors.

Hence, its follows [that] we have to give [a] teaching in the end [on the] significance of dreams.

Un ave, un perro, una serpiente, un pez, una letra o un número, significaba para ellos algo muy semejante que existe en el más álla en el mundo suprafisico.

Por esta causa, se impone la Teosofía Mexicana, donde aún están existentes esos cuadros en pleno estado de pureza con bastante más exactitud que las cosas adulteradas del Egipto.

Toros, hombres, mujeres y niños, eran al par que seres vivos, una poderosa simbología.

Si un telegrafista en su transmisión pone un punto y una raya, ya sabe que ha transmitido una A.

Si sigue colocando puntos y rayas, ha puesto el nombre de ANA o sea el de una mujer que lleva este nombre y nada más.

Pero cuando un egipcio ponía un Pez, este signo significaba Ciencia.

Claro es, todo el que sueña en un pez o lo ve, significa para el que algo que le ocupa o espera esta en relacion con un algo científico.

Los gitanos, que han vulgarizado estas cosas, han escrito libros con significaciones de sueños y oráculos, pero todos ellos están plagados de errores.

De aquí que, a continuación demos a conocer para alguna finalidad, significados de sueños.

---

[323] Literally 'se impone' means "come in; grow up; impose oneself; assert oneself"

[324] Literally 'espera' means "wait; delay; stay; patience; hope, expect; wait, tarry; stay; watch; anticipate; trust"

[325] Literally 'vulgarizado' means "popularize, vulgarize, make vulgar, coarsen"

Here they are:

Chopping wood	I make legitimate[326] friends and enemies.
Bones	Evil[327] and persecution
Bird bones	Understanding
Fruit	Wisdom that comes to me
Leaf[328]	The remedy makes me better[329]
Serpent	City
Man	Reason
Woman	Selfishness/Egoism
Vineyard	My spiritual things shall be settled[330].
Fig tree	My material things shall be settled.
Thorns[331]	A curse[332]
Briars[333]	Destruction
Bread	Spiritual Food
Rooster, cat or tiger	A woman [or spouse] cheating on me
Horse	Something from the past will be repeated.
Heart	I expect good things
Eyes	I am going to learn something new
Debt[334]	There must be obedience
Hands	Power
Sea/Ocean	Increase of internal development
Sun	I will be loved (good time).
Ox	I expect something good.
Mice	Fall into the hand of a greedy [person].

Hélos aqui :

Cortar leña	Me hacen justicia amigos y enemigos.
Huesos	Maldad y persecución
Huesos de aves	Entendimiento
Fruta	Sabiduría que me llega
Hojas	El remedio me hace provecho
Serpiente	Ciudad
Hombre	Razón
Mujer	Egoismos
Viñedo	Se arreglarán mis cosas espirituales.
Higuera	Se arreglarán mis cosas materiales
Espinas	Una maldición
Abrojos	Destrucción
Pan	Alimento espiritual
Gallo, gato o tigre	Una mujer me engaña
Caballo	Algo del pasado se va a repetir.
Corazón	Me esperan cosas buenas
Ojos	Voy a aprender algo nuevo
Debito	Hay que ser obediente
Manos	Poder
Mar	Aumento de desarrollo interno.
Sol	Seré amado (buena época).
Buey	Algo bueno debo esperar.
Ratones	Caeré en manos de un avaro.

---

[326] Literally 'justicia' means "justice, equality, rightness; righteousness; legitimacy; execution"

[327] Literally 'Maldad' means "evil, wickedness, badness"

[328] Literally 'Hojas' means "leaf, blade; sheet; form; bill; foil"

[329] Literally 'provecho' means "profit, earnings, financial gain; benefit, avail; financial income; advantage, privilege"

[330] Literally 'arreglarán' means "arrange, settle; fix; order, sort; tidy; quadrate; accommodate; regulate; posh up"

[331] Literally 'Espinas' means "thorn, spine, prickle; splinter; bone; fishbone; doubt"

[332] Literally 'maldición' means "curse, damn, malediction"

[333] Literally 'Abrojos' means "Thistles, Crowfoot, Briars"

[334] Literally 'Debito' means "debit, liability, debt, obligation"

Golden Idols	I am on my path, in my teachings.	Idolos Dorados	Estoy en mi camino, en mis enseñanzas.
Silver Idols	I am good at everything	Idolos de plata	Estoy bien del todo
Simple Gold	My love is rewarded[335]	Oro simple	Mi amor es recompensado
Copper	I must have better considerations with my neighbor.	Cobre	Debo tener más consideraciones con mi prójimo.
Stones	Increased faith	Piedras	Aumento de fe
Ships[336]	New lessons will come to me	Buques	Me vendrán enseñanzas nuevas
Eagle	Same meaning as above	Aguila	Igual significado que la anterior.
Lion	Very soon I will have power	León	Muy pronto tendré poder
Sheep	I am protected from the invisible.	Oveja	Me protegen desde el invisible.
Angel	Must use Mantrams	Angel	Debo utilizar Mantrams
Angel on horseback	Must make[337] Mantrams with knowledge of their significance.	Angel a caballo	Debo hacer Mantrams con conocimiento de sa significado.
Wall	White light.	Pared	Luz blanca.
Red Wall	Love	Pared roja	Amor
Ruby	In [the] superior planes [they] are with me	Rubí	En planos superiores están conmigo
Staff/Wand	The power of White Magic approaches me	Bastón	Se me acerca el poder de Magia Blanca
Hollow Cane/Staff	Black magic.	Bastón hueco	Magia negra.
Egypt	It is there [where I will] complete my studies.	Egipto	Está allí el completo de mis estudios.
Mexico	There I must study Nordic Theosophy	México	Allí debo estudiar Teosofía Nórdica
Sack/Bag[338]	I expected mourning[339]	Saco	Me espera luto
Blood	I am being lied to	Sangre	Me están mintiendo
Smoke	Curses that I receive	Humo	Maldiciones que me llegan
Mountain	Divine love	Montaña	Amor divino
Cross	Temptations	Cruz	Tentaciones
Palm [tree or leaf]	Divine truths	Palma	Verdades divinas
Rainbow	Birth of a new being.	Arco Iris	Nacimiento de un nuevo sér.
Wings	Material and spiritual protection	Alas	Proteccion material y espiritual

---

[335] Literally 'recompensado' means "guerdon, recompense, reward, requite"

[336] Literally 'Buques' means "ship, vessel"

[337] Literally 'hacer' means "make; manufacture; create; construct, build; fashion, shape; compose; emit; wage, conduct (war, battle); prepare, do; cause; perform; effect; force; render; fabricate; behave, act in a particular manner; live through; be"

[338] Literally 'Saco' means "sack; sac, bag; carrier bag; coat"

[339] Literally 'luto' means "mourning, bereavement; black"

Through these significances that we give, the student of Kabalah must reach greater and greater concepts.

By predicting or by wanting to learn the fate of anyone, we must avail ourselves of all the factors, that is to say how much the cards tell us in relation to their numbers and to the dreams which the consultant expresses.

The only way[340] Practical Kabalah can be [done] is with all the factors together.

We have reached the end of our Course of Kabalah.

Despite our efforts with this and other knowledge [all of it] is to prepare our Disciples for incomparably greater knowledge, it is not possible for us to further extend this course.

"Natura nom fecit saltus"[341] – says a latin proverb, [and one] should adapt oneself to this because [it] is the Law of Life.

Our policy[342] is to bring[343] everyone to the middle of the Path with a slow, but firm and safe, [pace] towards what is best (in order to not fall [along the way]).

We know that when the Law is awakened on one side, the white side, the [opposite] pair is awakened on the tenebrous side, and whosoever persistently[344] wants to be good, has to suffer the ordeal of evil advancing toward them [which] one has to dominate and overcome.

El estudiante de Cábala, mediante esos significados que damos, debe ensancharlos y llegar a conceptos mayores.

Al predecirse o al quererse conocer la suerte de cual-quiera, debemos valernos de todos los factores es decir de cuanto digan las cartas en relacion con les números y con los ensueños que exprese el consultante.

Con todos los factores reunidos es como únicamente puede hacerse Cábala Práctica.

Hemos llegado al final de nuestro Curso de Cábala.

A pesar de que nuestro afán con estos y otros conocimientos es el de preparar a nuestros Discípulos para conocimientos incomparablemente mayores, no nos es posible hacer más extenso el presente Curso.

"Natura non facit saltus"[345] – dice un proverbio latino, a él hay que ajustarse porque es la Ley de la Vida.

Nuestra norma es llevar a todos con alguna lentitud, pero firmes y seguros, para no caer, a lo mejor, en mitad del Sendero.

Sabemos que cuando la Ley se despierta de un lado, el lado blanco, se despierta al par el lado tenebroso, y el que quiere con insistencia ser bueno, ha de sufrir la prueba del mal avanza hacia él dominándolo y venciéndolo.

---

[340] Literally 'es como únicamente' means "is [the] only [way] how"

[341] Latin meaning: "Nature does not make jumps"

[342] Literally 'norma' means "norm; prescript; rule; yardstick; policy; establish norms"

[343] Literally 'llevar' means "carry, transport; take; convey; wear; win; lead; bear; spend; hunch, hump; heave; carry off; deliver; live through; encroach on"

[344] Literally 'insistencia' means "insistence, emphasis, insistently, persistently, earnestly, strongly"

---

[345] Originalmente: "Natura nom fecit saltus"

Let's go [foward] then, walking carefully.

When the time comes, the prepared disciple will stand and then convert themselves into the hero who has to pass [through] the narrow gate of Initiation.

Vayamos pues, con pies de plomo.

Cuando la hora suene, el discípulo preparado se erguira y entonces se convertirá en el héroe que ha de pasar la estrecha puerta de la Iniciación.

———

Editor's Appendix   # Apéndice del Editor

Table of the Tarot Cards and their correspondences according to Krumm-Heller

Tabla de las cartas del Tarot y sus correspondencias según Krumm Heller

Card 1: the Magician
Rune: Fa, that is to say the creator, the factor, the father, the divine essence as [the] impulse of life.
Significance: fire or "Light", because in the beginning was the Light of the Spirit.
Correspondence: [not given, but Fire].

Card 2: Popess, Priestess
Rune: [not given].
Significance: fame, reward, intelligence, the people, the masses and consultation.
Correspondence: [not given, but Moon].

Card 3: the Empress
Rune: DORN or THORN.
Significance: [not given].
Correspondence: [not given, but Venus].

Card 4: [the Emperor,] the calm, focused man
Rune: OS.
Significance: Upright [it] signifies [a] blond/fair[1] and wealthy husband, takeover[2], hypocrisy; [being] on [the beneficial] side [of the] Law; reversed [it means] shipwreck, ill-will, abuse of force/strength and temporal.
Correspondence: Scorpio & Jupiter

Card 5: the Pope, Priest
Rune: Rita, the Law.
Significance: Upright the card is fortune, wealth, inspiration and teaching, reversed [it] signifies marriage.
Correspondence: [not given, but Aries].

Carta 1: el Mago
Runa: Fa, es decir el creador, el factor, el padre, la esencia divina como impulso de la vida.
Significando: fuego o "Luz", pues al principio fue la Luz del Espiritu.
Correspondencia: [no se da, pero Fuego].

Carta 2: Papisa, Sacerdotisa
Runa: [no se da].
Significando: fama, recompensa, inteligencia, el pueblo, las masas y consulta.
Correspondencia: [no se da, pero la Luna].

Carta 3: la Emperatriz
Runa: DORN o TORN.
Significando: [no se da].
Correspondencia: [no se da, pero Venus].

Carta 4: [el Emperador,] el hombre quietos, concentradas
Runa: OS.
Significando: De cabeza significa marido rubio y rico, toma de posesión, hipocresía; de lado Ley; al revés naufragio, mala voluntad, abuso de fuerza y temporal.
Correspondencia: Escorpion & Jupiter.

Carta 5: El Papa, Sacerdote
Runa: Rita, la Ley.
Significando: Cayendo bien la carta es fortuna, riqueza, inspiracion y enseñanza, al reves significa casamiento.
Correspondencia: [no se da, pero Aries].

---

[1] Literally 'rubio' means "fair, light; blond; dusky; blond, one who has light-colored hair"
[2] Literally 'toma de posesión' means "entry, inauguration, takeover"

Card 6: the Lover
Rune: Kaum.
Significance: "Divine Love". Upright it is the day, reversed [it is] night, as well as material love.
Correspondence: Taurus.

Card 7: the Chariot of Triumph
Rune: an **X** like a cross.
Significance: triumph, success, good husband [or spouse], divine protection. Reversed it signifies disgust, struggles, enemies and intrigues.
Correspondence: Gemini.

Card 8: Justice
Rune: Rita.
Significance: [not given].
Correspondence: Cancer.

Card 9: the Hermit, the Sage
Rune: Hagal.
Significance: [being] on the good side, wisdom and [a] successful[3] process, upsidedown [it signifies a] simple process, slander[4].
Correspondence: [not given, but Leo].

Card 10: the Wheel of Fortune
Rune: EH.
Significance: good position, augmentation of fortune and upsidedown [it signifies] failure and fatal disease.
Correspondence: Virgo.

Carta 6: el Enamorado
Runa: Kaun.
Significando: "Amor Divino". De cabeza es el dia, al reves la noche, tambien el amor material.
Correspondencia: Toro.

Carta 7: el Carro del Triunfo
Runa: una **X** como una cruz.
Significando: el triunfo, exito, esposo bueno, protección divina. Se cae de cabeza significa disgusto, lucha, enemigos e intrigas.
Correspondencia: Los Gemelos.

Carta 8: la Justicia
Runa: Rita.
Significando: [no se da].
Correspondencia: Cancer.

Carta 9: el Ermitaño, el Sabio
Runa: Hagal.
Significando: por el lado bueno, sabiduria y proceso ganado, al reves proceso simple, calumnia.
Correspondencia: [no se da, pero Leo].

Carta 10: la Rueda de la Fortuna
Runa: EH.
Significando: buena posicion, aumento de fortuna y al reves fracaso y enfermedad mortal.
Correspondencia: Virgo.

---

[3] Literally 'ganado' means "gain, acquire; profit, earn; add; win; defeat; capture, possess; reach, arrive; prosper, succeed; flourish, thrive"
[4] Literally 'calumnia' means "calumny, slander, libel; defamation, slur"

Card 11: Power, force/strength
Rune: [not given].
Significance: force/strength, tenacity and resolution. When upsidedown it announces accidents.
Correspondence: Mars.

Carta 11: el Poder, la fuerza
Runa: [no se da].
Significando: fuerza, tenacidad y resolucion. Cuando cae de cabeza anuncia accidentes.
Correspondencia: Marte.

Card 12: THE HANGED MAN
Rune: /\
Significance: Upright it signifies warning[5], change and sacrifice, reversed [it signifies] discord[6].
Correspondence: Libra.

Carta 12: EL AHORCADO
Runa: /\
Significando: Caida bien significa advertencia, cambio y sacrificio, al revés discordia.
Correspondencia: Libra.

Card 13: Death
Rune: SIG.
Significance: [Upright] it signifies nothingness[7], conclusion of diseases and pains, that is to say: promise[8] of [good] health; and only [with the] head upside down is [it] bad.
Correspondence: Scorpio [& Mars, and Water].

Carta 13: La Muerte
Runa: SIEG.
Significando: Significa la nada, conclusión de enfermedades y penas, es decir: esperanza de salud; y sólo caída de cabeza es mala.
Correspondencia: Escorpion [& Marte, y Agua].

Card 14: Reincarnation
Rune: /\/
Significance: Upright it signifies Temperance[9] and heartache[10], spirituality; and reversed [it signifies] disgrace[11].
Correspondence: [not given, but Scorpio].

Carta 14: Reencarnación
Runa: /\/
Significando: Caída bien significa Templanza y penas de amor, espiritualidad; y al revés deshonra.
Correspondencia: [no se da, pero Escorpion].

---

[5] Literally 'advertencia' means "warning, caution; caveat, admonition; reminder; premonition"
[6] Literally 'discordia' means "discord, disharmony; dissension, disagreement"
[7] Literally 'nada' means "nothingness, nought; nil, naught"
[8] Literally 'esperanza' means "hope, promise, expectation, prospect; anticipation; confidence"
[9] Literally 'Templanza' means "temperance, moderation, calmness"
[10] Literally 'penas de amor' means "pains/pangs of love, love pains, heartache, romantic woes"
[11] Literally 'deshonra' means "defile; discredit; disgrace, dishonor"

Card 15: Baphomet, Lucifer

Rune: God ᛉ

Significance: Upright significance is: depression and loss; reversed [it signifies] illness and insanity. It is the black magician who harms[12] us.

Correspondence: Sagittarius.

Carta 15: el Bafometo, Lucifer

Runa: Dios ᛉ

Significando: El significado es: caida bien, depresión y pérdidas; al revés enfermedad y locura. Es el mago negro que nos hace daño.

Correspondencia: Sagitario.

Card 16: Lightning [or the Ray]/ House of God

Rune: [not given].

Significance: Upright [it] signifies good, prompt resolution and losses, reversed [it signifies] disgrace and deception.

Correspondence: Capricorn.

Carta 16: El Rayo/ Casa de Dios

Runa: [no se da].

Significando: Significando caída bien, pronta resolución y pérdidas, al revés desgracia y decepción.

Correspondencia: Capricornio.

Card 17: Star

Rune: SIG.

Significance: Upright it signifies hope, death of a relative and redemption; reversed [it means] theft[13].

Correspondence: Mercury.

Carta 17: Estrella

Runa: SIG.

Significando: Caída al derecho significa esperanza, muerte de un pariente y redencion; al revés robo.

Correspondencia: Mercurio.

Card 18: A moon/the sun

Rune: ↑ [TYR]

Significance: Upright it signifies deception[14], occult enemies [and] harmful vices and backwards [or reversed it signifies] repentance. The name of the Arian [card] is "Blind Vices."

Correspondence: Aquarius.

Carta 18: Una luna/el sol

Runa: ↑ [TYR]

Significando: Caída bien significa engano, enemigos ocultos vicios daninos y al revés arrepentimiento. El nombre de la Aria es "Vicios Ciegos".

Correspondencia: Acuario.

---

[12] Literally 'daño' means "harm, injury, damage; hazard; jeopardy; bruise; nuisance; eradication"

[13] Literally 'robo' means "steal, rob, thieve; remove; draw; walk away"

[14] Literally 'engano' means "deceit, double cross, betrayal; spoofing; cheat, deceive, swindle; betray, be disloyal"

Card 19: THE SUN/Spiritual Life

Rune: ᛉ [BAR]

Significance: [Upright it] signifies [good] luck, money, marriage[15], fire and reversed [it signifies] prison[16].

Correspondence: [not given, but Pisces].

Card 20: The Final Judgment

Rune: Mystery [M].

Significance: The significance of the card is "[good] fortune", public posts which honor us, "eternal life" and "verdict[17] of a pending trial".

Correspondence: Saturn.

Card 21 (or 0): The Lunatic [or Fool]/The Chaste Innocent

Rune: Life.

Significance: The significance of the card is "errors of the Past".

Correspondence: Neptune [and Air].

Card 22 (or 21): The World

Rune: the Rune of Equilibrium.

Significance: "[good] Fortune", "success", and reversed, that is to say upside down [it signifies], "break and disputes."

Correspondence: the Sun.

Card 23: the King of Clubs

Significance: the Lord of Karma.

Correspondence: [Saturn & the Sun].

Card 24: the Queen of Clubs

Significance: "A Woman who protects us." Reversed, [it signifies] a new man hinders the work you intend to do [and] a woman [is] in our favor.

Correspondence: Saturn [& the Moon].

Carta 19: EL SOL/Vida Espiritual

Runa: ᛉ [BAR]

Significando: Significa suerte, dinero, casamiento, fuego y al revés prision.

Correspondencia: [no se da, pero Piscis].

Carta 20: El Juicio Final

Runa: Misterio [M].

Significando: El significado de la carta es "fortuna", púestos publicos con que nos honran, "vida eterna" y "sentencia de un juicio pendiente".

Correspondencia: Saturno.

Carta 21 (o 0): El Loco/El Casto Inocente

Runa: Vida.

Significando: El significado de la carta es: "errores del Pasado."

Correspondencia: Neptuno [y Aire].

Carta 22 (o 21): El Mundo

Runa: la Runa del Equilibrio.

Significando: "Fortuna", "suerte", y al revés, es decir caída de cabeza, "rompimiento y disputas".

Correspondencia: el Sol.

Carta 23: Rey de Bastos

Significando: el Señor del Carma.

Correspondencia: [Saturno & el Sol].

Carta 24: la Dama de Bastos

Significando: "Una Mujer que nos protegerá." Al revés, un hombre nue obstaculiza la labor que pretende hacer una mujer a nuestro favor.

Correspondencia: Saturno [& la Luna].

---

[15] Literally 'casamiento' means "wedding, marriage; match; cassation"

[16] Literally 'prision' means "prison, jail; imprisonment"

[17] Literally 'sentencia' means "sentence, judgement, judgment, verdict"

Card 25: The Knight of Clubs
Significance: "Travel and separation" in a good sense. Reversed [it signifies] "Difference with another person" and "obstacles that are opposed to our plans.".
Correspondence: Saturn & Mars.

Carta 25: El Caballero de Bastos
Significando: "Viajes y separación" en buen sentido. Al revés "Diferencia con otra persona", y "obstáculos que se oponen a nuestros planes."
Correspondencia: Saturno & Marte.

Card 26: the Page of Clubs
Significance: "Good news", and reversed, [it signifies] "bad [news]".
Correspondence: [Saturn & Mercury].

Carta 26: el Paje de Bastos
Significando: "Buenas noticias", y de cabeza, "malas".
Correspondencia: [Saturno & Mercurio].

Card 27: the 10 of Clubs
Significance: "Might", and reversed [it] always indicates "punishment".
Correspondence: the Moon.

Carta 27: el 10 de Bastos
Significando: "Poderío", y al revés indicará siempre "penas".
Correspondencia: la Luna.

Card 28: the 9 of Clubs
Significance: "Delayed[18] success" and reversed [it signifies] "Difficulties".
Correspondence: Mercury.

Carta 28: el 9 de Bastos
Significando: "Tardanza del exito", y al revés "Dificultades".
Correspondencia: Mercurio.

Card 29: the 8 of Clubs
Significance: "Field trip" and reversed [it signifies] "Insecurity", but can also be threatening "Revolutions".
Correspondence: Venus.

Carta 29: el 8 de Bastos
Significando: "Salida al campo", y al revés "Inseguridad", puede ser y también amenaza "Revoluciones".
Correspondencia: Venus.

Card 30: the 7 of Clubs
Significance: [Upright, it signifies] "Power" or reversed [it signifies] "Doubt", which means that "Faith" is the Great Power in opposition to Doubt. This carefully[19] enclosed triangle is also "Harmony".
Correspondence: Sun.

Carta 30: el 7 de Bastos
Significando: "Poder" o de cabeza la "Duda", lo que significa que la Fe es el Gran Poder en oposicion de la Duda. Es también "Armonia" ese triangulo encerrado cuidadosamente.
Correspondencia: Sol.

---

[18] Literally 'Tardanza' means "backwardness, delay, tardiness"
[19] Literally 'cuidadosamente' means "carefully, cautiously; meticulously"

Card 31: the 6 of Clubs
Significance: "Dignity"and "Home Life".
Correspondence: Mars .

Carta 31: el 6 de Bastos
Significando: "Dignidad" y "Vida casera".
Correspondencia: Marte.

Card 32: the 5 of Clubs
Significance: "Think".
Correspondence: Jupiter.

Carta 32: el 5 de Bastos
Significando: "Pensar".
Correspondencia: Jupiter.

Card 33: the 4 of Clubs
Significance: "Advancement by means of the work."
Correspondence: Mars [typo for Saturn?].

Carta 33: el 4 de Bastos
Significando: "Adelanto por medio del trabajo".
Correspondencia: Marte.

Card 34: 3 of Clubs
Significance: "Surprise" and reversed [it] signifies "Temporary discomfort".
Correspondence: Uranus.

Carta 34: el 3 de Bastos
Significando: "Sorpresa" y al revés significa "Molestias pasajeras".
Correspondencia: Urano.

Card 35: 2 of Clubs
Significance: "Bonanza", albeit with some opposition, but under this sign [of the cross X or + which] we have to overcome
Correspondence: [Neptune].

Carta 35: el 2 de Bastos
Significando: "Bonanza", aunque con cierta oposicion, pero bajo este signo [del cruz X o +] hemos de vencer
Correspondencia: [Neptuno]

Card 36: Ace of Clubs
Significance: "Position", "The Office" and "Well being". Reversed [it means] "Weakness" of the same.
Correspondence: the Earth.

Carta 36: el As de Bastos
Significando: "La posición", "El Oficio" y el "Bienestar". Al revés "Debilidad" de lo mismo.
Correspondencia: la Tierra.

Card 37: the King of Cups
Significance: "Protection by superiors" and if it falls upsidedown [then it] tells us "Beware of your superiors".
Correspondence: Jupiter & the Sun.

Carta 37: Rey de Copas
Significando: "Proteccion por superiores" y si cae de cabeza nos dice "Cuidado de tus superiores".
Correspondencia: Júpiter & el Sol.

Card 38: the Queen of Cups
Significance: "The realization of our desires", this card is always favorable.
Correspondence: Jupiter & the Moon.

Carta 38: la Dama de Copas
Significando: "La realización de nuestros deseos", siempre es favorable esta carta.
Correspondencia: Júpiter & la Luna.

Card 39: The Knight of Cups
Significance: "Arrival of surprise", and reversed [it signifies] "Deception[20]".
Correspondence: Jupiter & Mars.

Carta 39: El Caballero de Copas
Significando: "Llegada de sorpresa", y al revés "Engaño".
Correspondencia: Jupiter & Marte.

Card 40: the Jack [or Page] of Cups
Significance: "An employment[21] is expected and the purpose is achieved." Reversed [it signifies] "Failed attempt".
Correspondence: Jupiter & Mercury.

Carta 40: la Sota de Copas
Significando: "Se espera uno empleo y se logra el propósito". Al revés "Fracasa el intento".
Correspondencia: Jupiter & Mercurio.

Card 41: the 10 of Cups
Significance: the 10 Sephiroth; "Grace, Clemency, Might[22]". If it is reversed, it signifies the contrary.
Correspondence: the Moon.

Carta 41: el 10 de Copas
Significando: los 10 Sefirotes; La Gracia, La Clemencia, El Poderío. Si cae de cabeza es al revés, significa pues todo lo contrario.
Correspondencia: la Luna.

Card 42: the 9 of Cups
Significance: "Birth, Fertility"; and reversed [it signifies] "Sterility".
Correspondence: Mercury.

Carta 42: el 9 de Copas
Significando: Nacimiento, Fertilidad; y al revés Esterilidad.
Correspondencia: Mercurio.

Card 43: the 8 of Cups
Significance: [good] Luck, but [good] Luck in Competition[23].
Correspondence: Venus.

Carta 43: el 8 de Copas
Significando: Suerte, pero Suerte en el Juego.
Correspondencia: Venus.

Card 44: the 7 of Cups
Significance: "Happy Marriage" while the Triad is up; reversed [it signifies] "Marriage [that] does not agree".
Correspondence: the Sun.

Carta 44: el 7 de Copas
Significando: Matrimonio Feliz, mientras la Triada está arriba; al caer al revés, Matrimonia aue no se aviene.
Correspondencia: el Sol.

---

[20] Literally 'Engaño' means "deceit, double cross, betrayal; spoofing; cheat, deceive, swindle; betray, be disloyal"
[21] Literally 'empleo' means "use; employment, occupation; business; investment; post, appointment"
[22] Literally 'Poderío' means "might; power, strength"
[23] Literally 'Juego' means "game, sport; court; gambling; set; service"

Card 45: the 6 of Cups
Significance: "Protection and Salary Increase"; and reversed [it is] "Treason[24]".
Correspondence: Mars.

Carta 45: el 6 de Copas
Significando: Protección y Aumento de Salario; y al revés Traición.
Correspondencia: Marte.

Card 46: the 5 of Cups
Significance: "Heritage/Inheritance[25] or Gain"; [and] reversed [it signifies] the "Loss of a Relative".
Correspondence: Jupiter.

Carta 46: el 5 de Copas
Significando: Herencia o Ganancia; al revés la Pérdida de un Pariente.
Correspondencia: Jupiter.

Card 47: the 4 of Cups
Significance: "New Relationships"; and reversed [it signifies] "A Traitor who tries to harm[26] us".
Correspondence: Saturn.

Carta 47: el 4 de Copas
Significando: Nuevas Relaciones; y al revés Un Traidor que nos trata de perjudicar.
Correspondencia: Saturno.

Card 48: 3 of Cups
Significance: "Wedding[27] Commitment[28]" and reversed [it signifies] "Unhappy[29] Love" or "Sweetheart who will not marry". For the Occultist, [this] is always a card of [good] lucky.
Correspondence: Uranus.

Carta 48: el 3 de Copas
Significando: Compromiso de casamiento y al revés Amor es Desgraciados o Novios qae no se casan. Para el Ocultista es siempre una carta de suerte
Correspondencia: Urano.

Card 49: 2 of Cups
Significance: "Love and Desire", reversed [it] is reversed.
Correspondence: Neptune.

Carta 49: el 2 de Copas
Significando: Amor y Deseo, caiga como caiga.
Correspondencia: Neptuno.

---

[24] Literally 'Traición' means "treason, betrayal, treachery"
[25] Literally 'Herencia' means "heritage, inheritance; apanage, provision for the subsistence of royal descendants (as in land, regular income, etc.); heirdom; heredity"
[26] Literally 'perjudicar' means "damage, cause harm, cause injury; prejudice"
[27] Literally 'casamiento' means "wedding, marriage; match; cassation"
[28] Literally 'Compromiso' means "obligation, commitment; pledge, committal; date, meeting; compromise"
[29] Literally 'Desgraciados' means "miserable, unhappy; unfortunate, unlucky"

Card 50: Ace of Cups (The Holy Grail)
Significance: "the Table of the Lord's Supper", or that "food will be provided for us", but it is the daily food that we receive from the Great God who filled this Grail-Earth with his gifts which he gives us [such as] his fruits as a result of constant work and honor[30]. In this symbol of the earth is represented our common mother, Gaia [or Gaio], our mother, who is an inexhaustible[31] Chalice.
Correspondence: the Earth.

Card 51: the King of Swords
Significance: a warning: "BE CAREFUL OF ATTORNEYS[32]". Reversed it signifies: "Evil men will cause you harm".
Correspondence: the Sun & Mars.

Card 52: the Queen of Swords
Significance: [not given].
Correspondence: [Mars & the Moon].

Card 53: The Knight of Swords
Significance: "War or Military[33]". Reversed, "Have done unthinkable things".
Correspondence: Mars.

Card 54: the Page of Swords
Significance: "There are spies after you". Watch out nonetheless[34] when it is reversed, the meaning is always the same.
Correspondence: [Mars & Mercury].

Carta 50: el As de Copas (el Santo Grial)
Significando: la Mesa de la Santa Cena, o sea que nos van a brindar una comida, pero es la comida diaria que recibimos del Gran Dios, que llena con sus dádivas este Grial Tierra que nos brinda sus frutos como producto de un trabajo constante y honrado. En este símbolo de la tierra esta representada nuestra madre común, la Gea [o Gaio], nuestra madre, que es un Cáliz inagotable.
Correspondencia: la Tierra.

Carta 51: Rey de Espadas
Significando: una advertencia: "CUIDATE DE LOS ABOGADOS". Caída al revés significa: Hombres malos te causarán daño.
Correspondencia: el Sol & Marte.

Carta 52: la Dama de Espadas
Significando: [no se da].
Correspondencia: [Marte & la Luna].

Carta 53: El Caballero de Espadas
Significando: Guerra o Militar. Al revés, Haber hecho cosas impensadas.
Correspondencia: Marte.

Carta 54: el Paje de Espadas
Significando: Hay espías tras de usted. Cuidado no importa como caiga, el significado es siempre el mismo.
Correspondencia: [Marte & Mercurio].

---

[30] Literally 'honrado' means "honest, truthful; honored; righteous; honorable, respectable; honor; grace"
[31] Literally 'inagotable' means "never failing; inexhaustible"
[32] Literally 'ABOGADOS' means "lawyer, attorney, barrister; solicitor, one who offers legal advice to clients and may present petitions to the lower courts but is not a member of the bar"
[33] Literally 'Militar' means "military; soldierly; regimental; service"
[34] Literally 'no importa' means "never mind, it doesn't matter, it makes no odds"

Card 55: the 10 of Swords
Significance: Upright it is "advantage, joy". Reversed [it signifies] the opposite.
Correspondence: Moon.

Card 56: the 9 of Swords
Significance: "Justice and Confidence". The opposite if [it is] reversed: [although it] has good significance if the card falls into the circle of the Present.
Correspondence: Mercury.

Card 57: the 8 of Swords
Significance: "Irresolution[35]" and "dispute".
Correspondence: Venus.

Card 58: the 7 of Swords
Significance: "Hope" and "Success". It [signifies] the opposite, if it is reversed.
Correspondence: Sun.

Card 59: the 6 of Swords
Significance: "Security and Good Contract[36]", reversed [it signifies]: "Theft/Robbery and Disputes".
Correspondence: [Mars].

Card 60: the 5 of Swords
Significance: "Extension and. Augmentation[37]". Reversed [it signifies], "Loss and Decrease".
Correspondence: Jupiter.

Carta 55: el 10 de Espadas
Significando: Caída bien es ventaja, alegría. Al revés lo contrario.
Correspondencia: Luna.

Carta 56: el 9 de Espadas
Significando: Justicia y Confianza. Lo contrario si cae mal: es buen significado si esa carta cae en el círculo del Presente.
Correspondencia: Mercurio.

Carta 57: el 8 de Espadas
Significando: Irresolucion y disputa.
Correspondencia: Venus.

Carta 58: el 7 de Espadas
Significando: Esperanza y Exito. Lo contrario siempre, si cae mal.
Correspondencia: Sol.

Carta 59: el 6 de Espadas
Significando: Seguridad y Contrato Bueno, al revés: Robo y Disputas.
Correspondencia: [Marte].

Carta 60: el 5 de Espadas
Significando: Extensión y Aumento. Al revés, Pérdida y Disminucion.
Correspondencia: Júpiter.

---

[35] Literally 'Irresolucion' means "hesitation, indecision, irresolution"
[36] Literally 'Contrato' means "agreement, contract; engagement"
[37] Literally 'Aumento' means "augmentation, growth, increase; addition, supplement; upturn, upward trend"

Card 61: the 4 of Swords
Significance: "Triumph over enemies". Reversed [it is] "Embarrassement/Hindrance[38]".
Correspondence: Saturn.

Card 62: 3 of Swords
Significance: "New Union", and if [it is] reversed, "Separation".
Correspondence: Uranus.

Card 63: 2 of Swords
Significance: "Friendship", [it] is a very good card, but reversed [it] signifies "Infidelity", it is passing/fleeting[39].
Correspondence: Neptune.

Card 64: Ace of Swords
Significance: "Dignity, Rank and Honors"; and reversed, "Attacks", [or] "crazy Loves".
Correspondence: the Sun.

Card 65: the King of Pentacles
Significance: "[A] protective[40] man", and reversed "[a] man who discredits".
Correspondence: Mercury & the Sun.

Card 66: the Queen of Pentacles
Significance: ["A protective woman", and reversed "a woman who discredits"].
Correspondence: Mercury & the Moon.

Carta 61: el 4 de Espadas
Significando: Triunfo sobre los enemigos. Al revés Embarazo.
Correspondencia: Saturno.

Carta 62: el 3 de Espadas
Significando: Nueva Unión, y si contrario, Separación.
Correspondencia: Urano.

Carta 63: el 2 de Espadas
Significando: Amistad, es una carta muy buena, aunque al revés significa Infidelidad, es ella pasajera.
Correspondencia: Neptuno.

Carta 64: el As de Espadas
Significando: Dignidad, Rango y Honores; y al revés Ataques, Amores locos.
Correspondencia: el Sol.

Carta 65: el Rey Oros
Significando: Hombre protector, y al revés Hombre que descredita.
Correspondencia: Mercurio & Sol.

Carta 66: la Reina Oros
Significando: [Mujer protector, y al revés Mujer que descredita].
Correspondencia: Mercurio & Luna.

---

[38] Literally 'Embarazo' means "pregnancy; embarrassment; hinder, prevent"
[39] Literally 'pasajera' means "transient, provisional, temporary, impermanent; passing, fleeting"
[40] Literally 'protector' means "protective; patronizing; protector, guardian; defender; embankment"

Card 67: The Knight of Pentacles
Significance: [not given].
Correspondence: Mars & Mercury.

Carta 67: El Caballero Oros
Significando: [No se da].
Correspondencia: Marte & Mercurio.

Card 68: the Page of Pentacles
Significance: "Useful Things" or the contrary [if] it is reversed; and also "Love with [a] lad", reversed [it] is: "Lad [who] is pretentious[41]".
Correspondence: Mercury.

Carta 68: el Paje Oros
Significando: Cosas Utiles o lo contrario segun como caiga; y tabien Amores con muchacho, al revés es: Muchacho es un pretensioso.
Correspondencia: Mercurio.

Card 69: the 10 of Pentacles
Significance: "Houses and Property"; reversed: "Maritime travel".
Correspondence: the Moon.

Carta 69: el 10 Oros
Significando: Casa y Propiedad; al revés: Viaje marítimo.
Correspondencia: la Luna.

Card 70: the 9 of Pentacles
Significance: "Lottery Prize[42]". Now we must look at what place falls.
Correspondence: all the planets.

Carta 70: el 9 Oros
Significando: "Premio de Lotería". Ahora hay que fijarse en qué lugar cae.
Correspondencia: todos los planetas.

Card 71: the 8 of Pentacles
Significance: "Idea for realization", and reversed: "Critical situation".
Correspondence: Venus.

Carta 71: el 8 Oros
Significando: "Idea por realizar", y al revés: Situación crítica.
Correspondencia: Venus.

Card 72: the 7 of Pentacles
Significance: "Gain less Overseas".
Correspondence: all the planets except Neptune.

Carta 72: el 7 Oros
Significando: Ganancia menos en Ultramar.
Correspondencia: todos los planetas menos Neptuno.

Card 73: the 6 of Pentacles
Significance: "Sparsity[43]".
Correspondence: all the planets except Mars.

Carta 73: el 6 Oros
Significando: Escasez.
Correspondencia: todos los planetas menos Marte.

---

[41] Literally 'pretensioso' means "pretentious, presumptuous, conceited"
[42] Literally 'Premio' means "reward, prize, award; premium; accolade; wage"
[43] Literally 'Escasez' means "scantiness, sparseness; parsimony, stinginess; tightness; shortage, dearth; famine; poverty"

Card 74: the 5 of Pentacles
Significance: "Good or bad Loves" according to how [the card] falls.
Correspondence: Jupiter.

Carta 74: el 5 Oros
Significando: Amores Buenos o malos según como caiga.
Correspondencia: Jupiter.

Card 75: the 4 of Pentacles
Significance: "Honorableness[44]"; and reversed [it signifies] the contrary.
Correspondence: Saturn.

Carta 75: el 4 Oros
Significando: Honorabilidad; y lo contrario al revés.
Correspondencia: Saturno.

Card 76: 3 of Pentacles
Significance: warns us [of] "an upcoming trip" with favorable success or unfavorable [success], according to how [the card] falls.
Correspondence: Uranus.

Carta 76: el 3 Oros
Significando: nos advierte un próximo viaje con éxito favorable o desfavorable, según como caiga.
Correspondencia: Urano.

Card 77: 2 of Pentacles
Rune: the Rune of Equilibrium.
Significance: "A card/letter".
Correspondence: Neptune.

Carta 77: el 2 Oros
Runa: la Runa del Equilibrio.
Significando: Una carta.
Correspondencia: Neptuno.

Card 78: Ace of Pentacles
Significance: always "good" and always gives us "Success".
Correspondence: the Sun.

Carta 78: el As de Oros
Significando: siempre bueno y nos ofrece siempre Éxito.
Correspondencia: el Sol.

---

[44] Literally 'Honorabilidad' means "honorableness, honor"

Summary of Krumm-Heller's Astrological Associations for the Major Arcana:

Arcana	Astrological Association
1	Fire or "Light", the Light of the Spirit
2	[the Moon]
3	[the Venus]
4	Scorpio & Jupiter
5	[Aries]
6	Taurus
7	Gemini
8	Cancer
9	[Leo]
10	Virgo
11	Mars
12	Libra
13	Scorpio [& Mars, and Water]
14	[Scorpio]
15	Sagittarius
16	Capricorn
17	Mercury
18	Aquarius
19	[Pisces]
20	Saturn
21 or 0	Neptune [and Air]
22 or 21	the Sun

Resumen de Asociaciones Astrológica de Krumm-Heller para los Arcanos Mayores:

Arcanos	Asociacion Astrológica
1	Fuego o "Luz", la Luz del Espiritu
2	[la Luna]
3	[Venus]
4	Escorpion & Jupiter
5	[Aries]
6	Toro
7	Los Gemelos
8	Cancer
9	[León]
10	Virgo
11	Marte
12	Libra
13	Escorpion [& Marte, y Agua]
14	[Escorpion]
15	Sagitario
16	Capricornio
17	Mercurio
18	Acuario
19	[Piscis]
20	Saturno
21 o 0	Neptuno [y Aire]
22 o 21	el Sol

Summary of Krumm-Heller's Astrological Associations for the Minor Arcana:

Card/Suit	General Astrological Association
Clubs	Saturn
Cups	Jupiter
Swords	Mars
Pentacles	Mercury
Kings	the Sun
Queens	the Moon
Knights	Mars
Pages or Jacks	Mercury
10s	the Moon
9s	Mercury
8s	Venus
7s	the Sun
6s	Mars
5s	Jupiter
4s	Saturn
3s	Uranus
2s	Neptune
Aces	the Earth or Sun

Resumen de Asociaciones Astrológica de Krumm-Heller para los Arcanos Menores:

Carta	Asociacion Astrológica General
Bastos	Saturno
Copas	Júpiter
Espadas	Marte
Oros	Mercurio
Reyes	el Sol
Reinas	la Luna
Caballeros	Marte
Pajes o Sotas	Mercurio
10es	la Luna
9es	Mercurio
8es	Venus
7es	el Sol
6es	Marte
5es	Júpiter
4es	Saturno
3es	Urano
2es	Neptuno
Ases	la Tierra o Sol

Comparison of Tarot Associations

	Krumm-Heller	Gnostic Egyptian Tarot[45]
1	the Magician	The Magician
2	Popess, Priestess	The Priestess
3	the Empress	the Empress
4	[the Emperor]	the Emperor
5	the Pope, Priest	The Hierophant
6	the Lover	Indecision
7	the Chariot of Triumph	Triumph
8	Justice	Justice
9	the Hermit, the Sage	The Hermit
10	the Wheel of Fortune	Retribution
11	Power, force/strength	Persuasion
12	THE HANGED MAN	The Apostolate
13	Death	Immortality
14	Reincarnation	Temperance
15	Baphomet, Lucifer	Passion
16	Lightning [or the Ray] or House of God	Fragility
17	Star	Hope
18	a moon or the sun	Twilight
19	THE SUN or Spiritual Life	Inspiration
20	The Last Judgment	Resurrection
21 or 0	The Lunatic or The Chaste Innocent	Transmutation
22 or 21	The World	Return

Comparación de las Asociaciones del Tarot

	Krumm-Heller	Tarot Gnostico Egyptico[46]
1	el Mago	El Mago
2	Papisa, Sacerdotisa	La Sacerdotisa
3	la Emperatriz	la Emperatriz
4	[La Emperador]	La Emperador
5	El Papa, Sacerdote	El Jerarca
6	el Enamorado	La Indecision
7	el Carro del Triunfo	El Triunfo
8	la Justicia	La Justicia
9	el Ermitaño, el Sabio	El Eremita
10	la Rueda de la Fortuna	La Retribucion
11	el Poder, la fuerza	La Persuasion
12	EL AHORCADO	El Apostolado
13	La Muerte	La Inmortalidad
14	Reencarnación	La Temperancia
15	el Bafometo, Lucifer	La Pasion
16	El Rayo o Casa de Dios	La Fragilidad
17	Estrella	La Esperanza
18	una luna o el sol	El Crepusculo
19	EL SOL o Vida Espiritual	La Inspiracion
20	El Juicio Final	La Resurreccion
21 o 0	El Loco o El Casto Inocente	La Transmutacion
22 o 21	El Mundo	El Regreso

[45] This is the Tarot found in *The Kabalah of Prediction* (originally published in 1947) by Jesus Iglesias Janeiro, but with the 21 & 22 cards modified by Samael Aun Weor.

[46] Este es el Tarot encuentra en *La Cábala de Predicción* (publicado originalmente en 1947) por Jesús Iglesias Janeiro, pero con los 21 y 22 cartas modificadas por Samael Aun Weor.

	Krumm-Heller	Gnostic Egyptian Tarot[47]		Krumm-Heller	Tarot Gnostico Egyptico[52]
23	King of Clubs	THE TILLER[48] [or LABORER]	23	Rey de Bastos	EL LABRADOR
24	Queen of Clubs	THE WEAVER	24	Dama de Bastos	LA TEJEDORA
25	Knight of Clubs	THE ARGONAUT[49]	25	Caballero de Bastos	EL ARGONAUTA
26	Page of Clubs	THE PRODIGY	26	Paje de Bastos	EL PRODIGIO
27	10 of Clubs	THE UNEXPECTED	27	10 de Bastos	LO INESPERADO
28	9 of Clubs	UNCERTAINTY	28	9 de Bastos	LA INCERTIDUMBRE
29	8 of Clubs	DOMESTICITY	29	8 de Bastos	LA DOMESTICIDAD
30	7 of Clubs	EXCHANGE[50]	30	7 de Bastos	EL INTERCAMBIO
31	6 of Clubs	IMPEDIMENTS	31	6 de Bastos	LOS IMPEDIMENTOS
32	5 of Clubs	MAGNIFICENCE	32	5 de Bastos	LA MAGNIFICENCIA
33	4 of Clubs	ALLIANCE	33	4 de Bastos	LA ALIANZA
34	3 of Clubs	INNOVATION	34	3 de Bastos	LA INNOVACION
35	2 of Clubs	DISTRESS[51]	35	2 de Bastos	EL DESCONSUELO
36	Ace of Clubs	INITIATION	36	As de Bastos	LA INICIACION

---

[47] This is the Tarot found in *The Kabalah of Prediction* (originally published in 1947) by Jesus Iglesias Janeiro, but with the 21 & 22 cards modified by Samael Aun Weor.
[48] Literally 'LABRADOR' means "farmer, farm worker, yeoman, cottager, haymaker"
[49] Literally 'ARGONAUTA' means "Argonaut, adventurer in Greek mythology who traveled to Colchis by ship in search of the Golden Fleece"
[50] Literally 'INTERCAMBIO' means "exchange, swap, interchange; cartel"
[51] Literally 'DESCONSUELO' means "frustration, act of frustrating; condition of being frustrated; aggravation; grief, heartbreak, despair, disconsolation"

---

[52] Este es el Tarot encuentra en *La Cábala de Predicción* (publicado originalmente en 1947) por Jesús Iglesias Janeiro, pero con los 21 y 22 cartas modificadas por Samael Aun Weor.

	Krumm-Heller	Gnostic Egyptian Tarot[53]		Krumm-Heller	Tarot Gnostico Egyptico[61]
37	King of Cups	ART AND SCIENCE	37	Rey de Copas	EL ARTE Y LA CIENCIA
38	Queen of Cups	DUPLICITY[54]	38	Dama de Copas	LA DUPLICIDAD
39	Knight of Cups	TESTIMONY	39	Caballero de Copas	EL TESTIMONIO
40	Jack of Cups	PREMONITION[55]	40	Sota de Copas	EL PRESENTIMIENTO
41	10 of Cups	RESTLESSNESS[56]	41	10 de Copas	EL DESASOSIEGO
42	9 of Cups	PREEMINENCE[57]	42	9 de Copas	LA PREEMINENCIA
43	8 of Cups	HALLUCINATION	43	8 de Copas	LA ALUCINACION
44	7 of Cups	THOUGHT	44	7 de Copas	EL PENSAMIENTO
45	6 of Cups	REGENERATION	45	6 de Copas	LA REGENERACION
46	5 of Cups	PATRIMONY[58]	46	5 de Copas	EL PATRIMONIO
47	4 of Cups	CONJECTURE[59]	47	4 de Copas	LA CONJETURA
48	3 of Cups	CONSUMMATION[60]	48	3 de Copas	LA CONSUMACION
49	2 of Cups	VERSATILITY	49	2 de Copas	LA VERSATILIDAD
50	Ace of Cups	AFFINITY	50	As de Copas	LA AFINIDAD

---

[53] This is the Tarot found in *The Kabalah of Prediction* (originally published in 1947) by Jesus Iglesias Janeiro, but with the 21 & 22 cards modified by Samael Aun Weor.
[54] Literally 'DUPLICIDAD' means "duplicity, being two-faced, double dealing"
[55] Literally 'PRESENTIMIENTO' means "presentiment, premonition, advance perception; presage; misgiving"
[56] Literally 'DESASOSIEGO' means "uneasiness, disquietude; anxiety"
[57] Literally 'PREEMINENCIA' means "Preeminence (high status importance owing to marked superiority)"
[58] Literally 'PATRIMONIO' means "patrimony, legacy, heritage; birthright"
[59] Literally 'CONJETURA' means "guess, conjecture, surmise"
[60] Literally 'CONSUMACION' means "Consummation, culmination, completion"

---

[61] Este es el Tarot encuentra en *La Cábala de Predicción* (publicado originalmente en 1947) por Jesús Iglesias Janeiro, pero con los 21 y 22 cartas modificadas por Samael Aun Weor.

	Krumm-Heller	Gnostic Egyptian Tarot[62]		Krumm-Heller	Tarot Gnostico Egyptico[67]
51	King of Swords	ADVICE	51	Rey de Espadas	EL ASESORAMIENTO
52	Queen of Swords	PREMEDITATION	52	Dama de Espadas	LA PREMEDITACION
53	Knight of Swords	RESENTMENT	53	Caballero de Espadas	EL RESENTIMIENTO
54	Page of Swords	EXAMINATION	54	Paje de Espadas	EL EXAMEN
55	10 of Swords	CONTRITION[63]	55	10 de Espadas	LA CONTRICION
56	9 of Swords	PILGRIMAGE	56	9 de Espadas	EL PEREGRINAJE
57	8 of Swords	RIVALRY	57	8 de Espadas	LA RIVALIDAD
58	7 of Swords	RECAPACITATION[64]	58	7 de Espadas	LA RECAPACITACION
59	6 of Swords	REVELATION	59	6 de Espadas	LA REVELACION
60	5 of Swords	EVOLUTION	60	5 de Espadas	LA EVOLUCION
61	4 of Swords	SOLITUDE	61	4 de Espadas	LA SOLEDAD
62	3 of Swords	PROSCRIPTION[65]	62	3 de Espadas	LA PROSCRIPCION
63	2 of Swords	COMMUNION	63	2 de Espadas	LA COMUNION
64	Ace of Swords	VEHEMENCE[66]	64	As de Espadas	LA VEHEMENCIA

---

[62] This is the Tarot found in *The Kabalah of Prediction* (originally published in 1947) by Jesus Iglesias Janeiro, but with the 21 & 22 cards modified by Samael Aun Weor.
[63] Literally 'CONTRICION' means "Contrition (sincere penitence or remorse)"
[64] Literally 'RECAPACITACION' means "retraining, refresher"
[65] Literally 'PROSCRIPCION' means "banishment, proscription, prohibition"
[66] Literally 'VEHEMENCIA' means "vehemence, passion, fervor, force"

---

[67] Este es el Tarot encuentra en *La Cábala de Predicción* (publicado originalmente en 1947) por Jesús Iglesias Janeiro, pero con los 21 y 22 cartas modificadas por Samael Aun Weor.

	Krumm-Heller	Gnostic Egyptian Tarot[68]
65	King of Pentacles	APPRENTICESHIP
66	Queen of Pentacles	PERPLEXITY
67	Knight of Pentacles	FRIENDSHIP
68	Page of Pentacles	SPECULATION
69	10 of Pentacles	CHANCE
70	9 of Pentacles	COOPERATION
71	8 of Pentacles	AVARICE[69]
72	7 of Pentacles	PURIFICATION
73	6 of Pentacles	LOVE AND DESIRE
74	5 of Pentacles	THE OFFERING
75	4 of Pentacles	GENEROSITY[70]
76	3 of Pentacles	THE DISPENSER
77	2 of Pentacles	DISORIENTATION
78	Ace of Pentacles	REBIRTH[71]

	Krumm-Heller	Tarot Gnostico Egyptico[72]
65	Rey de Oros	EL APRENDIZAJE
66	Reina de Oros	LA PERPLEJIDAD
67	Caballero de Oros	LA AMISTAD
68	Paje de Oros	LA ESPECULACION
69	10 de Oros	EL AZAR
70	9 de Oros	LA COOPERACION
71	8 de Oros	LA AVARICIA
72	7 de Oros	LA PURIFICACION
73	6 de Oros	EL AMOR Y EL DESEO
74	5 de Oros	LA OFRENDA
75	4 de Oros	LA GENEROSIDAD
76	3 de Oros	EL DISPENSADOR
77	2 Oros	LA DESORIENTACION
78	As de Oros	EL RENACIMIENTO

[68] This is the Tarot found in *The Kabalah of Prediction* (originally published in 1947) by Jesus Iglesias Janeiro, but with the 21 & 22 cards modified by Samael Aun Weor.
[69] Literally 'AVARICIA' means "avarice; miserliness, parsimony; greed"
[70] Literally 'GENEROSIDAD' means "generosity, benevolence, munificence; largesse, generous giving of gifts; liberality"
[71] Literally 'RENACIMIENTO' means "revival, rebirth, renaissance, renascence"

[72] Este es el Tarot encuentra en *La Cábala de Predicción* (publicado originalmente en 1947) por Jesús Iglesias Janeiro, pero con los 21 y 22 cartas modificadas por Samael Aun Weor.

Franco-Egyptian Tarot

This section is a collection of extracts from two French writers on Egyptian Tarot: Paul Christian and Robert Falconnier.

Christian (who's real name was Jean-Baptiste Pitois) was apparently the first of the modern occultist to refer to the 22 Trumps of the Tarot as "Arcana", and many occultists followed suit after him. In 1863, Christian published his first book *L'Homme rouge des Tuileries [The red Man from Tuileries]*, and then another book, *Historie de la Magie, du monde Surnaturel et de la fatalité a travers les Temps et les Peuples [History of Magic, of the Supernatural world and of fate/fatality through Times and Peoples]* in 1870. In both of these books, Christian described the 22 Major Aracana and gave their 'Egyptian' associations. Christian was also a Librarian and as a result seems to have been able to review some rare documents on occult subjects. French sources also claim that he was a neighbor of Eliphas Levi and greatly benefited from conversations with him on esoteric and occult subjects.

In 1896, Falconnier published *Les XXII Lames Hermétiques du Tarot Divinatoire [The 22 Hermetic Plates of the Divinitory Tarot]*. This book has Egyptian style Tarot plates which were drawn by Otto Wegener and which often seem to conform or complement those descriptions given by Christian in his previous works. These drawings certainly seem to have influenced Jesus Iglesias Janeiro's Tarot in *La Cabala de Prediccion [The Kabalah of Prediction]*, first published in 1947. Janeiro's Tarot eventually became the 'official' Tarot of the International Gnostic Movement of Samael Aun Weor.

It has also been suggested that Papus' *Le Tarot Divinatoire* (which is the origin of the Tarot drawn by Gabriel Goulinat and mentioned throughout Krumm-Heller's *Course of Aryan-Egyptian Kabalah* as "Papus' cards") published in 1909, was a response or rebuttal to Falconnier's book for various reasons, including the idea that prediction was possible .

We have two reasons why we are presenting these extracts:

1st. To show the influence these cards and their descriptions have had on Krumm-Heller and on Papus (whose cards are refered to in this *Course of Aryan-Egyptian Kabalah*).

2nd. To help readers see the influence these cards and their descritions have had on Janeiro and on the 'official' Gnostic-Egyptian Tarot.

After reviewing these translations, it should be quite clear, in reviewing the article 'The Secrets of Masonry 2' (about the Pytharogean Theorum and its Kabalistic significance)[73], that Krumm-Heller was translating portions of the Tarot descriptions from Christian's *History of Magic* into Spanish when describing the esoteric significance of the different numbers.

Those who have studied Eliphas Levi will also notice a strong influence on both Christian and Falconnier (in some cases almost exactly repeating him, although arguably applying his principles differently). In an attempt to highlight this, we have <u>underlined</u> and footnoted the similar quotes from Levi that we have been able to identify. This should help the reader see a trend of influence.

---

[73] See Ch.6 'The Rose Cross Secrets of Occult Masonry' in *The Gnostic and Estoeric Mysteries of Freemasonry, Lucifer and the Great Work*

As a final note, both Christian and Falconnier have a different numbering for the Tarot than that of the Gnostic Movement of Samael Aun Weor, so we have modified their numbering in order to simplify the Gnostic student's study of these descriptions.

The 22 Arcana and their Astrological Associations by Various Authors[74]

		Eliphas Levi (1850s-1870s)	Paul Christian (1860s-1870s)	Robert Falconnier (1890s)	Arnoldo Krumm-Heller (1920s-1940s)	J. Iglesias Janeiro (1940s)	Samael Aun Weor (1950s-1970s)
1	א	[The Sun, the earth]	[not given]	[not given]	[not given]	Sun in Leo	[not given]
2	ב	The Moon [the air]	The Moon	The Moon	[The Moon]	Moon in Cancer	The Moon
3	ג	Venus [the water]	Venus	Venus	[Venus]	Jupiter in Sagittarius	Venus
4	ד	Jupiter [the fire]	Jupiter	Jupiter	Scorpio & Jupiter	Uranus in Aquarius	Jupiter
5	ה	[Mars]	Aries, Mars	Mars, Aries	[Aries]	Mercury in Virgo	Mars, the Warrior of Aries
6	ו	[Saturn]	Taurus, the Moon	Moon, Taurus	Taurus	Venus in Taurus	Venus of Taurus
7	ז	[Mercury]	Gemini, the Sun	The Sun, Gemini	Gemini	Neptune in Pisces	Mercury of Gemini
8	ח	[not given]	Cancer, Venus	Venus, Cancer	Cancer	Saturn in Capricorn	Saturn
9	ט	[not given]	Leo, Jupiter	Jupiter, Leo	[Leo]	Mars in Aries	The Sun of Leo
10	י	[not given]	Virgo, Mercury	Mercury, Virgo	Virgo	Pluton in Scorpio	Mary or Virgo
11	כ	Mars	Mars	Mars	Mars	Sun in Aries	Mars
12	ל	[not given]	Libra, the Moon	The Moon, Libra	Libra	Moon in Taurus	[Libra]
13	מ	[not given]	[not given]	[not given]	Scorpio [& Mars]	Mercury in Gemini	[not given]
14	נ	[not given]	Scorpio, the Sun	The Sun, Scorpio	Scorpio	Jupiter in Cancer	[not given]
15	ס	[not given]	Sagittarius, Saturn	Saturn, Sagittarius	Sagittarius	Neptune in Leo	[not given]
16	ע	[not given]	Capricorn, Jupiter	Jupiter, Capricorn	Capricorn	Mercury in Virgo	[not given]
17	פ	Mercury	Mercury	Mercury	Mercury	Saturn in Libra	[not given]
18	צ	[not given]	Aquarius, Venus	Venus, Aquarius	Aquarius	Uranus in Scorpio	[not given]
19	ק	The Sun	Pisces, Jupiter	Jupiter, Pisces	[Pisces]	Pluto in Sagittarius	[not given]
20	ר	Saturn	Saturn	Saturn	Saturn	Mars in Capricorn	[not given]
21	ש	[not given]	[not given]	"The Eclipse"	Neptune	Neptune in Aquarius	[not given]
22	ת	The Sun	The Sun	The Sun	The Sun	Venus in Pisces	[not given]

[74] Note: Arcana 21 & 22 have been modified for all of these to correspond to 'Le Mat'/'Le Fou' for 21 and 'Le Monde' for 22.

[Introduction][75]

The Science of the Willpower, principle of all Wisdom and source of all Power, is contained in twenty-two *Arcana* or symbolic hieroglyphs, each attribute of which veils [in] one sense, while the whole composes an *Absolute doctrine*, that is summarized in the memory through its correspondence with the Letters of the sacred Language and with the Numbers which are linked to these Letters. Each *Letter* and each *Number*, when the sight contemplates them or one's speech utters them, expresses a reality of the *Divine world*, of the *Intellectual world* and of the *Physical world*. Each *arcanum*, rendered visible and tangible through one of its paintings, is the formula for a law of human activity in its correspondence with the spiritual forces and the material forces the combination of which produces the phenomenon of life.

[Introduction][76]

La Science de la Volonté, principe de toute Sagesse et source de toute Puissance, est contenue en vingt-deux *Arcanes* ou hiéroglyphes symboliques, dont chaque attribut voile un sens, et dont l'ensemble compose une *Doctrine absolue*, qui se résume dans la mémoire par sa correspondance avec les Lettres de la Langue sacrée et avec les Nombres qui se lient à ces Lettres. Chaque *Lettre* et chaque *Nombre*, quand le regard les contemple ou que la parole les profère, exprime une réalité du *Monde divin*, du *Monde intellectuel* et du *Monde physique* (p. 20). Chaque *arcane*, rendu visible et tangible par une de ces peintures, est la formule d'une loi de l'activité humaine dans son rapport avec les forces spirituelles et les forces matérielles don't la combinaison produit les phénomènes de la vie.

---

[75] This is from Christian (1870)

[76] Ceci est de Christian (1870)

LAME I   (A = 1)   LE MAGE

ARCANUM I. — LETTER **Athoïm** (A) — NUMBER 1.

A = 1 expresses in the *Divine world* the absolute Being, who contains and from whom eminate infinite possibilities. — In the *Intellectual world*, the Unity, principle and synthesis of numbers; Willpower, principle of actions. — In the *Physical world*, Man, the highest placed of [all] relative beings, [who is] called to elevate himself, through a perpetual expansion of his faculties, in the concentric spheres of the Absolute.

Arcanum 1 is depicted[77] by the Magus, [the] perfect type of man, that is to say [man] in full possession of his physical and moral faculties. He is represented standing: this is the attitude of the willpower which will carry out[78] the action. His robe[79] is white, image of original or reconquered purity. A serpent biting its tail serves as a belt: this is the symbol of eternity. His forehead is wrapped[80] with a circle of gold: gold signifies light; the circle expresses the universal circumference within which created things gravitate. The right hand of the Magus holds a golden scepter, the representation of command, and is raised towards heaven, as a sign of aspiration to science, wisdom, and strength/force[81]. The left hand extends the index finger towards the earth, in order to signify that the mission of the perfect man is to reign over the material world. This double gesture also expresses that the human will must reflect, down here, the divine will, in order to produce the [greater] good and to prevent [greater] evil. In front of the Magus, upon a cubic stone, are placed a cup, a sword[82] and a shekel[83], a gold coin in the center of which is engraved a cross.

---

[77] Literally 'figuré' means "represent; feature, figure; show, lay; figure to oneself"
[78] Literally 'procéder' means "proceed, behave, carry out"
[79] Literally 'robe' means "dress, gown, frock"
[80] Literally 'ceint' means "put on, don, girded"
[81] Literally 'force' means "strength, force, power; potency; iron; manpower, might"
[82] Literally 'glaive' means "sword, two-edged sword"
[83] Literally 'sicle' means "shekel, coin and monetary unit of Israel"

ARCANE I. — LETTRE **Athoïm** (A) — NOMBRE 1.

A = 1 exprime dans le *Monde divin* l'Etre absolu, qui contient et d'où émane l'infini des possibles. — Dans le *Monde intellectuel*, l'Unité, principe et synthèse des nombres ; la Volonté, principe des actes. — Dans le *Monde physique*, l'Homme, le plus haut placé des êtres relatifs, appelé à s'élever, par une perpétuelle expansion de ses facultés, dans les sphères concentriques de l'Absolu.

L'arcane 1 est figuré par le Mage, type de l'homme parfait, c'est-à-dire en pleine possession de ses facultés physiques et morales. Il est représenté debout : c'est l'attitude de la volonté qui va procéder à l'action. Sa robe est blanche, image de la pureté originelle ou reconquise. Un serpent se mordant la queue lui sert de ceinture : c'est le symbole de l'éternité. Son front est ceint d'un cercle d'or : l'or signifie lumière; le cercle exprime la circonférence universelle dans laquelle gravitent les choses créées. La main droite du Mage tient un sceptre d'or, figure du commandement, et s'élève vers le ciel, en signe d'aspiration à la science, à la sagesse, à la force. La main gauche étend l'index vers la terre, pour signifier que la mission de l'homme parfait est de régner sur le monde matériel. Ce double geste exprime encore que la volonté humaine doit refléter ici-bas la volonté divine, pour produire le bien et empêcher le mal. Devant le Mage, sûr une pierre cubique, sont posés une coupe, un glaive et un sicle, monnaie d'or au centre de laquelle est gravée une croix.

The cup signifies the mixture of the passions which contribute to happiness or to misfortune, according to whether we are their masters or their slaves. The sword symbolizes the work, the struggle[84] that [allows us] to traverse the obstacles [along the path], and the tests that submit us to pain[85]. The shekel, sign of a determined value, depicts aspirations realized, works accomplished, the sum of power conquered through perseverance and the efficacy of the willpower. The cross, seal of the infinite, which marks the shekel, expresses[86] the future ascension of this power in the spheres of the future.

Remember, son of the Earth, that man, like God, must constantly[87] act. To will nothing, to do nothing, is no less fatal[88] than willing or doing evil.[89] If the *Magus* appears among the fateful signs of your *Horoscope*, he announces that a firm will and faith in yourself, guided by reason and the love of justice, will lead you to the goal you want to attain and will preserve you from the perils of the road.

La coupe signifie le mélange des passions qui contribuent au bonheur ou au malheur, selon que nous sommes leurs maîtres ou leurs esclaves. Le glaive symbolise le travail, la lutte qui traverse les obstacles, et les épreuves que nous fait subir la douleur. Le sicle, signe d'une valeur déterminée, figure les aspirations réalisées, les œuvres accomplies, la somme de puissance conquise par la persévérance et l'efficacité de la volonté. La croix, sceau de l'infini, dont le sicle est marqué, énonce la future ascension de cette puissance dans les sphères de l'avenir.

Souviens-toi, fils de la Terre, que l'homme doit, comme Dieu, agir sans cesse. Ne rien vouloir, ne rien faire, n'est pas moins funeste que vouloir ou faire le mal.[90] Si le *Mage* apparaît parmi les signes fatidiques de ton *Horoscope*, il annonce qu'une ferme volonté et la foi en toi-même, guidées par la raison et l'amour de la justice, te conduiront au but que tu veux attaindre et te préserveront des périls du chemin.

PLATE I   (A = 1)   THE MAGUS

Hieroglyphic symbolism.

LAME I   (A = 1)   LE MAGE

Symbolisme hiéroglyphique.

---

[84] Literally 'lutte' means "fight, combat, war, battle; wrestle, contest, buffet; strive, struggle, cope"
[85] Literally 'douleur' means "pain, ache; sorrow, distress, grief; soreness; misery, afterpains"
[86] Literally 'énonce' means "declare firmly, express; enunciate, posit"
[87] Literally 'sans cesse' means "constantly, ever, forever, non-stop"
[88] Literally 'funeste' means "terrible, dreadful, baneful, baleful; disastrous"
[89] Editor's note: Compare Levi "To do nothing, is as fatal as to do evil, but it is more cowardly." from Axiom 16 in Ch. 1 of Book 2 of the *Keys to the Great Mystery*

---

[90] Note de l'éditeur: Comparez Levi « Ne rien faire, c'est aussi funeste que de faire le mal, mais c'est plus lâche. » de l'Axiome XVI du Chap. 1 du Livre II dans *La Clef des Grands Mystères*

The Magus is standing, in the attitude of the willpower [which is] ready-to-act, clothed in white (sign of purity), crowned with a golden circle (sign of eternal light), he holds in his right hand a scepter, surmounted by a circle (an emblem of the fecundated[91] intelligence [or intelligent understanding]), he raises it towards heaven in order to indicate his aspiration for wisdom, for science and for moral strength, the left hand is extended towards the earth, in order to indicate that he wants dominate matter[92]; in front of him, upon a cube (image of the perfect solid) is a cup full of human passions, a sword (weapon of the brave who fight against error), a golden shekel (symbol of the reward gained by voluntary labor), he has for his belt a serpent biting its tail (which symbolizes Eternity). The ibis on the cube is the emblem of Vigilance.

Number 1 signifies the Divine unity which is found as the whole when it is multiplied by itself, it is the synthesis of numbers.

SACERDOTAL SENTENCES: The human will is the reflection of the Divine power, to will is to create. The moral struggle is the law of the human spirit; to fight for the light is to conquer the absolute and <u>nothing resists man, when he knows the truth, and wills the just.</u>[93] *The comet means that the true Magus is the messenger of God.*

Le Mage est debout, dans l'attitude de la volonté prête à agir, vêtu de blanc, signe de pureté, couronné d'un cercle d'or, signe de la lumière éternelle, il tient dans la main droite un sceptre, surmonté d'un cercle, emblème de l'intelligence fécondante, il l'élève vers le ciel pour indiquer son aspiration à la sagesse, à la science et à la force morale, la main gauche est étendue vers la terre, pour indiquer qu'il veut dominer la matière ; devant lui, sur un cube, image du solide parfait, se trouve une coupe, pleine des passions humaines, un glaive, arme des braves qui combattent l'erreur, un sicle d'or, symbole dé la récompensé acquise par le travail volontaire, il a pour ceinture un serpent se mordant la queue, qui symbolise l'Eternité. L'ibis sur le cube est l'emblème de la Vigilance.

Nombre 1 signifie l'unité Divine qui se retrouve au total quand on la multiplie par elle-même, il est la synthèse des nombres.

SENTENCES SACERDOTALES: La volonté humaine est le reflet de la puissance Divine, vouloir c'est créer. La lutte morale est la loi de l'esprit humain; combattre pour la lumière c'est conquérir l'absolu et <u>rien ne résiste à l'homme, lorsqu'il sait le vrai, et veut le juste.</u>[94] *La comète signifie que le vrai Mage est l'envoyé de Dieu.*

---

[91] Literally 'fécondante' means "fertilized, fecundated; pregnant, impregnated"

[92] Literally 'matière' means "matter, material"

[93] Editor's note: Compare Levi "Nothing resists the willpower of man, when he knows the truth and wills the good." from Axiom I in Ch. 1 of Book 2 of the *Keys to the Great Mystery*

---

[94] Note de l'éditeur: Comparez Levi « Rien ne résiste à la volonté de l'homme, lorsqu'il sait le vrai et veut le bien. » de l'Axiome I du Chap. 1 du Livre II dans *La Clef des Grands Mystères*

LAME II (B = 2) LE SANCTUAIRE

ARCANUM II. — LETTER **Beïnthin** (B) — NUMBER 2.

B = 2 expresses in the *Divine world* the consciousness of the absolute Being which embraces the three terms of all manifestation: the past, the present, [and] the future. — In the *Intellectual world*, the Binary, reflection of the Unity; the Science, perception of choices [both] visible and invisible. — In the *Physical world*, Man, Woman (molder[95] of Man), and to unify himself with her in order to accomplish an equal destiny.

Arcanum II is depicted by a woman seated on the threshold[96] of the temple of Isis, between two columns. The column which is set up[97] to her right is red; this color signifies the pure spirit and its luminous[98] ascent above matter. The column on the left is black, and depicting the night of chaos, the captivity of the impure spirit within the bonds of matter. The woman is crowned with a tiara[99] surmounted by the lunar crescent, and enveloped in a veil whose folds fall upon her face. On her chest she carries the solar cross, and on her knees [is] an open book which she half-covers with her cloak[100]. This symbolic ensemble personifies the occult Science which awaits the initiate at the threshold of the sanctuary of Isis, in order to communicate to him the universal secrets of Nature.

ARCANE II. — LETTRE **Beïnthin** (B) — NOMBRE 2.

B = 2 exprime, dans le *Monde divin* la conscience de l'Etre absolu qui embrasse les trois termes de toute manifestation : le passé, le présent, le futur. — Dans le *Monde intellectuel*, le Binaire, reflet de l'Unité ; la Science, perception des choses visibles et invisibles. — Dans le *Monde physique*, l'Homme, la Femme, moule de l'Homme, et s'unifiant avec lui pour accomplir une égale destinée.

L'arcane II est figuré par une femme assise au seuil du temple d'Isis, entre deux colonnes. La colonne qui se dresse à sa droite est rouge; cette couleur signifie l'esprit pur et sa lumineuse ascension au-dessus de la matière. La colonne de gauche est noire, et figure la nuit du chaos, la captivité de l'esprit impur dans les liens de la matière. La femme est couronnée d'une tiare surmontée du croissant lunaire, et enveloppée d'un voile dont les plis tombent sur sa face. Elle porte sur sa poitrine la croix solaire, et sur ses genoux un livre ouvert qu'elle couvre à demi de son manteau. Cet ensemble symbolique personnifie la Science occulte qui attend l'initié au seuil du sanctuaire d'Isis, pour lui communiquer les secrets de la Nature universelle.

---

[95] Literally 'moule' means "mold, press; shape, cast; mill, grind"

[96] Literally 'seuil' means "sill; step, threshold, doorstep"

[97] Literally 'dresse' means "draw up, set right; raise, lift; rear, erect; put up, set up; train, break in; tame, shape, draft; lay, dress"

[98] Literally 'lumineuse' means "luminous, glowing, bright"

[99] Literally 'tiare' means "tiara, crown, coronet"

[100] Literally 'manteau' means "coat, overcoat, topcoat; mantle, wrap; pall, cloak"

The solar cross (analogous to the indian *Lingam* (1)[101], signifies the fecundation of matter by the spirit; it also expresses (as [a] seal of the infinite) that science proceeds from God, and that it is boundless as its source. The veil enveloping the tiara and falling upon the face expresses that the truth eludes[102] the eyes of a profane curiosity. The book, half hidden under the cloak, signifies that the mysteries are only revealed in solitude, to the sage who collects[103] himself in silence within the full[104] and calm possession of himself.

Remember, son of the Earth, that the spirit is enlightened by seeking God with the eyes of the Willpower. God said, "May the light be!" And the light inundated[105] space. Man must say: "May the Truth be manifest, and may Good come to me!"[106] And if that man possesses a sound will, [then] he will see the Truth shine[107], and, guided by it, he will attain all the good to which he aspires. If arcanum II appears on your Horoscope, strike resolutely at the door of the future, and it will be open for you; but study the path [for a] long time where you are about to enter. Turn your face toward the Sun of Justice, and the science of the true will be given unto you.

La croix solaire (analogique au *Lingam* indien (1)[108], signifie la fécondation de la matière par l'esprit; elle exprime aussi, comme sceau de l'infini, que la science procède de Dieu, et qu'elle est sans bornes comme sa source. Le voile enveloppant la tiare et retombant sur la face énonce que la vérité se dérobe aux regards d'une profane curiosité. Le livre à demi caché sous le manteau signifie que les mystères ne se révèlent que dans la solitude, au sage qui se recueille en silence dans la pleine et calme possession de lui-même.

Souviens-toi, fils de la Terre, que l'esprit s'éclaire en cherchant Dieu avec les yeux de la Volonté. Dieu a dit : « Que la lumière soit ! » et la lumière a inondé l'espace. L'homme doit dire : «'Que la Vérité se manifeste, et que le Bien m'arrive! »[109] Et si l'homme possède une saine volonté, il verra luire la Vérité, et, guidé par elle, il atteindra tout bien auquel il aspire. Si l'arcane II apparaît sur ton Horoscope, frappe résolument à la porte de l'avenir, et il te sera ouvert; mais étudie longtemps la voie où tu vas entrer. Tourne ta face vers le Soleil de Justice, et la science du vrai te sera donnée.

---

[101] (1) The *Lingam* was the figurative sign of the union of the two sexes. Sacred antiquity attached no shameful thought to the contemplation of the reproductive organs; the monuments of Mithra, among the Persians, are proof of this. The corruption of customs later relegated to these symbols into the secret sanctuaries of initiation, but customs did not become better.
[102] Literally 'se dérobe' means "shirk, shrink, evade, back down, elude, flinch, ooze away, fend off, balk"
[103] Literally 'recueille' means "gather, collect; garner, obtain, take in; reflect, meditate, contemplate"
[104] Literally 'pleine' means "full, solid; plump; replete"
[105] Literally 'inondé' means "flood, inundate, flow; deluge, swamp; submerge, overflow; float"
[106] Editor's note: Compare Levi "It is through willpower that the intelligence [or intelligent understanding] sees. If the will is healthy, the vision is just [or right]. God said: "May the light be!" and the light is; the willpower says: "May the world be as I wish to see it!" and the intelligence [or intelligent understanding] sees it as the willpower has willed [it]." from Axiom 2 in Ch. 1 of Book 2 of the *Keys to the Great Mystery*
[107] Literally 'luire' means "gleam, glisten, glimmer, glint"

---

[108] (l) Le *Lingam* était le signe figuratif de l'union des deux sexes. L'antiquité sacrée n'attachait aucune pensée honteuse à la contemplation des organes reproducteurs ; les monuments de Mithra, chez les Perses, en sont la preuve. La corruption des mœurs fut reléguer plus tard ces symboles dans les sanctuaires secrets de l'initiation, mais les mœurs n'en devinrent pas meilleures.
[109] Note de l'éditeur: Comparez Levi « C'est par la volonté que l'intelligence voit. Si la volonté est saine, la vue est juste. Dieu a dit : Que la lumière soit! et la lumière est; la volonté dit : Que le monde soit comme je veux le voir! et l'intelligence le voit comme la volonté a voulu. » de l'Axiome X du Chap. 1 du Livre II dans *La Clef des Grands Mystères*

Keep silence over your plans[110] so as not to give them up to the contradiction of men.

Garde le silence sur tes desseins, afin de ne point les livrer à la contradiction des hommes.

| PLATE II | (B = 2) | THE SANCTUARY | LAME II | (B = 2) | LE SANCTUAIRE |

Hieroglyphic symbolism.

Symbolisme hiéroglyphique.

The occult science between two columns of the temple which represent Good and Evil, she is crowned with the lunar crescent and has [her] face veiled, which signifies that the truth is not visible for the Profane, she has on her chest the solar Cross (emblem of universal generation) and holds on her knees a papyrus which she covers with her cloak in order to indicate that the mysteries of the sacred science are only unveiled[111] for the Initiates. The tiara which covers her head signifies the power of intelligence [or intelligent understanding] enlightened by wisdom (lunar crescent), she is seated, which means that the science united with wisdom and with willpower, is immutable[112].

Number 2 [is the] symbol of the union of man and of woman and the reflection of the unity.

La science occulte entre deux colonnes du temple qui représentent le Bien et le Mal, elle est couronnée du croissant lunaire et a la face voilée, ce qui signifie que la vérité n'est pas visible pour le Profane, elle a sur la poitrine la Croix solaire emblème de la génération universelle et tient sur ses genoux un papyrus qu'elle couvre de son manteau pour indiquer que les mystères de la science sacrée ne se dévoilent qu'aux Initiés. La tiare qui la coiffe signifie la puissance de l'intelligence éclairée par la sagesse (croissant lunaire), elle est assise, ce qui veut dire que la science unie à la sagesse et à la volonté, est immuable.

Nombre 2 symbole de l'union de l'homme et de la femme et reflet de l'unité.

---

[110] Literally 'desseins' means "intention, design, plan; goal, purpose"
[111] Literally 'dévoilent' means "unveil, disclose, reveal, uncover, uncloak, unfold, spill, light, bare, tip; tell tales"
[112] Literally 'immuable' means "immuable, unchanging, constant"

SACERDOTAL SENTENCES: <u>To will the possible is almost to create it,</u>[113] command matter and it will obey you; <u>to will evil and to do it is the suicide of the soul;</u>[114] to will good and to do it is to make oneself immortal, since love is stronger than hatred and will vanquish death.

Astral Influx of the Moon.

SENTENCES SACERDOTALES: <u>Vouloir le possible c'est presque le créer,</u>[115] commande à la matière et elle t'obéira; <u>vouloir le mal et le faire est le suicide de l'âme;</u>[116] vouloir le bien et le faire c'est se rendre immortel, car l'amour est plus fort que la haine et vaincra la mort.

Influx astral de la Lune.

---

[113] Editor's note: Compare Levi "To affirm and to will what must be, is to create; to affirm and to will what must not be, is to destroy." from Axiom 12 in Ch. 1 of Book 2 of the *Keys to the Great Mystery*

[114] Editor's note: Compare Levi "To will evil, is to will death. A perverse willpower is the beginning of suicide." from Axiom 2 in Ch. 1 of Book 2 of the *Keys to the Great Mystery*

[115] Note de l'éditeur: Comparez Levi « Affirmer et vouloir ce qui doit être, c'est créer; affirmer et vouloir ce qui ne doit pas être, c'est détruire. » de l'Axiome XII dans Chap. 1 du Livre II dans *La Clef des Grands Mystères*

[116] Note de l'éditeur: Comparez Levi « Vouloir le mal, c'est vouloir la mort. Une volonté perverse est un commencement de suicide. » de l'Axiome II du Chap. 1 du Livre II dans *La Clef des Grands Mystères*

ב

LAME III   (G = 3)   LA NATURE

ב

ARCANUM III. — LETTER **Gomor** (G) — NUMBER 3.

G = 3 expresses, in the *Divine world* the supreme Power, equilibrated by the eternally active Intelligence [or Intelligent Understanding] and by absolute Wisdom. — In the *Intellectual world*, the universal fecundity of the Being. — In the *Physical world*, Nature working, the germination of acts which must [be] hatched[117] [by] the Willpower.

Arcanum III is depicted with the image of a woman seated in the center of a radiant sun; she is crowned by twelve stars and her feet rest upon the moon. This is the personification of universal fecundity. The sun is the embleme of the creative power; the crown of stars symbolizes (through the number 12) those Houses or stations which this star passes through[118], year after year, around the zodical zone. This woman, the heavenly Isis, or Nature, carries a scepter surmounted by a globe: this is the sign of her perpetual action on things [already] born and [those who are yet] to be born. With the other hand she has[119] an eagle (symbol of the heights upon which the growth of the spirit can soar[120]). — The moon under her feet depicts the infinity of Matter and its dominion by the Spirit.

Remember, son of the Earth, that <u>to affirm what is true and to will what is just is to create it; to affirm and to will the contrary is to devote oneself to destruction.</u>[121]

---

[117] Literally 'éclore' means "hatch, open"

[118] Literally 'parcourt' means "travel, tour, run through; voyage, roam, range; skim, scour; look over, read through, turn over; leaf, run down, look into"

[119] Literally 'porte' means "carry, bear, wear; have on, take; direct, hit; strike"

[120] Literally 'essor' means "soar, flight, development, soaring"

[121] Editor's note: Compare Levi "To affirm and to will what must be, is to create; to affirm and to will what must not be, is to destroy." from Axiom 12 in Ch. 1 of Book 2 of the *Keys to the Great Mystery*

ARCANE III. — LETTRE **Gomor** (G) — NOMBRE 3.

G = 3 exprime, dans le *Monde divin* la Puissance suprême, équilibrée par l'Intelligence éternellement active et par la Sagesse absolue. — Dans le *Monde intellectuel*, la fécondité universelle de l'Être. — Dans le *Monde physique*, la Nature en travail, la germination des actes qui doivent éclore de la Volonté.

L'arcane III est figuré par l'image d'une femme assise au centre d'un soleil rayonnant; elle est couronnée de douze étoiles et ses pieds reposent sur la lune. C'est la personnification de la fécondité universelle. Le soleil est l'emblème de la puissance créatrice; la couronne étoilée symbolise, par le nombre 12, celui des Maisons ou stations que cet astre parcourt, d'année en année, autour de la zone zodiacale. Cette femme, l'Isis céleste, ou la Nature, porte un sceptre surmonté d'un globe: c'est le signe de sa perpétuelle action sur les choses nées et à naître. De l'autre main elle porte un aigle, symbole des hauteurs sur lesquelles peut s'élever l'essor de l'esprit. — La lune placée sous ses pieds figure l'infinité[122] de la Matière et sa domination par l'Esprit.

Souviens-toi, fils de la Terre, qu'<u>affirmer ce qui est vrai et vouloir ce qui est juste, c'est déjà le créer; affirmer et vouloir le contraire, c'est se vouer soi-même à la destruction.</u>[123]

---

[122] A l'origine "l'infimité"

[123] Note de l'éditeur: Comparez Levi « Affirmer et vouloir ce qui doit être, c'est créer; affirmer et vouloir ce qui ne doit pas être, c'est détruire. » de l'Axiome XII du Chap. 1 du Livre II dans *La Clef des Grands Mystères*

If arcanum III manifests itself among the fateful signs of your Horoscope, hope for the success of your undertakings, provided you know how to unite the fecundating activity with the rectitude of spirit that makes the works fruitful.

Si l'arcane III se manifeste parmi les signes fatidiques de ton Horoscope, espère le succès de tes entreprises, pourvu que tu saches unir l'activité qui féconde à la rectitude d'esprit qui fait fructifier les œuvres.

PLATE III   (G = 3)   NATURE

LAME III   (G = 3)   LA NATURE

Hieroglyphic symbolism.

Symbolisme hiéroglyphique.

Nature is represented by a woman sitting on a cube with covered eyes (emblem of the visions of Hermes); her feet rest upon the moon emblem of matter subject to the spirit, she is crowned with twelve stars that represent the course of the year, a radiant sun serves as her halo and symbolizes the creative power of intelligence [or intelligent understanding]; she holds a scepter surmounted by a globe with one hand (emblem of her dominating action upon the world), the other hand supports an eagle with its head turned towards her, which signifies the flight[124] and the power of the human soul returning to its initial principle: God.

La Nature est représentée par une femme assise sur un cube couvert d'yeux, emblème des visions d'Hermès ; ses pieds reposent sur la lune emblème de la matière soumise à l'esprit, elle est couronnée de douze étoiles qui représentent le cours de l'année, un soleil rayonnant lui sert d'auréole et symbolise la puissance créatrice de l'intelligence; elle tient d'une main un sceptre surmonté d'un globe, emblème de son action dominatrice sur le monde, l'autre main supporte un aigle la tête tournée vers elle, ce qui signifie le vol et la puissance de l'âme humaine faisant retour à son principe initial : Dieu.

Number 3, number of the universal trinity: Divine, spiritual and physical.

Nombre 3, nombre de la trinité universelle: Divine, spirituelle et physique.

SACERDOTAL SENTENCES: <u>To will what is just is to create, to will the opposite is to destroy,</u>[125] to affirm the truth is [one's] Duty, to deny it is only the [one's] Right.

SENTENCES SACERDOTALES: <u>Vouloir ce qui juste c'est créer, vouloir le contraire c'est détruire,</u>[126] affirmer la vérité est le Devoir, la nier n'est que le Droit.

---

[124] Literally 'vol' means "flight, flying; lift; robbery, thievery, stealing"

[125] Editor's note: Compare Levi "To affirm and to will what must be, is to create; to affirm and to will what must not be, is to destroy." from Axiom 12 in Ch. 1 of Book 2 of the *Keys to the Great Mystery*

---

[126] Note de l'éditeur: Comparez Levi « Affirmer et vouloir ce qui doit être, c'est créer; affirmer et vouloir ce qui ne doit pas être, c'est détruire. » de l'Axiome XII du Chap. 1 du Livre II dans *La Clef des Grands Mystères*

Nature is a perpetual rebirth. Consciousness is a divine mirror; to love and to create everything is therein; woe to the people whose loves are fruitless[127].

Astral Influx of Venus.

La nature est une perpétuelle renaissance. La conscience est un miroir divin; aimer et créer tout est là ; malheur aux peuples dont les amours sont infécondes.

Influx astral de Vénus.

---

[127] Literally 'infécondes' means "infertile, fruitless"

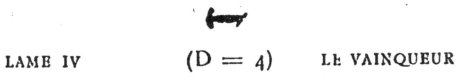

LAME IV   (D = 4)   LE VAINQUEUR

ARCANUM IV. — LETTER **Dinaïn** (D) — NUMBER 4.

D = 4 expresses, in the *Divine world* the perpetual and hierarchical realization of the possibilities[128] containted in the absolute Being. — In the *Intellectual world*, realization of the ideas of the contingent[129] Being, through the quadruple work of the spirit: Affirmation, Negation, Discussion, [and] Solution. — In the *Physical world*, the realization of acts directed by the science of the Truth, the love of Justice, the strength/force of the Willpower and the work of the Organs.

Arcanum IV is depicted by a man wearing a helmet surmounted by a crown. He sits on a cubic stone. His right hand raises a scepter, and his bent right leg rests on the other [leg] in the shape of a cross. The cubic stone, the figure of the perfect solid, signifies accomplishment [of] the human work. The crowned helmet is the emblem of the strength/force which has conquered power. This dominator is in possession of the scepter of Isis, and the stone (which serves him as throne) signifies matter tamed[130]. The cross traced by the position of his legs symbolizes the four elements and the expansion of the human power in every sense.

Remember, son of the Earth, that <u>nothing resists a firm will, which has for leverage the science of the true and the just.</u>[131] To fight in order to ensure its realization, is more than a right, it is a duty.

---

[128] Literally 'virtualités' means "virtualities, potentialities"
[129] Literally 'contingent' means "contingent (dependent for existence, occurrence, character, etc., on something not yet certain; conditional)"
[130] Literally 'domptée' means "tame, manage, master, gentle, school"
[131] Editor's note: Compare Levi "Nothing resists the willpower of man, when he knows the truth and wills the good." from Axiom 1, and "The dignity of man consists in doing what he wills, and in willing the good, in accordance with the science of the true. The good conforms to the true, which is [what is] just [or right]." in Ch. 1 of Book 2 of the *Keys to the Great Mystery*

ARCANE IV. — LETTRE **Dinaïn** (D) — NOMBRE 4.

D = 4 exprime, dans le *Monde divin* la réalisation perpétuelle et hiérarchique des virtualités contenues dans l'Etre absolu. — Dans le *Monde intellectuel*, la réalisation des idées de l'Etre contingent, par le quadruple travail de l'esprit : Affirmation, Négation, Discussion, Solution. — Dans le *Monde physique*, la réalisation des actes dirigés par la science de la Vérité, l'amour de la Justice, la force de la Volonté et le travail des Organes.

L'arcane IV est figuré par un homme coiffé d'un casque surmonté d'une couronne. Il est assis sur une pierre cubique. Sa main droite élève un sceptre, et sa jambe droite fléchie s'appuie sur l'autre en forme de croix. La pierre cubique, figure du solide parfait, signifie l'œuvre humaine accomplie. Le casque couronné est l'emblème de la force qui a conquis le pouvoir. Ce dominateur est en possession du sceptre d'Isis, et la pierre qui lui sert de trône signifie la matière domptée. La croix tracée par la position de ses jambes symbolise les quatre éléments et l'expansion de la puissance humaine en tous sens.

Souviens-toi, fils de la Terre, que <u>rien ne résiste à une volonté ferme, qui a pour levier la science du vrai et du juste.</u>[132] Combattre pour en assurer la réalisation, c'est plus qu'un droit, c'est un devoir.

---

[132] Note de l'éditeur: Comparez Levi « Rien ne résiste à la volonté de l'homme, lorsqu'il sait le vrai et veut le bien. » de l'Axiome I, et « La dignité de l'homme consiste à faire ce qu'il veut et à vouloir le bien, conformément à la science du vrai. Le bien conforme au vrai, c'est le juste. » du Chap. 1 du Livre II dans *La Clef des Grands Mystères*

The man who triumphs in this struggle only accomplishes his terrestrial mission; whosoever succumbs in devoting himself acquires immortality. If arcanum IV appears in your Horoscope, it signifies that the realization of your hopes depends upon a being more powerful than you: seek to know it, and you will have its support.

L'homme qui triomphe dans cette lutte ne fait qu'accomplir sa mission terrestre; celui qui succombe en se dévouant s'acquiert l'immortalité. Si l'arcane IV apparaît sur ton Horoscope, il signifie que la réalisation de tes espérances dépend d'un être plus puissant que toi : cherche à le connaître, et tu auras son appui.

PLATE IV   (D = 4)   THE CONQUEROR[133]

LAME IV   (D = 4)   LE VAINQUEUR

Hieroglyphic symbolism.

Symbolisme hiéroglyphique.

A man wearing a crowned helmet, symbolizing the conquered power, the cube is the emblem of the accomplished work, he holds the scepter of the Magi (emblem of the moral power acquired through sacred study), his left hand indicates matter tamed, the dove on the breast symbolizes innocence, the crossed legs signify the expansion of the power of the human Spirit in the three measurements of infinity (height, width, depth). The Cat on the cube symbolizes the thought of the magus who sees in the night of time.

Un homme coiffé d'un casque couronné, symbolise le pouvoir conquis, le cube est l'emblème du travail accompli, il tient le sceptre des Mages emblème de la puissance morale acquise par l'étude sacrée, sa main gauche indique la matière domptée, la colombe sur la poitrine symbolyse l'innocence, les jambes croisées signifient l'expansion de la puissance de l'Esprit humain dans les trois mesures de l'infini (hauteur, largeur, profondeur). Le Chat sur le cube symbolise la pensée du mage qui voit dans la nuit des temps.

Number 4, number of the strength/force, the unity completed by the trinity and [thereby] giving the perfect square (Affirmation, Negation, Discussion, Solution).

Nombre 4, nombre de la force, l'unité complétée par la trinité et donnant le carré parfait (Affirmation, Négation, Discussion, Solution).

SACERDOTAL SENTENCES: The Magus, in possession of the science of good and evil, must make use of the latter [or evil] only to build up the former [or good],[134] since evil is only the shadow of good, which alone exists.

SENTENCES SACERDOTALES: Le Mage en possession de la science du bien et du mal ne doit se servir de celui-ci que pour édifier celui-là,[135] car le mal n'est que l'ombre du bien, qui seul existe.

---

[133] Literally 'VAINQUEUR' means "victor, winner, conqueror, vanquisher"

[134] Editor's note: Compare Levi "One can and one must accept evil as [a] means of good; but one must never will it, nor do it, otherwise one would destroy with one hand what one creates with the other." from Axiom 4 in Ch. 1 of Book 2 of the *Keys to the Great Mystery*

[135] Note de l'éditeur: Comparez Levi « On peut et l'on doit accepter le mal comme moyen du bien ; mais il ne faut jamais ni le vouloir ni le faire, autrement on détruirait d'une main ce qu'on édifie de l'autre. » de l'Axiome IV du Chap. 1 du Livre II dans *La Clef des Grands Mystères*

Innocence is the inertia of good. Remember that whosoever harms[136] others hurts[137] themselves [or does evil to themselves].

Astral Influx of Jupiter.

L'innocence est l'inertie du bien. Souviens-toi que qui nuit à autrui fait du mal à soi-même.

Influx astral de Jupiter.

---

[136] Literally 'nuit' means "harm, injure, hurt, damage"
[137] Literally 'fait du mal' means "doing evil, does evil; hurts"

LAME V   (E = 5)   L'HIÉROPHANTE

ARCANUM V. — LETTER **Eni** (E) — NUMBER 5.

ARCANE V. — LETTRE **Eni** (E) — NOMBRE 5.

E = 5 expresses, in the *Divine world* the universal Law, regulator of the infinite manifestations of the Being in the unity of substance. — In the *Intellectual world*, Religion, connecting[138] the absolute Being to the relative Being, the Infinite to the Finite. — In the *Physical world*, the inspiration communicated through the vibrations of the astral fluid; the test of man by the liberty of action in the insurmountable[139] circle of the universal law.

E = 5 exprime, dans le *Monde divin* la Loi universelle, régulatrice des manifestations infinies de l'Etre dans l'unité de substance. — Dans le *Monde intellectuel*, la Religion, rapport de l'Etre absolu à l'Etre relatif, de l'Infini au Fini. — Dans le *Monde physique*, l'inspiration communiquée par les vibrations du fluide astral ; l'épreuve de l'homme par la liberté d'action dans le cercle infranchissable de la loi universelle.

Arcanum V is depicted with the image of the Hierophant (Master of the Sacred Mysteries). This prince of the occult doctrine is seated between the two columns of the sanctuary. He leans[140] on a cross with three crosses, and traces with the forefinger of his right hand, on his chest, the sign of silence. At his feet two men are prostrate, one dressed in red, the other clothed in black. The Hierophant, the supreme organ of the sacred science, represents the Genie of the good inspirations of the spirit and the conscousness; his gesture invites [us] to recollection, in order to hear the voice of heaven in the silence of the passions and instincts of the flesh. The right column symbolizes the divine law; the one on the left signifies the liberty to obey or to disobey [th divine law]. The cross with three transverses is the emblem of God penetrating the three worlds, in order to bring forth all the manifestations of universal life. The two prostrate men, one red and the other black, depict the Genie of Light and the one of Darkness, both of whom obey the Master of the Arcana.

L'arcane V est figuré par l'image de l'Hiérophante (Maître des Mystères sacrés). Ce prince de la doctrine occulte est assis entre les deux colonnes du sanctuaire. Il s'appuie sur une croix à trois traverses, et trace avec l'index de la main droite, sur sa poitrine, le signe du silence. A ses pieds sont prosternés deux hommes, l'un vêtu de rouge, l'autre vêtu de noir. L'Hiérophante, suprême organe de la science sacrée, représente le Génie des bonnes inspirations de l'esprit et de la conscience; son geste invite au recueillement, pour entendre la voix du ciel dans le silence des passions et des instincts de la chair. La colonne de droite symbolise la loi divine; celle de gauche signifie la liberté d'obéir ou de désobéir. La croix à trois traverses est l'emblème de Dieu pénétrant les trois mondes, pour y faire éclore toutes les manifestations de la vie universelle. Les deux hommes prosternés, l'un rouge, l'autre noir, figurent le Génie de la Lumière et celui des Ténèbres, qui obéissent tous deux au Maître des Arcanes.

---

[138] Literally 'rapport' means "connection, relation; link, communication, relevance; report, record; yield, profit; ratio; nexus, affinity"

[139] Literally 'infranchissable' means "impassable, insurmountable"

[140] Literally 'appuie' means "lean on, back up, support; favor; back, bolster; recline; side, second"

Remember, son of the Earth, that <u>before you say of a man that he is happy or unhappy, you must know what use he has made of his willpower,</u>[141] for every man creates his life in the image of his works. The Genie of Good is on your right, and that of Evil [is] on your left; their voice is only heard through thy consciousness: gather[142] thyself, and it will respond.

Souviens-toi, fils de la Terre, qu'<u>avant de dire d'un homme qu'il est heureux ou malheureux, il faut savoir quel usage il a fait de sa volonté,</u>[143] car tout homme crée sa vie à l'image de ses œuvres. Le Génie du Bien est à ta droite, et celui du Mal à ta gauche ; leur voix n'est entendue que de ta conscience : recueille-toi, et elle te répondra.

LAME V   (E = 5) THE HIEROPHANT

LAME V   (E = 5) L'HIÉROPHANTE

Hieroglyphic symbolism.

Symbolisme hiéroglyphique.

The high priest of Isis is represented seated between the columns of the Sanctuary, one hand on the angelic cross [which] symbolizes the penetration of the creative genie through the three worlds (Divine, Intellectual, and Physics), the two columns signify the law, and the liberty to obey or to disobey [it], the other hand, makes the sign of recollection and of silence (knowing and keeping quiet) at his feet two kneeling men personify good and evil submitting to the sovereign master of the arcana.

Number 5, the number of faith and the human hand (the 5 fingers).

Le grand prêtre d'Isis est représenté assis entre les colonnes du Sanctuaire, une main sur la croix ansée symbolise la pénétration du génie créateur à travers les trois mondes (Divin, Intellectuel, et Physique), les deux colonnes signifient la loi, et la liberté d'obéir ou de désobéir, l'autre main, fait le signe du recueillement et du silence (savoir et se taire) à ses pieds deux hommes agenouillés personnifient le bien et le mal soumis au souverain maître des arcanes.

Nombre 5, le nombre de la foi et de la main humaine (les 5 doigts).

---

[141] Editor's note: Compare Levi "Before declaring that a man [is] happy or unhappy, know what the direction of his willpower has made of him: Tiberius died every day at Capri, while Jesus proved his immortality and even his divinity on Calvary and upon the cross." from Axiom 22 in Ch. 1 of Book 2 of the *Keys to the Great Mystery*
[142] Literally 'recueille' means "gather, collect; garner, obtain, take in; reflect, meditate, contemplate"

---

[143] Note de l'éditeur: Comparez Levi « Avant de déclarer un homme heureux ou malheureux, sachez ce que l'a fait la direction de sa volonté : Tibère mourait tous les jours à Caprée, tandis que Jésus prouvait son immortalité et sa divinité même sur le Calvaire et sur la croix. » de l'Axiome XXII du Chap. 1 du Livre II dans *La Clef des Grands Mystères*

SACERDOTAL SENTENCES: Faith is the science of the just. Religion is the bond of absolute Being to relative being, and the connection of the infinite to the finite, the liberty of action is the test of man before God; judge not the happiness of a man until after his death. <u>The beautiful is the splendor of the true.</u>[144]

Astral Influx of Mars.
Cycle of Aries.

SENTENCES SACERDOTALES: La foi est la science du juste. La religion est le lien de l'Etre absolu à l'être relatif et le rapport de l'infini au fini, la liberté d'action est l'épreuve de l'homme devant Dieu; ne jugez du bonheur d'un homme qu'après sa mort. <u>Le beau est la splendeur du vrai.</u>[145]

Influx astral de Mars.
Cycle du Bélier.

---

[144] Editor's note: Compare Levi "The beauty of speech is the splendour of truth." from Ch. 1 of Book 2 of the *Keys to the Great Mystery*

[145] Note de l'éditeur: Comparez Levi « La beauté de la parole est une splendeur de vérité. » du Chap. 2 du Livre II dans *La Clef des Grands Mystères*

LAME VI   (U - V = 6)   L'ÉPREUVE

ARCANUM VI. — LETTER **Ur** (U,V) — NUMBER 6.

U, V = 6 expresses, in the *Divine world* the science of Good and of Evil. — In the *Intellectual world*, the equilibrium of Necessity and of Liberty. — In the *Physical world*, the antagonism of natural forces, the linking[146] of the effects with the causes.

Arcanum VI is depicted by a man standing motionless, placed at the angle formed by the junction of two roads. His eyes are fixed on the ground, his arms are crossed upon his chest. Two women, one on his right, the other on his left, put a hand on his shoulder, showing him one of the two roads. The woman on the right has her forehead surrounded by a circle of gold: she personifies Virtue. The one on the left is crowned with [a] vine branch, and represents the tempting Vice. Above and behind this group, the Genie of Justice (hovering in a dazzling aureole) stretches out its bow and directs the arrow of punishment towards Vice. The whole of this scene expresses the struggle between the passions and the consciousness.

Remember, son of the Earth, that for common men, the attraction of vice has more prestige than the austere beauty of virtue. If arcanum VI appears in your Horoscope, beware of your resolutions. Obstacles bar[147] the road of happiness [that is] before you [and] which you pursue; opposing choices[148] hang over you, and your willpower staggers[149] between opposing parties. Indecision is, in all things, more fatal than a bad choice. Advance or retreat, but do not hesitate, and know that <u>a chain of flowers is more difficult to break than a chain of iron.</u>[150]

---

[146] Literally 'enchaînement' means "linking, sequence, series; fetter, tying"
[147] Literally 'barrent' means "bar, block; obstruct, cancel out, cross; remove, delete; score off, stroke, rule out"
[148] Literally 'chances contraires' means "contrary chances, oppositing chances, bad luck"
[149] Literally 'chancelle' means "staggers, titters"
[150] Editor's note: Compare Levi "A chain of iron is easier to break than a chain of flowers." from Axiom 21 in Ch. 1 of Book 2 of the *Keys to the Great Mystery*

ARCANE VI. — LETTRE **Ur** (U,V) — NOMBRE 6.

U, V = 6 exprime, dans le *Monde divin* la science du Bien et du Mal. — Dans le *Monde intellectuel*, l'équilibre de la Nécessité et de la Liberté. — Dans le *Monde physique*, l'antagonisme des forces naturelles, l'enchaînement des effets aux causes.

L'arcane VI est figuré par un homme debout, immobile, placé à l'angle formé par la jonction de deux routes. Ses regards sont fixés à terre, ses bras se croisent sur sa poitrine. Deux femmes, l'une à sa droite, l'autre à sa gauche, lui posent une main sur l'épaule, en lui montrant une des deux routes. La femme placée à droite a le front ceint d'un cercle d'or: elle personnifle la Vertu. Celle de gauche est couronnée de pampre, et représente le Vice tentateur. Au-dessus et en arrière de ce groupe, le Génie de la Justice, planant dans une auréole fulgurante, tend son arc et dirige vers le Vice la flèche du châtiment. L'ensemble de cette scène exprime la lutte entre les passions et la conscience.

Souviens-toi, fils de la Terre, que, pour le commun des hommes, l'attrait du vice a plus de prestige que l'austère beauté de la vertu. Si l'arcane VI apparaît sur ton Horoscope, prends garde à tes résolutions. Les obstacles barrent devant toi la route du bonheur que tu poursuis ; les chances contraires planent sur toi, et ta volonté chancelle entre des partis opposés. L'indécision est, en toutes choses, plus funeste qu'un mauvais choix. Avance ou recule, mais n'hésite point, et sache qu'<u>une chaîne de fleurs est plus difficile à rompre qu'une chaîne de fer.</u>[151]

---

[151] Note de l'éditeur: Comparez Levi « Une chaîne de fer est plus facile à briser qu'une chaîne de fleurs. » de l'Axiome XXI du Chap. 1 du Livre II dans *La Clef des Grands Mystères*

PLATE VI   (U,V = 6)   THE TEST[152]

LAME VI   (U,V = 6)   L'ÉPREUVE

Hieroglyphic symbolism.

The Neophyte hesitates between two roads which two women (who symbolize Vice and Virtue) show him, in space a genie holds a bow directing its arrow towards vice (symbol of the punishment which awaits the man who preferred the easy way of the vice to the austere road of virtue). This arcana sums up the struggle of the consciousness against human passions.

Number 6, number of initiation through the test of the science of Good and of Evil, it is the equilibrium between heaven and earth, it is the perfect number which results from the assembly of its parts, the repercussion of the Ternary.

SACERDOTAL SENTENCES: <u>The will of the just man is the image of God's [will]</u>,[153] <u>the more the willpower struggles, the more it acquires power.</u>[154] <u>To conquer oneself is the supreme victory.</u>[155] Right equilibrates Duty.

Symbolisme hiéroglyphique.

Le Néophyte hésitant entre deux routes que lui montrent deux femmes qui symbolisent le Vice et la Vertu, dans l'espace un génie tenant un arc dirige sa flèche vers le vice, symbole du châtiment qui attend l'homme ayant préféré le chemin facile du vice à l'austère route de la vertu. Cet arcane résume la lutte de la conscience contre les passions humaines.

Nombre 6, nombre de l'initiation par l'épreuve de la science du Bien et du Mal, c'est l'équilibre entre le ciel et la terre, c'est le nombre parfait qui résulte de l'assemblage de ses parties, la répercussion du Ternaire.

SENTENCES SACERDOTALES: <u>La volonté de l'homme juste est l'image de celle de Dieu,</u>[156] <u>plus la volonté lutte, plus elle acquiert la puissance.</u>[157] <u>Se vaincre soi-même est la suprême victoire.</u>[158] Le Droit équilibre le Devoir.

---

[152] Literally 'ÉPREUVE' means "test, trial, examination; proof, print; pull, crucible"

[153] Editor's note: Compare Levi "The will of the just man is the will of God, and the law of nature." from Axiom 9 in Ch. 1 of Book 2 of the *Keys to the Great Mystery*

[154] Editor's note: Compare Levi "The more obstacles the willpower surmounts, the stronger it is. It is for this reason that Christ glorified poverty and sorrow." from Axiom 7 in Ch. 1 of Book 2 of the *Keys to the Great Mystery* and "…the willpower only [becomes] confident in itself through acts..." from Ch. 6 of *Dogma of High Magic*

[155] Editor's note: Compare Levi "The ultimate victory that a man can win over death is to triumph over the flavor of life, not by despair but by a more exalted hope, which is contained in faith, for all that is nice and honest, by the consent of the world. To learn to conquer oneself is therefore to learn to live, and the austerities of stoicism have never been a vain demonstration of liberty!" from Ch. 1 of *Dogma of High Magic*

---

[156] Note de l'éditeur: Comparez Levi « La volonté de l'homme juste, c'est la volonté de Dieu même, et c'est la loi de la nature. » de l'Axiome IX du Chap. 1 du Livre II dans *La Clef des Grands Mystères*

[157] Note de l'éditeur: Comparez Levi « Plus la volonté surmonte d'obstacles, plus elle est forte. C'est pour cela que le Christ a glorifié la pauvreté et la douleur. » de l'Axiome VII du Chap. 1 du Livre II dans *La Clef des Grands Mystères* et « …la volonté ne s'assure d'elle-même que par des actes… » du Chap. VI du *Dogme de la Haute Magie*

[158] Note de l'éditeur: Comparez Levi « La dernière victoire que l'homme puisse remporter sur la mort, c'est de triompher du goût de la vie, non par le désespoir, mais par une plus haute espérance, qui est renfermée dans la foi, pour tout ce qui est beau et honnête, du consentement de tout le monde. Apprendre à se vaincre, c'est donc apprendre à vivre, et les austérités du stoïcisme n'étaient pas une vaine ostentation de liberté! » du Chap. I du *Dogme de la Haute Magie*

The antagonism of forces creates the movement which is the universal life. <u>A chain of flowers is broken with more difficulty than a chain of iron.</u>[159]

Astral Influx of the Moon.
Cycle of Taurus.

L'antagonisme des forces crée le mouvement qui est la vie universelle. <u>Une chaîne de fleurs se brise plus difficilement qu'une chaîne de fer.</u>[160]

Influx astral de la Lune.
Cycle du Taureau.

---

[159] Editor's note: Compare Levi "A chain of iron is easier to break than a chain of flowers." from Axiom 21 in Ch. 1 of Book 2 of the *Keys to the Great Mystery*

[160] Note de l'éditeur: Comparez Levi « Une chaîne de fer est plus facile à briser qu'une chaîne de fleurs. » de l'Axiome XXI du Chap. 1 du Livre II dans *La Clef des Grands Mystères*

LAME VII $(Z = 7)$ LE TRIOMPHE

ARCANUM VII. — LETTER **Zaïn** (Z) — NUMBER 7.

Z = 7 expresses, in the *Divine world* the Septenary, the domination of the Spirit over Nature. — In the *Intellectual world*, the Priest and the Empire. — In the *Physical world*, the submission of the elements and of the forces of Matter to Intelligence [or Intelligent Understanding] and to the work of Man.

Arcanum VII is depicted by a chariot of war, in square form, surmounted by a starry canopy[161] supported by four columns. Upon this chariot advances a triumphant cuirassed[162] [man], holding [a] scepter and [a] sword in his hands. He is crowned with a circle of gold that flourishes three pentagrams or golden five-pointed stars. The square chariot symbolizes the work accomplished by the Willpower which has overcome obstacles. The four columns of the starry canopy are the four Elements subject to the master of the scepter and of the sword. On the square face of the front of the chariot is a sphere supported by two opened wings (a sign of the unlimited exaltation of human power in the infinity of space and time). The golden crown on the forehead of the triumphant [man] signifies the possession of the intellectual light which illuminates all the arcana of Fortune. The three stars that flourish [on his crown] symbolize Power equilibrated through Intelligence [or Intelligent Understanding] and Wisdom. Three squares[163] are drawn on the cuirass; they signify the rectitude of Judgment, of Willpower and of Action which gives the Strength/Force of which the cuirass is the emblem.

ARCANE VII. — LETTRE **Zaïn** (Z) — NOMBRE 7.

Z = 7 exprime, dans le *Monde divin*, le Septénaire, la domination de l'Esprit sur la Nature. — Dans le *Monde intellectuel*, le Sacerdoce et l'Empire. — Dans le *Monde physique*, la soumission des éléments et des forces de la Matière à l'Intelligence et au travail de l'Homme.

L'arcane VII est figuré par un char de guerre, de forme carrée, surmonté d'un baldaquin étoilé que soutiennent quatre colonnes. Sur ce char s'avance un triomphateur cuirassé, portant sceptre et glaive en ses mains. Il est couronné d'un cercle d'or que fleuronnent trois pentagrammes ou étoiles d'or à cinq pointes. Le char carré symbolise l'œuvre accompli par la Volonté qui a vaincu les obstacles. Les quatre colonnes du dais étoile figurent les quatre Eléments soumis au maître du sceptre et du glaive. Sur la face carrée que présente l'avant du char est tracée une sphère soutenue par deux ailes déployées, signe de l'exaltation illimitée de la puissance humaine dans l'infini de l'espace et du temps. La couronne d'or au front du triomphateur signifie la possession de la lumière intellectuelle qui éclaire tous les arcanes de la Fortune. Les trois étoiles qui la fleuronnent symbolisent la Puissance équilibrée par l'Intelligence et la Sagesse. Trois équerres sont tracées sur la cuirasse ; elles signifient la rectitude de Jugement, de Volonté et d'Action qui donne la Force dont la cuirasse est l'emblème.

---

[161] Literally 'baldaquin' means "baldachin, tester; permanent ornamental canopy over an alter or tomb (Architecture)"
[162] Literally 'cuirassé' means "cuirass, armor that protects the chest and back, cuirassier"
[163] Literally 'équerres' means "square, steel square (a tool used to produce right angles, also called a "framing" or "carpenter's" square)"

The rasied sword is the sign of victory. The scepter surmounted by a triangle (symbol of the Spirit), a square (symbol of Matter), and a circle (symbol of eternity), signifies the perpetual domination of Intelligence [or Intelligent Understanding] over the forces of Nature. Two sphinxes, one white, the other black, are harnessed to the chariot. The white symbolizes Good, the black symbolizes Evil, one conquered, the other defeated, and both become servants of the Magus who has triumphed over tests.

Remember, son of the Earth, that the empire of the world belongs to those who possess the sovereignty of the Spirit, that is to say, the light that illuminates the mysteries of life.[164] By breaking[165] [through] obstacles, you will crush your enemies, and all your vows will be realized, if you approach the future with an audacity armed with the consciousness of your right.

PLATE VII   (Z = 7)   TRIUMPH

Hieroglyphic symbolism.

A warrior mounted upon a cubic chariot whose four columns support a star canopy, the columns symbolize the four elements, the cubic chariot signifies the work [which is] edified through the willpower [that is] victorious over obstacles, the warrior is crowned with a gold circle (image of the eternal light);

L'épée haute est le signe de la victoire. Le sceptre surmonté d'un triangle, symbole de l'Esprit, d'un carré, symbole de la Matière, et d'un cercle, symbole de l'Eternité, signifie la perpétuelle domination de l'Intelligence sur les forces de la Nature. Deux sphinx, l'un blanc, l'autre noir, sont attelés au char. Le blanc symbolise le Bien, le noir symbolise le Mal, l'un conquis, l'autre vaincu, et devenus tous deux les serviteurs du Mage qui a triomphé des épreuves.

Souviens-toi, fils de la Terre, que l'empire du monde appartient à ceux qui possèdent la souveraineté de l'Esprit, c'est-à-dire la lumière qui éclaire les mystères de la vie.[166] En brisant les obstacles, tu écraseras tes ennemis, et tous tes vœux seront réalisés, si tu abordes l'avenir avec une audace armée de la conscience de ton droit.

LAME VII   (Z = 7)   LE TRIOMPHE

Symbolisme hiéroglyphique.

Un guerrier monté sur un char cubique dont les quatre colonnes supportent un dais étoile, les colonnes symbolisent les quatre éléments, le char cubique signifie l'œuvre édifié par la volonté victorieuse des obstacles, le guerrier est couronné d'un cercle d'or image de la lumière éternelle ;

---

[164] Editor's note: Compare Levi "The empire of the world, is the empire of the light." from Axiom 14 in Ch. 1 of Book 2 of the *Keys to the Great Mystery*
[165] Literally 'brisant' means "break, smash, shatter, wreck, bow down"

---

[166] Note de l'éditeur: Comparez Levi « L'empire du monde, c'est l'empire de la lumière. » de l'Axiome XIV du Chap. 1 du Livre II dans *La Clef des Grands Mystères*

he holds in one hand the sword (sign of victory), and in the other a scepter surmounted by a square (Matter) by a circle (Eternity) and by a triangle (Divinity), he wears a cuirass (emblem of strength/force), it is adorned with three squares which symbolize judgment, willpower and action; on the front of the chariot a sphere with wings spread out, indicates the exaltation of the intellectual power in the infinity of space and of time. Two sphinxes (harnessed to the chariot) are at rest, the black one is Evil, the other one, white, is Good; both submit to the Magus who emerged victorious from the tests.

Number 7, sacred number of magic, that of all the Geneses.

SACERDOTAL SENTENCES: Light is the Spirit of God and the source of all life; darkness[167] is the spirit of evil and the germ[168] of death; fight for light and you will triumph over the darkness which is error, evil and death.

Astral Influx of the Sun.
Cycle of Gemini.

il tient d'une main le glaive, signe de la victoire et de l'autre un sceptre surmonté d'un carré (La matière) d'un cercle (l'Eternité) et d'un triangle (la Divinité) il porte une cuirasse, emblème de la force, elle est ornée de trois équerres qui symbolisent le jugement, la volonté et l'action; une sphère aux ailes éployées, sur le devant du char, indique l'exaltation de la puissance intellectuelle dans l'infini de l'espace et du temps. Deux sphinx attelés au char, sont au repos, l'un noir est le Mal, l'autre blanc est le Bien ; tous deux soumis au Mage qui est sorti victorieux des épreuves.

Nombre 7, nombre sacré de la magie, celui de toutes les Genèses.

SENTENCES SACERDOTALES: La lumière est l'Esprit de Dieu et la source de toute vie, les ténèbres sont l'esprit du mal et le germe de la mort; combats pour la lumière et tu triompheras des ténèbres qui sont l'erreur, le mal et la mort.

Influx astral de la Soleil.
Cycle du Gémeaux.

---

[167] Literally 'ténèbres' means "darkness, gloom; obscurity, unclearness"
[168] Literally 'germe' means "germ; seed; sprout"

LAME VIII   (H = 8)   LA JUSTICE

ARCANUM VIII. — LETTER **Hélétha** (H) — NUMBER 8.

H = 8 expresses, in the *Divine world* absolute Justice. — In the *Intellectual world*, Attraction and Repulsion. — In the *Physical world*, the relative Justice, fallible[169] and bound[170], which emanates from men.

Arcanum VIII is depicted by a woman seated upon a throne, her forehead wrapped with a crown armed with spear-heads; she holds a sword with with the right hand, pointed up, and a scale in the left. It is the ancient symbol of Justice which weighs acts and which opposes evil, with [a] counterweight, the sword of atonement[171]. Justice, [having] emanated from God, is the equilibrating reaction that restores[172] order, that is to say, the equilibrium between right and duty. The sword here is a sign of protection for the good, and a threat to the wicked. The eyes of Justice are covered with a blindfold, in order to mark that she weighs and that she strikes, without taking into account the conventional differences which men establish among themselves.

Remember, son of the Earth, that achieving[173] victory and overcoming obstacles is only one part of the human task. In order to accomplish it in its entirety, one must establish an equilibrium between the forces which are put into play. Every action producing a reaction, the Willpower must anticipate the shock of opposing forces, in order to temper or cancel it. Every future is balanced between Good and Evil.

ARCANE VIII. — LETTRE **Hélétha** (H) — NOMBRE 8.

H = 8 exprime, dans le *Monde divin*, la Justice absolue. — Dans le *Monde intellectuel*, l'Attrait et la Répulsion. — Dans le *Monde physique*, la Justice relative, faillible et bornée, qui émane des hommes.

L'arcane VIII est figuré par une femme assise sur un trône, le front ceint d'une couronne armée de fers de lance : elle tient de la main droite un glaive, la pointe en haut, et de la gauche une balance. C'est l'antique symbole de la Justice qui pèse les actes et qui oppose au mal, pour contre-poids, le glaive de l'expiation. La justice, émanée de Dieu, est la réaction équilibrante qui reconstitue l'ordre, c'est-à-dire l'équilibre entre le droit et le devoir. Le glaive est ici un signe de protection pour les bons, et de menace pour les méchants. Les yeux de la Justice sont couverts d'un bandeau, pour marquer qu'elle pèse et qu'elle frappe, sans tenir compte des différences conventionnelles que les hommes établissent entre eux.

Souviens-toi, fils de la Terre, que remporter la victoire et dominer les obstacles franchis, ce n'est qu'une part de la tâche humaine. Pour l'accomplir tout entière, il faut établir l'équilibre entre les forces que l'on met en jeu. Toute action produisant une réaction, la Volonté doit prévoir le choc des forces contraires, pour le tempérer ou l'annuler. Tout avenir se balance entre le Bien et le Mal.

---

[169] Literally 'faillible' means "fallible, liable to err or make a mistake"

[170] Literally 'bornée' means "narrow minded; hidebound, thick witted; obtuse, parochial; narrow, restricted; bounded"

[171] Literally 'expiation' means "expiation, atonement"

[172] Literally 'reconstitue' means "reconstruct, put together, retrace, retrospect"

[173] Literally 'remporter' means "take, carry, obtain; win, achieve"

Every intelligence [or intelligent understanding] that does not know how to equilibrate itself resembles an aborted sun.[174]

Toute intelligence qui ne sait point s'équilibrer ressemble à un soleil avorté.[176]

PLATE VIII　　　(H = 8)　　　JUSTICE

LAME VIII　　　(H = 8)　　　LA JUSTICE

Hieroglyphic symbolism.

Upon three steps[175], which depict the three worlds, a woman [who's] forehead is wrapped with a crown of iron (symbol of inflexibility) is seated, her eyes are blindfolded in order to indicate that she does not take into account the social situations of the guily, [with] the Sword in one hand and the Scales in the other, she judges and punishes, the lion symbolizes the strength/force [which is] subject to justice and the sphinx [symbolizes] the eye of God who reads within the souls of the wicked. The winged tortoise symbolizes repentance which can rise to forgiveness despite the weight of crime, a divine genie symbolizes the justice of God who will judge the justice of Men.

Number 8, number of justice and of the equilibrating reaction, it is the harmony in the analogy of opposites, the first number which is divided into equal numbers, the complete number by itself.

Symbolisme hiéroglyphique.

Sur trois degrés qui figurent les trois mondes, une femme, le front ceint d'une couronne de fer, symbole de l'inflexibilité, est assise, elle a les yeux bandés, pour indiquer qu'elle ne tient pas compte des situations sociales des coupables, le Glaive d'une main et la Balance de l'autre elle juge et punit, le lion symbolise la force soumise à la justice et le sphinx l'œil de Dieu qui lit dans les âmes des méchants. La tortue ailée symbolise le repentir qui peut s'élever jusqu'au pardon malgré le poids du crime, un génie divin symbolise la justice de Dieu qui jugera la justice des Hommes.

Nombre 8, nombre de la justice et de la réaction équilibrante, c'est l'harmonie dans l'analogie des contraires, le premier nombre qui se divise en nombres égaux, le nombre complet par lui-même.

---

[174] Editor's note: Compare Levi "The great intelligences [or intelligent understandings] in whom the willpower is imbalanced resemble comets, which are aborted suns." from Axiom 15 in Ch. 1 of Book 2 of the *Keys to the Great Mystery*
[175] Literally 'degrés' means "degree; level, step; grade, rank; class"

---

[176] Note de l'éditeur: Comparez Levi « Les grandes intelligences dont la volonté s'équilibre mal ressemblent aux comètes, qui sont des soleils avortés. » de l'Axiome XV du Chap. 1 du Livre II dans *La Clef des Grands Mystères*

SACERDOTAL SENTENCES: <u>The willpower submitted to the absurd is rejected</u>[177] <u>by reason,</u>[178] the willpower must equilibrate the forces that it puts into play in order to temper or cancel the reaction of the contrary [forces]. <u>Intelligences [or Intelligent Understandings] whose willpower is not equilibrated are similar to aborted stars.</u>[179] Before judging your brother, make yourself judged by him.

Astral Influx of Venus.
Cycle of Cancer.

SENTENCES SACERDOTALES: <u>La volonté soumise à l'absurde est réprouvée de la raison,</u>[180] la volonté doit équilibrer les forces qu'elle met en jeu pour tempérer ou annuler la réaction des contraires. <u>Les intelligences dont la volonté ne s'équilibre pas sont semblables à des astres avortés.</u>[181] Avant de juger ton frère, fais-toi juger par lui.

Influx astral de Vénus.
Cycle du Cancer.

---

[177] Literally 'réprouvée' means "reprove, condemn, reprobate, rap"
[178] Editor's note: Compare Levi "When the will is vowed to the absurd, it is condemned by eternal reason." from Axiom 8 in Ch. 1 of Book 2 of the *Keys to the Great Mystery*
[179] Editor's note: Compare Levi "The great intelligences [or intelligent understandings] in whom the willpower is imbalanced resemble comets, which are aborted suns." from Axiom 15 in Ch. 1 of Book 2 of the *Keys to the Great Mystery*

---

[180] Note de l'éditeur: Comparez Levi « Lorsque la volonté est vouée à l'absurde, elle est réprouvée par l'éternelle raison. » de l'Axiome VIII du Chap. 1 du Livre II dans *La Clef des Grands Mystères*
[181] Note de l'éditeur: Comparez Levi « Les grandes intelligences dont la volonté s'équilibre mal ressemblent aux comètes, qui sont des soleils avortés. » de l'Axiome XV du Chap. 1 du Livre II dans *La Clef des Grands Mystères*

LAME IX   (T-H = 9)   LE SAGE

ARCANUM IX. — LETTER **Théla** (TH) — NUMBER 9.

TH = 9 expresses, in the *Divine world* absolute Wisdom. — In the *Intellectual world*, Prudence, director of Willpower. — In the *Physical world*, Circumspection[182], guide of Actions.

Arcanum IX is depicted by an old man walking [while] leaning on a staff[183] and carrying a lit lamp in front of himself, which he half-conceales under his cloak. This old man personifies the experience acquired in the work of life. The lit lamp signifies the light of intelligence [or intelligent understanding] which must extend over the past, the present, and the future. The cloak that half-conceales it signifies discretion. The staff symbolizes the support that prudence lends to the man who does not deliver[184] his thought.

Remember, son of the Earth, that Prudence is the armor of the Sage. Circumspection makes him avoid the pitfalls or the abysses, and anticipates[185] treason. Take it as a guide in all your acts, even in the smallest things. Nothing is indifferent here below; a pebble may cause the chariot of a master of the world to overturn. Remember that if the Speech is silver, [then] Silence is golden.

ARCANE IX. — LETTRE **Théla** (TH) — NOMBRE 9.

TH = 9 exprime, dans le *Monde divin*, la Sagesse absolue. — Dans le *Monde intellectuel*, la Prudence, directrice de la Volonté. — Dans le *Monde physique*, la Circonspection, guide des Actes.

L'arcane IX est figuré par un vieillard marchant appuyé sur un bâton et portant devant lui une lampe allumée, qu'il cache à demi sous son manteau. Ce vieillard personnifie l'expérience acquise dans le travail de la vie. La lampe allumée signifie la lumière de l'intelligence qui doit s'étendre sur le passé, le présent et l'avenir. Le manteau qui la cache à demi signifie discrétion. Le bâton symbolise le soutien que prête la prudence à l'homme qui ne livre point sa pensée.

Souviens-toi, fils de la Terre, que la Prudence est l'armure du Sage. La Circonspection lui fait éviter les écueils ou les abîmes, et pressentir la trahison. Prends-la pour guide dans tous tes actes, même dans les plus petites choses. Rien n'est indifférent ici-bas ; un caillou peut faire verser le char d'un maître du monde. Souviens-toi que si la Parole est d'argent, le Silence est d'or.

---

[182] Literally 'Circonspection' means "circumscription, prudence, wariness, cautiousness, carefulness, discretion, foresight"

[183] Literally 'bâton' means "stick, staff; club, baton; cane, pole; wand; ferule, rod or ruler used to punish children"

[184] Literally 'livre' means "deliver, hand over, yield, render up"

[185] Literally 'pressentir' means "presurmise, suppose in advance, sense in advance, perceive ahead of time; forebode, approach, sense, contact"

PLATE IX   (T-H = 9)   THE SAGE

LAME IX   (T-H = 9)   LE SAGE

Hieroglyphic symbolism.

An old man (symbol of wisdom) carries a lit lamp which represents intelligence [or intelligent understanding], he covers it with his cloak, which signifies discretion. He goes forward leaning on a staff (symbol of the strength/force acquired through experience).

Number 9, number of syntheses, image reflexing the three worlds (3 X 3 = 9).

SACERDOTAL SENTENCES: Prudence is the weapon[186] of the sages; do not show the light to the blind [because] they would not see it. <u>The education of the willpower is the law of nature.</u>[187] The Verb can do everything, but remember that if speech is silver, [then] silence is golden, bow down[188] before the Pharaoh, it is strength/force, kneel before the Hierophant, he is the law, straighten up[189] before Nature she is your right. Worship[190] the children, honor the elderly, they are the East and the West of life.

Astral Influx of Jupiter.
Cycle of the Lion.

Symbolisme hiéroglyphique.

Un vieillard symbole de la sagesse porte une lampe allumée qui représente l'intelligence, il la couvre de son manteau, ce qui signifie la discrétion. Il s'avance appuyé sur un bâton, symbole de la force acquise par l'expérience.

Nombre 9, nombre des synthèses, image réflexe des trois mondes (3 X 3 = 9).

SENTENCES SACERDOTALES: La prudence est l'arme des sages ; ne montre pas la lumière aux aveugles ils ne la verraient pas. <u>L'éducation de la volonté est la loi de la nature.</u>[191] Le Verbe peut tout, mais souviens-toi que si la parole est d'argent le silence est d'or, incline-toi devant le Pharaon, il est la force, agenouille-toi devant l'Hiérophante il est la loi, redresse-toi devant la Nature elle est ton droit. Adorez les enfants, honorez les vieillards, ils sont l'Orient et l'Occident de la vie.

Influx astral de Jupiter.
Cycle du Lion.

---

[186] Literally 'arme' means "weapon, arm; hardware, teardrop"
[187] Editor's note: Compare Levi "Human life and its innumerable difficulties have as [their] goal, in the order of eternal wisdom, the education of the willpower of man." from Ch. 1 of Book 2 of the *Keys to the Great Mystery*
[188] Literally 'incline' means "incline, bow, defer"
[189] Literally 'redresse' means "redress, re form, rectify; straighten up, right, unbend"
[190] Literally 'Adorez' means "adore, worship; love; enhance, treasure; feel a passionate attraction to"

---

[191] Note de l'éditeur: Comparez Levi « La vie humaine et ses difficultés innombrables ont pour but, dans l'ordre de la sagesse éternelle, l'éducation de la volonté de l'homme. » du Chap. 1 du Livre II dans *La Clef des Grands Mystères*

LAME X   (I-J-Y = 10)   LE SPHINX

ARCANUM X. — LETTER Ioïthi (I, J, Y) — NUMBER 10.

I, J, Y = 10 expresses, in the *Divine world* the active Principle which vivifies beings. — In the *Intellectual world*, the governing Authority. — In the *Physical world*, good or bad Fortune.

10 ROUE DE FORTUNE

Arcanum X is depicted by a wheel suspended on its axis between two columns. On the right, *Hermanubis*, Genie of Good, endeavors[192] to climb to the summit of the circumference. On the left, *Typhon*, Genie of Evil, is precipitated [downwards]. The Sphinx, in equilibrium on [top of] this wheel, holds a sword in its lion's claws. It personifies Destiny, always ready to strike to the right or to the left, and that, according to how the wheel turns under its impulse, lets the humblest rise and overturns the most haughty[193].

Remember, son of the earth, that <u>in order to be able to do[194], one must will; that in order to will effectively, one must dare; that in order to dare with success, one must know how to keep quiet until the moment of acting.</u>[195]

---

[192] Literally 'efforce' means "strive, endeavor, force oneself"

[193] Literally 'altiers' means "snobbish, haughty, proud"

[194] Literally 'pouvoir' means "power, authority, might; command, authorization; agency, rule; ability". Depending on the context, this could also mean "ability to do".

[195] Editor's note: Compare Levi "To attain *the sanctum regnum*, that is to say, the science and power of the magi, four things are indispensable: an intelligent understanding illuminated by study, an audacity which nothing can stop, a will which cannot be broken, and a discretion which nothing can corrupt nor intoxicate. TO KNOW , TO DARE, TO WILL, TO KEEP QUIET , here are the four verbs of the magus, inscribed upon the four symbolic forms of the sphinx." from Ch. 1 of *Dogma of High Magic*

ARCANE X. — LETTRE Ioïthi (I, J, Y) — NOMBRE 10.

I, J, Y = 10 exprime, dans le *Monde divin*, le Principe actif qui vivifie les êtres. — Dans le *Monde intellectuel*, l'Autorité gouvernante. — Dans le *Monde physique*, la bonne ou la mauvaise Fortune.

L'arcane X est figuré par une roue suspendue sur son axe entre deux colonnes. A droite, *Hermanubis*, Génie du Bien, s'efforce de monter au sommet de la circonférence. A gauche, *Typhon*, Génie du Mal, en est précipité. Le Sphinx, en équilibre sur cette roue, tient un glaive dans ses griffes de lion. Il personnifie le Destin toujours prêt à frapper à droite ou à gauche, et qui, selon que la roue tourne sous son impulsion, laisse monter les plus humbles et renverse les plus altiers.

Souviens-toi, fils de la Terre, que <u>pour pouvoir, il faut vouloir; que pour vouloir efficacement, il faut oser; que pour oser avec succès, il faut savoir se taire jusqu'au moment d'agir.</u>[196]

---

[196] Note de l'éditeur: Comparez Levi « Pour parvenir au *sanctum regnum*, c'est-à-dire à la science et à la puissance des mages, quatre choses sont indispensables: une intelligence éclairée par l'étude, une audace que rien n'arréte, une volonté que rien ne brise et une discrétion que rien ne puisse corrompre ou enivrer. SAVOIR, OSER, VOULOIR, SE TAIRE, voilà les quatre verbes du mage qui sont écrits dans les quatre formes symboliques du sphinx. » du Chap. I du *Dogme de la Haute Magie*

In order to acquire the right to possess the Science and the Ability to Do, one must will patiently, with an untiring[197] perseverance.[198] And, in order to maintain oneself on the heights of life, if you succeed in reaching them, one must have learned to fathom the most profound depths.

Pour acquérir le droit de posséder la Science et le Pouvoir, il faut vouloir patiemment, avec une infatigable persévérance.[199] Et, pour se maintenir sur les hauteurs de la vie, si tu parviens à les atteindre, il faut avoir appris à sonder d'un regard sans vertige les plus vastes profondeurs.

PLATE X   (I-J-Y = 10)   THE SPHINX

Hieroglyphic symbolism.

The wheel of destiny upon its axis, on the one side the God Kne-phta rises, genie of good, on the other Typhon, genie of evil, is precipitated [downwards], a winged Sphinx which represents the four forces of the human will (Knowing, daring, acting and keeping quiet), keeps itself in equilibrium which symbolizes the impenetrable power of God disposing human destinies according to the good or bad work of each one, it holds in its claws a javelin (emblem of supreme justice), at the foot of the support of the axis [there are] two serpents symbolizing the equilibrium resulting from the antagonism of contrary forces equal to each other.

Number 10, universal and absolute number, it contains all the others, being and not being (1. 0).

LAME X   (I-J-Y = 10)   LE SPHINX

Symbolisme hiéroglyphique.

La roue du destin sur son axe, d'un côté monte le Dieu Kné-phtâ, génie du bien, de l'autre Typhon, génie du mal, en est précipité, un Sphinx ailé qui représente les quatre forces de la volonté humaine (Savoir, oser, agir, se taire) au sommet se tient un sphinx en équilibre qui symbolise le pouvoir impénétrable do Dieu disposantes destinées humaines suivant l'œuvre bonne ou mauvaise de chacun, il tient dans ses griffes un javelot emblème de la justice suprême, au pied du support de l'axe deux serpents symbolisent l'équilibre résultant de l'antagonisme des forces contraires égales entre elles.

Nombre 10, nombre universel et absolu, il contient tous les autres, l'être et le non être (1. 0).

---

[197] Literally 'infatigable' means "indefatigable, tireless, unflagging, unremitting"

[198] Editor's note: Compare Levi "To have the right to always possess, one must will patiently and [for a] long time." from Axiom 5 in Ch. 1 of Book 2 of the *Keys to the Great Mystery*

---

[199] Note de l'éditeur: Comparez Levi « Pour avoir droit de posséder toujours, il faut vouloir patiemment et longtemps. » de l'Axiome V du Chap. 1 du Livre II dans *La Clef des Grands Mystères*

SACERDOTAL SENTENCES: <u>If the willpower is sound[200], [then] the spirit sees justly.[201] Accept the relative evil in order to arrive at the absolute good, but do not will it and never do it.[202]</u> To die to evil and to be reborn to good is the law. Whosoever is below will climb through virtue, like whosoever is above will fall through vice.

Astral Influx of Mercury.
Cycle of Virgo.

SENTENCES SACERDOTALES: <u>Si la volonté est saine, l'esprit voit juste.[203] Acceptez le mal relatif pour arriver au bien absolu, mais ne le veuillez pas et ne le faites jamais.[204]</u> Mourir pour le Mal et renaître pour le Bien telle est la loi. Celui qui est en bas montera par la vertu, comme celui qui est en haut tombera par le vice.

Influx astral de Mercure.
Cycle du Vierge.

---

[200] Literally 'saine' means "healthy, sound; salubrious, wholesome; good, sane, sweet"

[201] Editor's note: Compare Levi "It is through willpower that the intelligence [or intelligent understanding] sees. If the will is healthy, the vision is just [or right]." from Axiom 10 in Ch. 1 of Book 2 of the *Keys to the Great Mystery*

[202] Editor's note: Compare Levi "One can and one must accept evil as [a] means of good; but one must never will it, nor do it, otherwise one would destroy with one hand what one creates with the other. Good faith never justifies evil means; it corrects them when it undergoes them, and condemns them when it catches them." from Axiom 4 in Ch. 1 of Book 2 of the *Keys to the Great Mystery*

---

[203] Note de l'éditeur: Comparez Levi « C'est par la volonté que l'intelligence voit. Si la volonté est saine, la vue est juste. » de l'Axiome X du Chap. 1 du Livre II dans *La Clef des Grands Mystères*

[204] Note de l'éditeur: Comparez Levi « On peut et l'on doit accepter le mal comme moyen du bien ; mais il ne faut jamais ni le vouloir ni le faire, autrement on détruirait d'une main ce qu'on édifie de l'autre. La bonne foi ne justifie jamais les mauvais moyens ; elle les corrige lorsqu'on les subit, et les condamne lorsqu'on les prend. » de l'Axiome IV du Chap. 1 du Livre II dans *La Clef des Grands Mystères*

LAME XI   (CK = 20)   LA FORCE

ARCANUM XI. — LETTER **Caïtha** (C, K) — NUMBER 20.

C, K = 20 expresses, in the *Divine world* the Principle of all strength/force, spiritual or material. — In the *Intellectual world*, moral Strength/Force. — In the *Physical world*, organic Strength/Force.

Arcanum XI is depicted with the image of a young girl who, with her hands, effortless closes the mouth of a lion. It is the emblem of the strength/force communicated by faith in oneself and the innocence of life.

Remember, son of the Earth, that in order to be able to do, one must believe that one can. Advance with faith: the obstacle is a phantom. In order to become strong, one must impose silence on the weaknesses of the heart; one must study duty, which is the rule of law[205], and practice justice as if we loved it.

ARCANE XI. — LETTRE **Caïtha** (C, K) — NOMBRE 20.

C, K = 20 exprime, dans le *Monde divin*, le Principe de toute force, spirituelle ou matérielle. — Dans le *Monde intellectuel*, la Force morale. — Dans le *Monde physique*, la Force organique.

L'arcane XI est figuré par l'image d'une jeune fille qui ferme avec ses mains, sans efforts, la gueule d'un lion. C'est l'emblème de la force que communiquent la foi en soi-même et l'innocence de la vie.

Souviens-toi, fils de la Terre, que, pour pouvoir, il faut croire que l'on peut. Avance avec foi : l'obstacle est un fantôme. Pour devenir fort, il faut imposer silence aux faiblesses du cœur; il faut étudier le devoir, qui est la règle du droit, et pratiquer la justice comme si on l'aimait.

PLATEE XI   (CK = 20)   STRENGTH/FORCE   LAME XI   (CK = 20)   LA FORCE

Hieroglyphic symbolism.

A young girl effortlessly opens and closes the mouth of a lion, symbol of strength/force in itself gained through the education of the willpower and the experience of life.

Symbolisme hiéroglyphique.

Une jeune fille ouvre et ferme sans effort la gueule d'un lion, symbole de la force en soi-même acquise par l'éducation de la volonté et l'expérience de la vie.

---

[205] Literally 'la règle du droit' means "the rule of [one's] right"

SACERDOTAL SENTENCES: <u>Fear is only laziness of the will,</u>[206] <u>brave the Lion and the Lion will fear you.</u>[207] Error is only a phantom of the truth and vanishes before the courage of the strong, to believe that one can do, is power [or the ability to do]. <u>If you die for the fatherland [then] be proud, since no one is greater than you.</u>[208]

<u>Man has but one right, that of doing his duty.</u>[209]

Astral influx of Mars

SENTENCES SACERDOTALES: <u>La peur n'est qu'une paresse de la volonté,</u>[210] <u>bravez le Lion et le Lion vous craindra.</u>[211] L'erreur n'est qu'un fantôme de la vérité et s'évanouit devant le courage des forts, croire que l'on peut, c'est pouvoir. <u>Si tu meurs pour la patrie sois fier, car nul n'est plus grand que toi.</u>[212]

<u>L'homme n'a qu'un droit, celui de faire son devoir.</u>[213]

Influx astral de Mars.

---

[206] Editor's note: Compare Levi "Fear is nothing but laziness of the will, and it is for that reason that the cowards' opinion condemns [them]." from Axiom 19 in Ch. 1 of Book 2 of the *Keys to the Great Mystery*
[207] Editor's note: Compare Levi "Succeed in not being afraid [of] the lion, and the lion will fear you." from Axiom 20 in Ch. 1 of Book 2 of the *Keys to the Great Mystery*
[208] Editor's note: Compare Levi "Voluntary death from devotion is not suicide; it is the summit of willpower." from Axiom 18 in Ch. 1 of Book 2 of the *Keys to the Great Mystery*
[209] Editor's note: Compare Levi "The word GOD expresses the supreme personification of law, and consequently of duty; and if, by the word LIBERTY, one is willing to agree with us, [that it is] THE RIGHT TO DO ONE'S DUTY, [then] we (in our turn) will take it as a motto, and we shall repeat, without contradiction and without error: GOD AND LIBERTY. Since there is no liberty for man except in the order which results from the true and the good, one may say that the conquest of liberty is the great work of the human soul." from Ch. 1 of Book 2 of the *Keys to the Great Mystery*

[210] Note de l'éditeur: Comparez Levi « La peur n'est qu'une paresse de la volonté, et c'est pour cela que l'opinion flétrit les lâches. » de l'Axiome XIX du Chap. 1 du Livre II dans *La Clef des Grands Mystères*
[211] Note de l'éditeur: Comparez Levi « Arrivez à ne pas craindre le lion, et le lion vous craindra. » de l'Axiome XX du Chap. 1 du Livre II dans *La Clef des Grands Mystères*
[212] Note de l'éditeur: Comparez Levi « La mort volontaire par dévouement n'est pas un suicide; c'est l'apothéose de la volonté. » de l'Axiome XVIII du Chap. 1 du Livre II dans *La Clef des Grands Mystères*
[213] Note de l'éditeur: Comparez Levi « Le mot DIEU exprime la personnification suprême de la loi, et par conséquent du devoir; et si, par le mot LIBERTÉ, on veut entendre avec nous LE DROIT DE FAIRE SON DEVOIR, nous prendrons pour devise à notre tour, et nous répéterons sans contradiction et sans erreur : DIEU ET LA LIBERTÉ. Comme il n'y a de liberté pour l'homme que, dans l'ordre qui résulte du vrai et du bien, on peut dire que la conquête de la liberté est le grand travail de l'âme humaine. » du Chap. 1 du Livre II dans *La Clef des Grands Mystères*

ʒ

LAME XII   (L = 30)   LE SACRIFICE

ʒ

ARCANUM XII. — LETTER **Luzain** (L) — NUMBER 30.

L = 30 expresses, in the *Divine world* the revealed Law. — In the *Intellectual world*, the teaching of Duty. — In the *Physical world*, Sacrifice.

Arcanum XII is depicted with a man hanged by one foot on a gallows resting on two trees each having six branches cut off. The hands of this man are tied behind [his] back, and the fold of his arms forms the base of an overturned triangle whose head is the apex. It is the sign of violent death, suffered through a fatal accident, or for the attonement of a crime, or accepted by a heroic devotion to Truth and Justice. The twelve cut branches depict the extinction of life, the destruction of the twelve houses of the Horoscope. The upside-down triangle symbolizes a catastrophe.

Remember, son of the Earth, that devotion is a divine law of which no one is exempt; but do not expect hardly[214] anything but ingratitude from men. Hold your soul, then, ready to render its account to the Eternal, for if arcanum XII appears in your Horoscope, violent death will make its snares in your path. But if the world is waiting for your earthly life, do not expire without accepting this judgment[215] of God with resignation and without forgiving your most cruel enemies; since whoever does not forgive here will be condemned, beyond this life, to an eternal solitude.

ARCANE XII. — LETTRE **Luzain** (L) — NOMBRE 30.

L = 30 exprime, dans le *Monde divin*, la Loi révélée. — Dans le *Monde intellectuel*, l'enseignement du Devoir. — Dans le *Monde physique*, le Sacrifice.

L'arcane XII est figuré par un homme pendu par un pied à une potence qui repose sur deux arbres ayant chacun six branches coupées. Les mains de cet homme sont liées derrière le dos, et le pli de ses bras forme la base d'un triangle renversé dont sa tête est le sommet. C'est le signe de la mort violente, subie par un funeste accident, ou pour l'expiation d'un crime, ou acceptée par un héroïque dévouement à la Vérité et à la Justice. Les douze branches coupées figurent l'extinction de la vie, la destruction des douze maisons de l'Horoscope. Le triangle à sommet renversé symbolise une catastrophe.

Souviens-toi, fils de la Terre, que le dévouement est une loi divine dont nul n'est dispensé; mais n'attends guère qu'ingratitude de la part des hommes. Tiens donc ton âme toujours prête à rendre ses comptes à l'Eternel, car si l'arcane XII apparaît sur ton Horoscope, la mort violente dressera ses piéges sur ton chemin. Mais si le monde attente à ta vie terrestre, n'expire point sans accepter avec résignation cet arrêt de Dieu et sans pardonner à tes plus cruels ennemis; car quiconque ne pardonne point ici-bas sera condamné, au delà de cette vie, à une solitude éternelle.

---

[214] Literally 'guère' means "hardly, with difficulty; barely"
[215] Literally 'arrêt' means "arrest, stopping, cessation; halt, stop; break, pause, standstill; stand, end; stand off, letup; bus stop"

PLATE XII   (L = 30)   SACRIFICE   LAME XII   (L = 30)   LE SACRIFICE

Hieroglyphic symbolism.

Symbolisme hiéroglyphique.

A man hanging by one foot on a gallows supported by two trees, the twelve branches of which are cut, his hands are tied together, and let golden shekels escape, one of the legs is folded over the other.

Un homme pendu par un pied à une potence soutenue par deux arbres dont les douze branches sont coupées, ses mains sont liées et laissent échapper des sicles d'or, une des jambes est repliée sur l'autre.

The hanged man symbolizes the man who dies for [an] idea. His folded leg forms with the other a reversed triangle, which means that he dies [as a] victim of the wicked. His hands tied, dropping golden shekels, signify that ideas survive those who sacrifice themselves for them and that they will be contemplated[216] by others, which will make them emerge at the right moment. The twelve cut branches symbolize the signs of the zodiac that are constantly reborn in the course of time.

Le pendu symbolise l'homme qui meurt pour l'idée. Sa jambe repliée forme avec l'autre un triangle renversé, ce qui Veut dire qu'il meurt victime des méchants. Ses mains liées, laissant tomber des sicles d'or signifient que les idées survivent à celui qui se sacrifie pour elles et qu'elles seront recueillies par d'autres, qui les feront surgir au moment propice. Les douze branches coupées symbolisent les signes du zodiaque qui renaissent sans cesse, dans le cours des temps.

SACERDOTAL SENTENCES: To die for his faith by forgiving his enemies is to be born again eternally. The sacrifice of the body is the apotheosis[217] of the soul: which adds a page to progress [with] the sign of its blood.

SENTENCES SACERDOTALES: Mourir pour sa foi en pardonnant à ses ennemis, c'est renaître éternellement. Le sacrifice du corps est l'apothéose de l'âme : qui ajoute une page au progrès la signe de son sang.

Astral Influx of the Moon.
Cycle of Libra.

Influx astral de la Lune.
Cycle de la Balance.

---

[216] Literally 'recueillies' means "gather, collect; garner, obtain, take in; reflect, meditate, contemplate"
[217] Literally 'apothéose' means "apotheosis, elevation to high status"

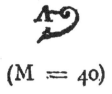

LAME XIII   (M = 40)   LA MORT

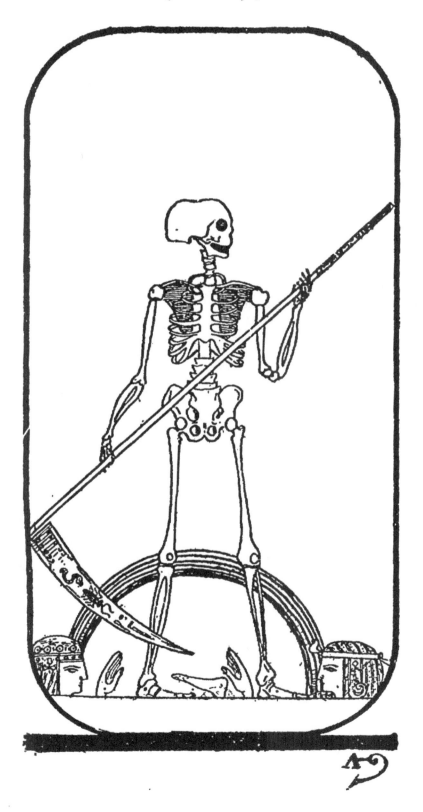

ARCANUM XII. — LETTER **Mataloth** (M) —
NUMBER 40.

M = 40 expresses, in the *Divine world* the perpetual movement of creation, destruction and renewal. — In the *Intellectual world*, the ascension of the Spirit into the divine spheres. — In the *Physical world*, natural death, that is to say, the transformation of human nature at the end of its last organic period.

Arcanum XIII is depicted by a skeleton mowing[218] heads in a meadow from where men's hands and feet emerge from all sides, as the scythe pursues its work. It is the emblem of the destruction and perpetual rebirth of all forms of Being in the domain of Time.

Remember, son of the Earth, that earthly things last a short time, and that the highest powers are mowed [down] like the grass of the field. The dissolution of your visible organs will arrive sooner than you expect; but do not dread it, for death is but the parturition[219] of another life. The universe constantly reabsorbs all that has emerged from its bosom [and] yet has not become spiritualized. But the liberation[220] of material instincts by a free and voluntary adherence of our soul to the laws of universal movement, constitutes in us the creation of a second man, of the celestial man, and begins our immortality.

ARCANE XIII. — LETTRE **Mataloth** (M) —
NOMBRE 40.

M = 40 exprime, dans le *Monde divin*, le mouvement perpétuel de création, destruction et renouvellement. — Dans le *Monde intellectuel*, l'ascension de l'Esprit dans les sphères divines. — Dans le *Monde physique*, la mort naturelle, c'est-à-dire la transformation de la nature humaine parvenue au terme de sa dernière période organique.

L'arcane XIII est figuré par un squelette fauchant des têtes dans un pré d'où sortent, de tous côtés, des mains et des pieds d'homme, à mesure que la faux poursuit son œuvre. C'est l'emblème de la destruction et de la renaissance perpétuelle de toutes les formes de l'Être dans le domaine du Temps.

Souviens-toi, fils de la Terre, que les choses terrestres durent peu de temps, et que les plus hautes puissances sont fauchées comme l'herbe des champs. La dissolution de tes organes visibles arrivera plus tôt que tu ne l'attends ; mais ne la redoute point, car la mort n'est que la parturition d'une autre vie. L'univers réabsorbe sans cesse tout ce qui, sorti de son sein, ne s'est point spiritualisé. Mais l'affranchissement des instincts matériels par une libre et volontaire adhésion de notre âme aux lois du mouvement universel, constitue en nous la création d'un second homme, de l'homme céleste, et commence notre immortalité.

---

[218] Literally 'fauchant' means "make hay, reap, mow; scythe, pick up; nip, whip; pick, bag; sneak, pinch"
[219] Literally 'parturition' means "parturition, birth"
[220] Literally 'affranchissement' means "enfranchisement, liberation; emancipation"

PLATE XIII   (M = 40)   DEATH   LAME XIII   (M = 40)   LA MORT

Hieroglyphic symbolism.

Symbolisme hiéroglyphique.

A skeleton armed with a scythe symbolizes death mowing men, whose heads, feet and hands are constantly reborn, on the horizon rises [a] rainbow, this arcana symbolizes the fictional end of the man who always reappears in his sons, nature reclaiming only organic matter. The rainbow symbolizes the immortality of the soul.

Un squelette armé d'une faux symbolise la mort fauchant les hommes, dont les têtes, les pieds et les mains renaissent sans cesse, à l'horizon se lève l'arc-en-ciel, cet arcane symbolise la fin fictive de l'homme qui renaît toujours dans ses fils, la nature ne reprenant que la matière organique. L'arc-en-ciel symbolise l'immortalité de l'âme.

SACERDOTAL SENTENCES: <u>Death is but a phantom of ignorance</u>[221] and the eyes that are closed in this world are reopened in another; the soul, part of the divine breath, is immortal. The sage does not fear death, since to die is to know. Happy [are] those who die young since they are quickly headed towards[222] the path of perfection.

SENTENCES SACERDOTALES: <u>La mort n'est qu'un fantôme de l'ignorance</u>[223] et les yeux que l'on ferme en ce monde se rouvrent dans un autre ; l'âme, parcelle du souffle divin est Immortelle. Le sage ne craint pas la mort, car mourir c'est savoir. Heureux ceux qui meurent jeunes car ils vont vite sur le chemin de la perfection.

---

[221] Editor's note: Compare Levi "Death does not exist for the sage: death is a phantom made horrible by the ignorance and weakness of the vulgar." from Ch. 20 of *Dogma of High Magic*
[222] Literally 'sur' means "on, upon; onto; over, after; toward"

[223] Note de l'éditeur: Comparez Levi « La mort n'existe pas pour le sage : la mort est un fantôme rendu horrible par l'ignorance et la faiblesse du vulgaire. » du Chap. XX du *Dogme de la Haute Magie*

LAME XIV   (N = 50)   LE SOLEIL

ARCANUM XIV. — LETTER **Naïn** (N) — NUMBER 50.

N = 50 expresses, in the *Divine world* the perpetual movement of life. — In the *Intellectual world*, the combination of ideas which create the moral life. — In the *Physical world*, the combination of the forces of Nature.

Arcanum XIV is depicted by the Genie of the Sun holding two urns, and pouring (from one into the other) the conductive[224] sap of life. It is the symbol of the combinations which constantly operate in all the kingdoms[225] of Nature.

Son of the Earth, consult your strengths/forces, not in order to retreat before your works, but in order to use obstacles, like water falling drop by drop uses the hardest stone.

PLATE XIV (N = 50) THE SUN

Hieroglyphic symbolism.

The genie of the sun transfers (from a golden vessel into a silver vessel) the elemental forces of nature, symbol of the great magical agent: the combined electric and magnetic fluid, an image of the perpetual fertilization of nature by light and the heat that is movement and life.

ARCANE XIV. — LETTRE **Naïn** (N) — NOMBRE 50.

N = 50 exprime, dans le *Monde divin*, le mouvement perpétuel de la vie. — Dans le *Monde intellectuel*, la combinaison des idées qui créent la vie morale. — Dans le *Monde physique*, la combinaison des forces de la Nature.

L'arcane XIV est figuré par le Génie du Soleil tenant deux urnes, et versant de l'une dans l'autre la séve conductrice de la vie. C'est le symbole des combinaisons qui s'opèrent sans cesse dans tous les règnes de la Nature.

Fils de la Terre, consulte tes forces, non pour reculer devant tes œuvres, mais pour user les obstacles, comme l'eau tombant goutte à goutte use la pierre la plus dure.

LAME XIV (N = 50) LE SOLEIL

Symbolisme hiéroglyphique.

Le génie du soleil transvasant d'un vase d'or dans un vase d'argent les forces élémentaires de la nature, symbole du grand agent magique : le fluide électrique et magnétique combinés, image de la fécondation perpétuelle de la nature par la lumière et la chaleur qui sont le mouvement et la vie.

---

[224] Literally 'conductrice' means "conductress; chauffeur, conductor, driver, cabby; operator"

[225] Literally 'règnes' means "reign, rule, period of time that a particular government is in control"

SACERDOTAL SENTENCES: <u>The Empire of the world is that of the Light.</u>[226] The Sun is the male of Nature and the principle of all life, it is the image of the splendor of God. Do not sow[227] precious stones before the blind, they would wound their feet and [they] would not see them.

Astral Influx of the Sun.
Cycle of the Scorpion.

SENTENCES SACERDOTALES: <u>L'Empire du monde est celui de la Lumière.</u>[228] Le Soleil est le mâle de la Nature et le principe de toute vie, il est l'image de la splendeur de Dieu. Ne sème pas de pierres précieuses devant les aveugles ils s'en blesseraient les pieds et ne les verraient pas.

Influx astral du Soleil.
Cycle du Scorpion.

---

[226] Editor's note: Compare Levi "The empire of the world, is the empire of the light." from Axiom XIV in Ch. 1 of Book 2 of the *Keys to the Great Mystery*
[227] Literally 'sème' means "sow; intersperse, scatter; spread; lose, miss"

[228] Note de l'éditeur: Comparez Levi « L'empire du monde, c'est l'empire de la lumière. » de l'Axiome XIV du Chap. 1 du Livre II dans *La Clef des Grands Mystères*

LAME XV   (X = 60)   LE THYPHON

ARCANUM XV. — LETTER **Xirôn** (X) — NUMBER 60.

X = 60 expresses, in the *Divine world*, Predestination. — In the *Intellectual world*, Mystery. — In the *Physical world*, Unexpected[229], Fatality.

Arcanum XV is depicted by Typhon, genie of catastrophes, rising from a burning chasm[230] and shaking[231] torches above the two men chained to his feet. It is the image of Fatality that bursts forth in certain lives (like the eruption of a volcano), and envelops the great as well as the small, the strong as well as the weak, the most skillful as well as [those with] the least foresight, in equality of the disaster.

Whoever you are, son of the Earth, contemplate the old oaks which defied the lightning [strike], and [also those] that the lightning [strike] broke after having respected them for more than a century. Stop believing in your wisdom and in your strength/force, if God has not permitted you to seize the key of the arcana which shackle[232] Fatality.

ARCANE XV. — LETTRE **Xirôn** (X) — NOMBRE 60.

X = 60 exprime, dans le *Monde divin*, la Prédestination. — Dans le *Monde intellectuel*, le Mystère. — Dans le *Monde physique*, l'Imprévu, la Fatalité.

L'arcane XV est figuré par Typhon, Génie des catastrophes, s'élevant d'un gouffre embrasé et secouant des torches au-dessus des deux hommes enchaînés à ses pieds. C'est l'image de la Fatalité qui éclate dans certaines vies comme l'éruption d'un volcan, et qui enveloppe les grands comme les petits, les forts comme les faibles, les plus habiles comme les moins prévoyants, dans l'égalité du désastre.

Qui que tu sois, fils de la Terre, contemple les vieux chênes qui défiaient la foudre, et que la foudre a brisés après les avoir respectés pendant plus d'un siècle. Cesse de croire à ta sagesse et à ta force, si Dieu ne t'a point permis de saisir la clef des arcanes qui enchaînent la Fatalité.

---

[229] Literally 'Imprévu' means "unforeseen, unexpected, unplanned, fortuitous"
[230] Literally 'gouffre' means "gulf, chasm, maw"
[231] Literally 'secouant' means "shake up, jolt; rock, shake; jog, jerk"
[232] Literally 'enchaînent' means "chain up, enchain, link up; concatenate, fetter; manacle, shackle"

PLATE XV   (X = 60)   TYPHON   LAME XV   (X = 60)   LE THYPHON

Hieroglyphic symbolism.

The genie of evil, of fatality and of chaos, it is represented by a hippopotamus with [the] head of [a] crocodile, with goat's feet, having the breasts of a woman and the sex [organ] of a man, a serpent comes out of the navel, which signifies that it give birth to nothing but evil, its bat wings indicate that it is the spirit of darkness. It emerges from chaos and ruins, with one hand it stirs the torch of destruction and in the other holds the scepter of division and of hatred, formed by an angle with the point at the bottom separated by a circle, the rest of the figure symbolizes the bestiality of the passions. At his feet are two men with goat's heads, symbolizing those who's vice chains and makes fall further below the beast. The horn on his nose indicates revolt against the Divine spirit and threatens heaven, their gesture indicates the supreme truth that while in evil, man can not do as much as he wills.

SACERDOTAL SENTENCES: <u>To serve evil is to serve death. A perverse willpower is the[233] beginning of suicide.[234] reason is the principle of order.[235]</u> Ignorance and error only infuse disorder into the night of chaos. Orient your life if you want to be master of your destiny, otherwise the sacred boat will capsize and you will be the prey of the Devourer.

Astral Influx of Saturn.
Cycle of Sagittarius.

---

[233] Literally 'un' means "a, an; one"
[234] Editor's note: Compare Levi "To will evil, is to will death. A perverse willpower is the beginning of suicide." from Axiom 2 in Ch. 1 of Book 2 of the *Keys to the Great Mystery*
[235] Editor's note: Compare Levi "Justice is the practice of reason." from Ch. 1 of Book 2 of the *Keys to the Great Mystery*

Symbolisme hiéroglyphique.

Le génie du mal, de la fatalité et du chaos, il est représenté par un hippopotame à tête de crocodile, à pieds de bouc, ayant les mamelles d'une femme et le sexe d'un homme, un serpent lui sort du nombril, ce qui signifie qu'il n'enfante rien que de mauvais, ses ailes de chauve-souris indiquent qu'il est l'esprit des ténèbres. Il surgit du chaos et des ruines, d'une main il agite la torche de la destruction et tient de l'autre le sceptre de la division et de la haine, formé par un angle la pointe en bas séparé par un cercle, le reste de la figure symbolise la bestialité des passions. A ses pieds sont deux hommes à tête de boucs, symbolisant ceux que le vice enchaîne et fait tomber plus bas que la bête. La corne qu'il a sur le nez indique la révolte contre l'esprit Divin et menace le ciel, leur geste indique la vérité suprême jusque dans le mal que l'homme ne peut faire autant qu'il le veut.

SENTENCES SACERDOTALES: <u>Servir le mal c'est servir la mort. Une volonté perverse est un commencement de suicide,[236] la raison est le principe de l'ordre.[237]</u> L'ignorance et l'erreur n'enfantent que le désordre dans la nuit du chaos. Oriente ta vie si tu veux être maître de ta destinée, sinon la barque sacrée chavirera et tu seras la proie de la Dévorante.

Influx astral de la Saturne.
Cycle de la Sagittaire.

---

[236] Note de l'éditeur: Comparez Levi « Vouloir le mal, c'est vouloir la mort. Une volonté perverse est un commencement de suicide. » de l'Axiome II du Chap. 1 du Livre II dans *La Clef des Grands Mystères*
[237] Note de l'éditeur: Comparez Levi « La justice, c'est la pratique de la raison. » du Chap. 1 du Livre II dans *La Clef des Grands Mystères*

LAME XVI   (0 = 70)   LA PYRAMIDE

ARCANUM XVI. — LETTER **Olélath** (O) — NUMBER 70.

O = 70 expresses, in the *Divine world* pride's punishment. — In the *Intellectual world*, the failure of the Spirit that tries to penetrate [into] the mystery of God. — In the *Physical world*, the collapses of fortune.

Arcanum XVI is depicted by a tower which lightning decapitates. A crowned man and a man without a crown are precipitated from its height with the debris of the battlements[238]. It is the symbol of the conflict of the material forces which can crush the great as well as the small, the kings as well as the subjects. It is, in fact, the emblem of rivalry, which leads (on both sides) only to a common ruin; sterilized projects, hopes that languish, aborted enterprises, ambitions struck down[239], deaths by catastrophe.

Remember, son of the Earth, that <u>every test of misfortune, accepted with resignation to the supreme Will of the Almighty, is an accomplished progression of which you will be eternally rewarded. To suffer is to work</u>[240] to free oneself from Matter, it is to re-clothe oneself with immortality.

ARCANE XVI. — LETTRE **Olélath** (O) — NOMBRE 70.

O = 70 exprime, dans le *Monde divin*, le châtiment de l'orgueil. — Dans le *Monde intellectuel*, la défaillance de l'Esprit qui tente de pénétrer le mystère de Dieu. — Dans le *Monde physique*, les écroulements de fortune.

L'arcane XVI est figuré par une tour que décapite la foudre. Un homme couronné et un homme sans couronne sont précipités de sa hauteur avec les débris des créneaux. C'est le symbole du conflit des forces matérielles qui peuvent broyer les grands comme les petits, les rois comme les sujets. C'est en core l'emblème des rivalités qui n'aboutissent, de part et d'autre, qu'à une ruine commune; des projets stérilisés, des espérances qui s'étiolent, des entreprises qui avortent, des ambitions foudroyées, des morts par catastrophe.

Souviens-toi, fils de la Terre, que <u>toute épreuve de l'infortune, acceptée avec résignation à la suprême Volonté du Tout-Puissant, est un progrès accompli dont tu seras éternellement récompensé. Souffrir, c'est travailler</u>[241] à se dégager de la Matière, c'est se revêtir d'immortalité.

---

[238] Literally 'créneaux' means "crenel, niche; gap, slot; window"
[239] Literally 'foudroyées' means "blasted, damaged as if by an explosive, stunned, struck, struck down"
[240] Editor's note: Compare Levi "To suffer is to work. A great pain suffered [or endured] is progress accomplished." from Axiom 17 in Ch. 1 of Book 2 of the *Keys to the Great Mystery*

---

[241] Note de l'éditeur: Comparez Levi « Souffrir, c'est travailler. Une grande douleur soufferte est un progrès accompli. » de l'Axiome XVII du Chap. 1 du Livre II dans *La Clef des Grands Mystères*

LAME XVI   (O = 70)   LA PYRAMIDE

Symbolisme hiéroglyphique.

Une Pyramide dont le faîte s'écroule sous l'éclair de la foudre, deux hommes dont l'un couronné, sont précipités dans le vide. This arcanum symbolizes the conflict of ill-directed forces and the collapse of human pride and of the false science: it is the spirit struck down by the astral fluid.

SACERDOTAL SENTENCES: <u>Light is a sacred fire, placed by nature at the service of the willpower; it enlightens the strong souls and strikes down the others.</u>[242] Beware of your actions and your words. Never do or say anything that is not approved of by your consciousness.

Astral Influx of Jupiter.
Cycle of Capricorn.

PLATE XVI   (O = 70)   THE PYRAMID

Hieroglyphic symbolism.

A pyramid whose ridge crumbles under the thunder of lightning, two men (one of which is crowned) are thrown into the void. Cet arcane symbolise le conflit des forces mal dirigées et l'écroulement de l'orgueil humain et de la fausse science: c'est l'esprit foudroyé par le fluide astral.

SENTENCES SACERDOTALES: <u>La lumière est un feu sacré, mis par la nature au service de la volonté ; elle éclaire les âmes fortes et foudroie les autres.</u>[243] Prends garde à tes actes et à tes paroles. Ne fais et ne dis jamais rien qui ne soit approuvé de ta conscience.

Influx astral de Jupiter.
Cycle du Capricorne.

---

[242] Editor's note: Compare Levi "The light is an electric fire placed by nature at the service of the willpower: it lights those who know how to use it, [and] it burns those who abuse it." from Axiom 13 in Ch. 1 of Book 2 of *The Key to the Great Mysteries*

[243] Note de l'éditeur: Comparez Levi « La lumière est un feu électrique mis par la nature au service de la volonté : elle éclaire ceux qui savent en user, elle brûle ceux qui en abusent. » de l'Axiome XIII du Chap. 1 du Livre II dans *La Clef des Grands Mystères*

♑

LAME XVII   (F P = 8o)   L'ÉTOILE

♑

ARCANUM XVII. — LETTER **Pilôn** (F, P) — NUMBER 80.

F, P = 80 expresses, in the *Divine world* Immortality. — In the *Intellectual world*, the interior Light that illuminates the Spirit. — In the *Physical world*, Hope.

Arcanum XVII is depicted by a flaming star, with eight rays, surrounded by seven other stars floating[244] above a naked girl who pours out[245] the universal fluids of Life, contained in two cups (one of gold, the other of silver), upon the earth. Near her, a butterfly lands on a rose. This young girl is the emblem of Hope who spreads her dew[246] on our saddest days. She is naked, in order to signify that hope remains with us when we are stripped of everything. Above this figure, the flaming star with eight rays symbolizes the revelation of Destiny, closed with seven seals which are the seven planets, represented by the seven other stars. The butterfly is the sign of the resurrection beyond the tomb.

Remember, son of the Earth, that Hope is Faith's sister. <u>In order to study the mysteries of the true Science, divest[247] yourself of your passions and of your errors, and their key will be given unto you.</u>[248] Then a ray of the divine Light will burst forth[249] from the occult Sanctuary in order to dissipate the darkness of your future and to show you the way of happiness.

---

[244] Literally 'planant' means "plane, smooth; hovering, floating"

[245] Literally 'épanche' means "unburden, outpour, free or relieve of a burden (weight, worry, etc.)"

[246] Literally 'rosée' means "dew, small drops of atmospheric moisture that form on cool surfaces (especially at night); pinkish, rose, rosaceous"

[247] Literally 'Dépouille' means "skin, strip, deprive, dispossess, dispoil, denude, comb, divest, milk"

[248] Editor's note: Compare Levi "Man, by freeing himself from his evil passions and their servitude, creates himself (in a certain way) a second time." from Ch. 1 of Book 2 of *The Key to the Great Mysteries*

[249] Literally 'jaillira' means "rear up; spurt out, gush forth, spout up; jet, fly out, spray out; squirt, flow; burst out"

ARCANE XVII. — LETTRE **Pilôn** (F, P) — NOMBRE 80.

F, P = 80 exprime, dans le *Monde divin*, l'Immortalité. — Dans le *Monde intellectuel*, la Lumière intérieure qui eclaire l'Esprit. — Dans le *Monde physique*, l'Espérance.

L'arcane XVII est figuré par une étoile flamboyante, à huit rayons, qu'entourent sept autres étoiles planant sur une jeune fille nue qui épanche sur la terre aride les fluides de la Vie universelle, contenus dans deux coupes, l'une d'or, l'autre d'argent. Près d'elle, un papillon se pose sur une rose. Cette jeune fille est l'emblème de l'Espérance qui répand sa rosée sur nos jours les plus tristes. Elle est nue, pour signifier que l'espérance nous reste quand nous sommes dépouillés de tout. Au-dessus de cette figure, l'étoile flamboyante à huit rayons symbolise l'apocalypse des Destins, fermée de sept sceaux qui sont les sept planètes, représentées par les sept autres étoiles. Le papillon est le signe de la résurrection au delà du tombeau.

Souviens-toi, fils de la Terre, que l'Espérance est sœur de la Foi. <u>Dépouille-toi de tes passions et de tes erreurs, pour étudier les mystères de la véritable Science, et leur clef te sera donnée.</u>[250] Alors un rayon de la divine Lumière jaillira du Sanctuaire occulte pour dissiper les ténèbres de ton avenir et te montrer la voie du bonheur.

---

[250] Note de l'éditeur: Comparez Levi « L'homme, en s'affranchissant des mauvaises passions et de leur servitude, se crée en quelque sorte une seconde fois lui-même. » du Chap. 1 du Livre II dans *La Clef des Grands Mystères*

Whatever happens in your life, never break the flowers of Hope, and you will [thus always be able to] pluck[251] the fruits of Faith.

Quoi qu'il advienne en ta vie, ne brise donc jamais les fleurs de l'Espérance, et tu cueilleras les fruits de la Foi.

PLATE XVII   (F P = 80)   THE STAR

LAME XVII   (F P = 80)   L'ÉTOILE

Hieroglyphic symbolism.

Symbolisme hiéroglyphique.

A young naked girl, symbolizing truth, one foot in the sea and the other on the earth, she pours[252] two cups that symbolize Goodness/Kindness[253] and Charity, the balm that relieves human ills. The sea represents the bitterness of the days of sadness, above this young girl is an eight-pointed star, double symbol of the Universe and of the Divine triad, in the center of which is found a white pyramid united to another black [pyramid which is] overturned and [they] touch each other at their bases. This is the emblem of the great occult law of magism, which is the [that of] analogy. (*What is above is like what is below*). Seven smaller stars represent the seven planetary types of man, near her [is] a flower (symbol of hope) where a moth drinks, image of adversity.

Une jeune fille nue, symbolisant vérité, un pied sur la mer et l'autre sur la terre, elle répand de deux coupes qui symbolisent la Bonté et la Charité, le baume qui soulage les maux humains. La mer représente l'amertume des jours de tristesse, au-dessus de cette jeune fille est une étoile à huit pointes, double symbole de l'Univers et de la triade Divine, au centre de laquelle se trouve une pyramide blanche unie à une autre noire renversée et se touchant par leurs bases. C'est là l'emblème de la grande loi occulte du magisme qui est l'analogie. (*Ce qui est en haut est comme ce qui est en bas*). Sept étoiles plus petites représentent les sept types planétaires de l'homme, près d'elle, une fleur, symbole de l'espérance, où s'abreuve un phalène, image de l'adversité.

SACERDOTAL SENTENCES: The man who has discovered the truth and wills to operate [with] justice breaks all obstacles. <u>Divest yourself of your vices and of your errors, you will know the true science and the key will be given unto you.</u> [254] Never break the flower of hope.

SENTENCES SACERDOTALES: L'homme qui à découvert la vérité et veut opérer la justice brise tous les obstacles. <u>Dépouille-toi de tes vices et de tes erreurs, tu connaîtras la vraie science et la clé t'en sera donnée.</u> [255] Ne brise jamais la fleur de l'espérance.

---

[251] Literally 'cueilleras' means "pick, pluck, gather; steal"
[252] Literally 'répand' means "spill, scatter; sprinkle, spray; shed"
[253] Literally 'bonté' means "kindness, goodness; gentleness, loving kindness; benignity, kind"
[254] Editor's note: Compare Levi "Man, by freeing himself from his evil passions and their servitude, creates himself (in a certain way) a second time." from Ch. 1 of Book 2 of *The Key to the Great Mysteries*

---

[255] Note de l'éditeur: Comparez Levi « L'homme, en s'affranchissant des mauvaises passions et de leur servitude, se crée en quelque sorte une seconde fois lui-même. » du Chap. 1 du Livre II dans *La Clef des Grands Mystères*

The science of numbers is the key to the movement of life which is the aspiration[256] and the respiration [of the universe]. Pity[257] is what is most divine in humanity.

Astral Influx of Mercury.

La science des nombres est la clé du mouvement de la vie qui est l'aspir et le respir. La pitié est ce qu'il y a de plus divin dans l'humanité.

Influx astral de Mercure.

---

[256] Literally 'aspir' means "inhale, aspirate; breathe, breathe in; yearn"

[257] Literally 'pitié' means "mercy, pity"

LAME XVIII   (T·S = 90)   **LA NUIT**

ARCANUM XVIII. — LETTER **Tsadi** (TS) — NUMBER 90.

TS = 90 expresses, in the *Divine world* the the abysses of the Infinite. — In the *Intellectual world*, the shadows that envelop the Spirit when it submits itself to the empire of the instincts. — In the *Physical world*, deceptions and hidden enemies.

Arcanum XVIII is depicted by a field which the half-veiled moon illuminates with a pale twilight. A tower stands on each side of a path that will lose itself in the desert horizon. In front of one of these towers is a crouching dog, and in front of the other a dog barking at the moon. Between these two animals crawls[258] a crayfish[259]. These towers symbolize the false security that does not presuppose[260] the hidden perils, [which are] more dreadful[261] than the perceived perils.

Remember, son of the Earth, that whosoever braves the unknown touches upon their [own] doom[262]. The hostile spirits (represented by the wolf [or black dog]) surround him with their traps[263]; the subservient[264] spirits (represented by the dog) hide their betrayals from him under base flatteries; and the lazy spirits (represented by the creeping crayfish) will pass without stirring to the side of one's ruin. Observe, listen, and know [how] to keep quiet.

ARCANE XVIII. — LETTRE **Tsadi** (TS) — NOMBRE 90.

TS = 90 exprime, dans le *Monde divin*, les abîmes de l'Infini. — Dans le *Monde intellectuel*, les ténèbres qui enveloppent l'Esprit quand il se soumet à l'empire des instincts. — Dans le *Monde physique*, les déceptions et les ennemis cachés.

L'arcane XVIII est figuré par un champ que la lune à demi voilée éclaire d'un pâle crépuscule. Une tour se dresse sur chaque bord d'un sentier qui va se perdre à l'horizon désert. Devant une de ces tours est un chien accroupi, et devant l'autre un chien aboyant à la lune. Entre ces deux animaux rampe une écrevisse. Ces tours symbolisent la fausse sécurité qui ne pressent point les périls cachés, plus redoutables que les périls aperçus.

Souviens-toi, fils de la Terre, que quiconque brave l'inconnu touche à sa perte. Les esprits hostiles, figurés par le loup, l'entourent de leurs embûches ; les esprits serviles, figurés par le chien, lui cachent leurs trahisons sous de basses flatteries ; et les esprits paresseux, figurés par l'écrevisse rampante, passeront sans s'émouvoir à côté de sa ruine. Observe, écoute, et sache te taire.

---

[258] Literally 'rampe' means "creep, crawl, trail"
[259] Literally 'écrevisse' means "crawfish, crayfish, freshwater crustacean which resembles a small lobster"
[260] Literally 'pressent' means "presurmise, suppose in advance, sense in advance, perceive ahead of time; forebode, approach, sense, contact"
[261] Literally 'redoutables' means "redoubtable, redoubted, dreadful, dread, formidable"
[262] Literally 'perte' means "loss; bereavement; waste, forfeit; miscarriage; ruination, perdition, doom; undoing, drain"
[263] Literally 'embûches' means "pitfall, snare"
[264] Literally 'serviles' means "servile, slavish; obsequious, subservient; menial, base"

PLATE XVIII (T S = 90) NIGHT LAME XVIII (T S = 90) LA NUIT

Hieroglyphic symbolism.

Two pyramids stand at the edge of a path, in front of them two dogs scream at the moon, below crawls a Scorpion, one of the pyramids is white and the other [is] black, which symbolizes true and false science.

The moon is the image of consciousness which must enlighten man in doubt, the two dogs are Good and Evil, and the scorpion is the emblem of Perversity, the great mystery of vice.

SACERDOTAL SENTENCES: Life is full of traps that you have to fight or avoid, but know that <u>not acting at all is almost doing evil. Inertia is cowardice of the soul.</u>[265] <u>A great pain suffered is progress accomplished.</u>[266]

Astral Influx of Venus.
Cycle of Aquarius.

Symbolisme hiéroglyphique.

Deux pyramides s'élèvent au bord d'un chemin, devant elles deux chiens qui hurlent à la lune, en bas rampe un Scorpion, une des pyramides est blanche et l'autre noire, ce qui symbolise la vraie et la fausse science.

La lune est l'image de la conscience qui doit éclairer l'homme dans le doute, les deux chiens sont le Bien et le Mal et le scorpion est l'emblème de la Perversité, le grand mystère du vice.

SENTENCES SACERDOTALES: La vie est remplie d'embûches que tu dois combattre ou éviter, mais sache que <u>ne point agir c'est presque faire le mal.</u>[267] <u>L'inertie est la lâcheté de l'âme. Une grande douleur soufferte est un progrès accompli.</u>[268]

Influx astral de Vénus.
Cycle du Verseau.

---

[265] Editor's note: Compare Levi "To do nothing, is as fatal as to do evil, but it is more cowardly." from Axiom 16 in Ch. 1 of Book 2 of the *Keys to the Great Mystery*
[266] Editor's note: Compare Levi "To suffer is to work. A great pain suffered [or endured] is progress accomplished." from Axiom 17 in Ch. 1 of Book 2 of the *Keys to the Great Mystery*

[267] Note de l'éditeur: Comparez Levi « Ne rien faire, c'est aussi funeste que de faire le mal, mais c'est plus lâche. » de l'Axiome XVI du Chap. 1 du Livre II dans *La Clef des Grands Mystères*
[268] Note de l'éditeur: Comparez Levi « Souffrir, c'est travailler. Une grande douleur soufferte est un progrès accompli. » de l'Axiome XVII du Chap. 1 du Livre II dans *La Clef des Grands Mystères*

LAME XIX $(Q = 100)$ **L'AMOUR**

ARCANUM XIX. — LETTER **Quitolath** (Q) — NUMBER 100.

Q = 100 expresses, in the *Divine world* the supreme Heaven. — In the *Intellectual world*, the sacred Truth. — In the *Physical world*, peaceful Happiness.

Arcanum XIX is depicted by a radiant sun, illuminating two little children, image of innocence, who are holding each other by the hand in the middle of a circle adorned[269] with flowers. It is the symbol of happiness promised by the simplicity of life and the moderation of desires.

Remember, son of the Earth, that the light of the Mysteries is a formidable[270] fluid, placed by Nature at the service of the Willpower. It illuminates those who know how to direct it; [and] it strikes[271] those who ignore its power or who abuse it.[272]

ARCANE XIX. — LETTRE **Quitolath** (Q) — NOMBRE 100.

Q = 100 exprime, dans le *Monde divin*, le Ciel suprême. — Dans le *Monde intellectuel*, la Vérité sacrée. — Dans le *Monde physique*, le Bonheur paisible.

L'arcane XIX est figuré par un soleil radieux, éclairant deux petits enfants, image de l'innocence, qui se tiennent par la main au milieu d'un cercle émaillé de fleurs. C'est le symbole du bonheur que promettent la simplicité de la vie et la modération des désirs.

Souviens-toi, fils de la Terre, que la lumière des Mystères est un fluide redoutable, mis par la Nature au service de la Volonté. Elle éclaire ceux qui savent la diriger; elle foudroie ceux qui ignorent son pouvoir ou qui en abusent.[273]

PLATE XIX	(Q = 100)	LOVE

LAME XIX	(Q = 100)	L'AMOUR

Hieroglyphic symbolism.

Beneath a radiant sun, a young man and a young girl hold each other by the hand in a circle of flowers; this arcanum symbolizes Love giving Happiness, the sign in the Sun is the emblem of universal generation.

Symbolisme hiéroglyphique.

Sous un soleil radieux, un jeune homme et une jeune fille se tiennent par la main, dans un cercle de fleurs; cet arcane symbolise l'Amour donnant le Bonheur, le signe dans le Soleil est l'emblème de la génération universelle.

---

[269] Literally 'émaillé' means "enamel, cover with a smooth and glossy coating (for ornament or protection)"
[270] Literally 'redoutable' means "redoubtable, redoubted, dreadful, dread, formidable"
[271] Literally 'foudroie' means "blast, lightening"
[272] Editor's note: Compare Levi "The light is an electric fire put at the service of the willpower by nature: it lights those who know how to use it, [and] it burns those who abuse it." from Axiom 13 in Ch. 1 of Book 2 of the *Keys to the Great Mystery*

---

[273] Note de l'éditeur: Comparez Levi « La lumière est un feu électrique mis par la nature au service de la volonté: elle éclaire ceux qui savent en user, elle brûle ceux qui en abusent. » de l'Axiome XIII du Chap. 1 du Livre II dans *La Clef des Grands Mystères*

SACERDOTAL SENTENCES: Love is what brings you closest to God, it is the sun of the soul and the great arcanum of life loves and gives life, but respects the woman [who is] free or slave and knows that to debase[274] women is [the same as] to prostitute your mother. Love is the attraction of complementary forces for[275] creation, it emanates directly from the Divine principle, it is eternal like Divinity[276] and must survive through the end of the worlds in order to create others!

Astral Influx of Jupiter.
Cycle of Pisces.

SENTENCES SACERDOTALES: L'amour est ce qui te rapproche le plus de Dieu, c'est le soleil de l'âme et le grand arcane de la vie, aime et donne la vie, mais respecte la femme libre ou esclave et sache qu'avilir la femme c'est prostituer ta mère. L'amour est l'attraction de forces complémentaires en vue d'une création, il émane directement du principe Divin, il est éternel comme lui et doit survivre à la fin des mondes pour en créer d'autres!

Influx astral de Jupiter.
Cycle des Poissons.

---

[274] Literally 'avilir' means "debase, depreciate, degrade"
[275] Literally 'en vue de' means "with [a] view to; in order to; against"
[276] Literally 'comme lui' means "like him, like it"

LAME XX   (R = 200)   LE RÉVEIL

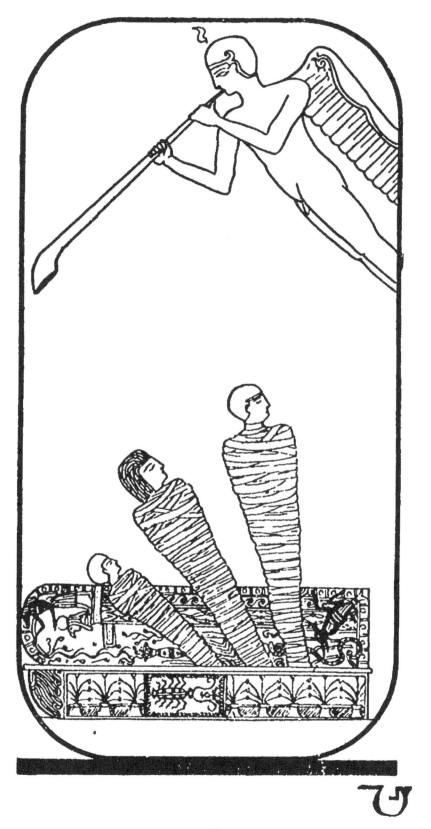

ARCANUM XX. — LETTER **Rasith** (R) — NUMBER 200.

R = 200 depicts the passage from the terrestrial life to the future life. A Genie sounds the bugle over a tomb that opens. A man, a woman, a child (collective symbol of the human trinity) rise from their funerary[277] sleep. It is the sign of change which is the end of all things, Good as well as Evil.

Remember, sons of the Earth, that every fortune is mobile, even that which seems the most stable. The ascension of the soul is the fruit which it must derive from its successive tests. Hope in suffering, but defy[278] yourself in prosperity. Do not fall asleep neither in idleness nor in oblivion. At the moment when you ignore, the wheel of Fortune will turn: you will be raised or precipitated by the Sphinx.

ARCANE XX. — LETTRE **Rasith** (R) — NOMBRE 200.

R = 200 figure le passage de la vie terrestre à la vie future. Un Génie sonne du clairon au-dessus d'un tombeau qui s'entr'ouvre. Un homme, une femme, un enfant, symbole collectif de la trinité humaine, se lèvent de leur couche funèbre. C'est le signe du changement qui est la fin de toute chose, du Bien comme du Mal.

Souviens-toi, fils de la Terre, que toute fortune est mobile, même celle qui parait le plus stable. L'ascension de l'âme est le fruit qu'elle doit tirer de ses épreuves successives. Espère dans la souffrance, mais défie-toi dans la prospérité. Ne t'endors ni dans la paresse ni dans l'oubli. Au moment que tu ignores, la roue de la Fortune va tourner : tu seras élevé ou précipité par le Sphinx.

PLATE XX   (R = 200) THE AWAKENING   LAME XX   (R = 200)   LE RÉVEIL

Hieroglyphic symbolism.

A genie sounding the trumpet above a sarcophagus from which a sort of human family emerges; which symbolizes the judgment of the dead and the awakening of the souls sleeping in error or inaction.

Symbolisme hiéroglyphique.

Un génie sonnant de la trompette au-dessus d'un sarcophage d'où sort une famille humaine ; ce qui symbolise le jugement des morts et le réveil des âmes endormies dans l'erreur ou l'inaction.

---

[277] Literally 'funèbre' means "funeral, mournful"
[278] Literally 'défie' means "challenge, defy, dare, pick a quarrel with, brave, baffle, take on, affront, confront"

SACERDOTAL SENTENCES: Know thou, son of the earth, that <u>after thy death thy fellow-citizens will judge thy life according to the use which thou hast made of thy willpower;</u>[279] always listen to the cry of your consciousness because it is the call of God. Weep over the living and not the dead; embalm the body of the sages so that they may remain as examples among you for a long time.

Astral Influx of Saturn.

SENTENCES SACERDOTALES: Sache fils de la terre qu'<u>après ta mort tes concitoyens jugeront ta vie d'après l'usage que tu auras fait de ta volonté;</u>[280] écoute toujours le cri de ta conscience car c'est l'appel de Dieu. Pleurez sur les vivants et non sur les morts; embaumez le corps des sages afin qu'ils restent longtemps comme exemples parmi vous.

Influx astral de Saturne.

---

[279] Editor's note: Compare Levi "Before declaring that a man [is] happy or unhappy, know what the direction of his willpower has made of him: Tiberius died every day at Capri, while Jesus proved his immortality and even his divinity on Calvary and upon the cross." from Axiom 22 in Ch. 1 of Book 2 of the *Keys to the Great Mystery*

[280] Note de l'éditeur: Comparez Levi « Avant de déclarer un homme heureux ou malheureux, sachez ce que l'a fait la direction de sa volonté : Tibère mourait tous les jours à Caprée, tandis que Jésus prouvait son immortalité et sa divinité même sur le Calvaire et sur la croix. » de l'Axiome XXII du Chap. 1 du Livre II dans *La Clef des Grands Mystères*

LAMB XXI (S = 300) L'ATHÉE

ARCANUM 0 [or XXI]. — LETTER **Sichen** (S) — NUMBER 300.

ARCANE 0 [ou XXI]. — LETTRE **Sichen** (S) — NOMBRE 300.

S = 300 depicts the punishment[281] which follows every fault. You see here a blind man loaded with a full satchel [282], and who is going to collide[283] with a broken obelisk, upon which rests[284] a crocodile with gaping jaws. This blind man is the symbol of the man who became the slave of Matter. His bag is full of his errors and of his faults. The broken obelisk is the ruin of his works; the crocodile is the emblem of a deadly[285] fatality, and of the inevitable Atonement.

S = 300 figure le châtiment qui suit toute faute. Tu vois ici un aveugle chargé d'une besace pleine, et qui va se heurter contre un obélisque brisé, sur lequel se pose en arrêt un crocodile à gueule béante. Cet aveugle est le symbole de l'homme qui s'est fait l'esclave de la Matière. Sa besace est remplie de ses erreurs et de ses fautes. L'obélisque brisé figure la ruine de ses œuvres; le crocodile est l'emblème d'une implacable fatalité, et de l'inévitable Expiation.

PLATE XXI   (S = 300)   THE ATHEIST   LAME XXI   (S = 300)   L'ATHÉE

Hieroglyphic symbolism.

Symbolisme hiéroglyphique.

A blind man, wearing a satchel, [with] a staff in his hand, advances towards a broken obelisk behind which a crocodile is waiting with [an] open mouth; this arcanum is the symbol of the Atheist who does not see the divine light, he carries the weight of his errors and of his faults, the staff can not serve him [in order] to guide himself and he goes into the void depicted by the crocodile, the broken obelisk represents the ruin of his works. *The astronomical figure of the Eclipse, symbolizes Doubt erasing[286] Faith.*

Un homme aveugle portant une besace, un bâton à la main, s'avance vers un obélisque brisé, derrière lequel attend, la gueule ouverte, un crocodile ; cet arcane est le symbole de l'Athée qui ne voit pas la lumière divine, il porte le poids de ses erreurs et de ses fautes, le bâton ne peut lui servir à se guider et il va au néant figuré par le crocodile, l'obélisque brisé représente la ruine de ses œuvres. *La figure astronomique de l'Eclipse, symbolise le Doute effaçant la Foi.*

---

[281] Literally 'châtiment' means "punishment, retribution, chastisement, corporal punishment"

[282] Literally 'besace' means "beggar's bag, wallet"

[283] Literally 'heurter' means "strike, hit, knock, jostle, collide with, bang into, bump, ram, stub, offend"

[284] Literally 'se pose' means "land, settle, put down, rest, sit, arise"

[285] Literally 'implacable' means "implacable, relentless, merciless; irreconcilable, remorseless; unrelenting, deadly"

[286] Literally 'effaçant' means "obliterate, efface, erase; delete, deface; extinguish; scratch, scrub"

SACERDOTAL SENTENCES: The starry sky is the book of universal life; whosoever refuses to read it, blinds themselves. The Atheist creates the fatality that becomes his punishment. If you do not believe in anything, you are but a living dead.

SENTENCES SACERDOTALES: Le ciel étoile est le livre de la vie universelle ; qui refuse d'y lire, s'aveugle soi-même. L'Athée crée la fatalité qui devient son châtiment. Si tu ne crois à rien, tu n'es qu'un mort vivant.

𝕷

LAME XXII　　　(T = 400)　　　LA COURONNE

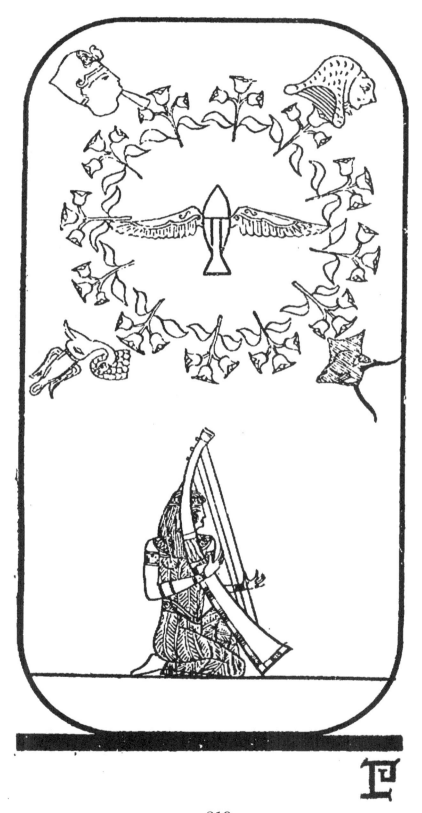

ARCANUM XXI [or XXII]. — LETTER **Thoth** (T) — NUMBER 400.

This supreme Arcanum of Magism is depicted by a crown of gold roses, surrounding a star and placed in a circle around which a man's head, a bull's head, a lion's head and an eagle's head. It is the sign which the Magus decorates himself who has reached the highest degree of initiation, and thereby placed in possession of a power whose ascensional degrees have no other limits than those of his intelligence [or intelligent understanding] and his wisdom.

Remember, son of the Earth, that the empire of the World belongs to the empire of the Light,[287] and that the empire of the Light is the throne that God reserves for the sanctified Willpower. Happiness is, for the Magus, the fruit of the science of Good and of Evil; but God only permits this imperishable fruit to be plucked by a man [who has become a] sufficient master of himself in order to approach it without coveting it.

ARCANE XXI [ou XXII]. — LETTRE **Thoth** (T) — NOMBRE 400.

Cet Arcane suprême du Magisme est figuré par une couronne de roses d'or, entourant une étoile et placée dans un cercle au tour duquel se rangent, à égale distance, une tête d'homme, une tête de taureau, une tête de lion et une tête d'aigle. C'est le signe dont se décore le Mage parvenu au plus haut degré de l'initiation, et mis par elle en possession d'un pouvoir dont les degrés ascensionnels n'ont d'autres limites que celles de son intelligence et de sa sagesse.

Souviens-toi, fils de la Terre, que l'empire du Monde appartient à l'empire de la Lumière,[288] et que l'empire de la Lumière est le trône que Dieu réserve à la Volonté sanctifiée. Le Bonheur est, pour le Mage, le fruit de la science du Bien et du Mal; mais Dieu ne permet de cueillir ce fruit impérissable qu'à l'homme assez maître de lui-même pour s'en approcher sans le convoiter.

PLATE XXII   (T = 400)   THE CROWN

Hieroglyphic symbolism.

A lotus crown having at the four corners a head: of [a] lion, of [a] man, of [an] eagle and of [a] bull, depicting the four winds of the spirit, in the middle [is] the primitive lingham (the supreme arcanum of the universal generation of the three worlds). The absolute in the infinite and the conjunction of the sexes.

LAME XXII   (T = 400)   LA COURONNE

Symbolisme hiéroglyphique.

Une couronne de lotus ayant aux quatre angles, une tête: de lion, d'homme, d'aigle et de taureau, figurant les quatre vents de l'esprit, au milieu, le lingham primitif, arcane suprême de la génération universelle des trois mondes. L'absolu dans l'infini et la conjonction des sexes.

---

[287] Editor's note: Compare Levi "The empire of the world, is the empire of the light." from Axiom 14 in Ch. 1 of Book 2 of the *Keys to the Great Mystery*

[288] Note de l'éditeur: Comparez Levi « L'empire du monde, c'est l'empire de la lumière. » de l'Axiome XIV du Chap. 1 du Livre II dans *La Clef des Grands Mystères*

The crown symbolizes the magic chain of beings, of things and of ideas; below, a young girl represents religion playing a three-stringed harp, image of the threefold divine harmony of man (soul, spirit, [and] body). It is also the symbol of primordial androgyny that the Kabalah translates with the latin formula: *Coagula et Solve.*

SACERDOTAL SENTENCES: God is the unique principle and the harmonic whole of the hidden forces of nature. The keys to the divine mystery of the science of Good and of Evil belong to the sage who has always had them beneath his gaze, [yet] never coveting them. Remember that the Right [angle] is for man, but that the Curve is for God, whosoever is born of God, returns to God.

Astral Influx of the Sun.

La couronne symbolise la chaîne magiquèdes êtres, des choses et des idées ; en bas, une jeune fille représente la religion jouant d'une harpe à trois cordes, image de la triple harmonie divine de l'homme (l'âme, l'esprit. le, corps). C'est aussi le symbole de l'androgyne primordial que la Kabbale traduit par la formule latine: *Coagula et Solve.*

SENTENCES SACERDOTALES: Dieu est le principe unique et l'ensemble harmonique des forces cachées de la nature. Les clés du mystère divin de la science du Bien et du Mal appartiennent au sage qui a su les regarder toujours, sans les convoiter jamais. Souviens-toi que la Droite est à l'homme, mais que la Courbe est à Dieu, qui né de Dieu, rentre en Dieu.

Influx astral du Soleil.

[Conclusion][289]

In summary, the doctrine of the Magi, emitted by the sentences which have just been read, and which are unfortunately incomplete, is reduced to the education of the human willpower and to its action upon the hidden forces of nature...

NOTE. — The realization of these predictions can be modified according to the willpower of statesmen[290], by virtue of the magical axiom: *Astra inclinant, non dominant et voluntati fatum cedat.[291]*

Let us now summarize these 22 Arcana with 22 titles in which the symbols are expressed.

The 1st is called *the Magus*, and symbolizes *the Willpower.*

The 2nd is called *the Door of the occult Sanctuary*, and symbolizes *the Science* which must guide the willpower.

The 3rd is called *Isis-Urania*, and symbolizes *the Action* which must manifest [as] willpower united with the science.

The 4th is called *the cubic Stone*, and symbolizes *the Realization* of human acts, the work accomplished.

The 5th is called *the Master of the Arcana*, and symbolizes *the Inspiration* that man receives from occult Powers.

The 6th is called *the Two Roads[292]*, and symbolizes *the Test*, to which all willpower is subjected in the presence of Good and Evil.

---

[289] The first two paragraphs come from Falconnier (1896), the rest is from Christian (1870).
[290] Literally 'hommes d'Etats' means "men of States"
[291] Latin meaning something like "The stars incline, [but] do not rule [absolutely] and fate yields to willpower.
[292] Literally 'Routes' means "road, way; course, route; path, pathway"

[Conclusion][293]

En résumé, la doctrine des Mages émise par les sentences que l'on vient de lire et qui sont malheusement incomplètes, se réduit à l'éducation de la volonté humaine et sa mise en action sur les forces cachées de la nature...

NOTA.— La réalisation de ces pronostics peut se modifier selon la volonté des hommes d'Etats, en vertu de l'axiome magique : *Astra inclinant, non dominant et voluntati fatum cedat.*

Résumons maintenant ces 22 Arcanes par 22 titres qui en expriment les symboles.

Le 1er se nomme *le Mage*, et symbolise *la Volonté.*

Le 2e se nomme *la Porte du Sanctuaire occulte*, et symbolise *la Science* qui doit guider la volonté.

Le 3e se nomme *Isis-Uranie*, et symbolise *l'Action* qui doit manifester la volonté unie à la science.

Le 4e se nomme *la Pierre cubique*, et symbolise *la Réalisation* des actes humains, l'œuvre accomplie.

Le 5e se nomme *le Maître des Arcanes*, et symbolise *l'Inspiration* que l'homme reçoit des Puissances occultes.

Le 6e se nomme *les Deux Routes*, et symbolise *l'Épreuve*, à laquelle est soumise toute volonté en présence du Bien et du Mal.

---

[293] Les deux premiers paragraphes viennent de Falconnier (1896), le reste est de Christian (1870).

The 7th is *the Chariot of Osiris*, and symbolizes *Victory*, that is to say, the choice of Good which is the fruit of truth and of justice.

The 8th is called *Themis*[294], and symbolizes *Equilibrium*, by analogy with the scale which is the attribute of Justice.

The 9th is called *the veiled Lamp*, and symbolizes *the Prudence* which maintains equilibrium.

The 10th is called *the Sphinx*, and symbolizes *Fortune*, happy or unhappy, which accompanies every life.

The 11th is called *the tamed Lion*, and symbolizes *the Force/Strength*, which every man is called to conquer through the development of his intellectual and moral faculties.

The 12th is called *the Sacrifice*, and symbolizes violent death.

The 13th is called *the Falx*[295], and symbolizes the *Transformation* of man, that is to say, his passage to the future life through natural death.

The 14th is called *the solar Genie*, and symbolizes *the Initiative* of man through willpower, science and action combined [together].

The 15th is called *Typhon*, and symbolizes *Fate/Fatality*[296], which strikes us with unexpected blows.

The 16th is called *the fulminated Tower*, and symbolizes *the Ruin* beneath every aspect that presents this idea.

Le 7e se nomme *le Char d'Osiris*, et symbolise *la Victoire*, c'est-à-dire le choix du Bien qui est le fruit de la vérité et de la justice.

Le 8e se nomme *Thémis*, et symbolise *l'Equilibre*, par analogie avec la balance qui est l'attribut de la Justice.

Le 9e se nomme *la Lampe voilée*, et symbolise *la Prudence* qui maintient l'équilibre.

Le 10e se nomme *le Sphinx*, et symbolise *la Fortune*, heureuse ou malheureuse, qui accompagne toute vie.

Le 11e se nomme *le Lion dompté*, et symbolise *la Force*, que tout homme est appelé à conquérir par le développement de ses facultés intellectuelles et morales.

Le 12e se nomme *le Sacrifice*, et symbolise la mort violente.

Le 13e se nomme *la Faulx*, et symbolise *la Transformation* de l'homme, c'est-à-dire son passage à la vie future par la mort naturelle.

Le 14e se nomme *le Génie solaire*, et symbolise *l'Initiative* de l'homme par la volonté, la science et l'action combinées.

Le 15e se nomme *Typhon*, et symbolise *la Fatalité*, qui nous frappe de coups imprévus.

Le 16e se nomme *la Tour foudroyée*, et symbolise *la Ruine* sous tous les aspects qui présente cette idée.

---

[294] Literally 'Thémis' means "Themis (in Greek mythology, Themis is goddess of law and order, daughter of Uranus and Gaia)"
[295] Literally 'Faulx' means "falx, a reaping-hook (such as the talons of birds of prey), sickle"
[296] Literally 'Fatalité,' means "destiny, fatality, fate"

The 17th is called *the Star of the Magi*, and symbolizes *the Hope* which leads to salvation through faith.

The 18th is called *Twilight*, and symbolizes *the Deceptions* which teach us our weakness.

The 19th is called *the resplendent Light*, and symbolizes earthly *Happiness*.

The 20th is called *the Awakening of the Dead*, and symbolizes *the Renewal* that changes Good into Evil, or Evil into Good, in the series of tests imposed on any career.

The 21st is called *the Crocodile*, and symbolizes *the Atonement* of errors or of voluntary faults.

The 22nd is called *the Crown of the Magi* and symbolizes *the Reward* awarded to every man who has fulfilled his mission on the earth by reflecting therein some traits of the image of God.

By linking one to the other and the 22 significations which emanate from these symbols successively, their collection summarizes in these terms the synthesis of Magism:

The human *Willpower* (I), enlightened by the *Science* (II) and manifested through *Action* (III), creates the *Realization* (IV) of a power which it [either] uses or abuses, according to its good or bad *Inspiration* (V), in the circle which is traced for him by the laws of the universal order. — After having overcome the *Test* (VI), which is imposed on it by divine Wisdom, it enters, through its *Victory* (VII), into possession of the work which it has created, and, constituting its *Equilibrium* (VIII) upon the axis of *Prudence* (IX), it dominates the oscillations of *Fortune* (X).

Le 17e se nomme *l'Etoile des Mages*, et symbolise *l'Espérance*, qui mène au salut par la foi.

Le 18e se nomme *le Crépuscule*, et symbolise *les Déceptions*, qui nous enseignent notre faiblesse.

Le 19e se nomme *la Lumière resplendissante*, et symbolise *le Bonheur* terrestre.

Le 20e se nomme *le Réveil des Morts*, et symbolise *le Renouvellement*, qui change le Bien en Mal, ou le Mal en Bien, dans la série des épreuves imposées à toute carrière.

Le 21e se nomme *le Crocodile*, et symbolise *l'Expiation* des erreurs ou des fautes volontaires.

Le 22e se nomme *la Couronne des Mages*, et symbolise *la Récompense* décernée à tout homme qui a rempli sa mission sur la terre en y reflétant quelques traits de l'image de Dieu.

En reliant l'une à l'autre et successivement les 22 signifiances qui émanent de ces symboles, leur ensemble résume en ces termes la synthèse du Magisme:

La *Volonté* humaine (I), éclairée par la *Science* (II) et manifestée par l'*Action* (III), crée la *Réalisation* (IV) d'un pouvoir dont elle use ou abuse, selon sa bonne ou mauvaise *Inspiration* (V), dans le cercle que lui tracent les lois de l'ordre universel. — Après avoir surmonté l'*Épreuve* (VI), qui lui est imposée par la Sagesse divine, elle entre, par sa *Victoire* (VII), en possession de l'oeuvre qu'elle a créée, et, constituant son *Équilibre* (VIII) sur l'axe de la *Prudence* (IX), elle domine les oscillations de la *Fortune* (X).

— The *Strength / Force* (XI) of man, sanctified through *Sacrifice* (XII), which is the voluntary offering of oneself upon the altar of devotion or expiation, [allow him to] triumph over Death; and his divine *Transformation* (XIII) raises him, beyond the grave, into the serene regions of infinite progress, opposing the reality of an immortal *Initiative* (XIV) to the eternal lie of *Fate* (XV). — The course of Time is measured by ruins; but, beyond each *Ruin* (XVI), one sees [either] the dawn of *Hope* (XVII) reappearing or the twilight of the *Deceptions* (XVIII). Man always aspires to that which escapes him, and the sun of *Happiness* (XIX) only rises for him behind the tomb, after the *Renewal* (XX) of his being through death which opens a higher sphere to him of willpower, intelligence [or intelligent understand] and action. — Every willpower which allows itself to be governed by the instincts of the body is an abdication of liberty and commits itself to the *Atonement* (0 [or XXI]) of its error or fault. — Every willpower, on the contrary, which unites with God in order to manifest the Truth and to work[297] Justice, enters, in this life, into participation with the divine power over beings and things, eternal *Reward* (XXI [or XXII]) of emancipated Spirits.

— La *Force* (XI) de l'homme, sanctifiée par le *Sacrifice* (XII), qui est l'offrande volontaire de soi-même sur l'autel du dévouement ou de l'expiation, triomphe de la Mort; et sa divine *Transformation* (XIII) l'élevant, outre-tombe, dans les régions sereines d'un progrès infini, oppose la réalité d'une immortelle *Initiative* (XIV) à l'éternel mensonge de la *Fatalité* (XV). — Le cours du Temps se mesure par des ruines; mais, au delà de chaque *Ruine* (XVI), on voit reparaître l'aurore de l'*Espérance* (XVII) ou le crépuscule des *Déceptions* (XVIII). L'homme aspire sans cesse à ce qui lui échappe, et le soleil du *Bonheur* (XIX) ne se lève pour lui que derrière la tombe, après le *Renouvellement* (XX) de son être par la mort qui lui ouvre une sphère plus haute de volonté, d'intelligence et d'action. — Toute volonté qui se laisse gouverner par les instincts du corps est une abdication de la liberté et se voue à l'*Expiation* (0 [ou XXI]) de son erreur ou de sa faute. — Toute volonté, au contraire, qui s'unit à Dieu pour manifester la Vérité et opérer la Justice, entre, dès cette vie, en participation de la puissance divine sur les êtres et les choses, *Récompense* (XXI [ou XXII]) éternelle des Esprits affranchis.

---

[297] Literally 'opérer' means "operate, carry out, run, effectuate"

Extract from
The Rosecross Magazine
Berlin, [June or July] of 1935

Extracto del
Revista Rosacruz
Bogotá, [Junio o Julio] de 1.935

Equilibrium

A professor at the University of Berlin has published a book entitled "De-Influence [or De-Suggestion]"; he says that we suffer [from] all of the suggestions that we have received in the past and [he] believes that our whole life is no more than an influenced[298] expression.

For him, in School, the lessons are merely [the] suggestion of the teacher, and the example of our parents and those around us [are] merely influencing[299] us in a given direction.

With that, says the author, we stop, we reduce[300] the expression of our inner potentialities and we shut ourselves off to our Subconsciousness.

The motto of the professor from berlin is thus: [LET US] DE-INFLUENCE OURSELVES; and in order to [do] this he gives a series of practices.

The arguments of this new school [of thought are] not without[301] reason, [especially] if we remember our Spiritualist Schools' way of being.

Theosophists, for example, have taken their teachings from India and seek[302] to imitate the Hindus in the renunciation of the personality.

El Equilibrio

Un profesor de la Universidad de Berlín ha publicado un libro titulado "La Desugestión"; en él dice que sufrimos todos de las sugestiones que recibimos en el pasado y cree que toda nuestra vida no resulta más que de una expresión sugestionada.

Para él en la Escuela, las lecciones son por mera sugestión del maestro, y el ejemplo de nuestros padres y de los que nos rodean no hace más que sugestionarnos en un sentido dado.

Con eso, dice el autor, frenamos, apocamos la expresión de nuestras potencialidades internas y hacemos callar a nuestro Subconsciente.

La divisa del profesor berlinés es, pues: DESUGESTIONARNOS; y para ello da una serie de prácticas.

No carecen de razón los argumentos de esa nueva escuela, si recordamos el modo de ser de nuestras Escuelas Espiritualistas.

Los teósofos, por ejemplo, han tomado sus enseñanzas de la India, y pretenden imitar a los indúes en la renunciación de la personalidad.

---

[298] Literally 'sugestionada' means "influenced, impacted"
[299] Literally 'sugestionarnos' means "influence; will"
[300] Literally 'apocamos' means "reduce, diminish, decrease, make smaller; create boundaries, limit, constrict (figurative)"
[301] Literally 'carecen' means "lack, be short of"
[302] Literally 'pretenden' means "purport, pretend; profess, allege, claim"

Kill[303] desire, is the main rule for the buddhists, despise[304] the gifts of the earth and [only have] ambition [for] things divine.

The Bible says it will be easier for a camel to pass through the eye of a needle than for a rich man to enter into the kingdom of Heaven.

The Nazarene, [in] all humility, shared with the less fortunate[305]; and those who called themselves disciples of him, as many religious orders take [a] vow of poverty (even if as a society, many of them handle millions) and pretend to comply with the advice of the Master, who asked his Apostles to leave everything they owned and only follow Him.

From the ideological point of view, this is beautiful and one imagines being very well secluded[306] in the countryside, without material concerns, without being [a] slave[307] to vile[308] money.

Most philosophers agree that money and wealth are the worst calamity in the world and one needs to educate oneself in order to be above the attractions of money.

From this point of view, my disciples are right, in repudiating[309] my advice, to offer my help in the conquest of material goods and to give them instructions on the means of educating the personality and putting them onto this path, [having an] advantage in the struggle for life.

Matar el deseo, es la regla principal de los budistas, despreciar los bienes de la tierra y ambicionar las cosas divinas.

La Biblia dice que será más fácil que un camello pase por el ojo de una aguja que un rico éntre al reino de los Cielos.

El Nazareno, todo humildad, compartía con los desheredados de la fortuna; y los que se dicen discípulos de él, como muchas órdenes religiosas, hacen voto de pobreza (aun cuando como sociedad, casi todas ellas manejan millones), pretendiendo así cumplir el consejo del Maestro, que pedía a sus Apóstoles que abandonaran todo lo que poseían y lo siguieran solo a El.

Desde el punto de vista ideológico, aquello es hermoso y se imagina estar uno muy bien recluido en el campo, sin preocupaciones materiales, sin necesidad de estar sujeto al vil dinero.

La mayoría de los filósofos están de acuerdo en que el dinero y las riquezas son la peor calamidad del mundo y que hay que educarse para estar por encima de los atractivos del dinero.

Desde este punto de vista, tienen razón mis discípulos, en repudiar mis consejos, al ofrecerles mi ayuda en la conquista de los bienes materiales y darles instrucciones sobre el medio de educar la personalidad y ponerlos por este medio, en ventaja en la lucha por la vida.

---

[303] Literally 'Matar' means "kill, murder; slaughter; homicide; butcher; postmark; destroy; file, smooth with a file; cancel; diminish; upset"

[304] Literally 'despreciar' means "despise, loathe; have contempt for, scorn, look down on"

[305] Literally 'los desheredados de la fortuna' means "the disinherited of the fortune"

[306] Literally 'recluido' means "confined; seclude, isolate, place in solitude; withdraw into solitude, isolate oneself; separate, make private, set apart"

[307] Literally 'sujeto' means "subject; thing; type; lot; fellow; secure, fasten; hold down, keep down; clip; anchor"

[308] Literally 'vil' means "low, vile, despicable, contemptible"

[309] Literally 'repudiar' means "repudiate, disavow; disown"

Now I will explain my point of view, leaving the disciples the liberty to follow the route that suits them... because our law is: "Do what you will[310], but remember that everything you do, you'll have to answer for", and "the Law of Consequence requires[311] your responsibility".

"Do what you will" means, 'do what your true SELF wills, your inner or Divine BEING', and that Being means, first of all, Equilibrium[312], [and] Harmony.

If, in order to achieve this equilibrium, money hinders[313] you, [then] throw it away; if, in order to obtain[314] harmony comfort bothers[315] you, [then] abandon it.

In [such a] way that this is a matter [specific] to each person[316], [it] is an issue that one must fix[317] oneself and not follow anyone [else's] suggestion, it comes from wherever it comes from.

In all times, the [members of the] Rose-cross [fraternity] were rich and lived in comfort.

Let us remember with respect to Cagliostro, or before him, Raymond Lullius, the musician Wagner, the poet Goethe, or the incomparable Nostradamus.

Ahora voy a exponer mi punto de vista, dejando al discípulo en libertad de seguir la ruta que le convenga... ya que nuestra ley es: "Haz lo que quieras, pero no olvides que de todo cuanto hagas, tendrás que dar cuenta", y "la Ley de Consecuencia te exigirá responsabilidad".

"Haz lo que quieras" quiere decir, haz lo que quiere tu verdadero SER[318], tu SER interno o Divino[319], y ese Ser[320] quiere decir Equilibrio, Armonía, ante todo.

Si para lograr ese equilibrio te estorba el dinero, arrójalo lejos de ti; si para conseguir armonía te molesta el confort, abandónalo.

De manera que esto es cuestión de cada cual, es un asunto que hay que solucionarlo consigo mismo y no seguir ninguna sugestión, venga ella de donde viniere.

Los Rosacruz en todos los tiempos fueron hombres ricos y vivían con comodidad.

Recordemos al respecto a Cagliostro, o anterior a él, a Raimundo Lulio, al músico Wagner, al poeta Goethe, o al incomparable Nostradamus.

---

[310] Literally 'quieras' means "want, will; wish; like; feel like"

[311] Literally 'exigirá' means "exact, demand, require; levy; need, necessitate; beg"

[312] Literally 'Equilibrio' means "equilibrium, balance, state in which all forces act in perfect opposition and cancel the effects of one another; equilibration, act of bringing into balance; poise"

[313] Literally 'estorba' means "obstruct, block; interfere; hinder, impede; thwart"

[314] Literally 'conseguir' means "obtain, acquire, come by; procure, secure; earn, achieve"

[315] Literally 'molesta' means "annoy, bother, harass, irritate; irksome, frustrating; tiresome"

[316] Literally 'de cada cual' means "of each, of each other, of everyone, of each person, of each individual"

[317] Literally 'solucionarlo' means "solve, find a solution, remove; sort out"

---

[318] Originalmente "verdadero YO"

[319] Originalmente "tu EGO interno o Divino"

[320] Originalmente "Ego"

All of them had wealth, but, and this is essential, none of them were **slaves of money**.

Wagner could not work if he was not in a comfortable room, because he needed luxury in order to get in tune with his subconscious.

Let us look at three different examples of imbalance:

First. **A businessman**[321], who works without seeing what collects money, nor other concerns [about] what make great profits.

He does not care [about] Science nor Art.

He feels contempt, antipathy[322], for those[323] who are devoted to books, he sees them [as being] beneath him; he does not conceive that life has another object [than] to make money, lots of money.

The more he earns, the more he wants, and a dreadful uneasiness overtakes him.

And every time he thinks about losing some of the acquired capital, **he sweats with fear**.

This is an imbalance, he is [going to] die unhappy with [a] hammer in [his] hand.

The second example[324] is **the library or laboratory man**, he believes he can fix everything with science; for him the businessman is a despicable ignorant [person], who walks[325] the wrong path in life.

Money is annoying, and every time [others] talk business, he feels offended.

Todos ellos poseían fortuna, pero, y esto es lo esencial, ninguno de ellos fue **esclavo del dinero**.

Wagner no podía trabajar si no estaba en una habitación confortable, pues él requería el lujo para ponerse a tono con su subconsciente.

Fijémonos en tres tipos distintos como ejemplo de desequilibrio:

Primero. **Un comerciante**, que trabaja sin más mira que reunir el dinero, ni otra inquietud que lograr grandes ganancias.

A él no le importa la Ciencia ni el Arte.

Para los hombres que se dedican a los libros siente desprecio, antipatía, los ve inferiores a él; no concibe que la vida tenga otro objeto que ganar dinero, mucho dinero.

Mientras más gana, más quiere, y se apodera de él una intranquilidad espantosa.

Y cada vez que piensa que puede perder algo del capital adquirido, **suda de miedo**.

Es un desequilibrado, es un infeliz que muere con el martillo en la mano.

El segundo tipo es el **hombre de biblioteca o de laboratorio**, que cree poder solucionar todo con la ciencia; para él el hombre de negocios, es un ignorante despreciable, que ha equivocado el camino de la vida.

El dinero le es molesto, y cada vez que le hablan de negocios se siente ofendido.

---

[321] Literally 'comerciante' means "trader, businessman, merchant, dealer"

[322] Literally 'antipatía' means "antipathy, dislike; unpleasantness"

[323] Literally 'los hombres' means "the men"

[324] Literally 'tipo' means "type, kind; sort; figure; print; character; disposition; genus; fellow, guy"

[325] Literally 'ha' means "have, possess; get; live"

He hoards[326] intellectual treasures.

The more he studies, the more he is convinced of their inability to solve the proposed problems.

He is full of other's ideas.

For some time he likes[327] an author, whom he [later] rejects[328] after finding another which likes more, but the result is the same: the internal restlessness of [an] unsatisfied man.

He reaches old age, undermined[329] by arteriosclerosis, his sight is no longer with him in order to read, and he renounces not having been occupied by something practical and not having gathered some capital.

The third example[330] is the **artist** or mystic, who lives in a hypothetical Nirvana, meditating and praying without hearing the voice of Science, without comparing issues of material life.

There will come a day when [this artist or mystic] will feel an immense void, and will recognize themselves as unilaterally imbalanced, [as someone] who has not managed to shake Heaven with their routine prayers.

These are three examples, different in their way of being, and yet similar in the end.

All three are imbalanced.

El acapara tesoros intelectuales.

Mientras más estudia, más se convence de su impotencia para resolver los problemas propuestos.

Se llena de ideas ajenas.

Por algún tiempo le satisface un autor, a quien repudia después al encontrar con otro que le gusta más, pero el resultado es la misma intranquilidad interna del hombre insatisfecho.

Llega a la vejez, minado por la arterieesclerosis, la vista ya no le acompaña para leer, y reniega de no haberse ocupado en algo práctico y de no haber reunido algún capital.

El tercer tipo es el del **artista** o místico, que vive en un Nirvana hipotético, meditando y orando sin escuchar la voz de la Ciencia, sin compartir los asuntos de la vida material.

Llegará un día, en que sentirá un inmenso vacío, y se reconocerá como un unilateral desequilibrado, que no logró conmover al Cielo con sus oraciones rutinarias.

Tres tipos, son estos, distintos por su modo de ser, y sin embargo, similares en la finalidad.

Los tres son desequilibrados.

---

[326] Literally 'acapara' means "monopolize, exercise exclusive control of a commodity or service in a particular market; hoard; overstock"
[327] Literally 'satisface' means "meet; satisfy, gratify; answer; indulge; provide; settle"
[328] Literally 'repudia' means "repudiate, disavow; disown"
[329] Literally 'minado' means "mine, attack; undermine"
[330] Literally 'tipos' means "type, kind; sort; figure; print; character; disposition; genus; fellow, guy"

On one of the ancient Temples of Initiation, I saw this sentence: "Pray in your oratory[331] and work in your laboratory", which translates into [these] vulgar phrases: "God helps those who help themselves".

The key, then, is to bring into balance these three states: material, intellectual and spiritual, and this certainly constitutes the goal[332] [of the] Rose Cross [fraternity].

All our efforts have no other objective than to gain[333] happiness, and we do not get it if we do not obtain liberty in all its aspects.

Let us liberate ourselves from others and from ourselves.

Let us liberate ourselves from the influences [or suggestions] of the environment, [let us] conquer our own individuality and [make] ourselves independent.

Let us be practical, we must not forget that we must take things as they are and not as we would like them to be.

We live in a medium[334], in a society where everything is struggling competitively, and unfortunately the basis of individual liberty is in economic independence.

It is sad, but the fact is no less true, that if we are surrounded by misery and poverty, that is to say, in a negative environment, [then] we can not put ourselves in a receptive state for superior things.

---

[331] Literally 'oratorio' means "oratory (a place of prayer, as a small chapel or a room for private devotions)"

[332] Literally 'finalidad' means "finality; end; purpose"

[333] Literally 'conquistar' means "conquer; win over; carry, take; capture, gain"

[334] Literally 'medio' means "half; middle; midst; mean; medium, average; means, way; ambience, atmosphere"

Just having dirty laundry or [an] empty stomach, [is enough] so that we feel weak, we are in imbalance, and as soon as we have eaten well, we have bathed and put on clean clothes, [then] we will be able to come up [with] new ideas and helpful inspirations.

[We,] the Rose Cross [brethren], [must] know practical life and the Path of Initiation, at all times, [and we] give our disciples practices in order to obtain[335] this triple state (material, intellectual and spiritual) of harmony.

This is necessary, at least during the preparatory period of the Rose Cross neophyte, but afterwards one is placed beyond all this.

Giving at the same time [both] mystical and material instructions, in accordance with the Law of Consequence, the Rose Cross [practitioner] does not misuse money, because on the contrary, a Rose Cross [practitioner] always uses it to do good.

Accept, then, my advice: attain[336] [your] fortune by any means, doing what you will, but never to the detriment of others, yet always in good and [in] harmony with everyone.

Men who have excelled in the fields of Art and Science were not the children of the rich but of the middle class and those less fortunate, but who managed to raise themselves up through constant effort and work.

Basta tener la ropa sucia o el estómago vacío, para que nos sintamos débiles, nos encontramos en desequilibrio, y tan pronto como hayamos comido bien, nos hayamos bañado y puesto ropa limpia, estaremos en condiciones de que nos vengan nuevas ideas e inspiraciones provechosas.

Conociendo la vida práctica y el Camino de Iniciación, los Rosacruz, en todos los tiempos, dieron prácticas para que sus discípulos logras en poner en armonía este triple estado, material, intelectual y espiritual.

Es necesario aquello, por lo menos durante el período preparatorio del neófito Rosacruz, ya que después se pondrá más allá de todo esto.

Dando al mismo tiempo instrucciones místicas y materiales, de acuerdo con la Ley de Consecuencia, no hará mal uso del dinero, el Rosacruz, pues al contrario, un Rosacruz lo empleará siempre en hacer el bién.

Aceptad, pues, mi consejo: lograd fortuna por cualquier medio, haciendo lo que queráis, pero nunca con perjuicio de terceros, sino siempre en bien y armonía con todos.

Los hombres que han sobresalido en el terreno de las Artes y las Ciencias no han sido los hijos de los ricos, sino los de la clase media y los desheredados de la fortuna, pero que lograron levantarse mediante el esfuerzo constante y el trabajo.

---

[335] Literally 'logras' means "get, obtain; achieve, attain; reach; win"

[336] Literally 'lograd' means "get, obtain; achieve, attain; reach; win"

And, among those born in the midst of comforts, [they] just do not appreciate the value of the opportunities that Fate has brought them, and [they have] a very human tendency to seek idleness[337] and sensual pleasures, abandoning and neglecting the study of the Sciences and the Arts, considering this of little or no importance, since they feel they have [the] characteristics[338] of nobility.

And this is a fundamental error that [should] be corrected, the young must be taught that [a] man is valued[339] by what he knows and what he does, and not by the value of [his] family caste.

Since they can refine[340] the caste (to which they belong) more, or [they can] degrade it, according to their activities.

There are thousands of examples that vain[341] young [people], from privileged families, have not lifted up their spirit and their consciousness, and therefore have brought dishonor therein.

However, there are many examples (and these are the most valuable) of the need which was [found] in young [people with a] categorical imperative that forced them to study, namely, were able (by this means) to elevate themselves to the highest social positions, in this way elevating their family, being useful to themselves and to society or [the] community to which they belong.

Y es que, los que nacieron en medio de comodidades, no saben apreciar el justo valor de las oportunidades que el Destino les ha deparado, y por una tendencia muy humana de buscar la holgazanería y los placeres sensuales, abandonan y desprecian el estudio de las Ciencias y de las Artes, considerando esto de poca o ninguna importancia, ya que ellos se sienten con rasgos de nobleza.

Y este es un error fundamental que hay que corregir, al joven hay que enseñarle que el hombre vale por lo que sabe y por lo que hace, y no por el valer o casta de familia.

Ya que él, según sus actividades, puede ennoblecer más la casta a que pertenece, o degradarla.

Miles de ejemplos hay de que jóvenes engreídos en los privilegios de familia, no han elevado su espíritu y su conciencia, y por lo tanto han venido a ser el desdoro de las mismas.

En cambio, muchos ejemplos hay también, y éstos son los más valiosos, de que la necesidad fue en los jóvenes el imperativo categórico que los obligó a estudiar, a saber, pudiendo por este medio elevarse a las más encumbradas posiciones sociales, elevando de esta manera a su familia, siendo útiles a sí mismos y a la sociedad o colectividad a que pertenecen.

---

[337] Literally 'holgazanería' means "idleness, inactivity"

[338] Literally 'rasgos' means "characteristic, trait; feature; quirk; streak; twist; vein"

[339] Literally 'vale' means "aid, help; protect; serve; avail; cause; earn; cost; be useful; be valid; score; amount; hold"

[340] Literally 'ennoblecer' means "ennoble, make noble, raise the level of excellence, refine; give someone a title of nobility"

[341] Literally 'engreídos' means "vain, conceited; bumptious; bighead, braggart, boaster"

The Rose Cross practices activate, augment and put into [a] state of permanent equilibrium, the economic, intellectual and spiritual parts [so as] to resolve social issues by themselves [which] other currents of thought have failed to resolve.

Huiracocha

Las prácticas Rosa Cruz activan, aumentan y ponen en estado de equilibrio permanente, la parte económica, intelectual y espiritual, resuelven de por sí la cuestión social que no han logrado resolver otras corrientes de pensamiento.

Huiracocha

Extract from
The Rosecross Magazine
Berlin, October 1932

Extracto del
Revista Rosacruz
Berlín, Octubre de 1.932

The Origin of Writing

In our Book *Logos Mantram Magic*, we prove that human words are of [a] Divine Origin.

This affirmation has caused the following question to emerge[342]: And Writing, is [it] also of [a] Divine Origin?

In fact, no.

Writing is purely of human importance[343].

In it, the law is injured[344].

[This] is a matter of "do not make any figures of what is above, in heaven, nor of what is contained below, on the earth."

So said the first men whose powerful minds did not need graphical symbols in order to translate a symbol, nor to comprehend a truth which was (beforehand) already clearly[345] manifested in their mind as [a] central point of[346] focus.

The fact that, much later, writing was necessary, was a clear sign of degeneration[347] among men.

Official science, in opposition to us, the Rose Cross [brethren], says that the Phoenicians were the inventors of Writing and the Jews [were] the first Monotheists.

El Origen de la Escritura

En nuestro Libro *Logos Mantram Magia*, probamos que las palabras humana es de Origen Divino.

Esta afirmación, ha hecho que brote la pregunta siguiente: Y la Escritura, es de Origen Divino También?

No, en efecto.

La escritura es puramente de trascendencia humana.

En ello se lesiona la ley.

Es aquello de "no hagas figura alguna de lo que hay arriba, en el cielo, ni de lo que esta abajo en la tierra".

Así decían los primeros hombres cuya mente poderosa no necesitaba de signos gráficos para traducir un símbolo ni para comprender una verdad que ya estaba, de antemano, bien manifiesta en su mente como punto y foco central.

El hecho de necesitar mas tarde la escritura, fue un signo evidente de decadencia entre los hombres.

La ciencia oficial, en oposición a nosotros los Rosa Cruz, dice que fueron los Fenicios los inventores de la Escritura y los Judíos los primeros Monoteístas.

---

[342] Literally 'brote' means "shoot, sprout; outbreak; upsurge; burst forth; grow quickly"

[343] Literally 'trascendencia' means "implications; momentousness; transcendence"

[344] Literally 'lesiona' means "injure, hurt; wound"

[345] Literally 'bien' means "well, excellently, in a good manner; appropriately, properly; nicely, pleasantly; alright, okay"

[346] Literally 'y' means "and"

[347] Literally 'decadencia' means "decadence, decay; decline; down grade"

[This] is completely false, [and] totally[348] deceitful[349].

Let us examine the surroundings[350] of the [North] Pole, both on the American side like [in] Greenland, [where] we find signs engraved on the Rocks, that (in all parts) have a marked similarity which constitutes these interesting Paleo-epigraphic[351] Rose Cross studies.

The first letter was X, as if saying to us, "the Cross in a twisting[352] form", all the others are derived from this letter.

Therefore, we must say with great pride, that the Rose Cross Science is the most ancient [science] in the [whole] world.

The first original peoples[353] or, if we could say, Paradise, existed in the North.

Back in the Ancient regions people could only see a night of the same length one day out of six months and for them [there] only existed two points, the Sun, culminating in the North and its descent[354] in the South.

Es falso, completamente, de toda falsedad.

Le examinamos los alrededores del Polo, tanto del lado Americano como por la Groenlandia, encontraremos signos grabados en las Rocas, que por todas partes, tienen una similitud notoria lo cual constituye esos estudios interesantes Paleo epigráficos Rosa Cruz.

La primera letra fue la X, como si dijéramos, la Cruz en forma de aspas, derivándose de esa letra todas las demás.

Por ello, debemos decir con verdadero orgullo, que la Ciencia Rosa cruz es la más antigua del mundo.

Los primeros pueblos originarios o, como si dijéramos, el Paraíso, existieron por el Norte.

Allá en las regiones Antiguas tuvieron que ver los pueblos Solo un dia de seis meses a una noche de la misma duración y para ellos solo existieron dos puntos, el Sol, culminando por el Norte y su caída en el Sur.

---

[348] Literally 'de toda' means "from all"

[349] Literally 'falsedad' means "falseness, dishonesty, deceitfulness"

[350] Literally 'alrededores' means "surroundings, environs; purlieus, neighborhood"

[351] Literally 'epigráficos' means "epigraphic, pertaining to epigraphs, pertaining to inscriptions"

[352] Literally 'aspas' means "wind, be twisted around, twist around; annoy, irritate"

[353] Literally 'pueblos' means "town, village; populace, common folk; people"

[354] Literally 'caída' means "fall, tumble; descent; decrease; collapse; slope; downfall, defeat, ruin"

They formed the first lines from above to below because of the annual return of the sun, but at the same time, they observed its daily trek[355], its exit and entry upon the horizon and from this they determined the transverse line forming the Cross with its antecedent[356].

Our Planet has captured several moons and each entry of a Moon, produced major catastrophes and significant weather changes.

The fact that the regions of the North froze, forcing the Peoples [of that region], after the catastrophe of Atlantis, to migrate to the South and [thus] the shape of the Cross, as an X, was made in its trajectory in order to be able to orient themselves.

We encounter those emigrations designated in all ancient peoples, and especially in the Toltecs of Mexico, who were the first settlers that established the Solar Cult with its Annual[357] God.

With the deciphering of the Palaeogeographical inscriptions, we have proof for the World that monism[358] was the first Deistic idea and that our key is the Only [key] in order to decipher human enigmas.

[Krumm-Heller]

Así formaron las primeras líneas de arriba hacia abajo a causa de la vuelta anual del sol, pero, al mismo tiempo, observaron su marcha diaria, su salida y entrada en el horizonte y de este modo deliberaron[359] la línea transversal formando con su antecedente la Cruz.

Nuestro Planeta se ha capturado varias lunas y cada entrada de una Luna, produjo grandes catástrofes y cambios significativos de clima.

El hecho de helarse las regiones del Norte, obligaron a los Pueblos, después de esta catástrofe de la Atlántida, a emigrar hacia el Sur y en esta trayectoria hicieron la forma de la Cruz, como una X, para poder orientarse.

Esas emigraciones la encontramos designadas en todos los pueblos antiguos, y sobre todo, en los toltecas de México, que fueron los primeros pobladores que establecieron el Culto Solar con su Dios Anual.

Con el descifrado de las inscripciones Paleogeográficas[360], probamos al Mundo, que el monismo fue la primera idea Deista y que nuestra clave es la Única para descifrar los enigmas humanos.

[Krumm-Heller]

---

[355] Literally 'marcha' means "march, long journey by foot; coordinated steps of soldiers; decampment; walkout; run; walk; hike; speed; running, functioning; track; way; tide; line"
[356] Literally 'antecedente' means "aforegoing, antecedent, something which precedes;"
[357] Literally 'Anual' means "annual; yearly, yearlong"
[358] Literally 'monismo' means "monism, theory that reality consists of a single element; oneness of the universe (Philosophy); doctrine that only one supreme being exists (Theology)"

---

[359] Originalmente "delineraron"
[360] Originalmente "Paleoepigráficas"

Extract from
The Rosecross Magazine
[no date]

[The] Chain of Well-Being
or Holy Divine Alliance

In recent years a magnetic chain has been greatly[361] abused by means of a letter[362], directed by an official of the American army, that was [supposed] to be reproduced nine times and that [then] had to be given to others [just] as many times as it traveled[363] [around] the world.

That official was an ignorant [person] because he did not know the occult laws, he did not know how to do it [properly] and for that [reason] the beneficial effect was almost null and, instead, the danger was great.

I am going to give[364] a chain of truly beneficial results that can injure[365] no one and will provide[366] a great benefit to all those [who] participate[367] in it.

ROSE CROSS READER:

"EVERY MORNING, UPON WAKING, PRONOUNCE THE WORD EHEYEH [אהיה] AND WITH THE SOUND OF THIS WORD TRY[368] [TO HAVE IT] GO FROM THE BRAIN TO THE BELLY.

Extracto del
Revista Rosacruz
[sin dato]

Cadena de Bienestar
o la Santa Alianza Divina

En los últimos años se ha abusado mucho de una cadena magnética mediante una carta, dirigida por un oficial del ejército americano, que había que reproducir nueve veces y que debía dar otras tantas veces la vuelta al mundo.

El oficial aquél era un ignorante pues desconocía las leyes ocultas, no lo supo hacer y por eso el efecto benéfico fue casi nulo y, en cambio, el peligro fue grande.

Voy a provocar yo una cadena de verdaderos resultados benéficos que a nadie puede perjudicar y sí proporcionar un beneficio grande a todos cuantos en ella participen.

LECTOR DE ROSA CRUZ:

"PRONUNCIA TODAS LAS MAÑANAS AL LEVANTARTE LA PALABRA EHEJEH [אהיה] Y TRATA DE QUE EL SONIDO DE ESTA PALABRA VAYA DEL CEREBRO AL VIENTRE.

---

[361] Literally 'mucho' means "a lot, very much, very many; very, extremely; long"

[362] Literally 'carta' means "letter; document; charter; epistle; map; card; playing card; menu"

[363] Literally 'vuelta' means "walking; detour; round; turn; spin; change; revolution"

[364] Literally 'provocar' means "provoke, incite, instigate; stimulate, arouse; cause, induce"

[365] Literally 'perjudicar' means "damage, cause harm, cause injury; prejudice"

[366] Literally 'proporcionar' means "proportion; provide, afford; furnish, supply; put up"

[367] Literally 'participen' means "participate, be involved, partake, take part; intervene; inform"

[368] Literally 'Trara' means "try, make a trial, attempt, attempt it, endeavor, endeavour; treat, cure;"

AT NIGHT PRONOUNCE CHAYITH [חיות], LIKE [YOU ARE] CALLING[369], AND THINK ABOUT INVOKING ANGELS WHICH DESCEND FROM HEAVEN ENVELOPING [YOU] IN THE SACRED FIRE AND, FINALLY, [WHEN YOU ARE] ALREADY IN THE BED, THINK OF THE FIRST COMMANDMENT: "I AM THE LORD, YOUR GOD"[370].

To those not versed in this [kabalistic] material, this will seem [like] nonsense and, especially, the author of the attacks directed against me and reproduced in several spiritualist magazines, will believe themselves to be authorized to laugh.

I will give some explanations.

EHEYEH [אהיה] is the name of one of the Sephiroth or one of the ten paths towards God[371], as recorded in the Hebrew text of the Bible in the Exodus, Ch. 3, v. 14[372], in which God orders Abraham saying to the people of Israel, "Eheyeh" which means: "I will be".

CHAYITH [חיות] we find in the book of Ezekiel, [in Chapter] 1, v. 5[373], where it is [used as a] name for the angels that appeared.

DE NOCHE PRONUNCIA, COMO LLAMANDO, CHAJJITH [חיות] Y PIENSA EN INVOCAR ANGELES QUE DESCIENDEN DEL CIELO ENVUELTOS EN FUEGO SAGRADO Y, FINALMENTE, PIENSA, YA EN LA CAMA, EN EL PRIMER MANDAMIENTO: "YO SOY DIOS, TU SEÑOR".

Esto parecerá a los no versados en esta materia un disparate y, sobre todo, el autor de los ataques dirigidos contra mí y reproducidos en varias revistas espiritas, se creerá autorizado para reírse.

Voy a dar algunas explicaciones.

EHEJEH [אהיה] es el nombre de uno de los Sefirotes o de uno de los diez caminos hacia Dios, según consta en el texto hebreo de la Biblia en el Éxodo, Cap. 3, vers. 14 [374], en que Dios ordena a Abraham diga al pueblo de Israel, "Ehejeh" que quiere decir: Yo seré.

CHAJJITH [חיות] lo encontramos en el libro de Ezequiel, 1, vers. 5[375], donde se llama así a los ángeles que aparecen.

---

[369] Literally 'LLAMANDO' means "call; name; invite; attract; knock; ring up; summon; recall"

[370] Literally 'YO SOY DIOS, TU SEÑOR' means "I AM GOD, YOUR LORD"

[371] Editor's note: It is the Name of God corresponding to Kether, the 1st Sephira.

[372] Exodus 3:14 "And God said unto Moses, I AM THAT I AM: and he said, Thus shalt thou say unto the children of Israel, I AM hath sent me unto you." (KJV)

ויאמר אלהים אל־משה אהיה אשר אהיה ויאמר כה תאמר
לבני ישראל אהיה שלחני אליכם: (HOT)

[373] Ezekiel 1:5 "Also out of the midst thereof came the likeness of four living creatures. And this was their appearance; they had the likeness of a man." (KJV)

ומתוכה דמות ארבע חיות דמות מראיהן דמות אדם להנה: (HOT)

---

[374] Éxodo 3:14 "Y respondió Dios á Moisés: YO SOY EL QUE SOY. Y dijo: Así dirás á los hijos de Israel: YO SOY me ha enviado á vosotros." (SRV)

ויאמר אלהים אל־משה אהיה אשר אהיה ויאמר כה תאמר
לבני ישראל אהיה שלחני אליכם: (HOT)

[375] Ezekiel 1:5 "Y en medio de ella, figura de cuatro animales. Y este era su parecer; había en ellos semejanza de hombre." (RSV)

ומתוכה דמות ארבע חיות וזה מראיהן דמות אדם להנה: (HOT)

This has been translated as 'animals' [in Spanish, and as 'living creatures' in English], which [is something that] would be [too] long to explain.

From the previous verse[376] [we learn that the Chayith] are taken [out of] the sacred fire; about which one should to think.

Now it will be asked: What value do simple words have or [what value is there in] the simple enunciation of the names of God?

[In] the same way that we take one word, we could take another; well, no [not in kabalah].

The sacred texts of the jews hold[377] that the hebrew alphabet and all alphabets proceed from heaven, Edward Stucken[378] (the famous orientalist) proved that this affirmation comes[379] from much older works than those of the jews.

Se ha traducido esto por animales, lo cual sería largo de explicar.

Del versículo anterior[380] se toma el fuego sagrado; en que se debe pensar.

Ahora se preguntará: ¿Qué valor tienen las simples palabras o la simple enunciación de los nombres de Dios?.

Lo mismo que tomamos una palabra podríamos tomar otra; pues, no.

Los textos sagrados de los judíos sostienen que él alfabeto hebreo y todos los alfabetos proceden del cielo, Eduardo Stueken, el famoso orientalista prueba que esta afirmación la traen obras mucho más antiguas que las de los judíos.

---

[376] Ezekiel 1:4 "And I looked, and, behold, a whirlwind came out of the north, a great cloud, and a fire infolding itself, and a brightness was about it, and out of the midst thereof as the color of amber, out of the midst of the fire."
[377] Literally 'sostienen ' means "sustain, uphold, support; maintain; bear; live"
[378] Eduard Stucken (1865-1936) was a German author of "Astralmythen der Hebräer, Babylonier und Ägypter [Astral myths of the Hebrews, Babylonians, and Egyptians]" (in 5 volumes) 1896-1907, in which Biblical heroes are connected with other famous myths of history, Stucken attempts to show, that Abraham is originally the constellation Orion, and Sarah that of Sirius, Abraham and Sarah being parallel figures to Osiris and Isis of Egyptian mythology. The accounts of Abraham go back, according to Stucken, to two Babylonian sources, the legend of "Etana" and "Istar's Journey to Hell."
[379] Literally 'traen' means "bring; carry; cover up; wear; get"

---

[380] Ezequiel 1:4 "Y miré, y he aquí un viento tempestuoso venía del aquilón, una gran nube, con un fuego envolvente, y en derredor suyo un resplandor, y en medio del fuego una cosa que parecía como de ámbar," (SRV)

In a papyrus one finds the following:

En un papiro se encuentra lo siguiente:

IN THE CELESTIAL SPACE THAT COVERS OUR EARTH THERE ARE FIGURES AND SIGNS THROUGH WHICH THE MOST FORMABLE SECRETS MAY BE DISCOVERED, AND IN THESE FIGURES RESIDE GREAT POWER, AND ARE AT THE SAME TIME THE LETTERS WITH WHICH THE NAMES OF GOD ARE WRITTEN THROUGH WHOM THE MOST HIGH COMMUNICATES HIS POWER.

EN EL ESPACIO CELESTIAL QUE CUBRE NUESTRA TIERRA HAY FIGURAS Y SEÑALES MEDIANTE LAS CUALES SE PUEDEN DESCUBRIRLOS MAS FORMIDABLES SECRETOS Y EN ESTAS FIGURAS RESIDE GRAN PODER Y SON AL MISMO TIEMPO LAS LETRAS CON QUE ESTAN ESCRITOS LOS NOMBRES DE DIOS MEDIANTE LOS CUALES EL ALTÍSIMO COMUNICA SU PODER.

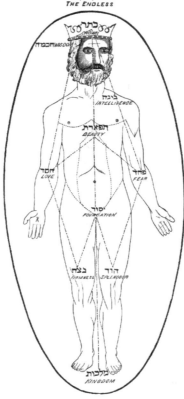

In such a way, the ancients were affirming the power that exists in the zodiacal figures, and that God manifests himself by means of them [which] can be evoked by us.

For the jews, the Sephiroth constituted part of the organism of Adam Kadmon, the divine man. (See [the] Jewish Encyclopedia).

On the other hand, the Sephiroth are the 10 paths to arrive at God and are at the same time ten names that correspond to the divinity.

The Torah, one of sacred books of the jews, mentions them saying:

"The Sephiroth receive (at the same time) the thoughts, the words and the facts of the men; in them it echos[381] the great divine power and the Sephiroth are the unique mediators between God and men".

De manera que los antiguos afirmaban ya el poder que existe en las figuras zodiacales, y que el Dios que se manifiesta por medio de ellas puede ser evocado por nosotros.

Para los judíos, los Sefirotes constituían parte del organismo del Adam Kadmon, el hombre divino. (Véase Jewish, Encyclopedia).

Por otra parte, los Sefirotes son los 10 caminos para llegar a Dios y son al mismo tiempo diez nombres que corresponden a la divinidad.

Dice la Torah — uno de los libros sagrados de los mencionados judíos:

"Los Sefirotes reciben a la par los pensamientos, las palabras y los hechos de los hombres; en ellos repercute el gran poder divino y los Sefirotes son los únicos mediadores entre Dios y los hombres".

---

[381] Literally 'repercute' means "have repercussions; rebound; echo"

[Editor's Insert]　　　　　**[Inserción del Editor]**

אין סוף
Aïn Soph.
THE WITHOUT END.

𝕷𝖊𝖋𝖙　　　　　𝕽𝖎𝖌𝖍𝖙

1
כתר
Kether.
א
אהיה
AïH'-YeH

2
בינה
Blnah.
ב
יה
YaH'

3
חכמה
'Hokhmah.
ג
יהוה
YeHoVaH

5
פחד
Pa'had.
ה
אלהים
ELoHIM

4
חסד
'Hesed.
ד
אלוה
ELO-aH'

6
תפארת
Tiphereth.
ו
יהוה
YeHoVaH

8 Hod.
הוד
ח
אלהים צבאות
E'loHIM
TZe'Ba-OTH

7 Ne-tza'h.
נצח
נ
יהוה צבאות
YeHoVaH
TZe'Ba-OTH

9
יסוד
Ye'sod.
ט
אל חי
El'HaY

10
מלכות
Malkhuth.
ו
אדני
A'Do-NaY̆

[End of Editor's Insert]　　　　　**[Fin de la Inserción del Editor]**

With the pronouciation of the names of God we attract upon ourselves tremendous forces and angels who come to the aid[382] of humans.

In such a way, according to these old texts, there is [some] relation between the zodiacal figures, the sephiroth and the fundamental letters or the vowels.

However; if an initiate knows this relationship [then] he can provoke and accumulate these forces.

This is obtained with amulets; but so that these amulets are powerful it is necessary to cause a vibration with a **MANTRAM** or with the articulation of the corresponding name of God.

Taking advantage of certain favorable constellations this spring we are going to make powerful amulets and to offer them to the readers so as to form a powerful chain by means of which they will attract blessings, success, [and] happiness upon themselves for the whole year.

The reader will have to pronounce the indicated **MANTRAM** and communicate it to three people interested[383] in our studies so that they write this to me and then, every month, I will give them the kabalistic **MANTRAM** that is the new name of God that corresponds.

The people will [thus] surely be safe from all misfortune and poverty.

"SAHASVARA"

What is "Sahasvara"?. Sahasvara is the sanscrit name that goes with the pineal gland, "gland pinealis" as the ancients called it because it has the form of [a] pine, that is to say [a] pine cone.

Con la pronunciación de los nombres de Dios atraemos sobre nosotros fuerzas tremendas y ángeles que vienen en socorro de los humanos.

De manera que, según estos textos antiguos, hay relación entre las figuras zodiacales, los sefirotes y las letras fundamentales o sean las vocales.

Ahora bien; si un iniciado conoce esta relación puede provocar y acumular estas fuerzas.

Esto se logra con amuletos; pero para que estos amuletos sean poderosos es necesario provocar una vibración con un **MANTRAM** o sea con la pronunciación del nombre de Dios correspondiente.

Aprovechando ciertas constelaciones favorables en esta primavera vamos a hacer unos amuletos poderosos y ofrecerlos a los lectores para que formen una cadena poderosa mediante la cual atraerán sobre ellos bendiciones, éxitos, bienandanza para todo el año.

El lector deberá pronunciar el **MANTRAM** indicado y comunicarlo a tres personas afines a nuestros estudios para que estas me escriban y entonces les daré cada mes el **MANTRAM** cabalístico o sea el nuevo nombre de Dios que corresponde.

Las personas estarán seguramente al abrigo de todo infortunio y pobreza.

"SAHASVARA"

¿Qué es "Sahasvara"?. Sahasvara es el nombre sánscrito que se le da a la glándula pineal, "glándula pinealis" como la llamaron los antiguos porque tiene forma de pino, es decir de fruta del pino.

---

[382] Literally 'en socorro' means "in distress; in relief; to help"
[383] Literally 'afines' means "related, kindred, cognate; allied"

This gland is one of the endocrine [glands], that is a gland that it secretes interiorily.

We know that we have two types of glands: those that expel[384] their secretions outside of the body, like the sweat[385] [glands], and those that expel their juice (let us say it thus) to the interior, towards the blood.

The pineal gland is the size of a chick-pea and weighs a fifth of a gram.

Kahn, the german sage, has presented irrefutable evidence that the pineal gland is the degenerated remains of a central eye.

There are animals that nowadays still have remains of [an] optic nerve and retina.

The small lizards conserve, even today, external signs of a central eye, and recent experiments have verified that small lizards have [a] sensitivity to light in that area.

Official science has always been dumbfounded[386], and continues to be dumbfounded by the mysterious gland [found in] the head.

The Rose Cross [fraternity] alone has solved the problem, only it is not possible to disclose it.

It is enough to know this: There are glands that secrete in the interior and their liquid is absorbed by the blood; there are those that expel their liquid, like sweat, outside the body.

If we took the sweat into the blood we would spontaneously become ill.

Esta glándula es una de las endocrinas, o sea una glándula que segrega interiormente.

Sabemos que tenemos dos clases de glándulas: las que expulsan sus secreciones fuera del cuerpo, como las sudoríparas, y las que expulsan su jugo, digámoslo así, al interior, hacia la sangre.

La glándula pineal tiene el tamaño de un garbanzo y pesa una quinta parte de un gramo.

Kahn, el sabio alemán, ha aportado pruebas irrefutables de que la glándula pineal es el resto degenerado de un ojo central.

Hay animales que hasta hoy día conservan en ella restos de nervio óptico y retina.

Las lagartijas conservan hasta hoy señales externas de un ojo central, y experiencias últimas han comprobado que las lagartijas tienen en ese punto sensibilidad para la luz.

La ciencia oficial se ha quebrado siempre, y sigue quebrándose la cabeza por la misteriosa glándula.

Únicamente el Rosa Cruz ha resuelto el problema, sólo que no es posible divulgarlo.

Baste con saber esto: Hay glándulas que segregan al interior y su líquido es absorbido por la sangre; y las hay que expulsan su líquido, como el sudor, fuera del cuerpo.

Si llevásemos el sudor a la sangre enfermaríamos espontáneamente.

---

[384] Literally 'expulsan' means "expel, eject; scavenge"
[385] Literally 'sudoríparas' means "sudoriparous, producing or secreting sweat (Physiology)"
[386] Literally 'quebrado' means "broken; rough, uneven; cracked; bankrupt"

Now conversely[387], the seminal glands, that are in direct relation with the pineal gland, secrete to the interior [of the body] and to them we must [attribute] the principle part of development, not only for the body but [also] for the mind.

To take thse secretions outside [of the body] (masturbation) is bad.

Nevertheless, nature indicates the sexual act to us.

…

All organic acts have their material and spiritual side and their effects in both planes.

In the moment of [performing the duties of] marriage[388] a supreme act of magic is realized and the spiritual state of giver and receiver influences in order to give major or minor range[389] to the magical operation.

The ancient initiates had their priestesses; the Incas [had] their princesses[390] for these ceremonies and they handled the great secret of the sexual magic.

We need women and we must make use of them for the supreme good, in order to obtain initiation.

HUIRACOCHA R+

Ahora a la inversa, las glándulas seminales, que están en relación directa con la glándula pineal, segregan al interior y a ellas debemos la parte principal del desarrollo, no sólo del cuerpo sino de la mente.

Llevar las secreciones fuera (masturbación) es malo.

Sin embargo la naturaleza nos indica el acto sexual.

…

Todos los actos orgánicos tienen su lado material y espiritual y sus efectos en ambos planos.

En el momento del connubio se realiza un acto supremo de magia y el estado espiritual del dador y receptor influye para dar mayor o menor alcance a la operación mágica.

Los antiguos iniciados tenían sus sacerdotisas; los Incas sus nustas para estas ceremonias y ellos manejaban el secreto magno de la magia sexual.

Nosotros necesitamos las mujeres y hemos de servirnos de ellas para el supremo bien, para lograr la iniciación.

HUIRACOCHA R+

---

[387] Literally 'inversa' means "inverse, reverse; converse"
[388] Literally 'connubio' means "matrimony, marriage, wedding, conjugality"
[389] Literally 'alcance' means "reach; range, scope; importance, significance; deficit; intelligence; chase, hunt; size; potency of drug; catch up, overtake; achieve, attain; gain, win; reach, arrive at; hit, strike; amount; perceive; bring, fetch; extend the arm outward"
[390] Literally 'nustas' means "princess, daughter of the king and queen"

Extract from
The Rosecross Magazine
[no date]

Extracto del
Revista Rosacruz
[sin dato]

The 72 Genii of the Kabalah and their Occult Value

Los 72 Genios de la Kabala y su Valor Oculto

Man is the human voice. A broken[391] faultering, [or] dissonant, voice presents us with a timid, unhappy, pessimistic man, lacking in character.

On the contrary, it is sufficient to hear a man talk with a sonorous, happy, optimistic voice, and [then] we feel that we are in front of[392] a good being, capable of something.

With the voice, we command[393], and with it, we humiliate, it is a very big bridge of communication that [allows] us to hold those that surrounds us.

Without respiration, the voice does not conceive[394], for this [it] the breath is also spirit.

In the hebrew and greek roots, voice and respiration and spirit, are identical and [it is] in German (which is one of the archaic dialects) that we can discover all the secrets of occultism.

Respiration is called "Atmen"; from sanskrit we know [that] "Atma" signifies the highest spiritual potency.

We have departed from the bosom of Atma and turned, on a spiral path, or Atma.

La voz humana es el hombre. Una vez quebrada, entrecortada, disonante, nos presenta a un hombre apocado, falto de carácter, triste, pesimista.

Al contrario, basta oír hablar a un hombre con una voz sonora, alegre, optimista, y sentimos que tenemos enfrente a un ser bueno, capaz de algo.

Con la voz, mandamos, y con ella, nos humillamos, ella es el puente de comunicación más grande que tenemos con los que nos rodean.

La voz sin respiración no se concibe, por eso también la respiración es espíritu.

En las raíces hebreas y griegas, voz y respiración y espíritu, son idénticos y en alemán, que es uno de los idiomas arcaicos, que por él solo podríamos descubrir todos los secretos del ocultismo.

Respiración se llama "Atmen"; del sánscrito conocemos el Atma que significa la potencia espiritual más alta.

Nosotros hemos salido del seno de Atma y volvemos, por un camino espiral, o Atma.

---

[391] Literally 'quebrada' means "broken; rough, uneven; cracked; bankrupt"

[392] Literally 'enfrente' means "face, stand opposite; stand face to face; in front; front to front"

[393] Literally 'mandamos' means "mandate, order, command; direct, instruct; draft; dictate; delegate; send, post; ordain"

[394] Literally 'concibe' means "conceive; form, shape; envisage, think of an idea"

In my book **ESOTERIC CONFERENCES**, which was published in the year 1913, I tried (with a long tuning fork that could destroy [things]) to make a certain tone vibrate an edifice and I could give the experimental proof that, with another tone, with a different sound, it could be reconstructed.

Children prove to us, when the time is right, [by] saying "AA aa", the influence or the relation that exists between the spoken tones and our organs.

It is not that they learn [this] from us; if we enclose them [somewhere], and the test has been done, without ever seeing a human being nor hearing the pronounciation of any voice, when they are going to deficate, they also exclaim[395] "Aa".

It resides, then, in the subconsciousness of humanity.

More tedious[396] observations have demonstrated than the rectum is contracted when the creature pronounces "Aa".

The same could be said with the "pee-pee" of children.

It is not [something] that only we use, no; the men of science, when there are uncovering new tribes, or have arrived at parts [of the world] where they have never stepped on civilized soil, [they have] found that the little savages [meaning the children] also said "pee-pee".

When children suffer from retention of urine, it is sufficient to give them the key of potable water, and the sound alone, will [have an] influence upon the bladder of the creature and the urine.

En mi libro **CONFERENCIAS ESOTÉRICAS,** que publiqué allá por el año 1913, probé que con un diapasón se podría destruir, haciendo vibrar cierto tono un edificio y podría dar la prueba experimental que, con otro tono, con diferente sonido, se podría construirlo de nuevo.

La influencia o la relación que existe entre los tonos hablados y nuestros órganos, nos lo prueban los niños, que cuando tienen una necesidad, dicen AA aa.

No es que lo aprendan de nosotros; si los encerrásemos, y se ha hecho la prueba, sin que jamás vean a un ser humano ni hayan oído pronunciar voz alguna, cuando van a defecar, también lanzan el grito aa.

Reside, pues, en el subconsciente de la humanidad.

Observaciones más prolijas han demostrado que el recto se contrae al pronunciar la criatura su aa.

Lo mismo se podría decir con el pi-pi de los niños.

No es que sólo lo usáramos nosotros, no; los hombres de ciencia, cuando han descubierto tribus nuevas, o han llegado a partes donde nunca pisó planta civilizada encontraron que los salvajes pequeños también decían pi-pi.

Cuando los niños sufren de retención de la orina, basta abrir la llave del agua potable, y el sonido solo, influye sobre la vejiga de la criatura y orina.

---

[395] Literally 'lanzan' means "throw, cast; send; sling; aim; shoot; pitch; release; launch; dart, dash"

[396] Literally 'prolijas' means "prolix, tedious; diffuse; discursive"

In 95% [of cases, this] gives [positive] results.

I have done the test and invite those who are willing to do so.

There are 10 divine names known in Holy Kabalah, each one of which represents an attribute of God.

These names, which bring [good] luck, and which we almost always encounter on amulets are: "Ehieh", "Jah", "Jeovah" (mark well, my esoteric disciples, the "H", in this mode of primitive writing, is at the end where it indicates to us the sound), "El", "Eloha", "Elohim Jeve" or "[Elohim] Sabaoth", "Shadai" and "Adonai".

The name "Jeovah", is not permited to be pronounced in public, and is a replacement for the Tetragrammaton [יהוה].

My teacher Papus[397] said, and I believe he repeats [it] in one of his works: "Each letter used in these names or sacred mantrams, holds an enlivening[398] force" and Dr. Nestler, the German translator of the works of Papus, added that "each of these vowels provokes or excites some [part of the] central nervous [system] of our organism".

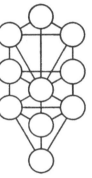

En 95% da resultado.

Yo he hecho la prueba e invito a que cuantos quieran lo hagan.

La Santa Cábala conocía 10 nombres divinos en los que, cada uno, representaba un atributo de Dios.

Estos nombres, que traen suerte, y que encontramos casi siempre sobre los amuletos son: Ehieh, Jah, Jeovah, fijarse bien, mis discípulos esotéricos, la hache, en el modo de escribir primitivo, es al final donde nos indica el sonido El, Eloha, Elohim Jeve o Sabaoth, Shadai y Adonai.

El nombre Jeováh, nunca se permitió pronunciarlo en público, y se reemplazaba por Tetragrammaton [יהוה].

Mi maestro Papus[399] decía, y creo lo repite en una de sus obras: Cada letra usada en estos nombres o mantrams sagrados, tiene una fuerza invivita y el Dr. Nestler, el traductor al alemán de las obras de Papus, añade que cada una de estas vocales provoca o irrita a algún centro nervioso de nuestro organismo.

---

[397] Editor's note: Compare "[#10] ...Simon the Magician is really a Black Magician [#14] HUIRACOCHA also believed that Simon the Magician was a great Gnostic Master, and he told us that everything that 'Papus' and other authors have taught in the past years about magic was taken from Simon the Magician."
— *Treatise of Sexual Alchemy* (1954), Ch. 17 by Samael Aun Weor

This implies that Papus taught black magic.

[398] Editor's note: This word 'invivita' does not have a translation, but the word 'vivita' means "alive and kicking", so we have chosen "enlivening" as a translation.

---

[399] Nota del editor: Comparemos "[#10] ...Simón el Mago es realmente un Mago Negro [#14] HUIRACOCHA también creyó que Simón el Mago era un gran Maestro Gnóstico, y nos dice que todo lo que Papus y otros autores enseñaron acerca de la magia en los últimos anos, era tomado de Simón el Mago",
— *Tratado del Alquimia Sexual* (1954) Cap. XVII, por Samael Aun Weor

Esto implica que Papus enseñó la Magia Negra.

Papus[400] says that the 72 sacred names of the Kabalah are curative mantrams and that in accordance with the vowel this can exercise [an] action upon the body.

Vehuiah, Jeliel, Sitael, Elemiah, Mehasiah, Lehahel, Achaiah, Cahatel, Haziel, Aladiah, Lauviah, Habaiah, Jesalel, Leuviah, Pahaliah, Melchael, Jecaiel, Melehel, Hahimah, Nith-Heich, Haaiah, Jerathel, Seeiah, Reiiel, Omael, Lecabel, Amiel, Haamiah, Rehahel, Jeiazel, Hahahel, Mikahel, Vehualiah, Jelahiah Sealieh, Ariel, Azaliah, Michael, Vehuel, Mehaiah, Poiel, Nemamiah, Jeialel, Nazael, Mizrael, Umebel, Jahhel, Ananel, Mehiel, Damabiah, Manakel, Ejael, Mehahel, Hariel, Hakamiah, Lanoiah, Caliel, Vasaniah, Jomiah, Lehaiah, Chavakiah, Menadel, Daniel, Hahasiah, Imamiah, Nanael, Nitbael, Nabujah, Rochel, Jabamiah, Jaiael, Miumiah.

The ancient rabbis treated only with the pronounciation of these names which today is confirmed through their values afterwards which we have seen that the blood flows to a derminated part [of the body] according to what words we make vibrate with [the vowels] I, E, O, U, A.

Papus[401] dice que los 72 nombres sagrados de la Cabala son mantrams curativos y que según la vocal se podría ejercer acción sobre el cuerpo.

Vehuiah, Jeliel, Sitael, Elemiah, Mehasiah, Lehahel, Achaiah, Cahatel, Haziel, Aladiah, Lauviah, Habaiah, Jesalel, Leuviah, Pahaliah, Melchael, Jecaiel, Melehel, Hahimah, Nith-Heich, Haaiah, Jerathel, Seeiah, Reiiel, Omael, Lecabel, Amiel, Haamiah, Rehahel, Jeiazel, Hahahel, Mikahel, Vehualiah, Jelahiah Sealieh, Ariel, Azaliah, Michael, Vehuel, Mehaiah, Poiel, Nemamiah, Jeialel, Nazael, Mizrael, Umebel, Jahhel, Ananel, Mehiel, Damabiah, Manakel, Ejael, Mehahel, Hariel, Hakamiah, Lanoiah, Caliel, Vasaniah, Jomiah, Lehaiah, Chavakiah, Menadel, Daniel, Hahasiah, Imamiah, Nanael, Nitbael, Nabujah, Rochel, Jabamiah, Jaiael, Miumiah.

Los antiguos rabinos sólo curaban con la pronunciación de estos nombres que hoy se confirman en su valía después que hemos visto que la sangre afluye a determinada parte según que hagamos vibrar palabras con I, E, O, U, A.

---

[400] Editor's note: Compare "In this path we will have to live all the twelve hours of which the great sage Apollonius spoke about. The Black Magician "Papus" tried to disfigure the 12 hours of Apollonius with teachings of Black Magic, liquidating all the millions of Kabalistic volumes that drift in the world. We have arrived at the conclusion that: all Kabalah is reduced to the 22 Major Arcanum of the Tarot and 4 Aces, which represent the 4 Elements of Nature.

On such a simple thing, scholars have written millions of volumes and theories that would turn anyone "crazy" who had the bad taste of becoming intellectualized with all that arsenal.

The worst of it is that in questions of Kabalah, the black magicians took over what they found, to disfigure the teaching and lead the world astray. The works of Papus are legitimate black magic."
– *Zodiacal Course* (1951) Ch. Sagittarius, by Samael Aun Weor

[401] Nota del editor: Comparemos "En esta senda tendremos que vivir todas las 12 Horas de que nos habló el Gran Sabio Apolonio. El Mago Negro "Papus" intentó desfigurar las 12 Horas de Apolonio con enseñanzas de Magia Negra, haciendo una liquidación de todos los millones de volúmenes kabalísticos que ruedan por el mundo. Llegamos a la conclusión de que: toda Kábala se reduce a los 22 Arcanos Mayores del Tarot y 4 Ases, que representan los 4 Elementos de la Naturaleza.

Sobre algo tan sencillo han levantado los eruditos, millones de volúmenes y teorías que volverían "loco" a todo aquel que tuviera el mal gusto de intelectualizarse con todo ese arsenal.

Lo peor del caso fue que en materia de Kábala, los Magos Negros se apoderaron de lo que encontraron para desfigurar la enseñanza y extraviar al mundo. Las obras de Papus son: legítima Magia Negra."
– *Curso Zodiacal* (1951) Cap. Sagitario, por Samael Aun Weor

These 72 names are the designations of genii and they give to the readers what can be used to seek[402], each time, [for whatever is] convenient.

For example: Achaiah; has 3 "A's" and one "I".

The "A" corresponds to the lungs and the "I" to the head, this indicates that those who have lung diseases should rhythmically repeat this mantram, [and] will succeed in healing this terrible evil, and everyone can study the different words that I have noted[403] [above].

It is true that, according to the kabalah, each of these names corresponds [to a] certain time of the year and of the day, but it would be too long in this article to treat this aspect, which is for esoteric students to whom we gladly give the key.[404]

Each one of the vowels holds its own rhythm given by nature and thus it is that the "A" that is the principle of life, it is the Atma, the Allah or the Brahma carrying (in its tonality) the superior octave of attention, surprise, affirmation.

I have already said that everything is dual and vibrates in two octaves, one higher and the other lower.

In the lower octave, is the negation, like in greek what is represented [as] repugnance, disgust, rage.

Estos 72 nombres son las designaciones de genios y los doy a los lectores para que los puedan usar buscando siempre la conveniente.

Por ejemplo: Achaiah; tiene 3 a y una i.

La a corresponde a los pulmones y la i a la cabeza, esto indica que los enfermos del pulmón, repitiendo rítmicamente este mantram, lo lograrán la curación de este terrible mal, y así cada uno puede estudiar las diferentes palabras que he apuntado.

Es verdad que según la cabala a cada uno de estos nombres corresponde cierta época del año y del día, pero sería demasiado largo en este artículo tratar este aspecto, que queda para estudiantes esotéricos a los que con gusto daré la clave.

Cada una de las vocales tiene su ritmo dado por la naturaleza y así la A que es el principio de la vida, es el Atma, el Allah o el Brama lleva en su tonalidad de la octava superior la atención, la sorpresa, la afirmación.

Ya he dicho que todo es dual y vibra en dos octavas, una alta y otra baja.

En la octava baja, es la negación, como en griego lo representa la repugnancia, el asco, la rabia.

---

[402] Literally 'buscando' means "search for, seek, look for; scout for; forage; call for, ask for"

[403] Literally 'apuntado' means "aim; level; point; write down; record; score; outline; mend, darn; tack down; prompt, provide a cue for an actor's forgotten lines; appear; sprout; fail to keep one's word; bet, place a wager"

[404] Editor's note: After this Article, we have included a number of tables including one with the correspondences given by Lazare Lenain in his book *La science cabalistique ou l'art de connaître les bons genies* (1832)

Look carefully: all the things hold two aspects, two octaves, two poles; there is black and white magic within the application of the same vowel.

The "E" is the expression of pain and of joy since the octave in which [it] vibrates, [is one] of doubt, in many peoples [it] vibrates as interrogation "eh?"

The "O" is the vowel of admiration, it is the circulation that includes everything, is the eternal, the great all, [it] is the closed circle that resolves everything, it is art, love, it is the heart not only [in its] material [form], but also [in its] ideal [form].

The "U" represents the fear, distress, fire, the different tonality can be experienced with [when] children they say: "Uh…! Get out of here!" in a low tone, and in the act of being frightened, but reversing it, [by] putting the 'H' in the [front of the] expression: "Huhu Huhu Huhu!", in the act of laughing by [the] little ones who are playing.

I am going to conclude, by giving three other very powerful mantrams that can always be used.

The first is the **O M** of the Hindus.

We already know that the O represents the All, the central heart of the universe and its pronunciation [or articulation] puts all the masters [into a state] like when we walk down the street [and] we hear the word **ATTENTION!**

Everyone turns their head towards where the voice is coming from and is fixed upon that which must hold [the] Attention!

For that reason we use it in all evocations and this is not [what] we have learned from the Hindus through the Theosophists.

Fijarse bien: todas las cosas tienen dos aspectos, dos octavas, dos polos; hay magia negra y blanca dentro de la aplicación de una misma vocal.

La E es la expresión del dolor y de la alegría según la octava en que vibra, de la duda, en muchos pueblos vibra en la interrogación ¿e?.

La O es la vocal de la admiración, es el círculo que todo lo incluye, es la eternidad, el gran todo, es el círculo cerrado que todo lo resuelve, es el arte, el amor, es el corazón no sólo material, sino también ideal.

La U representa el temor, la pena, el fuego la diferente tonalidad se puede experimentar con los niños cuando se les dice: ¡Uh....! ¡largo! en tono bajo, y en el acto se asustan, pero al revés, poniendo la hache en expiración: "¡Huhu Huhu Huhu!", en el acto ríen por muy pequeños que sean.

Voy, para concluir, a dar aún tres mantrams muy poderosos que se pueden usar siempre.

El primero es el **O M** de los indues.

Ya sabemos que la O representa el Todo, el corazón central del universo y su pronunciación pone a todos los maestros como cuando nosotros al pasar por la calle escuchamos de repente la palabra **¡ATENCIÓN!**.

Todo el mundo vuelve la cabeza hacia donde viene la voz y se fija en lo que debe tener. ¡Atención!.

Por eso en todas las evocaciones lo usamos y no es que lo hayamos aprendido de los indues por los teósofos.

One encounters in the **EDDA** of the Germans [something] like a mantram [we] already know.

The **O M** heard or pronounced, exerts an immediate action upon our Chakras or [upon the] nervous centers of the organism.

Leadbeater is now the first of the Theosophists that does justice to their merit and cites, in his work **[THE] CHAKRAS**, the square of Gichtel[405].

It is true that this again relates to Hindu studies, [but] I do not understand why.

…

I have been convinced: There is nothing, absolutely nothing of which Blavatsky or the other Theosophists bring, that are not in the **ROSE CROSS** works of the Middle Ages, published by the Germans, and I refer to the proof; it is only necessary [to take the] time to look for it.

The advantage that all the studies on Karma and Reincarnation, on the Monad, on the different planes, are even clearer in **ROSE CROSS** literature and free of an eastern technicalism, but with western clarity.

I am a friend of a hindu in Berlin, [who is] very wise, [and] professor of the Eastern University and who is intimate friends with Mahatma Gandi, this man who thoroughly knows all the things of India (his mother country) thinks just like I [do] in this sense.

I have often asked the question: Why have the Theosophists done just like the catholic friars and the old doctors who hid behind Latin and the Theosophists who today [hide] behind Hindu terminology?

Se encuentra en la **EDDA** de los germanos como mantram ya conocido.

La **O M** escuchada o pronunciada, ejerce una acción inmediata sobre nuestros Chacras o centros nerviosos del organismo.

Leadbeater es el primero ahora de los teósofos que hace justicia al mérito, y cita en su obra **CHACRAS** el cuadro de Gichtel.

Es verdad que lo relaciona otra vez con estudios indues, yo no comprendo porqué.

…

Me he convencido: No hay nada, absolutamente nada de lo que trae la Blavatsky o los demás teósofos, que no se encuentre en las obras **ROSA CRUZ** de la Edad Media, publicado por los alemanes, y me remito a la prueba; sólo necesito tiempo para buscar.

La ventaja que todos los estudios sobre Karma y Reencarnación, sobre la mónada, sobre los diferentes planos, están más claros en la literatura **ROSA CRUZ** y exento de un tecnicismo oriental, sino con claridad occidental.

Soy amigo acá en Berlín de un hindú, muy sabio, profesor de la Universidad Oriental y quien es íntimo amigo del Mahatma Gandi, este hombre que conoce a fondo todas las cosas de la India, su patria, opina lo mismo que yo en este sentido.

Yo me he hecho muchas veces la pregunta: ¿Por qué los teósofos han hecho lo mismo que los frailes católicos y los médicos antiguos que se escondían tras del latín y hoy los teósofos tras de un terminismo indú.

---

[405] Editor's note: Leadbeater mentions "…*Theosophia Practica* by the well known German mystic Johann Georg Gichtel, a pupil of Jakob Boehme, who probably belonged to the secret society of the Rosicucians" in Chapter 1 of *The Chakras*

Everything the catholic religion says can be said in spanish, german, english and french; but they insist on latin; it would be equal and less dangerous to formulate a prescription on our living tongues and to put white sugar, for example, instead of *"sacharis albi"*[406].

Todo lo que diga la religión católica se puede decir en español, alemán, inglés y francés; pero se empeñan en el latín; igual sería y menos peligroso formular una receta en nuestras lenguas vivas y poner azúcar blanca, por ejemplo, en vez de *"sacharis albi"*.

The master Therion presented in his 'book 4' the pronounciation of Aum with musical notes. I have never dared so much.

El maestro Therion da en su obra 4 la pronunciación del Aum con notas musicales. Yo nunca me habría atrevido a tanto.

To Therion I am bound by way of brother Yarker[407], from whom I received the 96th degree of occult masonry and this is why I should not criticize him.

A Therion me une el lazo amarrado por el hermano Yarker, del cual recibí el grado 96 de la masonería oculta y por eso no debo criticarlo.

Therion has launched the principle "Love is the Law, Love under Will"[408] let's stick[409] to this.

Therion ha lanzado el principio "Love is the Law, Love under Will[410] [Amor es la Ley, Amor debajo Voluntad]" atengámonos a ello.

---

[406] Editor's note: This is 'white sugar' in Latin.

[407] Editor's note: John Yarker was the head of the Memphis-Misraim Rite of "Egytpain" Masonry and gave Theodore Reuss the ability to work it and to give its degrees in 1905. Then in 1908, Reuss helped both Arnoldo Krumm-Heller and Gérard Encausse (aka Papus) join the Memphis-Misraim Rite and acquire the same abilities.

[408] Editor's note: Compare "Love is Law, but Conscious Love." from Ch.8 of *The Perfect Matrimony* by Samael Aun Weor. As well as the following excerpt:

"…The word Love, in itself, is a little abstract, [so] it is necessary to try to know what is that which we call Love.

Before all else, we must consult the Christian Gospel a bit. Jesus the great Kabir said, "In loving one another you will be my disciples." There are also other very interesting phrases of the Great Kabir: "Love God above all things," and "Love your neighbor as [you love] yourself," and "Do unto others as you would have them do unto you."

…In the Gnostic Esoteric Work, it has been said that we [should] feel affection towards the Work, but we could not if we don't comprehend. COMPREHENSION IS FUNDAMENTAL. Well, let's continue on, pursuing these examinations as follows: There are three kinds of Love.

…We must understand a little bit of background of this subject, because PURELY SEXUAL LOVE exists, PURELY EMOTIONAL LOVE exists and CONSCIOUS LOVE exists.

…Unquestionably, only Conscious Love deserves our veneration, but the existence of Conscious Love is indispensable, in all the work upon oneself, to eliminate from oneself those undesireable psychological elements that we carry in our interior…

…It is necessary [to have] Conscious Love…"
     – from the lecture *Transvaluation of the Esoteric Work* by Samael Aun Weor

[409] Literally 'atengámonos' means "go by; keep; stick"

[410] Comparemos: "Amor es Ley, pero Amor Consciente." del Cap. VIII de *El Matrimonio Perfecto* por Samael Aun Weor. Así como el extracto siguiente:

"…La palabra Amor, en sí misma, es un poco abstracta, necesitamos especificarla para saber que es eso que se llama Amor.

Ante todo, nos toca consultar un poco el Evangelio Crístico. El Gran Kabir Jesús dijo: "En que os améis los unos a los otros demostraréis que sois mis discípulos", También hay otra frase del Gran Kabir muy interesante: "Ama a Dios sobre todas las cosas" y "[Ama] al prójimo como a tí mismo" o "No hagáis a otros lo que no queráis que os hagan a vosotros."

…En el Trabajo Esotérico Gnóstico tiene (dije) que haber afecto por el Trabajo, pero no podría haberlo si no lo comprendiéramos; COMPRENSIÓN ES FUNDAMENTAL. Bueno, continuando hacia adelante, prosiguiendo con estas disquisiciones diremos lo siguiente: Hay tres clases de Amor.

…Nosotros debemos entender un poquito a fondo esta cosa, porque existe el AMOR PURAMENTE SEXUAL, existe el AMOR PURAMENTE EMOCIONAL y existe el AMOR CONSCIENTE.

…Incuestionablemente, sólo el Amor Consciente merece nuestra veneración, pero para que exista el Amor Consciente se hace indispensable, ante todo trabajar sobre sí mismo, para eliminar de sí mismo los elementos psíquicos indeseables que en nuestro interior cargamos…

…Se necesita del Amor Consciente…"
     – de la confencia 'La Transvalorización del Trabajo Esotèrico' por Samael Aun Weor

In the number of my Magazine corresponding to the 1st of January, I offered to return to Gichtel, [whom I have] already mentioned today.

I know that in Spain there are works of his and it would be very important for the disciples to investigate [these works] in the libraries.

Pardon [me], I am leaving the subject, and [so] I [shall] return to the three mantrams.

I said that the first is **O M** and it is for the reader to meditate upon why the frenchmen write it **A U M.**

Our "You" [Spanish: "Usted"], that we use every day to direct ourselves towards another person could be explained as "your mercy[411]" and I do not know at what time that [it began to be] used in spanish, [but] what I [do] know, is that it is a mantram that is powerful like the Aum.

The Sanskrit speaker knows that the "Ut" means 'high, elevated, soaring, beyond'; and "Utsaha" [means] 'force, energy'.

USTED is encountered in many Indian and German monuments, and we know that with them they called upon their gods.

And the third, **OHANSA**, or better, for the Spaniards; "Ojanza".

This last one makes the chakra of the pineal gland vibrate, and is of an immense power.

En el número de mi Revista correspondiente al 1° de enero, ofrezco volver sobre Gichtel, ya hoy lo menciono.

Sé que en España hay obras de él y sería muy importante que los discípulos indagasen en las bibliotecas.

Perdón, me estoy saliendo del tema, y vuelvo sobre los tres mantrams.

Ya dije que el primero es el **O M** y queda al lector meditar por qué los franceses escriben **A U M.**

Nuestro "Usted", que usamos todos los días para dirigirnos a otra persona podrá ser explicado como "vuestra merced" y no sé cuanto tiempo hace que se usa en español, lo que sé, es que es un mantram tan poderoso como el Aum.

El sánscrito conoce el Ut que significa alto, elevado, encumbrado, más allá; y Utsaha, fuerza, energía.

USTED se encuentra en muchos monumentos de la India y de los germanos, y sabemos que con ellos llamaban a sus dioses.

Y el tercero, **OHANSA**, o mejor, para los españoles; Ojanza.

Este último hace vibrar el chacra de la glándula pineal, y es de un poder inmenso.

---

[411] Literally 'vuestra merced' means "your mercy", but this is a title also which translates as "esquire" (the word 'usted' is a combination of the beginning part 'uest' of the first word and the end part 'ed' of the second word). The term 'esquire' is "an unofficial title of respect, having no precise significance, sometimes placed, especially in its abbreviated form, after a man's surname in formal written address: in the U.S., it is usually applied to lawyers; in Britain, it is applied to a commoner considered to have gained the social position of a gentleman."

On-Uste and **Ojanza**[412] enclose[413] the key of all occultism, and are the key of Initiation.

Use it, [dear] readers, according to how you feel the necessity, use one or the other; they will always purify you.

Let us not forget [that] the word "person" comes from latin and signifies "to appear", to produce sounds by some method.

The Theosophists have always spoken to us, when it was about the etimology about this word, about mumbling[414] or about the inferior quaternary, calling the superior triad individuality.

They have their reason for being, but Mrs. H.P. Blavatsky who (like us) belonged to **O.T.O.**[415] knows what I am talking [about].

What reason would [one] have to hide it?

[Krumm-Heller]

On-Uste y, **Ojanza,** encierran la clave de todo el ocultismo, y son la clave de la Iniciación.

Usadlo, lectores, según como sintáis la necesidad, ya uno u otro; siempre os purificarán.

No olvidemos la palabra "persona" viene del latín y significa "personare", producir sonidos por algún medio.

Los teósofos siempre nos han hablado, cuando se trataba de la etimología de esta palabra, de máscara o del cuaternario inferior, llamando la triada superior individualidad.

Aquello tiene su razón de ser, pero la señora H. P. Blavatsky que, como nosotros, pertenecía a la **O. T. O.** sabía lo que digo.

¿Qué razón tendría para ocultarlo?.

[Krumm-Heller]

---

[412] Editor's note: This would be pronounced "Oh-Han-Za" in English.

[413] Literally 'encierran' means "to shut up or in; to lock up or in; to lock away or up; To contain, to conclude, to comprehend; imprison; close on; surround, jail; confine, include"

[414] Literally 'máscara' means "mask; disguise; mascara; masticate, chew; munch; mumble"

[415] Editor's note: This appears to be incorrect because Blavatsky died in 1891, which was before the OTO was even in existence. In 1903, the AOTO was established by the Germans Theodor Reuss & Carl Kellner. After Kellner died (in June of 1905), Reuss then converted the AOTO into the OTO (in January of 1906) and began working with famous occultists of the time to promote it, including: John Yarker, Gérard Encausse (aka Papus), Krumm-Heller, Aleister Crowley and eventually even H. Spencer Lewis. Rudolf Steiner was also a member of John Yarker's Memphis-Mizraim "Egyptian" Rite Masonry, via Reuss, and this may be where Krumm-Heller assumes that Blavatsky was also connected.

Comparison of the 72 Names from
Reuchlin, Kircher, Lenain, Levi, Glahn and Krumm-Heller

	Johann Reuchlin (1517)	Kircher (1652)	Lazare Lenain (1823)	Eliphas Levi (1860s)	A. Frank Glahn (1909)	Arnoldo Krumm-Heller (1930s)[416]
1	והו Vehuiah Ps. 3:3 (KJV)	והויה Vehuiah Ps. 3:4[417] [Ps. 3:3 (KJV)]	והויה Vehuiah Ps. 3:3[418] [Ps. 3:3 (KJV)]	Vehuiah{1} והויה	Vehuiah Ps. 3:4	Vehuiah{1}
2	ילי Ieliel Ps. 22:19 (KJV)	יליאל Ieliel Ps. 21:20[419] [Ps. 22:19 (KJV)]	יליאל Jeliel Ps. 21:20[420] [Ps. 22:19 (KJV)]	Jéliel{3} יליאל	Jeliel Ps.22:20	Jeliel{2}
3	סיט Sitael Ps. 91:2 (KJV)	סיטאל Sitael 90:2[421] [Ps. 91:2 (KJV)]	סיטאל Sitaël Ps. 90:2[422] [Ps. 91:2 (KJV)]	Sitaël{5} סיט	Sitael Ps. 91:2	Sitael{3}
4	עלם Elemiah Ps. 6:4 (KJV)	עלמיה Nghelamiah Ps. 6:5[423] [Ps. 6:4 (KJV)]	עלמיה Elemiah Ps. 6:4[424] [Ps. 6:4 (KJV)]	Ch'Almaiah{2}	Elamiah Ps. 6:5	Elemiah{4}
5	מהש Mahasiah Ps. 34:4 (KJV)	מהשיה Mehasiah Ps. 33:5[425] [Ps. 34:4 (KJV)]	מהשיה Mahasiah Ps. 33:4[426] [Ps. 34:4 (KJV)]	Mahasiah{4} מהש	Mehasiah Ps. 34:5	Mehasiah{5}

[416] Editor's note: The number in {brackets} indicates the original ordering of these names as given by the Author and a star* indicates a typo or misspelling of the name when compared with the other columns.

[417] Given as Ps. 3:4 « *Et tu Domine susceptor meus et gloria mea et exaltans caput meum* », which is Ps. 3:3 in KJV

[418] Given as Ps. 3:3 « *Et tu Domine susceptor meus et gloria mea et exaltans caput meum* », which is Ps. 3:3 in KJV

[419] Given as Ps. 21:20 « *Tu autem Domine ne elongaveris auxilium tuum a me ad defensionem meam conspice* », which is Ps. 22:19 in KJV

[420] Given as Ps. 21:20 « *Tu autem Domine ne elongaveris auxilium tuum a me ad defensionem meam conspice* », which is Ps. 22:19 in KJV

[421] Given as Ps. 90:2 « *Dicam Domine, susceptor meus es, et refugium meum, Deus meus, sperabo in eum* », which is Ps. 91:2 in KJV

[422] Given as Ps. 90:2 « *Dicet Domino: Susceptor meus es tu et refugium meum: Deus meus, sperabo in eum* », which is Ps. 91:2 in KJV

[423] Given as 6:5 « *Convertere Domine, eripe animam meam salvum me fac propter misericordiam tuam* », which is Ps. 6:4 in KJV

[424] Given as Ps. 6:4 « *Convertere Domine, et eripe animam meam: salvum me fac propter misericordiam tuam* », which is Ps. 6:4 in KJV

[425] Given as 33 :5 « *Exquisivi Dominum, et exaudivit me, et ex omnibus tribulationibus meis eripuit me* », which is Ps. 34:4 in KJV

[426] Given as Ps. 33:4 « *Exquisivi Dominum, et exaudivit me: et ex omnibus tribulationibus meis eripuit me* », which is Ps. 34 :4 in KJV

	Johann Reuchlin (1517)	Kircher (1652)	Lazare Lenain (1823)	Eliphas Levi (1860s)	A. Frank Glahn (1909)	Arnoldo Krumm-Heller (1930s)[427]
6	ללה Lelahel Ps. 9:11 (KJV)	ללהאל Lelahel Ps. 9:12[428] [Ps. 9:11 (KJV)]	ללהאל Lelahel Ps. 9:11[429] [Ps. 9:11 (KJV)]	Lalahel{6} ללהאל	Lelahel Ps. 9:12	**Lehahel*{6} [~Lelahel]
7	אכא Achaiah Ps. 103:8 (KJV)	אכאיה Achaiah Ps. 102:8[430] [Ps. 103:8 (KJV)]	אכאיה Achaiah Ps. 102:8[431] [Ps. 103:8 (KJV)]	Achaiah{7} אכאיה	Achaiah Ps. 103:8	Achaiah{7}
8	כהת Cahethel Ps. 95:6 (KJV)	כהתאל Cahathel Ps. 94:6[432] [Ps. 95:6 (KJV)]	כהתאל Cahathel Ps. 94:6[433] [Ps. 95:6 (KJV)]	Cahetel{9} כהת	Kahatel Ps. 95:6	Cahatel{8}
9	הזי Haziel Ps. 25:6 (KJV)	הזיאל Haziel Ps. 24:6[434] [Ps. 25:6 (KJV)]	הזיאל Haziel Ps. 24:6[435] [Ps. 25:6 (KJV)]	Haziel{11} הזי	Haziel Ps. 25:6	Haziel{9}
10	אלד Aladiah	אלדיה Aladiah Ps. 32:22[436] [Ps. 33:22 (KJV)]	אלדיה Aladiah Ps. 32:22[437] [Ps. 33:22 (KJV)]	Aladiah{8} אלדיה	Aladiah Ps. 33:22	Aladiah{10}
11	לאו Lauiah Ps. 18:46 (KJV)	לאויה Laauiah Ps. 17:47[438] [Ps. 18:46 (KJV)]	לאויה Lauviah Ps. 17:50[439] [Ps. 18:46 (KJV)]	Laaviah{10} לאויה	Laauiah Ps. 18:47	Lauviah{11}

[427] Editor's note: The number in {brackets} indicates the original ordering of these names as given by the Author and a star* indicates a typo or misspelling of the name when compared with the other columns.

[428] Given as Ps. 9:12 « *Psallite Domino, qui habitat in Sion, annunciate, inter gentes studia eius* », which is Ps. 9:11 in KJV

[429] Given as Ps. 9:11 « *Psallite Domino, qui habitat in Sion: annuntiate inter gentes studia ejus* », which is Ps. 9 :11 in KJV

[430] Given as Ps. 102:8 « *Miserator et misericors Dominus, longanimus, et multum misericors* », which is Ps. 103:8 in KJV

[431] Given as Ps. 102:8 « *Miserator et misericors Dominus: longanimis, et misericors* », which is Ps. 103 :8 in KJV

[432] Given as Ps. 94:6 « *Venite adoremus et procidemus ante facem Domini, qui fecit nos* », which is Ps. 95:6 in KJV

[433] Given as Ps. 94:6 « *Venite adoremus, et procidamus: et ploremus ante Dominum, qui fecit nos* », which is Ps. 95:6 in KJV

[434] Given as Ps. 24:6 « *Reminiscere miserationum tuarum Domine, et misericordiarum tuarum quae a seculo sunt*», which is Ps. 25:6 in KJV

[435] Given as Ps. 24:6 « *Reminiscere miserationum tuarum, Domine, et misericordiarum tuarum quae a saeculo sunt* », which is Ps. 25:6 in KJV

[436] Given as Ps. 32:22 « *Fiat misericordia tua Domine super nos, quemadmodum speravimus in te*», which is Ps. 33:22 in KJV

[437] Given as Ps. 32:22 « *Fiat misericordia tua Domine super nos: quemadmodum speravimus in te* », which is Ps. 33:22 in KJV

[438] Given as Ps. 17 :47 « *Vivit Dominus, et benedictus Deus meus, et exaltetur Deus salutis meae* », which is Ps. 18:46 in KJV

[439] Given as Ps. 17:50 « *Vivit Dominus, et benedictus Deus meus, et exaltetur Deus salutis meae* », which is Ps. 18:46 in KJV

	Johann Reuchlin (1517)	Kircher (1652)	Lazare Lenain (1823)	Eliphas Levi (1860s)	A. Frank Glahn (1909)	Arnoldo Krumm-Heller (1930s)[440]
12	ההע Hahaiah Ps. 10:1 (KJV)	ההעיה Hahaiah Ps. 10:1[441] [Ps. 10:1 (KJV)]	ההעיה Hahaiah Ps. 9:22[442] [Ps. 10:1 (KJV)]	Hahaiah{12} ההעיה	Haiah Ps. 9:22	**Habaiah*{12} [~Hahaiah]
13	יזל Iezalel Ps. 98:4 (KJV)	יזלאל Iezalel Ps. 97:4[443] [Ps. 98:4 (KJV)]	יזלאל Iezalel Ps. 97:6[444] [Ps. 98:4 (KJV)]	Jezael{13} יזל	Jezalel Ps. 98:4	Jesalel{13}
14	מבה Mebahel Ps. 9:9 (KJV)	מבהאל Mebahel Ps. 9:9[445] [Ps. 9:9 (KJV)]	מבהאל Mebahel Ps. 9:10[446] [Ps. 9:10 (KJV)]	Mebahel{15} מבה	Mebahel Ps. 9:10	Mehahel*{53} [~Mebahel]
15	הרי Hariel Ps. 94:22 (KJV)	הריאל Hariel Ps. 2:2[447] [Ps. 94:22 (KJV)]	הריאל Hariel Ps. 93:22[448] [Ps. 94:22 (KJV)]	Hariel{17} הרי	Hariel Ps. 94:22	Hariel{54}
16	הקם Hakamiah Ps. 88:1 (KJV)	הקמיה Hakamiah Ps. 87:2[449] [Ps. 88:1 (KJV)]	הקמיה Hakamiah Ps. 87:1[450] [Ps. 88:1 (KJV)]	Hackamiah{14} הקמ	Hakamiah Ps. 88:2	Hakamiah{55}

[440] Editor's note: The number in {brackets} indicates the original ordering of these names as given by the Author and a star* indicates a typo or misspelling of the name when compared with the other columns.

[441] Given as Ps. 10:1 « *Ut quid Domine recessisti longe, de spicis in opportunitatibus, in tribulatione?* », which is Ps. 9:22 in KJV

[442] Given as Ps. 9:22 « *Ut quid Domine recessisti longe, de spicis in opportunitatibus, in tribulatione* », which is Ps. 10:1 in KJV

[443] Given as Ps. 97:4 « *Iubilate Domino omnis terrae, cantate, exultate, et psallite* », which is Ps. 98:4 in KJV

[444] Given as Ps. 97:6 « *Jubilate Deo omnis terra : cantate, et exultate, et psallite* », which is Ps. 98:4 in KJV

[445] Given as Ps. 9:9 « *Et factus est Dominus refugium pauperi, adiutor in opportunitatibus, in tribulatione.* », which is also Ps. 9:9 in KJV

[446] Given as Ps. 9:9 « *Et factus est Dominus refugium pauperis: adjutor in opportunitatibus, in tribulatione.* », which is Ps. 9:10 in KJV

[447] Given as Ps. 2:2 « *Et factus est mihi Dominus in refugium, et Deus meus in adiutorium spei meae* », which is Ps. 94:22 in KJV

[448] Given as Ps. 93:22 « *Et factus est mihi Dominus in refugium : et Deus meus in adjutorium spei meae* », which is Ps. 94:22 in KJV

[449] Given as Ps. 87:2 « *Domine Deus salutis meae, in die clamaui et nocte coram te* », which is Ps. 88:1 in KJV

[450] Given as Ps. 87:1 « *Domine Deus salutis meae, in die clamavi et nocte coram te* », which is Ps. 88:1 in KJV

	Johann Reuchlin (1517)	Kircher (1652)	Lazare Lenain (1823)	Eliphas Levi (1860s)	A. Frank Glahn (1909)	Arnoldo Krumm-Heller (1930s)[451]
17	לאו Louiah [or Loviah] Ps. 8:1 (KJV)	לאויה Louiah Ps. 8:2[452] [Ps. 8:1 (KJV)]	לאויה Lauviah Ps. 8:1[453] [Ps. 8:1 (KJV)]	Loviah{16} לאו	Lauviah Ps. 8:2	**Lanoiah*{56} [~Lauoiah]
18	כלי Caliel Ps. 35:24 (KJV)	כליאל Caliel Ps. 34:24[454] [Ps. 35:24 (KJV)]	כליאל Caliel Ps. 7:9[455] [Ps. 7:8 (KJV)]	Caliel{18} כלי	Kaliel Ps. 7:9	Caliel{57}
19	לוו Leuuiah [or Levuiah] Ps. 40:1 (KJV)	לוויה Leuiuiah Ps. 39:2[456] [Ps. 40:1 (KJV)]	לוויה Leuviah Ps. 39:1[457] [Ps. 40:1 (KJV)]	Leviviah{19}	Lewowoiah Ps. 40:2	Leuviah{14}
20	פהל Pahaliah Ps. 116:4 (KJV)	פהליה Pahaliah Ps. 119:2[458] [Ps. 116:4 (KJV)]	פהליה Pahaliah Ps. 119:2[459] [Ps. 120:2 (KJV)]	Pahaliah{21} פהל	Pahaliah Ps. 120:2	Pahaliah{15}
21	נלך Nelchael Ps. 31:14 (KJV)	נלכאל Nelchael Ps. 30:15[460] [Ps. 31:14 (KJV)]	נלכאל Nelchael Ps. 30:18[461] [Ps. 31:14-15 (KJV)]	Nelchael{23} נלכ	Nelchael Ps. 31:15	Melchael*{16} [~Nelchael]

[451] Editor's note: The number in {brackets} indicates the original ordering of these names as given by the Author and a star* indicates a typo or misspelling of the name when compared with the other columns.

[452] Given as Ps. 8:2 « *Domine Dominus noster, quam admirabile est nomen tuum in universa terra!* », which is Ps. 8:1 in KJV

[453] Given as Ps. 8:1 « *Domine Dominus noster, quam admirabile est nomen tuum in universa terra!* », which is Ps. 8:1 in KJV

[454] Given as Ps. 34:24 « *Iudica me secundum iustitiam tuam Domine Deus meus, et non supergaudeant mihi.* », which is Ps. 35:24 in KJV. Note that the Hebrew given by Kircher also corresponds to Ps. 35:24 KJV.

[455] Given as Ps. 7:9 « *Judica me Domine secundum justitiam meam, et sucundum innocentiam meam super me.* », which is Ps. 7:8 in KJV

[456] Given as Ps. 39:2 « *Exspectans exspectaui Dominum, & intendit mihi.* », which is Ps. 40:1 in KJV

[457] Given as Ps. 39:1 « *Exspectans exspectavi Dominum et intendit mihi* », which is Ps. 40:1 in KJV

[458] Given as Ps. 119:2 « *Et nomen Domini invocabo, o Domine, libera animam meam* », which is Ps. 116:4 in KJV

[459] Given as Ps. 119:2 « *Domine libera animam meam a labiis iniquis a lingua dolosa* », which is Ps. 120:2 in KJV

[460] Given as Ps. 30:15 « *Ego autem in te speravi Domine, dixi, Deus meus es tu.* », which is Ps. 31:14 in KJV

[461] Given as Ps. 30:18 « *Ego autem in te speravi Domine: dixi Deus meus es tu: in manibus tuis sortes meae* », which is Ps. 31:14-15 in KJV

	Johann Reuchlin (1517)	Kircher (1652)	Lazare Lenain (1823)	Eliphas Levi (1860s)	A. Frank Glahn (1909)	Arnoldo Krumm-Heller (1930s)[462]
22	ייי Ieiaiel Ps. 121:5 (KJV)	יייאל Ieiahel Ps. 120:5[463] [Ps. 121:5 (KJV)]	יייאל Ieiaiel Ps. 120:3[464] [Ps. 121:5 (KJV)]	Jejahiel{20} ייי	Jujuael Ps. 121:5	**Jecaiel*{17} [~Jejaiel]
23	מלה Melahel Ps. 121:8 (KJV)	מלהאל Melahel Ps. 120:8[465] [Ps. 121:8 (KJV)]	מלהאל Melahel Ps. 120:8[466] [Ps. 121:8 (KJV)]	Melahel{22} מלה	Melahel Ps. 121:8	Melehel{18}
24*	חהו Chaiuiah Ps. 147:11 (KJV)	ההויה Hahiuiah Ps. 35:5[467] [Ps. 147:11 (KJV)]	ההויה Hahiuiah Ps. 32:18[468] [Ps. 33:18 (KJV)]	Hahiviah{24} חהו	Hahiwoiah Ps. 33:18	**Hahimah*{19} [~Hahiwah or Hahiviah]
25	נתה Nithhaiah Ps. 9:1 (KJV)	נתהיה Nithaiah Ps. 9:2[469] [Ps. 9:1 (KJV)]	נתהיה Nith-Haiah Ps. 9:1[470] [Ps. 9:1 (KJV)]	Nithaiah{25} נתה	Nithaiah Ps. 9:2	Nith-Heich{20}
26	האא Haaiah Ps. 119:145 (KJV)	האאיה Haaiah Ps. 118:145[471] [Ps. 119:145 (KJV)]	האאיה Haaiah Ps. 118:145[472] [Ps. 119:145 (KJV)]	Haajah{27} האא	Haaiah Ps. 119:145	Haaiah{21}

[462] Editor's note: The number in {brackets} indicates the original ordering of these names as given by the Author and a star* indicates a typo or misspelling of the name when compared with the other columns.

[463] Given as Ps. 120:5 « *Dominus custodit te Dominus protectio tua super manum dexteram tuam* », which is Ps. 121:5 in KJV

[464] Given as Ps. 120:3 « *Dominus custodit te; Dominus proteclio tua, super manum dexteram tuam.* », which is Ps. 121:5 in KJV

[465] Given as Ps. 120:8 « *Dominus custodiat introitum tuum & exitum tuum ex hoc nunc & usque in seculum* », which is Ps. 121:8 in KJV

[466] Given as Ps. 120:8 « *Dominus custodiat introïtum tuum, et exitum tuum: et ex hoc nunc, et in seculum* », which is Ps. 121:8 in KJV

[467] Given as Ps. 35:5 « *beneplacitum est Domino super timentes eum & in eos qui sperant super misericordia eius* », which is Ps. 147:11 in KJV

[468] Given as Ps. 32:18 « *Ecce oculi Domini super metuentes eum: et in eis, qui sperant in misericordia ejus.* », which is Ps. 33:18 in KJV

[469] Given as Ps. 9:2 « *confitebor tibi Domine in toto corde meo narrabo omnia mirabilia tua* », which is Ps. 9:1 in KJV

[470] Given as Ps. 9:2 « *Confitebor tibi Domine in toto corde meo: narrabo omnia mirabilia tua* », which is Ps. 9:1 in KJV

[471] Given as Ps. 118:145 « *clamavi in toto corde exaudi me Domine iustificationes tuas requiram* », which is Ps. 119:145 in KJV

[472] Given as Ps. 118:145 « *Clamavi in toto corde exaudi meo, exaudi me Domine; justificationes tuas requiram* », which is Ps. 119:145 in KJV

	Johann Reuchlin (1517)	Kircher (1652)	Lazare Lenain (1823)	Eliphas Levi (1860s)	A. Frank Glahn (1909)	Arnoldo Krumm-Heller (1930s)[473]
27	ירת Ierathel Ps. 140:1 (KJV)	ירתאל Ierathel Ps. 139:1[474] [Ps. 140:1 (KJV)]	ירתאל Ierathel Ps. 139:1[475] [Ps. 140:1 (KJV)]	Jérathel{29} ירת	Jerathel Ps. 140:2	Jerathel{22}
28	שאה Seehiah Ps. 71:12 (KJV)	שאהיה Scheheiah Ps. 70:12[476] [Ps. 71:12 (KJV)]	שאהיה Séheiah Ps. 70:13[477] [Ps. 71:12 (KJV)]	Scheheiah{26} שאה	Scheaheiah Ps. 71:12	Seeiah{23}
29	ריי Reiaiel Ps. 54:4 (KJV)	רייאל Reiaiel Ps. 53:7[478] [Ps. 54:4 (KJV)]	רייאל Reiiel Ps. 53:7[479] [Ps. 54:4 (KJV)]	Réjajel{28} ריי	Rejiel Ps. 54:6	Reiiel{24}
30	אום Omael Ps. 71:5 (KJV)	ומאל Omael Ps. 70:5[480] [Ps. 71:5 (KJV)]	ומאל Omael Ps. 70:6[481] [Ps. 71:5 (KJV)]	Omael{30} אום	Osmael Ps. 71:5	Omael{25}
31	לכב Lecabel Ps. 71:16 (KJV)	לכבאל Lecabel Ps. 70:16[482] [Ps. 71:16 (KJV)]	לכבאל Lecabel Ps. 70:16[483] [Ps. 71:15-16 (KJV)]	Lecabel{31} לכב	Lekabel Ps. 71:16	Lecabel{26}

---

[473] Editor's note: The number in {brackets} indicates the original ordering of these names as given by the Author and a star* indicates a typo or misspelling of the name when compared with the other columns.

[474] Given as Ps. 139:1 « *eripe me Domine ab homine malo a viro iniquo eripe me* », which is Ps. 140:1 in KJV

[475] Given as Ps. 139:1 « *Eripe me Domine ab homine malo, à viro iniquo eripe me* », which is Ps. 140:1 in KJV

[476] Given as Ps. 70:12 « *Deus ne elongeris a me Deus meus in adiutorium meum respice* », which is Ps. 71:12 in KJV

[477] Given as Ps. 70:13 « *Deus ne elongeris à me: Deus meus in auxilium meum respice* », which is Ps. 71:12 in KJV

[478] Given as Ps. 53:7, but is actually 53:6 « *ecce enim Deus adiuvat me Dominus susceptor animae meae* », which is Ps. 54:4 in KJV

[479] Given as Ps. 53:7, but is actually 53:6 « *Ecce enim Deus adjuvat me: et Dominus susceptor est animae meae* », which is Ps. 54:4 in KJV

[480] Given as Ps. 70:5 « *quoniam tu es patientia mea Domine Domine spes mea a iuventute mea* », which is Ps. 71:5 in KJV

[481] Given as Ps. 70:5 « *Quoniam tu es patientia mea Domine: Domine spes mea à juventute mea* », which is Ps. 71:5 in KJV

[482] Given as Ps. 70:16 « *introibo in potentiam Domini Domine memorabor iustitiae tuae solius* », which is Ps. 71:16 in KJV

[483] Given as Ps. 70:16 « *Quoniam non cognovi litteraturam, introibo in potentiam Domini Domine memorabor iustitiae tuae solius* », which is Ps. 71:15-16 in KJV

	Johann Reuchlin (1517)	Kircher (1652)	Lazare Lenain (1823)	Eliphas Levi (1860s)	A. Frank Glahn (1909)	Arnoldo Krumm-Heller (1930s)[484]
32	ושר Vasariah Ps. 33:4 (KJV)	ושריה Vasariah Ps. 32:4[485] [Ps. 33:4 (KJV)]	ושריה Vasariah Ps. 32:4[486] [Ps. 33:4 (KJV)]	Vasariah{33} ושר	Vesariah Ps. 33:4	Vasaniah{58}
33*	יחו Iechuiah Ps. 94:11 (KJV)	יהויה Iehuiah Ps. 83:11[487] [Ps. 94:11 (KJV)]	יהויה Iehuiah Ps. 33:11[488] [Ps. 94:11 (KJV)]	Jejuiah {35} ייה	Jehuiah Ps. 33:1	**Jomiah{59} [~Johuiah]
34	להה Lehachiah Ps. 131:3 (KJV)	לההיה Lehaiah Ps. 130:3[489] [Ps. 131:3 (KJV)]	לההיה Lehaiah Ps. 130:5[490] [Ps. 131:3 (KJV)]	Lehahiah{32} לההיה	Leihaiah Ps. 131:3	Lehaiah{60}
35	כוק Chauakiah Ps. 116:1 (KJV)	כוקיה Chauakiah Ps. 114:1[491] [Ps. 116:1 (KJV)]	כוקיה Chauakiah Ps. 114:1[492] [Ps. 116:1 (KJV)]	Chavakiah{34} כוק	Kewakiah Ps. 116:1	Chavakiah{61}
36	מנד Manadel Ps. 26:8 (KJV)	מנדאל Menadel Ps. 25:8[493] [Ps. 26:8 (KJV)]	מנדאל Menadel Ps. 25:8[494] [Ps. 26:8 (KJV)]	Menadel{36} מנד	Menadel Ps. 26:8	Menadel{62}

[484] Editor's note: The number in {brackets} indicates the original ordering of these names as given by the Author and a star* indicates a typo or misspelling of the name when compared with the other columns.

[485] Given as Ps. 32:4 « *Quia rectum est verbum Domini & omnia opera eius in fide* », which is Ps. 33:4 in KJV

[486] Given as Ps. 32:4 « *Quia rectum est verbum Domini, et omnia opera ejus in fide* », which is Ps. 33:4 in KJV

[487] Given as Ps. 83:11, but is actually 93:11 « *Dominus scit cogitationes hominum quoniam vanae sunt* », which is Ps. 94:11 in KJV

[488] Given as Ps. 33:11, but is actually 93:11 « *Dominus scit cogitationes hominum quoniam vanae sunt* », which is Ps. 94:11 in KJV

[489] Given as Ps. 130:3 « *Speret Israhel in Domino ex hoc nunc & usque in seculum* », which is Ps. 131:3 in KJV

[490] Given as Ps. 130:5 « *Speret Israël in Domino; ex hoc nunc, et usque in saeculum* », which is Ps. 131:3 in KJV

[491] Given as Ps. 114:1 « *Dilexi quoniam exaudiut Dominus vocem depricationis meae* », which is very similar to Ps. 116:1 in KJV

[492] Given as Ps. 114:1 « *Dilexi quoniam exaudiet Dominus vocem orationis meae* », which is Ps. 116:1 in KJV

[493] Given as Ps. 25:8 « *Dilexi decorem domus tuae & locum habitationis gloriae tuae* », which is Ps. 26:8 in KJV

[494] Given as Ps. 25:8 « *Domine dilexi decorem domus tuae & locum habitationis gloriae tuae* », which is Ps. 26:8 in KJV

	Johann Reuchlin (1517)	Kircher (1652)	Lazare Lenain (1823)	Eliphas Levi (1860s)	A. Frank Glahn (1909)	Arnoldo Krumm-Heller (1930s)[495]
36	מנד Manadel Ps. 26:8 (KJV)	מנדאל Menadel Ps. 25:8[496] [Ps. 26:8 (KJV)]	מנדאל Menadel Ps. 25:8[497] [Ps. 26:8 (KJV)]	Menadel{36} מנד	Menadel Ps. 26:8	Menadel{62}
37	אני Aniel Ps. 80:19 (KJV)	אניאל Aniel Ps. 79:4[498] [Ps. 80:19 (KJV)]	אניאל Aniel Ps. 79:8[499] [Ps. 80:19 (KJV)]	Aniel{37} אני	Aniel Ps. 80:8	Amiel*{27} [~Anniel]
38*	חעם Chaamiah Ps. 91:9 (KJV)	העמיה Haamiah Ps. 90:9[500] [Ps. 91:9 (KJV)]	העמיה Haamiah Ps. 90:9[501] [Ps. 91:9 (KJV)]	Haamiah{39} העמ	Haamiah Ps. 91:9	Haamiah{28}
39	רהע Rehael Ps. 30:10 (KJV)	רהעאל Rehael Ps. 29:11[502] [Ps. 30:10 (KJV)]	רהעאל Rehael Ps. 29:13[503] [Ps. 30:10 (KJV)]	Réhael{41} רהע	Rehael Ps. 30:11	Rehahel{29}
40	ייז Ieiazel Ps. 88:14 (KJV)	ייזאל Ieiazel Ps. 87:15[504] [Ps. 88:14 (KJV)]	ייזאל Ieiazel Ps. 87:15[505] [Ps. 88:14 (KJV)]	Jajazel{38} ייז	Jeiazel Ps. 88:15	Jeiazel{30}
41	הההה Hahahel Ps. 120:2 (KJV)	הההאל Hahael Ps. 119:1[506] [Ps. 120:2 (KJV)]	הההאל Hahahel Ps. 119:2[507] [Ps. 120:2 (KJV)]	Haahel{40} [הה]האל	Hahael Ps. 120:2	Hahahel{31}

[495] Editor's note: The number in {brackets} indicates the original ordering of these names as given by the Author and a star* indicates a typo or misspelling of the name when compared with the other columns.

[496] Given as Ps. 25:8 « *Dilexi decorem domus tuae & locum habitationis gloriae tuae* », which is Ps. 26:8 in KJV

[497] Given as Ps. 25:8 « *Domine dilexi decorem domus tuae & locum habitationis gloriae tuae* », which is Ps. 26:8 in KJV

[498] Given as Ps. 79:4 « *Domine Deus converte nos, ostende faciem tuam & salvi erimus* », which is Ps. 80:19 in KJV

[499] Given as Ps. 79:8 « *Deus ad vertutem converte nos: et ostende faciem tuam et salvi erimus* », which is Ps. 80:19 in KJV

[500] Given as Ps. 90:9 « *Quoniam tu es, Domine, spes mea altissimum posuisti refugium tuum* », which is Ps. 91:9 in KJV

[501] Given as Ps. 90:9 « *Quoniam tu es Domine spes mea: altissimum posuisti refugium tuum* », which is Ps. 91:9 in KJV

[502] Given as Ps. 29:11 « *Audivit me Dominus & misertus est mei, Dominus factus est adiutor meus* », which is Ps. 30:10 in KJV

[503] Given as Ps. 29:13 « *Audivit me Dominus, et misertus est mei: Dominus factus est adiutor* », which is Ps. 30:10 in KJV

[504] Given as Ps. 87:15 « *Ut quid Domine repellis animam meam, avertis faciem tuam a me* », which is Ps. 88:14 in KJV

[505] Given as Ps. 87:15 « *Ut quid Domine repellis orationem meam: avertis faciem tuam à me* », which is Ps. 88:14 in KJV

[506] Given as Ps. 119:1, but is actually 119:2 « *Domine libera animam meam a labiis iniquis, & a lingua dolosa* », which is Ps. 120:2 in KJV

[507] Given as Ps. 119:2 « *Domine libera animam meam à labiis iniquis, et à linguâ dolosâ* », which is Ps. 120:2 in KJV

	Johann Reuchlin (1517)	Kircher (1652)	Lazare Lenain (1823)	Eliphas Levi (1860s)	A. Frank Glahn (1909)	Arnoldo Krumm-Heller (1930s)[508]
42	מיך Michael Ps. 121:7 (KJV)	מיכאל Michael Ps. 120:7[509] [Ps. 121:7 (KJV)]	מיכאל Mikael Ps. 120:7[510] [Ps. 121:7 (KJV)]	Michael{42} מכא	Michael Ps. 121:7	**Mikahel{32}
43	וול Veualiah Ps. 88:13 (KJV)	ווליה Veualiah Ps. 87:14[511] [Ps. 88:13 (KJV)]	ווליה Veualiah Ps. 87:14[512] [Ps. 88:13 (KJV)]	Vavaliah{43} וול	Wevaliah Ps. 88:14	Vehualiah{33}
44	ילה Ielahiah Ps. 119:108 (KJV)	ילהיה Ielaiah Ps. 118:108[513] [Ps. 119:108 (KJV)]	ילהיה Ielahiah Ps. 118:108[514] [Ps. 119:108 (KJV)]	Jelaiah{45} יל[ה]	Jelaiah Ps. 119:108	Jelahiah{34}
45	סאל Sealiah Ps. 94:18 (KJV)	סאליה Sealhiah Ps. 93:18[515] [Ps. 94:18 (KJV)]	סאליה Sealiah Ps. 93:18[516] [Ps. 94:18 (KJV)]	Seathiah{47} סאל	Sealiah Ps. 94:18	Sealieh{35}
46	ערי Ariel Ps. 145:9 (KJV)	עריאל Nghariel Ps. 114:9[517] [Ps. 145:9 (KJV)]	עריאל Ariel Ps. 144:9[518] [Ps. 145:9 (KJV)]	Ngariel{44} ערי	Ariel Ps. 145:9	Ariel{36}

---

[508] Editor's note: The number in {brackets} indicates the original ordering of these names as given by the Author and a star* indicates a typo or misspelling of the name when compared with the other columns.

[509] Given as Ps. 120:7 « *Dominus custodit te ab omni malo, & custodiat animam tuam [Dominus]* », which is Ps. 121:7 in KJV

[510] Given as Ps. 120:7 « *Dominus custodit te ab omni malo; custodiat animam tuam Dominus* », which is Ps. 121:7 in KJV

[511] Given as Ps. 87:14 « *Et ego ad te Domine clamavi, & mane oratio mea praeveniet te* », which is Ps. 88:13 in KJV

[512] Given as Ps. 87:14 « *Et ego ad te Domine clamavi: et manè oratio mea praeveniet te* », which is Ps. 88:13 in KJV

[513] Given as Ps. 118:108 « *Voluntaria oris mei beneplacita sunt Domino, & iudicia tua doce me* », which is Ps. 119:108 in KJV

[514] Given as Ps. 118:108 « *Voluntaria oris mei bene placita fac Domine: et judicia tua doce me* », which is Ps. 119:108 in KJV

[515] Given as Ps. 93:18 « *Si dicebam motus est pes meus, misericordia tua Domine adiuvabat me* », which is Ps. 94:18 in KJV

[516] Given as Ps. 93:18 « *Si dicebam, motus est pes meus: misericordia tua Domine adjuvabat me* », which is Ps. 94:18 in KJV

[517] Given as Ps. 114:9, but is actually 144:9 « *Bonus Dominus universis, & miserationes eius super omnia opera eius* », which is Ps. 145:9 in KJV

[518] Given as Ps. 144:9 « *Suavis Dominus universis: et miserationes ejus super omnia opera ejus* », which is Ps. 145:9 in KJV

	Johann Reuchlin (1517)	Kircher's Bible Verse Number [Corrected]	Lazare Lenain (1823)	Eliphas Levi (1860s)	A. Frank Glahn (1909)	Arnoldo Krumm-Heller (1930s)[519]
47	עשל Asaliah Ps. 92:5 (KJV)	עשליה Asaliah Ps. 91:6[520] [Ps. 92:5 (KJV)]	עשליה Asaliah Ps. 104:25[521] [Ps. 104:24 (KJV)]	Azaliah{46} עשליה	Asaliah Ps. 104:24	Azaliah{37}
48	מיה Mehiel Ps. 98:2 (KJV)	מיהאל Mehiel Ps. 97:2[522] [Ps. 98:2 (KJV)]	מיהאל Mihael Ps. 97:3[523] [Ps. 98:2 (KJV)]	Mehiel{48}	Mihael Ps. 98:2	**Michael{38} [~Mihael]
49	והו Vehuel Ps. 145:3 (KJV)	והואל Vehuel Ps. 144:3[524] [Ps. 145:3 (KJV)]	והואל Vehuel Ps. 144:3[525] [Ps. 145:3 (KJV)]	Vehuel{49} והו	Vehuel Ps. 145:3	Vehuel{39}
50	דני Daniel Ps. 145:8 (KJV)	דניאל Daniel Ps. 85:15[526] [Ps. 145:8 (KJV)]	דניאל Daniel Ps. 102:8[527] [Ps. 103:8 (KJV)]	Daniel{51} דני	Daniel Ps. 103:8	Daniel{63}
51*	החש Hachasiah Ps. 104:31 (KJV)	ההשיה Hahasiah Ps. 103:31[528] [Ps. 104:31 (KJV)]	ההשיה Hahasiah Ps. 103:32[529] [Ps. 104:31 (KJV)]	Hahasiah{53} ההס	Hahasiah Ps. 104:31	Hahasiah{64}

[519] Editor's note: The number in {brackets} indicates the original ordering of these names as given by the Author and a star* indicates a typo or misspelling of the name when compared with the other columns.

[520] Given as Ps. 91:6 « *Quam magnificata sunt opera tua Domine, nimis profundae factae sunt cogitationes tuae* », which is Ps. 92:5 in KJV

[521] Given as Ps. 104:25, but is actually 103:24 « *Quam magnificata sunt opera tua Domine! omnia in sapientia fecisti: impleta est terra possessione tua* », which is Ps. 104:24 in KJV

[522] Given as Ps. 97:2 « *Notum fecit Dominus salutare suum, in conspectu [gentium] revelavit iustitiam suam* », which is Ps. 98:2 in KJV

[523] Given as Ps. 97:2 « *Notum fecit Dominus salutare suum: in conspectu gentium revelavit justitiam suam* », which is Ps. 98:2 in KJV

[524] Given as Ps. 144:3 « *Magnus Dominus & laudabilis nimis, & magnitudinis eius non est finis* », which is Ps. 145:3 in KJV

[525] Given as Ps. 144:3 « *Magnus Dominus et laudabilis nimis et magnitudinis ejus non est finis* », which is Ps. 145:3 in KJV

[526] Given as Ps. 85:15 (86:15 KJV), but is actually 144:8 « *Miserator & misericors Dominus patiens, & multum misericors* », which is Ps. 145:8 in KJV

[527] Given as Ps. 102:8 « *Miserator et misericors Dominus: longanimis et multum misericors* », which is Ps. 103:8 in KJV

[528] Given as Ps. 103:31 « *Sit gloria Domini in seculum, laetabitur Dominus in operibus suis* », which is Ps. 104:31 in KJV

[529] Given as Ps. 103:32 « *Sit gloria Domini in saeculum: laetabitur Dominus in operibus suis* », which is Ps. 104:31 in KJV

	Johann Reuchlin (1517)	Kircher (1652)	Lazare Lenain (1823)	Eliphas Levi (1860s)	A. Frank Glahn (1909)	Arnoldo Krumm-Heller (1930s)[530]
52	עמם Imamiah Ps. 7:17 (KJV)	עממיה Nghimamiah Ps. 7:18[531] [Ps. 7:17 (KJV)]	עממיה Imamiah Ps. 7:18[532] [Ps. 7:17 (KJV)]	Nghimamiah{50} עממ	Omamiah Ps. 7:18	Imamiah{65}
53	אננ Nanael Ps. 119:75 (KJV)	ננאל Nanael Ps. 118:75[533] [Ps. 119:75 (KJV)]	ננאל Nanael Ps. 118:75[534] [Ps. 119:75 (KJV)]	Nanael{52}	Nanael Ps. 119:75	Nanael{66}
54	נית Nithael Ps. 103:19 (KJV)	ניתאל Nithael Ps. 102:19[535] [Ps. 103:19 (KJV)]	ניתאל Nithael Ps. 102:19[536] [Ps. 103:19 (KJV)]	Nithael{54}	Nithael Ps. 103:19	Nitbael{67}
55	מבה Mebahiah Ps. 102:12 (KJV)	מבהיה Mebaiah Ps. 103:13[537] [Ps. 102:12 (KJV)]	מבהיה Mebahiah Ps. 101:13[538] [Ps. 102:12 (KJV)]	Mebaiah{55} מבה	Mebaiah Ps. 102:13	Mehaiah*{40} [~Hebaiah]
56	פוי Poiel Ps. 145:14 (KJV)	פויאל Pouiel Ps. 144:14[539] [Ps. 145:14 (KJV)]	פויאל Poiel Ps. 144:15[540] [Ps. 145:14 (KJV)]	Poviel{57} פוי	Poviel Ps. 145:14	Poiel{41}

[530] Editor's note: The number in {brackets} indicates the original ordering of these names as given by the Author and a star* indicates a typo or misspelling of the name when compared with the other columns.

[531] Given as Ps. 7:18 « *Confitebor Domino secundum iustitiam eius, & psallam Nomini Domini altissimi* », which is Ps. 7:17 in KJV

[532] Given as Ps. 7:18 « *Confitebor Domino secundum justitiam ejus: et psallam nomini Domini altissimi* », which is Ps. 7:17 in KJV

[533] Given as Ps. 118:75 « *Cognovi Domine, quia aquitas iudicia tua, & veritate humiliasti me* », which is Ps. 119:75 in KJV

[534] Given as Ps. 118:75 « *Cognovi Domine quia aequitas judicia tua: et veritate tua humiliasti me* », which is Ps. 119:75 in KJV

[535] Given as Ps. 102:19 « *Dominus in coelo paravit sedem suam, & regnum ipsius omnibus dominabitur* », which is Ps. 103:19 in KJV

[536] Given as Ps. 102:19 « *Dominus in coelo paravit sedem suam: et regnum ipsius omnibus dominabitur* », which is Ps. 103:19 in KJV

[537] Given as Ps. 103:13, but is actually 101:13 « *Tu autem Domine in aeternum permanes, & memoriale tuum in generationem & generationem* », which is Ps. 102:12 in KJV

[538] Given as Ps. 101:13 « *Tu autem Domine in aeternum permanes: et memoriale tuum in generationem* », which is Ps. 102:12 in KJV

[539] Given as Ps. 144:14 « *Allevat Dominus, [omnes] qui corruunt, & erigit omnes elisos* », which is Ps. 145:14 in KJV

[540] Given as Ps. 144:15 « *Allevat Dominus omnes qui corruunt: et erigit omnes elisos* », which is Ps. 145:14 in KJV

	Johann Reuchlin (1517)	Kircher (1652)	Lazare Lenain (1823)	Eliphas Levi (1860s)	A. Frank Glahn (1909)	Arnoldo Krumm-Heller (1930s)[541]
57	נמם Nemamiah Ps. 115:11 (KJV)	נממיה Nemamiah Ps. 113:9[542] [Ps. 115:11 (KJV)]	נממיה Nemamiah Ps. 113:19[543] [Ps. 115:11 (KJV)]	Nemamiah{59}	Nemamiah Ps. 115:11	Nemamiah{42}
58	ייל Ieialel Ps. 6:3 (KJV)	יילאל Ieialel Ps. 6:4[544] [Ps. 6:3 (KJV)]	יילאל Ieialel Ps. 6:3[545] [Ps. 6:3 (KJV)]	Jejalel{56}	Jejaliel ייל Ps. 6:4	Jeialel{43}
59*	הרח Harachel Ps. 113:3 (KJV)	הרהאל Harahel Ps. 112:3[546] [Ps. 113:3 (KJV)]	הרהאל Harahel Ps. 112:3[547] [Ps. 113:3 (KJV)]	Harael{58} הרה	Harahel Ps. 113:3	**Nazael{44} [~Hazael or Harael]
60	מצר Mizrael [or Mitzrael] Ps. 145:17 (KJV)	מצראל Mitsraël Ps. 144:17[548] [Ps. 145:17 (KJV)]	מצראל Mitzrael Ps. 144:18[549] [Ps. 145:17 (KJV)]	Mitsrael{60}	Mizrael Ps. 145:17	Mizrael{45}
61	ומב Vmabel [or Umabel] Ps. 113:2 (KJV)	ומבאל Vmabael Ps. 122:1[550] [Ps. 113:2 (KJV)]	ומבאל Umabael Ps. 122:2[551] [Ps. 113:2 (KJV)]	UMABEL{61}	Umabel Ps. 113:2	Umebel{46}

---

[541] Editor's note: The number in {brackets} indicates the original ordering of these names as given the Author and a star* indicates a typo or misspelling of the name when compared with the other columns.

[542] Given as Ps. 113:9, but is actually 113:19 « *Qui timent Dominum, speraverunt in [Domino] eo[rum], adiutor & protector eorum est* », which is Ps. 115:11 in KJV

[543] Given as Ps. 113:19 « *Qui timent Dominum speraverunt in Domino: adiutor eorum et protector eorum est* », which is Ps. 115:11 in KJV

[544] Given as Ps. 6:4 « *Et anima mea turbata est valde, [et] tu Domine usquequo* », which is Ps. 6:3 in KJV

[545] Given as Ps. 6:3 « *Et anima mea turbata est valde; sed tu Domine usque quo?* », which is Ps. 6:3 in KJV

[546] Given as Ps. 112:3 « *A solis ortu usque ad occasum, laudabile nomen Domini* », which is Ps. 113:3 in KJV

[547] Given as Ps. 112:3 « *A solis ortu usque ad occasum, laudabile nomen Domini* », which is Ps. 113:3 in KJV

[548] Given as Ps. 144:17 « *Iustus Dominus in omnibus viis suis, & sanctus in omnibus operibus suis* », which is Ps. 145:17 in KJV

[549] Given as Ps. 144:18 « *Justus Dominus in omnibus viis suis: et sanctus in omnibus operibus suis* », which is Ps. 145:17 in KJV

[550] Given as Ps. 122:1, but is actually 112:2 « *Sit nomen Domini benedictum ex hoc, nunc, & usque in seculum* », which is Ps. 113:2 in KJV

[551] Given as Ps. 122:2 « *Sit nomen Domini benedictum, ex hoc nunc et usque in saeculum* », which is Ps. 113:2 in KJV

	Johann Reuchlin (1517)	Kircher (1652)	Lazare Lenain (1823)	Eliphas Levi (1860s)	A. Frank Glahn (1909)	Arnoldo Krumm-Heller (1930s)[552]
62	יהה Iahhael Ps. 119:159 (KJV)	יההאל Iahahel Ps. 118:159[553] [Ps. 119:159 (KJV)]	יההאל Iah-hel Ps. 118:159[554] [Ps. 119:159 (KJV)]	JABAHEL{63}	Jahahel Ps. 119:159	Jahhel{47}
63	ענו Anauel Ps. 100:2 (KJV)	ענואל Nghanauel Ps. 99:2[555] [Ps. 100:2 (KJV)]	ענואל Anauel Ps. 2:11[556] [Ps. 2:11 (KJV)]	NGAMAVEL{65}	Anianuel Ps. 2:11	Ananel*{48} [~Anauel]
64*	מהי Mechiel Ps. 33:18 (KJV)	מהיאל Mehiel Ps. 32:18[557] [Ps. 33:18 (KJV)]	מהיאל Mehiel Ps. 32:18[558] [Ps. 33:18 (KJV)]	MÉHIEL{68}	Mehiel Ps. 33:18	Mehiel{49}
65	דמב Damabiah Ps. 90:13 (KJV)	דמביה Damabiah Ps. 89:13[559] [Ps. 90:13 (KJV)]	דמביה Damabiah Ps. 89:15[560] [Ps. 90:13 (KJV)]	DAMABIAH{70}	Damabiah Ps. 90:13	Damabiah{50}
66	מנק Mauakel [typo for Manakel] Ps. 38:21 (KJV)	מנקאל Mankel Ps. 21:12[561] [Ps. 38:21 (KJV)]	מנקאל Manakel Ps. 37:22[562] [Ps. 38:21 (KJV)]	MAUZEL{72}	Menakel Ps. 38:22	Manakel{51}

[552] Editor's note: The number in {brackets} indicates the original ordering of these names as given by the Author and a star* indicates a typo or misspelling of the name when compared with the other columns.

[553] Given as Ps. 118:159 « *Vide quoniam dilexi mandata tua Domine, in misericordia tua vivifica me* », which is Ps. 119:159 in KJV

[554] Given as Ps. 118:159 « *Vide quoniam dilexi mandata tua dilexi Domine, in misericordiâ tuâ vivifica me* », which is Ps. 119:159 in KJV

[555] Given as Ps. 99:2 « *Servite Domino in laetitia, introite in conspectu eius in exultatione* », which is Ps. 100:2 in KJV

[556] Given as Ps. 2:11 « *Servite Domino in timore: et exultate ei cum tremore* », which is Ps. 2:11 in KJV

[557] Given as Ps. 32:18 « *Ecce oculi Domini super metuentes eum, & in eis, qui sperant super misericordia eius* », which is Ps. 33:18 in KJV

[558] Given as Ps. 32:18 « *Ecce oculi Domini super metuentes eum: et in eis, qui sperant super misericordia ejus* », which is Ps. 33:18 in KJV

[559] Given as Ps. 89:13 « *Convertere Domine usquequo, & deprecabilis esto super servos tuos* », which is Ps. 90:13 in KJV

[560] Given as Ps. 89:15 « *Convertere Domine, et usque qua? et deprecabilis esto super servos tuos* », which is Ps. 90:13 in KJV

[561] Given as Ps. 21:12, but is actually 37:22 « *Ne derelinquas me Domine Deus meus, ne discesseris a me* », which is Ps. 38:21 in KJV

[562] Given as Ps. 37:22 « *Ne derelinquas me Domine Deus meus; ne discesseris à me* », which is Ps. 38:21 in KJV

	Johann Reuchlin (1517)	Kircher (1652)	Lazare Lenain (1823)	Eliphas Levi (1860s)	A. Frank Glahn (1909)	Arnoldo Krumm-Heller (1930s)[563]
67	איע Eiael Ps. 37:4 (KJV)	איעאל Eiael Ps. 36:4[564] [Ps. 37:4 (KJV)]	איעאל Eïael Ps. 36:4[565] [Ps. 37:4 (KJV)]	EIAEL{67}	Eiael Ps. 37:4	Ejael{52}
68*	חבו Chabuiah Ps. 106:1 (KJV)	הבויה Habuiah Ps. 105:1[566] [Ps. 106:1 (KJV)]	הבויה Habuhiah Ps. 105:1[567] [Ps. 106:1 (KJV)]	HATVIAH{69}	Habuiah Ps. 106:5	**Nabujah*{68} [~Habujah]
69*	ראה Roehel Ps. 16:5 (KJV)	ראחאל Rochel Ps. 15:5[568] [Ps. 16:5 (KJV)]	ראחאל Rochel Ps. 15:5[569] [Ps. 16:5 (KJV)]	ROCHEL{71}	Rochel Ps. 16:5	Rochel{69}
70	יבם Iabamiah Gen 1:1 (KJV)	יבמיה Iabamiah Gen 1:1[570] [Gen 1:1 (KJV)]	יבמיה Jabamiah Gen 1:1[571] [Gen 1:1 (KJV)]	JABAMIAH{62}	Jobanuiah 1st Mos. 1:1	Jabamiah{70}
71	היי Haiaiel Ps. 109:30 (KJV)	הייאל Haiaiel Ps. 108:30[572] [Ps. 109:30 (KJV)]	הייאל Haiaiel Ps. 108:29[573] [Ps. 109:30 (KJV)]	HAÏAEL{64}	Haiaiel Ps. 109:30	Jaiael{71}

[563] Editor's note: The number in {brackets} indicates the original ordering of these names as given by the Author and a star* indicates a typo or misspelling of the name when compared with the other columns.

[564] Given as Ps. 36:4 « *Delectare in Domino, & dabit tibi petitiones cordis tui* », which is Ps. 37:4 in KJV

[565] Given as Ps. 36:4 « *Delectare in Domino et dabit tibi petitiones cordis tui* », which is Ps. 37:4 in KJV

[566] Given as Ps. 105:1 « *[Alleluia] Confitemini Domino, quoniam bonus, quoniam in seculum misericordia eius* », which is Ps. 106:1 in KJV

[567] Given as Ps. 105:1 « *Confitemini Domino, quoniam bonus: quoniam in saeculum misericordia ejus* », which is Ps. 106:1 in KJV

[568] Given as Ps. 15:5 « *Dominus pars hereditatis meae & calicis mei, tu es, qui restitues hereditatem meam mihi* », which is Ps. 16:5 in KJV

[569] Given as Ps. 15:5 « *Dominus pars haereditatis meae, et calicis mei: tu es, qui restitues haereditatem meam mihi* », which is Ps. 16:5 in KJV

[570] Given as Gen. 1:1 « *In principio creavit Deus coelum & terram* », which is also Gen. 1:1 in KJV

[571] Given as Gen. 1:1 « *Au commencement Dieu créa le ciel et la terre* », which is also Gen. 1:1 in KJV

[572] Given as Ps. 108:30 « *Confitebor Domino nimis in ore meo, & in medio multorum laudabo eum* », which is Ps. 109:30 in KJV

[573] Given as Ps. 108:29 « *Confitebor Domino nimis in ore meo: et in medio multorum laudabo eum* », which is Ps. 109:30 in KJV

	Johann Reuchlin (1517)	Kircher (1652)	Lazare Lenain (1823)	Eliphas Levi (1860s)	A. Frank Glahn (1909)	Arnoldo Krumm-Heller (1930s)[574]
72	מום Mumiah Ps. 116:7 (KJV)	מומיה Mumiah Ps. 114:7[575] [Ps. 116:7 (KJV)]	מומיה Mumiah Ps. 114:7[576] [Ps. 116:7 (KJV)]	NUMIAH{66}	Mumuiah Ps. 116:7	Miumiah{72}

---

[574] Editor's note: The number in {brackets} indicates the original ordering of these names as given by the Author and a star* indicates a typo or misspelling of the name when compared with the other columns.

[575] Given as Ps. 114:7 « *Convertere Domine [anima mea] in requiem tuam, quia Dominus benefecit tibi* », which is Ps. 116:7 in KJV

[576] Given as Ps. 114:7 « *Convertere anima mea in requiem tuam: quia Dominus benefecit tibi* », which is Ps. 116:7 in KJV

Comparison of the Names and Attributes of Lazare Lenain[577] and Krumm-Heller

	Lenain's Name and Bible Verse Number [Corrected] (1823)	Attributes Given by Lenain[578]	Arnoldo Krumm-Heller (1930s)[579]
1	והויה Vehuiah Ps. 3:3[580] [Ps. 3:3 (KJV)]	1) 20th – 24th of March [Aries I]; 2) 20th of March, 31st of May, 11th of August, 22nd of October, 2nd of January;[581] 3) 00:00 – 00:20	Vehuiah{1}
2	יליאל Jeliel Ps. 21:20[582] [Ps. 22:19 (KJV)]	1) 25th – 29th of March [Aries II]; 2) 21st of March, 1st of June, 12th of August, 23rd of October, 3rd of January; 3) 00:20 – 00:40	Jeliel{2}
3	סיטאל Sitaël Ps. 90:2[583] [Ps. 91:2 (KJV)]	1) 30th of March – 3rd of April [Aries III]; 2) 22nd of March, 2nd of June, 13th of August, 24th of October, 4th of January; 3) 00:40 – 01:00	Sitael{3}
4	עלמיה Elemiah Ps. 6:4[584] [Ps. 6:4 (KJV)]	1) 4th – 8th of April [Aries IV]; 2) 23rd of March, 3rd of June, 14th of August, 25th of October, 5th of January; 3) 01:00 – 01:20	Elemiah{4}
5	מהשיה Mahasiah Ps. 33:4[585] [Ps. 34:4 (KJV)]	1) 9th – 13th of April [Aries V]; 2) 24th of March, 4th of June, 15th of August, 26th of October, 6th of January; 3) 01:20 – 01:40	Mehasiah{5}

[577] This information in taken from *La science cabalistique ou l'art de connaître les bons genies* (1832) by Lazare Lenain

[578] Editor's note: According to Lenain, the 1st Attribute corresponds to the genie who governs the physique of the person, the 2nd corresponds to the genie who governs the morality of the person and the 3rd corresponds to the genie who governs the soul and spirit of the person.

[579] Editor's note: The number in {brackets} indicates the original ordering of these names as given by Krumm-Heller and a star* indicates a typo or misspelling of the name when compared with the other columns.

[580] Given as Ps. 3:3 « *Et tu Domine susceptor meus et gloria mea et exaltans caput meum* », which is Ps. 3:3 in KJV

[581] Editor's Note: According to Lenain, "Through the calculation of the preceeding table [2nd group of dates listed here], the first revolution of the 72 genii begins from March 20th at midnight until May 31st; the second, from May 31st to August 11th; the third, from August 11th to October 22nd; the fourth, from October 22nd to January 2nd, and so forth… [the fifth from January 2nd to March 15th, all 72 day periods]" from p.35-36 in *La science cabalistique ou l'art de connaître les bons genies* (1832) by Lazare Lenain

[582] Given as Ps. 21:20 « *Tu autem Domine ne elongaveris auxilium tuum a me ad defensionem meam conspice* », which is Ps. 22:19 in KJV

[583] Given as Ps. 90:2 « *Dicet Domino: Susceptor meus es tu et refugium meum: Deus meus, sperabo in eum* », which is Ps. 91:2 in KJV

[584] Given as Ps. 6:4 « *Convertere Domine, et eripe animam meam: salvum me fac propter misericordiam tuam* », which is Ps. 6:4 in KJV

[585] Given as Ps. 33:4 « *Exquisivi Dominum, et exaudivit me: et ex omnibus tribulationibus meis eripuit me* », which is Ps. 34 :4 in KJV

	Lenain's Name and Bible Verse Number [Corrected] (1823)	Attributes Given by Lenain[586]	Arnoldo Krumm-Heller (1930s)[587]
6	ללהאל Lelahel Ps. 9:11[588] [Ps. 9:11 (KJV)]	1) 14th – 18th of April [Aries VI]; 2) 25th of March, 5th of June, 16th of August, 27th of October, 7th of January; 3) 01:40 – 02:00	**Lehahel*{6} [~Lelahel]
7	אכאיה Achaiah Ps. 102:8[589] [Ps. 103:8 (KJV)]	1) 19th – 23rd of April [Aries/Taurus]; 2) 26th of March, 6th of June, 17th of August, 28th of October, 8th of January; 3) 02:00 – 02:20	Achaiah{7}
8	כהתאל Cahethel Ps. 94:6[590] [Ps. 95:6 (KJV)]	1) 24th – 28th of April [Taurus II]; 2) 27th of March, 7th of June, 18th of August, 29th of October, 9th of January; 3) 02:20 – 02:40	Cahatel{8}
9	הזיאל Haziel Ps. 24:6[591] [Ps. 25:6 (KJV)]	1) 29th of April – 3rd of May [Taurus III]; 2) 28th of March, 8th of June, 19th of August, 30th of October, 10th of January; 3) 02:40 – 03:00	Haziel{9}
10	אלדיה Aladiah Ps. 32:22[592] [Ps. 33:22 (KJV)]	1) 4th – 8th of May [Taurus IV]; 2) 29th of March, 9th of June, 20th of August, 31st of October, 11th of January; 3) 03:00 – 03:20	Aladiah{10}
11	לאויה Lauviah Ps. 17:50[593] [Ps. 18:46 (KJV)]	1) 9th – 13th of May [Taurus V]; 2) 30th of March, 10th of June, 21st of August, 1st of November, 12th of January; 3) 03:20 – 03:40	Lauviah{11}

[586] Editor's note: According to Lenain, the 1st Attribute corresponds to the genie who governs the physique of the person, the 2nd corresponds to the genie who governs the morality of the person and the 3rd corresponds to the genie who governs the soul and spirit of the person.

[587] Editor's note: The number in {brackets} indicates the original ordering of these names as given by Krumm-Heller and a star* indicates a typo or misspelling of the name when compared with the other columns.

[588] Given as Ps. 9:11 « *Psallite Domino, qui habitat in Sion: annuntiate inter gentes studia ejus* », which is Ps. 9 :11 in KJV

[589] Given as Ps. 102:8 « *Miserator et misericors Dominus: longanimis, et misericors* », which is Ps. 103 :8 in KJV

[590] Given as Ps. 94:6 « *Venite adoremus, et procidamus: et ploremus ante Dominum, qui fecit nos* », which is Ps. 95:6 in KJV

[591] Given as Ps. 24:6 « *Reminiscere miserationum tuarum, Domine, et misericordiarum tuarum quae a saeculo sunt* », which is Ps. 25:6 in KJV

[592] Given as Ps. 32:22 « *Fiat misericordia tua Domine super nos: quemadmodum speravimus in te* », which is Ps. 33:22 in KJV

[593] Given as Ps. 17:50 « *Vivit Dominus, et benedictus Deus meus, et exaltetur Deus salutis meae* », which is Ps. 18:46 in KJV

	Lenain's Name and Bible Verse Number [Corrected] (1823)	Attributes Given by Lenain[594]	Arnoldo Krumm-Heller (1930s)[595]
12	ההעיה Hahaiah Ps. 9:22[596] [Ps. 10:1 (KJV)]	1) 14th – 18th of May [Taurus VI]; 2) 31st of March, 11th of June, 22nd of August, 2nd of November, 13th of January; 3) 03:40 – 04:00	**Habaiah*{12} [~Hahaiah]
13	יזלאל Iezalel Ps. 97:6[597] [Ps. 98:4 (KJV)]	1) 19th – 23rd of May [Taurus/Gemini]; 2) 1st of April, 12th of June, 23rd of August, 3rd of November, 14th of January; 3) 04:00 – 04:20	Jesalel{13}
*14	מבהאל Mebahel Ps. 9:9[598] [Ps. 9:10 (KJV)]	1) 24th – 28th of May [Gemini II]; 2) 2nd of April, 13th of June, 24th of August, 4th of November, 15th of January; 3) 04:20 – 04:40	Mehahel*{53} [~Mebahel]
15	הריאל Hariel Ps. 93:22[599] [Ps. 94:22 (KJV)]	1) 29th of May – 2nd of June [Gemini III]; 2) 3rd of April, 14th of June, 25th of August, 5th of November, 16th of January; 3) 04:40 – 05:00	Hariel{54}
16	הקמיה Hakamiah Ps. 87:1[600] [Ps. 88:1 (KJV)]	1) 3rd – 7th of June [Gemini IV]; 2) 4th of April, 15th of June, 26th of August, 6th of November, 17th of January; 3) 05:00 – 05:20	Hakamiah{55}
17	לאויה Lauviah Ps. 8:1[601] [Ps. 8:1 (KJV)]	1) 8th – 12th of June [Gemini V]; 2) 5th of April, 16th of June, 27th of August, 7th of November, 18th of January; 3) 05:20 – 05:40	**Lanoiah*{56} [~Lauoiah]
*18	כליאל Caliel Ps. 7:9[602] [Ps. 7:8 (KJV)]	1) 13th – 17th of June [Gemini VI]; 2) 6th of April, 17th of June, 28th of August, 8th of November, 19th of January; 3) 05:40 – 06:00	Caliel{57}

[594] Editor's note: According to Lenain, the 1st Attribute corresponds to the genie who governs the physique of the person, the 2nd corresponds to the genie who governs the morality of the person and the 3rd corresponds to the genie who governs the soul and spirit of the person.

[595] Editor's note: The number in {brackets} indicates the original ordering of these names as given by Krumm-Heller and a star* indicates a typo or misspelling of the name when compared with the other columns.

[596] Given as Ps. 9:22 « *Ut quid Domine recessisti longe, de spicis in opportunitatibus, in tribulatione* », which is Ps. 10:1 in KJV

[597] Given as Ps. 97:6 « *Jubilate Deo omnis terra : cantate, et exultate, et psallite* », which is Ps. 98:4 in KJV

[598] Given as Ps. 9:9 « *Et factus est Dominus refugium pauperis: adjutor in opportunitatibus, in tribulatione.* », which is Ps. 9:10 in KJV

[599] Given as Ps. 93:22 « *Et factus est mihi Dominus in refugium : et Deus meus in adjutorium spei meae* », which is Ps. 94:22 in KJV

[600] Given as Ps. 87:1 « *Domine Deus salutis meae, in die clamavi et nocte coram te* », which is Ps. 88:1 in KJV

[601] Given as Ps. 8:1 « *Domine Dominus noster, quam admirabile est nomen tuum in universa terra!* », which is Ps. 8:1 in KJV

[602] Given as Ps. 7:9 « *Judica me Domine secundum justitiam meam, et sucundum innocentiam meam super me.* », which is Ps. 7:8 in KJV

	Lenain's Name and Bible Verse Number [Corrected] (1823)	Attributes Given by Lenain[603]	Arnoldo Krumm-Heller (1930s)[604]
19	לוויה Leuviah Ps. 39:1[605] [Ps. 40:1 (KJV)]	1) 18th – 22nd of June [Gemini/Cancer]; 2) 7th of April, 18th of June, 29th of August, 9th of November, 20th of January; 3) 06:00 – 06:20	Leuviah{14}
*20	פהליה Pahaliah Ps. 119:2[606] [Ps. 120:2 (KJV)]	1) 23rd – 27th of June [Cancer II]; 2) 8th of April, 19th of June, 30th of August, 10th of November, 21st of January; 3) 06:20 – 06:40	Pahaliah{15}
21	נלכאל Nelchael Ps. 30:18[607] [Ps. 31:14-15 (KJV)]	1) 28th of June – 2nd of July [Cancer III]; 2) 9th of April, 20th of June, 31st of August, 11th of November, 22nd of January; 3) 06:40 – 07:00	Melchael*{16} [~Nelchael]
22	ייאל Ieiaiel Ps. 120:3[608] [Ps. 121:5 (KJV)]	1) 3rd – 7th of July [Cancer IV]; 2) 10th of April, 21st of June, 1st of September, 12th of November, 23rd of January; 3) 07:00 – 07:20	**Jecaiel*{17} [~Jejaiel]
23	מלהאל Melahel Ps. 120:8[609] [Ps. 121:8]	1) 8th – 12th of July [Cancer V]; 2) 11th of April, 22nd of June, 2nd of September, 13th of November, 24th of January; 3) 07:20 – 07:40	Melehel{18}
*24	ההויה Hahiuiah Ps. 32:18[610] [Ps. 33:18]	1) 13th – 17th of July [Cancer VI]; 2) 12th of April, 23rd of June, 3rd of September, 14th of November, 25th of January; 3) 07:40 – 08:00	**Hahimah*{19} [~Hahiwah or Hahiviah]

[603] Editor's note: According to Lenain, the 1st Attribute corresponds to the genie who governs the physique of the person, the 2nd corresponds to the genie who governs the morality of the person and the 3rd corresponds to the genie who governs the soul and spirit of the person.

[604] Editor's note: The number in {brackets} indicates the original ordering of these names as given by Krumm-Heller and a star* indicates a typo or misspelling of the name when compared with the other columns.

[605] Given as Ps. 39:1 « *Exspectans exspectavi Dominum et intendit mihi* », which is Ps. 40:1 in KJV

[606] Given as Ps. 119:2 « *Domine libera animam meam a labiis iniquis a lingua dolosa* », which is Ps. 120:2 in KJV

[607] Given as Ps. 30:18 « *Ego autem in te speravi Domine: dixi Deus meus es tu: in manibus tuis sortes meae* », which is Ps. 31:14-15 in KJV

[608] Given as Ps. 120:3 « *Dominus custodit te; Dominus proteclio tua, super manum dexteram tuam.* », which is Ps. 121:5 in KJV

[609] Given as Ps. 120:8 « *Dominus custodiat introïtum tuum, et exitum tuum: et ex hoc nunc, et in seculum* », which is Ps. 121:8 in KJV

[610] Given as Ps. 32:18 « *Ecce oculi Domini super metuentes eum: et in eis, qui sperant in misericordia ejus.* », which is Ps. 33:18 in KJV

	Lenain's Name and Bible Verse Number [Corrected] (1823)	Attributes Given by Lenain[611]	Arnoldo Krumm-Heller (1930s)[612]
25	נתהיה Nith-Haiah Ps. 9:1[613] [Ps. 9:1]	1) 18th – 22nd of July [Cancer VII]; 2) 13th of April, 24th of June, 4th of September, 15th of November, 26th of January; 3) 08:00 – 08:20	Nith-Heich{20}
26	האאיה Haaiah Ps. 118:145[614] [Ps. 119:145]	1) 23rd – 27th of July [Leo I]; 2) 14th of April, 25th of June, 5th of September, 16th of November, 27th of January; 3) 08:20 – 08:40	Haaiah{21}
27	ירתאל Ierathel Ps. 139:1[615] [Ps. 140:1]	1) 28th of July – 1st of August [Leo II]; 2) 15th of April, 26th of June, 6th of September, 17th of November, 28th of January; 3) 08:40 – 09:00	Jerathel{22}
28	שאהיה Séheiah Ps. 70:13[616] [Ps. 71:12]	1) 2nd – 6th of August [Leo III]; 2) 16th of April, 27th of June, 7th of September, 18th of November, 29th of January; 3) 09:00 – 09:20	Seeiah{23}
29	רייאל Reiiel Ps. 53:7[617] [Ps. 54:4]	1) 7th – 11th of August [Leo IV]; 2) 17th of April, 28th of June, 8th of September, 19th of November, 30th of January; 3) 09:20 – 09:40	Reiiel{24}
30	ומאאל Omael Ps. 70:6[618] [Ps. 71:5]	1) 12th – 16th of August [Leo V]; 2) 18th of April, 29th of June, 9th of September, 20th of November, 31st of January; 3) 09:40 – 10:00	Omael{25}
31	לכבאל Lecabel Ps. 70:16[619] [Ps. 71:15-16]	1) 17th – 21st of August [Leo VI]; 2) 19th of April, 30th of June, 10th of September, 21st of November, 1st of February; 3) 10:00 – 10:20	Lecabel{26}

[611] Editor's note: According to Lenain, the 1st Attribute corresponds to the genie who governs the physique of the person, the 2nd corresponds to the genie who governs the morality of the person and the 3rd corresponds to the genie who governs the soul and spirit of the person.

[612] Editor's note: The number in {brackets} indicates the original ordering of these names as given by Krumm-Heller and a star* indicates a typo or misspelling of the name when compared with the other columns.

[613] Given as Ps. 9:2 « *Confitebor tibi Domine in toto corde meo: narrabo omnia mirabilia tua* », which is Ps. 9:1 in KJV

[614] Given as Ps. 118:145 « *Clamavi in toto corde exaudi meo, exaudi me Domine; justificationes tuas requiram* », which is Ps. 119:145 in KJV

[615] Given as Ps. 139:1 « *Eripe me Domine ab homine malo, à viro iniquo eripe me* », which is Ps. 140:1 in KJV

[616] Given as Ps. 70:13 « *Deus ne elongeris à me: Deus meus in auxilium meum respice* », which is Ps. 71:12 in KJV

[617] Given as Ps. 53:7, but is actually 53:6 « *Ecce enim Deus adjuvat me: et Dominus susceptor est animae meae* », which is Ps. 54:4 in KJV

[618] Given as Ps. 70:5 « *Quoniam tu es patientia mea Domine: Domine spes mea à juventute mea* », which is Ps. 71:5 in KJV

[619] Given as Ps. 70:16 « *Quoniam non cognovi litteraturam, introibo in potentiam Domini Domine memorabor iustitiae tuae solius* », which is Ps. 71:15-16 in KJV

Lenain's Name and Bible Verse Number [Corrected] (1823)		Attributes Given by Lenain[620]	Arnoldo Krumm-Heller (1930s)[621]
32	ושריה Vasariah Ps. 32:4[622] [Ps. 33:4]	1) 22nd – 26th of August [Leo/Virgo]; 2) 20th of April, 1st of July, 11th of September, 22nd of November, 2nd of February; 3) 10:20 – 10:40	Vasaniah{58}
33	יהויה Iehuiah Ps. 33:11[623] [Ps. 94:11]	1) 27th – 31st of August [Virgo II]; 2) 21st of April, 2nd of July, 12th of September, 23rd of November, 3rd of February; 3) 10:40 – 11:00	**Jomiah{59} [~Johuiah]
34	לההיה Lehaiah Ps. 130:5[624] [Ps. 131:3]	1) 1st – 5th of September [Virgo III]; 2) 22nd of April, 3rd of July, 13th of September, 24th of November, 4th of February; 3) 11:00 – 11:20	Lehaiah{60}
35	כוקיה Chauakiah Ps. 114:1[625] [Ps. 116:1]	1) 6th – 10th of September [Virgo IV]; 2) 23rd of April, 4th of July, 14th of September, 25th of November, 5th of February; 3) 11:20 – 11:40	Chavakiah{61}
36	מנדאל Menadel Ps. 25:8[626] [Ps. 26:8]	1) 11th – 15th of September [Virgo V]; 2) 24th of April, 5th of July, 15th of September, 26th of November, 6th of February; 3) 11:40 – 12:00	Menadel{62}
37	אניאל Aniel Ps. 79:8[627] [Ps. 80:19]	1) 16th – 20th of September [Virgo VI]; 2) 25th of April, 6th of July, 16th of September, 27th of November, 7th of February; 3) 12:00 – 12:20	Amiel*{27} [~Anniel]
38	העמיה Haamiah Ps. 90:9[628] [Ps. 91:9]	1) 21st – 25th of September [Virgo/Libra]; 2) 26th of April, 7th of July, 17th of September, 28th of November, 8th of February; 3) 12:20 – 12:40	Haamiah{28}

---

[620] Editor's note: According to Lenain, the 1st Attribute corresponds to the genie who governs the physique of the person, the 2nd corresponds to the genie who governs the morality of the person and the 3rd corresponds to the genie who governs the soul and spirit of the person.

[621] Editor's note: The number in {brackets} indicates the original ordering of these names as given by Krumm-Heller and a star* indicates a typo or misspelling of the name when compared with the other columns.

[622] Given as Ps. 32:4 « *Quia rectum est verbum Domini, et omnia opera ejus in fide* », which is Ps. 33:4 in KJV

[623] Given as Ps. 33:11, but is actually 93:11 « *Dominus scit cogitationes hominum quoniam vanae sunt* », which is Ps. 94:11 in KJV

[624] Given as Ps. 130:5 « *Speret Israël in Domino; ex hoc nunc, et usque in saeculum* », which is Ps. 131:3 in KJV

[625] Given as Ps. 114:1 « *Dilexi quoniam exaudiet Dominus vocem orationis meae* », which is Ps. 116:1 in KJV

[626] Given as Ps. 25:8 « *Domine dilexi decorem domus tuae & locum habitationis gloriae tuae* », which is Ps. 26:8 in KJV

[627] Given as Ps. 79:8 « *Deus ad vertutem converte nos: et ostende faciem tuam et salvi erimus* », which is Ps. 80:19 in KJV

[628] Given as Ps. 90:9 « *Quoniam tu es Domine spes mea: altissimum posuisti refugium tuum* », which is Ps. 91:9 in KJV

	Lenain's Name and Bible Verse Number [Corrected] (1823)	Attributes Given by Lenain[629]	Arnoldo Krumm-Heller (1930s)[630]
39	רהעאל Rehael Ps. 29:13[631] [Ps. 30:10]	1) 26th – 30th of September [Libra II]; 2) 27th of April, 8th of July, 18th of September, 29th of November, 9th of February; 3) 12:40 – 13:00	Rehahel{29}
40	ייזאל Ieiazel Ps. 87:15[632] [Ps. 88:14]	1) 1st – 5th of October [Libra III]; 2) 28th of April, 9th of July, 19th of September, 30th of November, 10th of February; 3) 13:00 – 13:20	Jeiazel{30}
41	הההאל Hahahel Ps. 119:2[633] [Ps. 120:2]	1) 6th – 10th of October [Libra IV]; 2) 29th of April, 10th of July, 20th of September, 1st of December, 11th of February; 3) 13:20 – 13:40	Hahahel{31}
42	מיכאל Mikael Ps. 120:7[634] [Ps. 121:7]	1) 11th – 15th of October [Libra V]; 2) 30th of April, 11th of July, 21st of September, 2nd of December, 12th of February; 3) 13:40 – 14:00	**Mikahel{32}
43	וליה Veualiah Ps. 87:14[635] [Ps. 88:13]	1) 16th – 20th of October [Libra VI]; 2) 1st of May, 12th of July, 22nd of September, 3rd of December, 13th of February; 3) 14:00 – 14:20	Vehualiah{33}
44	ילהיה Ielahiah Ps. 118:108[636] [Ps. 119:108]	1) 21st – 25th of October [Libra/Scorpio]; 2) 2nd of May, 13th of July, 23rd of September, 4th of December, 14th of February; 3) 14:20 – 14:40	Jelahiah{34}
45	סאליה Sealiah Ps. 93:18[637] [Ps. 94:18]	1) 26th – 30th of October [Scorpio II]; 2) 3rd of May, 14th of July, 24th of September, 5th of December, 15th of February; 3) 14:40 – 15:00	Sealieh{35}

[629] Editor's note: According to Lenain, the 1st Attribute corresponds to the genie who governs the physique of the person, the 2nd corresponds to the genie who governs the morality of the person and the 3rd corresponds to the genie who governs the soul and spirit of the person.

[630] Editor's note: The number in {brackets} indicates the original ordering of these names as given by Krumm-Heller and a star* indicates a typo or misspelling of the name when compared with the other columns.

[631] Given as Ps. 29:13 « *Audivit me Dominus, et misertus est mei: Dominus factus est adiutor* », which is Ps. 30:10 in KJV

[632] Given as Ps. 87:15 « *Ut quid Domine repellis orationem meam: avertis faciem tuam à me* », which is Ps. 88:14 in KJV

[633] Given as Ps. 119:2 « *Domine libera animam meam à labiis iniquis, et à linguâ dolosâ* », which is Ps. 120:2 in KJV

[634] Given as Ps. 120:7 « *Dominus custodit te ab omni malo; custodiat animam tuam Dominus* », which is Ps. 121:7 in KJV

[635] Given as Ps. 87:14 « *Et ego ad te Domine clamavi: et manè oratio mea praeveniet te* », which is Ps. 88:13 in KJV

[636] Given as Ps. 118:108 « *Voluntaria oris mei bene placita fac Domine: et judicia tua doce me* », which is Ps. 119:108 in KJV

[637] Given as Ps. 93:18 « *Si dicebam, motus est pes meus: misericordia tua Domine adjuvabat me* », which is Ps. 94:18 in KJV

	Lenain's Name and Bible Verse Number [Corrected] (1823)	Attributes Given by Lenain[638]	Arnoldo Krumm-Heller (1930s)[639]
46	עריאל Ariel Ps. 144:9[640] [Ps. 145:9]	1) 31st of October – 4th of November [Scorpio III]; 2) 4th of May, 15th of July, 25th of September, 6th of December, 16th of February; 3) 15:00 – 15:20	Ariel{36}
47*	עשליה Asaliah Ps. 104:25[641] [Ps. 104:24]	1) 5th – 9th of November [Scorpio IV]; 2) 5th of May, 16th of July, 26th of September, 7th of December, 17th of February; 3) 15:20 – 15:40	Azaliah{37}
48	מיהאל Mihael Ps. 97:3[642] [Ps. 98:2]	1) 10th – 14th of November [Scorpio V]; 2) 6th of May, 17th of July, 27th of September, 8th of December, 18th of February; 3) 15:40 – 16:00	**Michael{38} [~Mihael]
49	והואל Vehuel Ps. 144:3[643] [Ps. 145:3]	1) 15th – 19th of November [Scorpio VI]; 2) 7th of May, 18th of July, 28th of September, 9th of December, 19th of February; 3) 16:00 – 16:20	Vehuel{39}
50*	דניאל Daniel Ps. 102:8[644] [Ps. 103:8]	1) 20th – 24th of November [Scorpio/Sagittarius]; 2) 8th of May, 19th of July, 29th of September, 10th of December, 20th of February; 3) 16:20 – 16:40	Daniel{63}
51	ההשיה Hahasiah Ps. 103:32[645] [Ps. 104:31]	1) 25th – 29th of November [Sagittarius II]; 2) 9th of May, 20th of July, 30th of September, 11th of December, 21st of February; 3) 16:40 – 17:00	Hahasiah{64}

---

[638] Editor's note: According to Lenain, the 1st Attribute corresponds to the genie who governs the physique of the person, the 2nd corresponds to the genie who governs the morality of the person and the 3rd corresponds to the genie who governs the soul and spirit of the person.

[639] Editor's note: The number in {brackets} indicates the original ordering of these names as given by Krumm-Heller and a star* indicates a typo or misspelling of the name when compared with the other columns.

[640] Given as Ps. 144:9 « *Suavis Dominus universis: et miserationes ejus super omnia opera ejus* », which is Ps. 145:9 in KJV

[641] Given as Ps. 104:25, but is actually 103:24 « *Quam magnificata sunt opera tua Domine! omnia in sapientia fecisti: impleta est terra possessione tua* », which is Ps. 104:24 in KJV

[642] Given as Ps. 97:2 « *Notum fecit Dominus salutare suum: in conspectu gentium revelavit justitiam suam* », which is Ps. 98:2 in KJV

[643] Given as Ps. 144:3 « *Magnus Dominus et laudabilis nimis et magnitudinis ejus non est finis* », which is Ps. 145:3 in KJV

[644] Given as Ps. 102:8 « *Miserator et misericors Dominus: longanimis et multum misericors* », which is Ps. 103:8 in KJV

[645] Given as Ps. 103:32 « *Sit gloria Domini in saeculum: laetabitur Dominus in operibus suis* », which is Ps. 104:31 in KJV

Lenain's Name and Bible Verse Number [Corrected] (1823)		Attributes Given by Lenain[646]	Arnoldo Krumm-Heller (1930s)[647]
52	עממיה Imamiah Ps. 7:18[648] [Ps. 7:17]	1) 30th of November – 4th of December [Sagittarius III]; 2) 10th of May, 21st of July, 1st of October, 12th of December, 22nd of February; 3) 17:00 – 17:20	Imamiah{65}
53	ננאאל Nanael Ps. 118:75[649] [Ps. 119:75]	1) 5th – 9th of December [Sagittarius IV]; 2) 11th of May, 22nd of July, 2nd of October, 13th of December, 23rd of February; 3) 17:20 – 17:40	Nanael{66}
54	ניתאל Nithael Ps. 102:19[650] [Ps. 103:19]	1) 10th – 14th of December [Sagittarius V]; 2) 12th of May, 23rd of July, 3rd of October, 14th of December, 24th of February; 3) 17:40 – 18:00	Nitbael{67}
55	מבהיה Mebahiah Ps. 101:13[651] [Ps. 102:12]	1) 15th – 19th of December [Sagittarius VI]; 2) 13th of May, 24th of July, 4th of October, 15th of December, 25th of February; 3) 18:00 – 18:20	Mehaiah*{40} [~Hebaiah]
56	פויאל Poiel Ps. 144:15[652] [Ps. 145:14]	1) 20th – 24th of December [Sagittarius/Capricorn]; 2) 14th of May, 25th of July, 5th of October, 16th of December, 26th of February; 3) 18:20 – 18:40	Poiel{41}
57	נממיה Nemamiah Ps. 113:19[653] [Ps. 115:11]	1) 25th – 29th of December [Capricorn II]; 2) 15th of May, 26th of July, 6th of October, 17th of December, 27th of February; 3) 18:40 – 19:00	Nemamiah{42}

---

[646] Editor's note: According to Lenain, the 1st Attribute corresponds to the genie who governs the physique of the person, the 2nd corresponds to the genie who governs the morality of the person and the 3rd corresponds to the genie who governs the soul and spirit of the person.

[647] Editor's note: The number in {brackets} indicates the original ordering of these names as given by Krumm-Heller and a star* indicates a typo or misspelling of the name when compared with the other columns.

[648] Given as Ps. 7:18 « *Confitebor Domino secundum justitiam ejus: et psallam nomini Domini altissimi* », which is Ps. 7:17 in KJV

[649] Given as Ps. 118:75 « *Cognovi Domine quia aequitas judicia tua: et veritate tua humiliasti me* », which is Ps. 119:75 in KJV

[650] Given as Ps. 102:19 « *Dominus in coelo paravit sedem suam: et regnum ipsius omnibus dominabitur* », which is Ps. 103:19 in KJV

[651] Given as Ps. 101:13 « *Tu autem Domine in aeternum permanes: et memoriale tuum in generationem* », which is Ps. 102:12 in KJV

[652] Given as Ps. 144:15 « *Allevat Dominus omnes qui corruunt: et erigit omnes elisos* », which is Ps. 145:14 in KJV

[653] Given as Ps. 113:19 « *Qui timent Dominum speraverunt in Domino: adiutor eorum et protector eorum est* », which is Ps. 115:11 in KJV

Lenain's Name and Bible Verse Number [Corrected] (1823)		Attributes Given by Lenain[654]	Arnoldo Krumm-Heller (1930s)[655]
58	ייליאל Ieialel Ps. 6:3[656] [Ps. 6:3]	1) 30th of December – 3rd of January [Capricorn III]; 2) 16th of May, 27th of July, 7th of October, 18th of December, 28th of February; 3) 19:00 – 19:20	Jeialel{43}
59	הרהאל Harahel Ps. 112:3[657] [Ps. 113:3]	1) 4th – 8th of January [Capricorn IV]; 2) 17th of May, 28th of July, 8th of October, 19th of December, 1st of March; 3) 19:20 – 19:40	**Nazael{44} [~Hazael or Harael]
60	מצראל Mitzrael Ps. 144:18[658] [Ps. 145:17]	1) 9th – 13th of January [Capricorn V]; 2) 18th of May, 29th of July, 9th of October, 20th of December, 2nd of March; 3) 19:40 – 20:00	Mizrael{45}
61	ומבאל Umabael Ps. 122:2[659] [Ps. 113:2]	1) 14th – 18th of January [Capricorn VI]; 2) 19th of May, 30th of July, 10th of October, 21st of December, 3rd of March; 3) 20:00 – 20:20	Umebel{46}
62	יההאל Iah-hel Ps. 118:159[660] [Ps. 119:159]	1) 19th – 23rd of January [Capricorn/Aquarius]; 2) 20th of May, 31st of July, 11th of October, 22nd of December, 4th of March; 3) 20:20 – 20:40	Jahhel{47}
63*	ענואל Anauel Ps. 2:11[661] [Ps. 2:11]	1) 24th – 28th of January [Aquarius II]; 2) 21st of May, 1st of August, 12th of October, 23rd of December, 5th of March; 3) 20:40 – 21:00	Ananel*{48} [~Anauel]
64	מהיאל Mehiel Ps. 32:18[662] [Ps. 33:18]	1) 29th of January – 2nd of February [Aquarius III]; 2) 22nd of May, 2nd of August, 13th of October, 24th of December, 6th of March; 3) 21:00 – 21:20	Mehiel{49}

---

[654] Editor's note: According to Lenain, the 1st Attribute corresponds to the genie who governs the physique of the person, the 2nd corresponds to the genie who governs the morality of the person and the 3rd corresponds to the genie who governs the soul and spirit of the person.

[655] Editor's note: The number in {brackets} indicates the original ordering of these names as given by Krumm-Heller and a star* indicates a typo or misspelling of the name when compared with the other columns.

[656] Given as Ps. 6:3 « Et anima mea turbata est valde; sed tu Domine usque quo? », which is Ps. 6:3 in KJV

[657] Given as Ps. 112:3 « A solis ortu usque ad occasum, laudabile nomen Domini », which is Ps. 113:3 in KJV

[658] Given as Ps. 144:18 « Justus Dominus in omnibus viis suis: et sanctus in omnibus operibus suis », which is Ps. 145:17 in KJV

[659] Given as Ps. 122:2 « Sit nomen Domini benedictum, ex hoc nunc et usque in saeculum », which is Ps. 113:2 in KJV

[660] Given as Ps. 118:159 « Vide quoniam dilexi mandata tua dilexi Domine, in misericordiâ tuâ vivifica me », which is Ps. 119:159 in KJV

[661] Given as Ps. 2:11 « Servite Domino in timore: et exultate ei cum tremore », which is Ps. 2:11 in KJV

[662] Given as Ps. 32:18 « Ecce oculi Domini super metuentes eum: et in eis, qui sperant super misericordia ejus », which is Ps. 33:18 in KJV

	Lenain's Name and Bible Verse Number [Corrected] (1823)	Attributes Given by Lenain[663]	Arnoldo Krumm-Heller (1930s)[664]
65	דמביה Damabiah Ps. 89:15[665] [Ps. 90:13]	1) 3rd – 7th of February [Aquarius IV]; 2) 23rd of May, 3rd of August, 14th of October, 25th of December, 7th of March; 3) 21:20 – 21:40	Damabiah{50}
66	מנקאל Manakel Ps. 37:22[666] [Ps. 38:21]	1) 8th – 13th of February [Aquarius V]; 2) 24th of May, 4th of August, 15th of October, 26th of December, 8th of March; 3) 21:40 – 22:00	Manakel{51}
67	איעאל Eïael Ps. 36:4[667] [Ps. 37:4]	1) 13th – 17th of February [Aquarius VI]; 2) 25th of May, 5th of August, 16th of October, 27th of December, 9th of March; 3) 22:00 – 22:20	Ejael{52}
68	הבויה Habuhiah Ps. 105:1[668] [Ps. 106:1]	1) 18th – 22nd of February [Aquarius/Pisces]; 2) 26th of May, 6th of August, 17th of October, 28th of December, 10th of March; 3) 22:20 – 22:40	**Nabujah*{68} [~Habujah]
69	ראחאל Rochel Ps. 15:5[669] [Ps. 16:5]	1) 23th – 27th of February [Pisces II]; 2) 27th of May, 7th of August, 18th of October, 29th of December, 11th of March; 3) 22:40 – 23:00	Rochel{69}
70	יבמיה Jabamiah Gen 1:1[670] [Gen 1:1]	1) 28th of February – 4th of March [Pisces III]; 2) 28th of May, 8th of August, 19th of October, 30th of December, 12th of March; 3) 23:00 – 23:20	Jabamiah{70}
71	הייאל Haiaiel Ps. 108:29[671] [Ps. 109:30]	1) 5th – 9th of March [Pisces IV]; 2) 29th of May, 9th of August, 20th of October, 31st of December, 13th of March; 3) 23:20 – 23:40	Jaiael{71}

[663] Editor's note: According to Lenain, the 1st Attribute corresponds to the genie who governs the physique of the person, the 2nd corresponds to the genie who governs the morality of the person and the 3rd corresponds to the genie who governs the soul and spirit of the person.

[664] Editor's note: The number in {brackets} indicates the original ordering of these names as given by Krumm-Heller and a star* indicates a typo or misspelling of the name when compared with the other columns.

[665] Given as Ps. 89:15 « *Convertere Domine, et usque qua? et deprecabilis esto super servos tuos* », which is Ps. 90:13 in KJV

[666] Given as Ps. 37:22 « *Ne derelinquas me Domine Deus meus; ne discesseris à me* », which is Ps. 38:21 in KJV

[667] Given as Ps. 36:4 « *Delectare in Domino et dabit tibi petitiones cordis tui* », which is Ps. 37:4 in KJV

[668] Given as Ps. 105:1 « *Confitemini Domino, quoniam bonus: quoniam in saeculum misericordia ejus* », which is Ps. 106:1 in KJV

[669] Given as Ps. 15:5 « *Dominus pars haereditatis meae, et calicis mei: tu es, qui restitues haereditatem meam mihi* », which is Ps. 16:5 in KJV

[670] Given as Gen. 1:1 « *Au commencement Dieu créa le ciel et la terre* », which is also Gen. 1:1 in KJV

[671] Given as Ps. 108:29 « *Confitebor Domino nimis in ore meo: et in medio multorum laudabo eum* », which is Ps. 109:30 in KJV

	Lenain's Name and Bible Verse Number [Corrected] (1823)	Attributes Given by Lenain[672]	Arnoldo Krumm-Heller (1930s)[673]
72	מומיה Mumiah Ps. 114:7[674] [Ps. 116:7]	1) 10th – 14th of March [Pisces V]; 2) 30th of May, 10th of August, 21st of October, 1st of January, 14th of March; 3) 23:40 – 00:00	Miumiah{72}
		1&2) 15th – 19th of March[675] [Pisces VI];	

---

[672] Editor's note: According to Lenain, the 1st Attribute corresponds to the genie who governs the physique of the person, the 2nd corresponds to the genie who governs the morality of the person and the 3rd corresponds to the genie who governs the soul and spirit of the person.

[673] Editor's note: The number in {brackets} indicates the original ordering of these names as given by Krumm-Heller and a star* indicates a typo or misspelling of the name when compared with the other columns.

[674] Given as Ps. 114:7 « *Convertere anima mea in requiem tuam: quia Dominus benefecit tibi* », which is Ps. 116:7 in KJV

[675] Editor's Note: According to Lenain, these remaining 5 days "are consecrated, by the Egyptians and the Persians, to five divinities, named Epagomenal, which they call the *sacred Pentad* (1). The modern kabalists attribute these five final days to the intelligences that preside over the four elements (according to the ancients), to the four cardinal points, to the four quarters of the circle which correspond to the equinoxes, to the solstices and to the four seasons: one day remains, it is consecrated to the great principal (God); when the year is bissextile [ie when there is a leap year], there are two [days]: number attributed to the genie of man.

Orpheus, in his theology, admits 360 gods or genii, as many as there are of degrees in the circle and [as there are days] in the year, five of which are subtracted and consecrated to five divinities; being: Osiris, Apollo [or Horus], Isis, Typhon and Venus [Aphrodite, Astarte or Hathor]." from p.33 in *La science cabalistique ou l'art de connaître les bons genies* (1832) by Lazare Lenain

(1) See l'*Origine des Cultes* [the *Origin of Religious Worship*], by Dupuis, 1st volume, edition of the 3rd year, pages 233, 328 and 565.

French Author's Significance of the Arcana

Numeric Value	Kabalistic Value	Square Hebrew:	Hebrew Letter Name:	Eliphas Levi's Chapters from *Dogma* (1855):	Paul Christian Associated Letter:	Paul Christian Associations for the Arcana (1870):	Robert Falconnier Associated Name of Arcana (1896)*:
1	1	א	Aleph	The Recipient	A	The Magus, Willpower	The Magus
2	2	ב	Beth	The Columns of the Temple	B	The Door of the Occult Sanctuary, the Science	The Sanctuary of the Occult Science
3	3	ג	Gimel	The Triangle of Solomon	G	Isis-Urania, Action	Nature or Isis
4	4	ד	Dalet	The Tetragram	D	The Cubic Stone, Realization	The Conqueror
5	5	ה	Heh	The Pentagram	E	The Master of the Arcana, Inspiration	The Hierophant
6	6	ו	Vau	Magical Equilibrium	U,V	The Two Roads, the Tests	The Test or Ordeal
7	7	ז	Zayin	The Flaming Sword	Z	The Chariot of Osirs, Victory	Triumph
8	8	ח	Cheth	Realization	H	Themis, Equilibrium	Justice
9	9	ט	Teth	Initiation	Th	The Veiled Lamp, Prudence	The Sage
10	10	י	Yod/Jod	The Kabalah	I,J,Y	The Sphinx, Fortune	The Sphinx
11	20	כ	Kaf/Kaph	The Magic Chain	C,K	The Tamed Lion, Strength or Force	Strength or Force
12	30	ל	Lamed	The Great Work	L	Sacrifice	Sacrifice
13	40	מ	Mem/Men	Necromancy	M	The Falx, Transformation	Death
14	50	נ	Nun	Transmutations	N	The Solar Genie, Initiative	The Sun
15	60	ס	Samech	Black Magic	X	Typhon, Fate/Fatality	Typhon
16	70	ע	Ayin	Effigyisms	O	The Fulminated Tower, Ruin	The Pyramid
17	80	פ	Pei	Astrology	P	The Star of the Magi, Hope	The Star
18	90	צ	Tzadik	Love Potions and Spells	Ts	Twilight, Deceptions	The Night
19	100	ק	Kuf/Qoph	The Stone of the Philosophers	Q	The Resplendent Light, Happiness	Love
20	200	ר	Resh/Reish	The Universal Medicine	R	The Awakening of the Dead, Renewal	The Awakening
21	300	ש	Shin	Divination	S	The Crocodile, Atonement	The Atheist
22	400	ת	Tav	Summary and General Key of the 4 Occult Sciences (Kabalah, Magic, Alchemy and Magentism or Occult Medicine)	T	The Crown of the Magi, Reward	The Crown

*These have been modified to correspond to the Gnostic numbering of the Arcana

Sources: "Dogma de la Haute Magie"(1855) by Éliphas Lévi, "Historie de la Magie, du monde Surnaturel et de la fatalité a travers les Temps et les Peuples" (1870) by Paul Christian [Jean-Baptiste Pitois], and "Les XXII Lames Hermétiques du Tarot Divinatoire" (1896) by Robert Falconnier

High Masonic Alphabet of the Egyptian Magi

Numeric Value	Kabalistic Value	Square Hebrew:	Hebrew Letter Name:	Alphabet of the Magi:	Dr. Bataille's Egyptian Magi Letter Name:	Dr. Bataille's Associated Modern Letter:	Dr. Bataille's High Masonic Letter Meaning (1894):
1	1	א	Aleph		Athoïm	A	the Magus
2	2	ב	Beth		Beïnthin	B	the Door of the occult Sanctuary
3	3	ג	Gimel		Gomor	G	Isis
4	4	ד	Dalet		Dinaïn	D	the cubic Stone
5	5	ה	Heh		Eni	E	the Master of the Arcana
6	6	ו	Vau		Ur	U,V	the Two Paths
7	7	ז	Zayin		Zaïn	Z	the Chariot of Osiris
8	8	ח	Cheth		Hélétha	H	Themis [law & order]
9	9	ט	Teth		Théla	Th	the veiled Lamp
10	10	י	Yod/Jod		Ioïthi	I,J,Y	the Sphinx
11	20	כ	Kaf/Kaph		Caïtha	C,K	the tamed Lion
12	30	ל	Lamed		Luzaïn	L	the Sacrifice
13	40	מ	Mem/Men		Mataloth	M	the Sickle
14	50	נ	Nun		Naïn	N	the Solar Genie
15	60	ס	Samech		Xirôn	X	Typhon
16	70	ע	Ayin		Olélath	O	the fulminated Tower
17	80	פ	Pei		Pilôn	P	the Star of the Magi
18	90	צ	Tzadik		Tsadi	Ts	Twilight
19	100	ק	Kuf/Qoph		Quitolath	Q	the resplendant Light
20	200	ר	Resh/Reish		Rasith	R	the Awakening of the Dead
21	300	ש	Shin		Sichen	S	the Crocodile
22	400	ת	Tav		Thoth	T	the Crown of the Magi
23	(500)	ך	final Kaph				
24	(600)	ם	final Mem				
25	(700)	ן	final Nun				
26	(800)	ף	final Pei				
27	(900)	ץ	final Tzadik				

"...American high-masons ...used the letters of a secret magical alphabet to mark the divisions of a document... Each letter has a corresponding hierogliphic, a secret, a symbolic name and a motto..."
- Docteur Bataille [Gabriel Jogand-Pagès]

*Sources: "Traicté des chiffres ou Secrètes manières d'escrire" (1587) by Blaise de Vigenère, and 'L'Alphabet du Magism Palladique dit Alphabet des Mages d'Égypte' by Docteur Bataille [Gabriel Jogand-Pagès] in "REVUE MENSUELLE Religieuse, Politique, Scientifique" from Issue No. 3 (March 1894)

Daath Gnosis: Bilingual Translations

"The Book of the Virgin of Carmel" by Samael Aun Weor

"Universal Charity" by Samael Aun Weor

"Gnostic Christification" by Samael Aun Weor

"Logos Mantram Magic" by Krumm-Heller (Huiracocha)

"The Reconciliation of Science and Religion" by Eliphas Levi

"The Bible of Liberty" by Eliphas Levi

"The Initiatic Path in the Arcanum of the Tarot & Kabalah"
   by Samael Aun Weor

"Esoteric Course of Kabalah" by Samael Aun Weor

"Magic, Alchemy and the Great Work" by Samael Aun Weor

"Dogma of High Magic" by Eliphas Levi

"The Awakening of Man" by Samael Aun Weor

"Gnostic Rosicrucian Astrology" by Krumm-Heller (Huiracocha)

"The Kabalistic and Occult Philosophy of Eliphas Levi" Vol.1 by
   Eliphas Levi

"The Kabalistic and Occult Philosophy of Eliphas Levi" Vol.2
   by Eliphas Levi *

"Gnostic Rosicrucian Kabalah" by Krumm-Heller (Huiracocha) *

"Ritual of High Magic" by Eliphas Levi *

* Current projects for future publication from Daath Gnostic Publishing

Daath Gnosis: Reprints[1]

"The Psychology of Man's Possible Evolution" by P.D. Ouspensky
(English-Español)

"In Search of the Miraculous" Vol. 1 & 2 by P.D. Ouspensky
(English-Español)

"Mystical Kabalah" by Dion Fortune *(English - Español)*

"Rito Memphis y Misraim Guias del Aprendiz, Compañero, y
Maestro" by Memphis y Misraim Argentina *(Español)*

"The Theosophical ZOHAR" by Nurho de Manahar *(English)*

"The Oragean Version" by C. Daly King *(English)*

"La Science Cabalistique" by Lazare Lenain *(Français)* *

"The Fourth Way" by P.D. Ouspensky *(English - Español)* *

Daath Gnosis: Study Guides

"Gnostic Egyptian Tarot Coloring Book" *(English - Español)*

"The Gnostic Kabalistic Verb" *(English - Español)*

"The Gnostic and Esoteric Mysteries of Freemasonry,
Lucifer and the Great Work" *(English - Español)*

"The Kabalistic and Occult Tarot of Eliphas Levi" *(English)*

"Esoteric Studies in Masonry" Vol. 1 *(English - Français)*

"Esoteric Studies in Masonry" Vol. 2 *(English - Français)* *

* Current projects for future publication from Daath Gnostic Publishing

---

[1] These are books which were 1) either originally in English and have been republished by Daath Gnosis in
order to either make them bilingual or 2) provide access to difficult to find documents in their original language.

A word about **"Daath Gnostic Publishing – Art, Science, Philosophy and Mysticism (A.S.P.M)"** and our motivation:

> In an attempt to integrate the large amount of enlightening material on the subject of GNOSIS into the English language and to provide a way:
> - for non-English speakers to give lectures & assignments to English speaking students (and vice versa) and be able to reference specific topics or quotes, and
> - for English speakers to access materials previously unavailable in English (or not critically translated into English)
>
> we have decided to translate and publish these materials for the serious Gnostic Students.

Almost all our publications are bilingual, giving access to the original source material and the translation so that the reader can decide for themselves what the meaning of each sentence is.

We are also working on Study Guides that are a combination of Gnostic Materials from multiple sources which provide further insight when taken together.

Because of the need for a practical GNOSIS in these revolutionary times, we have focused on, and continue to benefit from, the writing and teachings of Samael Aun Weor. We encourage you to study his materials, they are wonderful.

In *Endocrinology and Criminology* (1959), at the end of Ch. 15, he says:

"Before delivering ourselves to the development of occult powers, we need to study ourselves and make a persona-logical and psycho-pathological diagnosis of our own personality.

After discovering our own particular Psycho-bio-typo-logical "I", it is necessary for us to reform ourselves with intellectual culture.

A Pedagogic[2] Psychotherapy is necessary in order to reform ourselves.

"Antes de entregarnos al desarrollo de los poderes ocultos necesitamos estudiarnos a sí mismos, y hacer un diagnóstico persona-lógico y psico-patológico de nuestra propia personalidad.

Después de haber descubierto nuestro propio yo Psico-Biotipológico, necesitamos reformarnos con la cultura intelectual.

Necesitamos una Psicoterapia Pedagógica para reformarnos.

---

[2] Pedagogy: 1) the function or work of a teacher; teaching. 2) the art or science of teaching; education; instructional methods.

The four gospels of Jesus Christ are the best Pedagogic Psychotherapy.

It is necessary to totally study and practice all the teachings contained in the four gospels of Jesus Christ.

Only after reforming ourselves morally can we deliver ourselves to the development of the chakras, discs or magnetic wheels, of the astral body.

It is also urgent to study the best authors of Theosophy, Rosicrucianism, Psychology, Yoga, etc., etc."

In *The Seven Words* (1953), about a third of the way through, he says:

"I dare to affirm that all the books which have been written in the world on Theosophism, Rosicrucianism, Spiritualism, etc., are completely antiquated for the new AQUARIAN Era, and therefore they should be revised in order to extract from them only what is essential.

Here I, AUN WEOR, deliver to humanity, the authentic message that the WHITE LODGE sends to humanity for the new AQUARIAN Era.

God has delivered to men the wisdom of the Serpent. What more do they want?

This science is not mine; this science is from God; my person is not worth anything; the work is everything, I am nothing but an emissary."

So let us practice the Science of the Serpent, *la magia amorosa*, while we study and extract only what is essential from the Esoteric texts of the past, in order to synthesize the truth within ourselves.

If you are interested:
- in receiving a list of our currently available materials,
- or would like to suggest a better translation for anything we publish,
- or if you would like to take the responsibility and time to translate or proofread a chapter or a book (in English, French or Spanish),
- or would like to suggest or submit materials for publication,
- or would like to inquire about purchasing Gnostic Tarot Deck(s)

please send us an email at:

GnosticStudies@gmail.com

Or join our group for the latest updates:

http://groups.yahoo.com/group/DaathGnosis/

Daath דעת
Gnostic ☥
Publishing

Art - Arte
Science - Ciencia
Philosophy - Filosofía
Mysticism - Misticismo